Chinese Complaint Systems

Complaint systems have existed in China for many years, and in 2004, a debate took place in the People's Republic of China (PRC) over the Letters and Visits System (*xinfang zhidu*), which was designed to allow people to register complaints with the upper levels of the government. However, both parties generally overlooked several different complaint systems that had preceded the letters and visits system during China's history. Indeed, despite the rich heritage of numerous complaint systems throughout China's past, most studies of complaint systems in China have paid little attention to the origins, development, practices, impact, and nature of similar institutions in the *longue durée* of Chinese history.

Presenting a comprehensive study of complaint systems in Chinese history from early times to the present, this important book fills the gap in existing literature on complaint systems in China. Drawing on primary sources, Qiang Fang analyzes the significance of continuities and changes in historical complaint systems for contemporary China, where the state continues to be nominally strong, but actually fragile. Unlike other major theories of popular resistance to the state in China, such as "everyday resistance," "rightful resistance," and resistance "as legal rights," this book develops the theory that behind Chinese complaint systems, there was a mentality of "natural resistance" that has been deeply embedded in Chinese culture, political philosophy, and folk religion for millennia. Given this history, Fang concludes that it is likely that some form of complaint system will continue to exist, and by helping to mitigate the increasing demands of the Chinese state on the Chinese, will serve to strengthen the state.

An essential contribution understanding the strengths, weaknesses, and various roles of the letters and visits system in contemporary China, as well as the systems that have preceded it throughout China's long history, this book will be of huge interest to students and scholars of Chinese history, politics, and law.

Qiang Fang is Associate Professor in the Department of History at the University of Minnesota Duluth, USA.

Routledge studies in the modern history of Asia

1 **The Police in Occupation Japan**
Control, corruption and resistance to reform
Christopher Aldous

2 **Chinese Workers**
A new history
Jackie Sheehan

3 **The Aftermath of Partition in South Asia**
Tai Yong Tan and Gyanesh Kudaisya

4 **The Australia–Japan Political Alignment**
1952 to the present
Alan Rix

5 **Japan and Singapore in the World Economy**
Japan's economic advance into Singapore, 1870–1965
Shimizu Hiroshi and Hirakawa Hitoshi

6 **The Triads as Business**
Yiu Kong Chu

7 **Contemporary Taiwanese Cultural Nationalism**
A-chin Hsiau

8 **Religion and Nationalism in India**
The case of the Punjab
Harnik Deol

9 **Japanese Industrialisation**
Historical and cultural perspectives
Ian Inkster

10 **War and Nationalism in China**
1925–1945
Hans J. van de Ven

11 **Hong Kong in Transition**
One country, two systems
Edited by Robert Ash, Peter Ferdinand, Brian Hook and Robin Porter

12 **Japan's Postwar Economic Recovery and Anglo-Japanese Relations, 1948–1962**
Noriko Yokoi

13 **Japanese Army Stragglers and Memories of the War in Japan, 1950–1975**
Beatrice Trefalt

14 **Ending the Vietnam War**
The Vietnamese communists' perspective
Ang Cheng Guan

15 **The Development of the Japanese Nursing Profession**
Adopting and adapting Western influences
Aya Takahashi

16 **Women's Suffrage in Asia**
Gender nationalism and democracy
Louise Edwards and Mina Roces

17 **The Anglo-Japanese Alliance, 1902–1922**
Phillips Payson O'Brien

18 **The United States and Cambodia, 1870–1969**
From curiosity to confrontation
Kenton Clymer

19 **Capitalist Restructuring and the Pacific Rim**
Ravi Arvind Palat

20 **The United States and Cambodia, 1969–2000**
A troubled relationship
Kenton Clymer

21 **British Business in Post-Colonial Malaysia, 1957–70**
'Neo-colonialism' or 'disengagement'?
Nicholas J. White

22 **The Rise and Decline of Thai Absolutism**
Kullada Kesboonchoo Mead

23 **Russian Views of Japan, 1792–1913**
An anthology of travel writing
David N. Wells

24 **The Internment of Western Civilians under the Japanese, 1941–1945**
A patchwork of internment
Bernice Archer

25 **The British Empire and Tibet**
1900–1922
Wendy Palace

26 **Nationalism in Southeast Asia**
If the people are with us
Nicholas Tarling

27 **Women, Work and the Japanese Economic Miracle**
The case of the cotton textile industry, 1945–1975
Helen Macnaughtan

28 **A Colonial Economy in Crisis**
Burma's rice cultivators and the world depression of the 1930s
Ian Brown

29 **A Vietnamese Royal Exile in Japan**
Prince Cuong De (1882–1951)
Tran My-Van

30 **Corruption and Good Governance in Asia**
Nicholas Tarling

31 **US–China Cold War Collaboration, 1971–1989**
S. Mahmud Ali

32 **Rural Economic Development in Japan**
From the nineteenth century to the Pacific War
Penelope Francks

33 **Colonial Armies in Southeast Asia**
Edited by Karl Hack and Tobias Rettig

34 **Intra Asian Trade and the World Market**
A.J.H. Latham and Heita Kawakatsu

35 **Japanese–German Relations, 1895–1945**
War, diplomacy and public opinion
Edited by Christian W. Spang and Rolf-Harald Wippich

36 **Britain's Imperial Cornerstone in China**
The Chinese maritime customs service, 1854–1949
Donna Brunero

37 **Colonial Cambodia's 'Bad Frenchmen'**
The rise of French rule and the life of Thomas Caraman, 1840–1887
Gregor Muller

38 **Japanese–American Civilian Prisoner Exchanges and Detention Camps, 1941–45**
Bruce Elleman

39 **Regionalism in Southeast Asia**
Nicholas Tarling

40 **Changing Visions of East Asia, 1943–93**
Transformations and continuities
R.B. Smith
(edited by Chad J. Mitcham)

41 **Christian Heretics in Late Imperial China**
Christian inculturation and state control, 1720–1850
Lars P. Laamann

42 **Beijing – A Concise History**
Stephen G. Haw

43 **The Impact of the Russo-Japanese War**
Edited by Rotem Kowner

44 **Business–Government Relations in Prewar Japan**
Peter von Staden

45 **India's Princely States**
People, princes and colonialism
Edited by Waltraud Ernst and Biswamoy Pati

46 **Rethinking Gandhi and Nonviolent Relationality**
Global perspectives
Edited by Debjani Ganguly and John Docker

47 **The Quest for Gentility in China**
Negotiations beyond gender and class
Edited by Daria Berg and Chloë Starr

48 **Forgotten Captives in Japanese Occupied Asia**
Edited by Kevin Blackburn and Karl Hack

49 **Japanese Diplomacy in the 1950s**
From isolation to integration
Edited by Iokibe Makoto, Caroline Rose, Tomaru Junko and John Weste

50 **The Limits of British Colonial Control in South Asia**
Spaces of disorder in the Indian Ocean region
Edited by Ashwini Tambe and Harald Fischer-Tiné

51 **On The Borders of State Power**
Frontiers in the greater Mekong sub-region
Edited by Martin Gainsborough

52 **Pre-Communist Indochina**
R.B. Smith
(edited by Beryl Williams)

53 **Communist Indochina**
R.B. Smith
(edited by Beryl Williams)

54 **Port Cities in Asia and Europe**
Edited by Arndt Graf and Chua Beng Huat

55 **Moscow and the Emergence of Communist Power in China, 1925–30**
The Nanchang Rising and the birth of the Red Army
Bruce A. Elleman

56 **Colonialism, Violence and Muslims in Southeast Asia**
The Maria Hertogh controversy and its aftermath
Syed Muhd Khairudin Aljunied

57 **Japanese and Hong Kong Film Industries**
Understanding the origins of East Asian film networks
Kinnia Shuk-ting

58 **Provincial Life and the Military in Imperial Japan**
The phantom samurai
Stewart Lone

59 **Southeast Asia and the Vietnam War**
Ang Cheng Guan

60 **Southeast Asia and the Great Powers**
Nicholas Tarling

61 **The Cold War and National Assertion in Southeast Asia**
Britain, the United States and Burma, 1948–1962
Matthew Foley

62 **The International History of East Asia, 1900–1968**
Trade, ideology and the quest for order
Edited by Antony Best

63 **Journalism and Politics in Indonesia**
A critical biography of Mochtar Lubis (1922–2004) as editor and author
David T. Hill

64 **Atrocity and American Military Justice in Southeast Asia**
Trial by army
Louise Barnett

65 **The Japanese Occupation of Borneo, 1941–1945**
Ooi Keat Gin

66 **National Pasts in Europe and East Asia**
P.W. Preston

67 **Modern China's Ethnic Frontiers**
A journey to the West
Hsiao-ting Lin

68 **New Perspectives on the History and Historiography of Southeast Asia**
Continuing explorations
Michael Aung-Thwin and Kenneth R. Hall

69 **Food Culture in Colonial Asia**
A taste of empire
Cecilia Leong-Salobir

70 **China's Political Economy in Modern Times**
Changes and economic consequences, 1800–2000
Kent Deng

71 **Science, Public Health and the State in Modern Asia**
Edited by Liping Bu, Darwin Stapleton and Ka-che Yip

72 **Russo-Japanese Relations, 1905–1917**
From enemies to allies
Peter Berton

73 **Reforming Public Health in Occupied Japan, 1945–52**
Alien prescriptions?
Christopher Aldous and Akihito Suzuki

74 **Trans-Colonial Modernities in South Asia**
Edited by Michael S. Dodson and Brian A. Hatcher

75 **The Evolution of the Japanese Developmental State**
Institutions locked in by ideas
Hironori Sasada

76 **Status and Security in Southeast Asian States**
Nicholas Tarling

77 **Lee Kuan Yew's Strategic Thought**
Ang Cheng Guan

78 **Government, Imperialism and Nationalism in China**
The Maritime Customs Service and its Chinese staff
Chihyun Chang

79 **China and Japan in the Russian Imagination, 1685–1922**
To the ends of the Orient
Susanna Soojung Lim

80 **Chinese Complaint Systems**
Natural resistance
Qiang Fang

81 **Martial Arts and the Body Politic in Meiji Japan**
Denis Gainty

Chinese Complaint Systems

Natural resistance

Qiang Fang

Routledge
Taylor & Francis Group
LONDON AND NEW YORK

First published 2013
by Routledge
2 Park Square, Milton Park, Abingdon, Oxon OX14 4RN

Simultaneously published in the USA and Canada
by Routledge
711 Third Avenue, New York, NY 10017

Routledge is an imprint of the Taylor & Francis Group, an informa business

British Library Cataloguing in Publication Data
A catalogue record for this book is available from the British Library

Library of Congress Cataloging in Publication Data
Fang, Qiang, 1968–
Chinese complaint systems : natural resistance / Qiang Fang.
p. cm. – (Routledge studies in the modern history of Asia)
Includes bibliographical references and index.
1. Petition, Right of–China–History. 2. Political participation–China–History. 3. China–Politics and government. I. Title.
JQ1516.F37 2013
323.4'80951–dc23 2012034648

ISBN: 978-0-415-81181-1 (hbk)
ISBN: 978-0-203-06982-0 (ebk)

Typeset in Times New Roman
by Wearset Ltd, Boldon, Tyne and Wear

To my wife Duan Jing, my son Hanru, and to all aggrieved complainants in China

Contents

Acknowledgments

A Chinese saying states: "It takes ten years to sharpen a sword." Since early 2003, I have spent the past decade working on this book. Throughout those arduous but always meaningful years, there are many people and institutions to whom I want to express my sincere gratitude. First of all, my greatest debt is to my mentor Professor Roger Des Forges, a prominent scholar of Chinese history at the University at Buffalo, for his extraordinary guidance, encouragement and patience from the very beginning to the end. He generously read and meticulously revised each draft, and helped clarify and improve the book at every stage. Without his endeavor, this book would not have seen today.

I am highly appreciative of the financial support magnanimously offered by these institutions. The History Department at the University at Buffalo provided me with a dissertation travel grant to conduct research in China between 2003 and 2004. Grants from both the University of Minnesota and the University of Minnesota Duluth also allowed me to read additional archives in Wuhan and Taiwan. Their supports made my research visits possible.

While I was working in China, my family and many friends had given me huge assistance with my research. My father, Fang Zhenguo, a military veteran, helped me collect newspaper reports and shared his complaint experience in the 1970s. My brothers, Fang Liang and Fang Hong, introduced and accompanied me to meet with many former or current officials of the letters and visits offices in Shanghai and Hubei province. Those interviews with officials were crucial to this book as they greatly helped me learn the internal structure and function of the letters and visits offices. Zhou Shuanzhu, a friend of my brother Fang Liang, assisted me to interview officials in both Shijiazhuang and Pingshan county in Hebei province. Chen Guangxi, a friend and the former party secretary of Weishi county in Henan, helped me hold talks with several township officials and heads of the letters and visits office. These interviews expanded my understanding of China's complaint systems in contemporary China and the way that Chinese local officials dealt with people's complaints. Wang Shoufa, my long-time friend, introduced a couple of complainants to me who gave me important information about their own complaint experiences. I am also thankful to those scholars for their valuable suggestions and advice on my research such as Yang Yifan, a researcher at the Chinese Academy of Social Science, He Weifang, a law professor at Peking University, Ying Xing, a professor at the Chinese University of Politics and Law, Tao Dongfeng, a friend and professor at the Capital Normal University, and Liang Zhiping, a legal scholar in Beijing.

In particular, I deeply thank Ms. Stephanie Rogers, the senior editor and publisher at Routledge, for her strong interest, support, and patience in this book, and her professionalism in overseeing every aspect of the publication. I furthermore appreciate the two anonymous reviewers. Their highly detailed and extremely insightful suggestions significantly improved the final outcome in many ways. I also appreciate others on the publication team, including Leanne Hinves, Hannah Mack, Allie Hargreaves, Phillippa Nichol, and Sue Littleford.

As always, I owe more than I can say to my beloved wife Jing Duan, who is the most important companion and best friend, has given her constant support and help unconditionally. My cherished son Hanru's wonderful smiles have helped me walk through the darkest part of this publication. I want to thank my little boy for being such a joy and laughter, and always giving me love and hope.

Permissions

I am very grateful to both the Cambridge University Press and the *Journal of Asian History* for their permissions to reprint the materials in Chapter 1 and Chapter 2 that have been previously published by the *Journal of Asian Studies* (Vol. 68, No. 4, 2009, pp. 1105–35) and the *Journal of Asian History* (46/2012, pp. 97–116).

Introduction

A national debate

In 2004, there was a debate in the People's Republic of China (PRC) over the Letters and Visits System (*xinfang zhidu*),[1] designed to allow people with complaints to register them with the upper levels of the government. Yu Jianrong, a sociologist in the Chinese Academy of Social Sciences who had compiled a "first report" on the system, argued that it had fatal flaws and should be eliminated.[2] Yu's rationale was that the system had political as well as legal functions and hampered the effort to make the judicial system more independent of the administrative and political systems. This argument immediately drew much criticism from both officials and scholars across the country. Chen Shuangquan, vice chairman of the Legal Committee of the Sichuan People's Congress, contended that the letters and visits system had deep roots in the PRC political structure and could not be abolished just like that. Kang Xiaoguang, a political scientist at Qinghua University, specified that the letters and visits system was indispensable precisely because of the absence of any genuine judicial independence in China.[3] Ying Xing, a legal scholar at the Chinese University of Politics and Law in Beijing also defended the system. He argued that, given problems in the Administrative Litigation and Reconsideration systems, also designed to protect the rights of citizens, the letters and visits system remained an important alternative venue for people to lodge complaints against the abuses of local officials.[4]

Despite their differences, both sides in this debate tended to assume that the letters and visits system was unique to China. In fact, similar forms of complaint systems have existed in many times and places in world history. Lex Heerma van Voss correctly argues, "Petitions are demands for a favor, or for the redressing of an injustice" and "writing petitions was a common human experience."[5] Likewise, social psychologists Jonathan Haidt and Craig Joseph also acknowledge certain universalities. "To the extent that there are similarities across cultures," they point out, "…[it is] because all cultures face similar problems."[6] Indeed, notwithstanding the cultural, political, and institutional differences, many countries around the world in both the past and the present have developed certain forms of complaint systems.

In ancient Egypt, for example, a peasant whose barley and donkeys had been seized by the son of a local official had to complain nine times to a high steward before having his grievance taken care of. He was finally successful because of his persistence and eloquence.[7] The archives of the Holy Roman Empire contain about 20,000 to 30,000 supplications written by commoners to the Frankfurt council between 1600 and 1810. Some complainants, like Chinese complainants to Beijing, traveled long distances from Frankfurt to Vienna.[8] In England, both the king and early Parliament accepted people's complaints and remedied grievances and injustices as early as the twelfth century,[9] when even "skipping" complaints by peasants that skipped the required levels of local notables and directly reached to the king were also fairly common.[10] Today, British subjects can appeal to the High Court, functioning as an administrative court (i.e., a body that will listen to complaints against administrative personnel), against any government decisions that they feel have effectively infringed their rights.[11] Similar practices can also be found in many other cultures such as colonial India and North America.[12] In all of these cases, there were common institutional problems in existing channels for redress that led to the perceived need for some kind of separate complaint system

In the West in recent times one such system involves a special official to handle popular complaints against other officials. In 1809, the Swedish legislature appointed such an official who was called an "ombudsman." The institution subsequently spread to other parts of the world including the United States where, since 1965, there has been reported a "remarkable burgeoning of interest in ombudsmanship."[13] By mid-2003, about 110 countries were said to have "classical" and "hybrid" ombudsman institutions.[14] In the West, ombudsmen exist not just in public organizations such as governments and schools but also in private enterprises such as newspapers and commercial industries. As in the case of Chinese letters and visits, such arrangements do not always work out as planned. One study examines the role of newspaper ombudsmen in redressing consumers' complaints in North America, concluding that they work best as "facilitators" of communication and less well as "mediators."[15] Aside from ombudsmen, it is quite common for aggrieved Americans to complain to many different authorities, including federal, state, and city government organs, congressmen, and company presidents.[16] Archives show that in the Great Depression, many desperate Americans wrote letters directly to Present Roosevelt for assistance.[17] Although the differences of various complaint systems among different polities and cultures await further study, we may observe that many countries, be they democratic or authoritarian, have their own complaint systems. Thus, if separate complaint systems are seen to be compatible with the ideals of judicial independence, democracy, and the rule of law in many other countries, why should they, as Yu argues, necessarily be harmful to such principles in China?

In addition, both parties to the debate in China have focused on the letters and visits system in the PRC and have generally overlooked several different kinds of complaint systems that preceded it during China's long recorded history.

Indeed, despite the rich heritage of numerous complaint systems in Chinese history, most Western as well as Chinese studies of one or more complaint systems in the PRC and earlier periods have paid little systematic attention to the origins, development, practices, impact, and nature of similar institutions in the *longue durée* of Chinese history.

Existing scholarship

Generally speaking, present scholarship on Chinese complaint systems can be categorized into three schools based on the periods and specific systems they have examined: studies of specific complaint systems in the recent period; studies of the letters and visits system in the PRC; and studies of individual complaint systems prior to the establishment of the PRC.

In the first school, scholars such as Kevin O'Brien and Liangjiang Li have broadened our understanding of what they call the "rightful resistance" of farmers' complaints to the Administrative Court regarding local tax burdens and alleged corruption in village elections.[18] Focusing on collective resistance in China, Yongshun Cai argues that the "government's perception of costs and benefits plays a crucial role in shaping the outcome of popular resistance."[19] After comparing the activities of letters and visits offices with those of arbitration committees in the 1990s, Isabelle Thireau and Hua Linshan find that people who sought aid from letters and visits offices were more likely to be poor while those who appealed to arbitration committees tended to be better-off. Thus the former institution appears to have the beneficial effect of marginally leveling the playing field of Chinese justice.[20] In his study of a veteran's petition in 2002, Neil J. Diamant goes back to previous veterans' petitions in the early PRC to gain perspective. He concludes that the gap between the veterans' high expectations of good government and the harsh reality they had faced, a gap that had resulted in their petitions in the past, continues into the present.[21] Xi Chen challenges the conventional view that commoners in authoritarian states can only resort to disruptive tactics for bargaining power. He argues that the "troublemaking" tactics employed by Chinese complainants "may include but are not restricted to disruption."[22]

Another analyst in this first group, Carl Minzner, provides a highly detailed comparison of the 1995 and 2005 *Regulations Regarding Letters and Visits*. He suggests that the system, which he identifies as a "quasi-formal petitioning institution," "operates as a dysfunctional proxy for formal legal institutions." Minzner convincingly argues that, instead of carrying out political reforms, many Chinese leaders have chosen to try to "perfect the formal legal system" in an effort to solve problems associated with the letters and visits institutions.[23]

Some Chinese specialists such as Yu Jianrong and Ying Xing also focus on specific complaint systems in the recent period. Unlike Yu Jianrong whose studies have centered exclusively on the contemporary period and have called for the abolition of the letters and visits system due to its fundamental flaws,[24] Ying Xing has examined a specific set of farmers' complaints against relocation in Sichuan province in the 1980s and 1990s to explore how the bottom-up power (letters and visits) and top-down power (government and administration) interacted.[25] He concludes that the system should be maintained.

The second school of research examines the letters and visits system in the PRC in general. For example, Laura M. Luehrmann has surveyed the history of the letters and visits system from 1949 to 1996. Comparing the system with similar ones elsewhere in the world, she has concluded that it has tended, on balance, to sustain the government's legitimacy rather than to create centrifugal pressures.[26] Diao Jiecheng, taking advantage of his position as an official of the National Letters and Visits Bureau, has written *A Brief History of People's Letters and Visits* (*renmin xinfang shilüe*), which offers a highly comprehensive account of the origin and development of PRC's principal complaint system from the 1920s to the early 1990s.[27]

Scholars in the third school have done research on Chinese complaint systems in earlier periods. They have generally focused on a specific complaint system or on a certain period. Chinese legal scholars Yang Yifan and Liu Ducai probe into the origin, function, and evolution of the Petition Box (*guihan*), one of the early Chinese complaint systems.[28] The historian Jonathan Ocko described the operation of the capital appeal system in the Qing dynasty, largely in the Jiaqing reign (1796–1820). He argued that in that limited period, at least, the system actually offered more opportunities for dissatisfied criminal suspects to gain redress than did contemporary legal systems in the West.[29] Similarly, legal historian Huang Yuansheng has studied the establishment and the effectiveness of a novel complaint system—the Administrative Court—in the early republic (1912–1928). On the basis of some 186 cases, Huang argues that the Institution, designed to hear appeals against official abuses, was not "totally useless" as some other scholars have suggested.[30]

Some scholars who look to the past center their studies on larger and more violent collective complaints, protests, and rebellions. Guangyuan Zhou examines a tax protest in Sichuan province in the 1870s, which began with collective complaints. Although the late Qing state harshly suppressed the protest, it also acknowledged its legitimacy in a time of increasing official corruption by executing two officials. Unfortunately, Zhou observes, this was more a symbolic effort to warn, educate, and persuade other corrupt officials than part of a systematic effort to root out corruption.[31] Elizabeth J. Perry has analyzed ten public protests from the Taiping rebellion in the late Qing to the 1989 Tiananmen demonstrations. Believing that the Confucian concept of the "Mandate of Heaven" has long legitimated many rebellions, Perry sees a linkage between public protests in the "late imperial period" and those of more recent times.[32]

There is no denying that these focused studies have enriched our understanding of the history of Chinese complaint systems and laid important foundations for this research, but some of them have offered premature and tangential conclusions. If Yu Jianrong had been aware of similar complaint systems in other countries, including self-styled democratic ones, he might not have been so quick to conclude that the system in China is at odds with the ideal of judicial independence. If Ying Xing had taken account of the republican Administrative Court, he might not have so readily characterized the 1989 Administrative Litigation Law (*xingzheng susongfa*) as a "quiet revolution (*jingqiaoqiao de geming*) after a millennial Chinese "tradition of rule by man" (*renzhi chuantong*)."[33] Although those who resort to the letters and visits system constitute a relatively small and impoverished cohort in the larger context of the entire Chinese population, their disillusionment may easily contribute to a general process of disenchantment that might eventually undermine the authority of the state. Some scholars, relying solely on the *Rites of the Zhou* (*Zhouli*), a book most likely written in the Han dynasty (206 BCE–220 CE) and a banished official's personal account, argue that certain complaint forms like the Red Stone (*feishi*, literally, lung stone) existed in the Eastern Zhou period (771–246 BCE). But other sources show that the Red Stone was not established until a much later time and the only verifiable means of complaining to the Zhou state was to appeal to the palace gate (*yique*).[34]

In accord with the popular saying "to know one area, one must study the whole territory; to know one era, one must study the whole record," I have undertaken a comprehensive study of complaint systems in Chinese history from early times to the present. It is, I believe, an essential first step in understanding the strengths, weaknesses, and various roles of the letters and visits system in contemporary China. Such a comprehensive study of Chinese complaint systems should help explain why the PRC leaders, like most of their predecessors, continue to allow skipping complaints even when they have been forbidden by the law. It should help us understand why many complainants today still try to block the leader's vehicle even when such measures seem rarely to have positive results.

Formal and informal complaint systems

First of all, I must address the thorny problem of the complex relationship between complaint systems that typically have no enforcement capability and the formal legal system that has such authority. Two legal scholars, David Engel working on Thailand and Carl Minzner working on China, have acknowledged this problem. In his study of the 1970s' judicial system in Chiangmai, northern Thailand, Engel argues that, despite the legal "reform" started in the early twentieth century, many people continued to use "conventional" means, such as going to the local headman, to settle their disputes instead of appealing to the "modern" court. Aware of the long-standing legitimacy of such practices, local Thai officials considered people's complaints, both civil and criminal, unless they were too big to be solved locally.[35] In the case of China, Minzner shows how the PRC letters and visits system overlaps with the judicial and administrative systems because both national and provincial letters and visits regulations create a multistage procedure for complaining about administrative decisions that is parallel to established judicial and administrative hierarchies as well as to that established by the Administrative Litigation Law and the Administrative Reconsideration Law (*xingzheng fuyifa*).[36]

In Chinese history, too, formal and informal legal systems tended to intermingle, and various complaint systems functioned between the formal and the informal, the judicial and the political, the legal and the customary, and the past and the present. At the risk of oversimplification, we may trace the relationships of complaint systems with administrative and legal structures through several major periods. Chinese complaint systems began informally with several related institutions such as complaints to the palace gate (*yique*), complaints through the official cart (*gongche shangshu*), and complaints at the red stone (*feishi*) and they developed gradually from the Eastern Zhou to the Southern and Northern Dynasties (770 BCE–580 CE). From the Sui dynasty (581–618) through the Qing dynasty (1644–1911), the complaint systems became more formal and systematic, but, at the same time, became more closely integrated into the formal administrative and legal system. In other words, the same formal bureaucracy handled both complaints and legal cases of the first instance and of review. After the Republic of China was founded in 1912, the government created complaint systems (e.g., Complaint Laws and the Administrative Court) outside the formal legal system which was itself more clearly distinguished from the administrative system. But the distinction between the complaint system and the legal/administrative system became blurred again in the early PRC when the People's Republic abolished most of the republican legal system. The situation has changed yet again since the PRC began its legal reform in 1978. With the establishment of the administrative court in 1989 and the publication of the *Regulations Regarding Letters and Visits* in 1995, the distinction between the two systems has become clearer once again. It is perhaps the very hybrid and dynamic nature of these institutions—informal and formal, judicial and political, customary and codified, ancient and renewed—that explains their persistence despite changes in other aspects of the state and society.

Three complaint systems

In addition to clarifying relations between complaint systems and other law-like systems, I shall distinguish among the various kinds of complaint systems that existed over time in China. Jonathan Ocko studied what he called "capital appeals (*jingkong*, literally, appeal to the state capital)" in the Qing as distinct from other forms such as "skipping complaints (*yuesu*)" and "direct complaints (*zhisu*)."[37] Other scholars such as Luehrmann, Ying Xing, and Minzner who focus on the PRC, use various terms such as "complaint," "petition," or "mass petition" to describe the activities of those aggrieved at local official action or inaction. In this study, taking account of all kinds of complaint systems over the entire course of Chinese history, I shall divide them into the three categories that seem to make the most sense over the longest period of time: gradual/regular complaints (*zhuji shangsu*), skipping complaints, and direct complaints. Gradual/regular complaint refers to a kind of step-by-step complaint authorized by almost all laws from as early as the Sui to as recently as the PRC today.[38] Skipping complaints were and are made by complainants who have bypassed at least one level of the state hierarchy and brought their complaints to the higher level without specific authorization. From the Sui through the Qing, skipping complaints were generally considered criminal and those who mounted them were subject to harsh penalties, although the contents of the complaints were handled variously and the laws were not always enforced. In China today, as Minzner and a Human Rights Watch report have shown, many "retrievers" from local governments at the county level regularly go to Beijing to capture those who have jumped over them to go to the capital but even those complainants are not always prosecuted for their alleged crimes.[39] Aggrieved people who made or make direct complaints skip all required legal steps in the judicial and administrative ladders and complain directly to the heads of state, including kings, sons of heaven, august lords, khans, generalissimos, and chairmen. Even today, some complainants still go straight to top leaders such as presidents and prime ministers without dealing first with any of the intermediate levels of local and provincial government.

Natural resistance

While studying rural complaints in the PRC, O'Brien and Li coined the important term "rightful resistance" because many such complainants routinely invoke laws and regulations as the basis for their charges and operate through established legal channels.[40] Although the precise concept may be new, the principle of "rightful resistance" has actually long been practiced and observed in Chinese history. Ever since the Sui and Tang when the rulers systematized the process of lodging complaints, many complainants had registered their complaints through legal or "rightful" steps such as regular/gradual complaints and even some skipping and direct complaints. But in my research I have found that the theory of "rightful resistance" does not provide full answers to the following questions: Why do so many complainants ignore "rightfulness" by making skipping and direct complaints that are illegal? Why are many complainants prepared to risk harsh punishments by continuing their illicit complaints? And why do some complainants commit self-immolation after repeated failures to have their grievances addressed and wrongs rectified? To answer such questions, we perhaps need a more fundamental and capacious theory that I would like to call "natural resistance."

Like rightful resistance, natural resistance is a form of protest and contention, but, unlike rightful resistance, natural resistance operates outside the existing laws and regulations. Invoking both religious and secular principles, aggrieved complainants often consciously or unconsciously neglect the laws and regulations that require them to proceed through lawful steps in seeking justice for official malfeasance. Natural resistance is composed of four independent but also interconnected elements: heavenly (or natural) principles, people as the root of the state, republicanism, and natural response of intense injustice.

As one of the oldest notions in Chinese history dating from the early Zhou period, heavenly principles (*tianli*) have long been revered by both rulers and the ruled in China. Most schools of thought, embraced by elites and commoners, hold that heaven is ultimately just, righteous, and benevolent, at least in the long term.[41] *The Book of Documents* and the Confucian scholars who edited them claimed that "heaven hears as the people hear, heaven sees as the people see" and that heaven loves the people.[42] Heavenly principles, whether specified in detail or invoked in general,[43] have been regarded as representing heaven's will and as transcending human laws.[44] Some popular "natural principles" such as "a life for a life" have been firmly embedded in the minds of complainants over time. Moreover, most Chinese believe that any violations of heavenly principles (e.g., injustices) will result in eventual heavenly retribution if not punished by humans according to the human laws. Owing to profound beliefs in heaven and heavenly principles, many complainants, after infringement of heavenly principles occurred, would consider it their natural right to complain to the government, especially the rulers—the "sons of heaven" and supposedly the ultimate authorities under heaven. For most rulers in Chinese history, any harm to heavenly principles was tantamount to damaging heavenly harmony that might draw anger from heaven in the forms of natural disasters. Thus, many rulers tended to acknowledge this natural right of resistance to injustice by permitting certain non-regular or even illegal complaints.

"People as the root of the state (*minben*) was another critical concept in Chinese culture and politics originating in the Zhou dynasty and persisting through the ages. Even under the supposedly novel polities of the Republic and People's Republic, many top leaders continued to invoke the ancient concept as a basis of legitimacy. They generally accept that because the people are the root of the state rulers should take care of them so that the state will enjoy peace (*bengu bangning*).[45] In that sense, rulers and officials should assume responsibility to serve as "parental officials" (*fumuguan*) and treat the people as their children.[46] As reflected in Mencius' popular words "people are more important than rulers (*mingui junqing*)," many Chinese rulers in successive dynasties and the republics tended to be quite attentive to people's natural right to complain. Complainants, for their part, would naturally be willing to bring their complaints to their "parents," especially the rulers, for satisfaction. After all, no one is better equipped to assist the people than the rulers in a family state (*guojia*), the Chinese word for both dynasties and nation states.

After the establishment of the Republic of China (ROC) in 1912, government leaders such as Sun Yat-sen advocated the Western concept of republicanism (using the term *gongche* dating from the Zhou period to translate the Western term). According to Sun and others, the people should be in charge (*minzhu*) of the people's state (*minguo*). From then on to the PRC, republican principles such as "heaven bestows freedom" and "officials are public servants" have further enhanced people's natural right (*minquan*) to complain. Because they are now the masters, many complainants believe that it is their natural right to complain about and to their "servants" (in Mao's phrase officials should "serve the people," *weirenmin fuwu*). In the Republic and People's Republic, unlike from the Sui to the Qing, neither rulers nor the people expect complainants who skip the lawful steps to be punished.

The fourth component of natural resistance is the complainants' natural response to injustice. For most complainants who ignore the laws and insist on registering their complaints illegally at higher levels, the damages imposed on them and their families by official injustice are so intolerable that their complaints are simply a natural response rather than ones based on certain laws, be they natural or positive. If rightful means cannot redress their grievances, some complainants will try illegal ways, endure all hardships, and bear all burdens, continuing their journey until they succeed or die. When all rational means fail, some desperate complainants, from the Tang to today, take extreme actions such as self-immolation to express their outrage.

As the common term "natural" suggests, natural resistance in China shares some features with natural law in the West. For example, both consider that heaven and nature [in natural resistance] and Yahwe/God/Allah [in natural law] play important roles. Both heaven and God represent something higher than any human law and possibly something just, humane, and good.[47] Second, heavenly principles and divine rights that support natural resistance and natural law have been found in (or instilled into) all humans' minds.[48] Third, both heavenly principles [in natural resistance] and God's Law [in natural law] were (and are) often believed to be eternal and unchanging.[49]

However, the above three similarities were (and are) accompanied by the following fundamental differences between the two notions. For example, heaven/nature in natural resistance is different from God in natural law. Heaven in Chinese history and culture was the abode of super-*human* forces, but, unlike God in the West, it was not a super*natural* force that created the universe out of nothing or intervened unilaterally in history.[50] From the Zhou and Han times, heaven, earth, and humans were thought to interact to produce both cosmic and historical change. Some later Confucian scholars such as Liu Zongzhou (1578–1645) even argued that "Heaven cannot fulfill itself without human participation."[51] This reflects a quite different conception of the supreme force from that of the Western religious tradition in which God was omnipotent and inscrutable.[52] In addition, unlike God in natural law, heaven in natural resistance is not the only source of legitimate popular action. As we have seen, the idea of *minben*/people as the root became a key Confucian concept that played a very important role in natural resistance because aggrieved complainants consider it as their natural right to complain to parental officials and rulers, even for purposes and by methods not sanctioned by law.

Natural resistance is similar in some respects to other forms of popular resistance, but it also differs in certain ways. In invoking the cause of justice above the rule of law, it is similar to civil disobedience.[53] In countenancing illegality in the pursuit of equity it differs from labor movements dependent on legal strikes to advance their cause.[54] Natural resistance like collective action can take on national and transnational forms, but it emphasizes individual and local contention more than national or transnational mobilization.[55] Like "everyday resistance," natural resistance can often be a "weapon of the weak," but may often take more overt and active forms. Natural resistance is like rightful resistance in speaking truth to power, but it tends to be mostly individual, spontaneous, constant, and customary, while rightful resistance may typically be more collective, planned, episodic, and legal.[56] Or, to complicate the matter, natural resistance can be both individual and collective,[57] both spontaneous and planned, both endemic and epidemic, and both legal and illegal. Natural resistance embraces both religious and secular values, the boundaries of which are often blurred. But it encompasses a combination of heavenly principles, *minben*, parental ruler/official, and republicanism, and seems to have less to do with religious icons, celebrated dates, or sacred documents that often legitimate social movements.[58]

Despite the persistence of sophisticated complaint systems and continued emphasis on the legitimacy of complaints justified by widespread belief in natural resistance, many—perhaps most—grievances lodged through China's perennial complaint systems remained unsatisfied. As we shall see, although each major dynasty or polity had its special characteristics, it also shared fundamental problems with other dynasties or polities. They included political corruption, judicial dependency, restricted venues for voicing grievances, internal problems of the complaint institution (e.g., limited power), excessive distrust of local officials, and unwarranted faith in central authorities. China experienced certain changes in its legal system at the turn of the twentieth century due partly to Western influence, but political corruption and numerous wars still created many grievances in the republic.[59] In the early PRC, institutionalized complaint systems were marginalized by popular mobilization; in the reform period since 1979, numerous problems have arisen from administrative decentralization and bureaucratic pragmatism.

When studying the labor movements in the early nineteenth century, the famed historian E. P. Thompson argued that a variety of factors such as the English Jacobin tradition, the exploitative and oppressive relationship intrinsic to the Industrial Revolution, and the hardship and exposure to "irresponsible and unlicensed competition" contributed to the persistence of revolts of English workers in this period.[60] Likewise, I may suggest, the persistence of Chinese complainants' natural resistance and rulers' tolerance of illegitimate complaints can be explained by a mixture of ingrained beliefs in heavenly principles, *minben*, and later republicanism by the rulers and the ruled as well as natural responses of harms to the complainants and their families.

Content of chapters

In Chapter 1, I examine the origin of complaint systems in the earliest recorded times and the development of those institutions over two millennia to the late Qing. We shall find that the complaint systems probably began informally in the Zhou, were further articulated in the Han, and developed into a part of the formal legal system during the Jin and Tang. The enhanced legitimacy of complaint systems was balanced by restrictions on skipping appeals and other extreme forms of dissent from the Tang through the Qing. In this period, as in later ones, many complainants never got satisfaction for their grievances, but the state continued to allow public expressions of complaints and complainants continued to mount appeals in line with the fundamental belief in a natural right to complain.

The second chapter explores the period between 1898 and 1911 when the late Qing rulers were under Western pressure to undertake various "reforms." On the one hand, the royal court showed rare lenience to skipping appealers and it also introduced the ideas of many putatively Western institutions, such as an Administrative Court, and ideas, such as "respecting people's dignity." On the other hand, it justified many of the reforms in its complaint systems by seeking precedents in Chinese history. This effort to "sell" the reforms by appeals to history also influenced the nature and fate of the reforms that resonated long after the fall of the Qing in 1911.

Chapter 3 deals with the complaint systems in the early republican period (1912–1928). In line with plans of the late Qing period, the early republic created an Administrative Court and passed an Administrative Litigation Law. To better protect its citizens from official violations of their "[natural] rights," the early republican government established a Department for Disciplining Government whose mission was to supervise the Administrative Court and entertain people's complaints against officials. People in this period could also continue to use informal means to complain. With many judges strongly believing in the ideal of the "rule of law (*fazhi*)," the complaint systems in this period arguably experienced their "golden age" in theoretical terms, but they were confined largely to the capital (Beijing).

Chapter 4 discusses what I have chosen to call the late republican period (1928–1949) under the rule of the Guomindang (GMD or KMT). While the GMD remained a largely military regime under one-party rule, it provided some people with more means to complain. The Administrative Court continued to take formal charge of accepting people's lawsuits against both local and central government officials. Other organs of the National Government (*guomin zhengfu*), including the Legislative Yuan and the Supervisory Yuan, and local people's congresses, were allowed to accept informal complaints from the people. Some cases show that Chiang Kai-shek could take people's natural resistance seriously and ordered officials to conduct detailed investigations. Although noted for its own forms of corruption and authoritarianism bordering on fascism, the GMD actually abolished a fee that had been charged by the early republican Administrative Court and that had forced many poor complainants to back off from lodging their complaints.

Chapters 5 probes into conditions in the PRC, from 1949 to 1982. Under the aura of what I may call "Revolutionary Idealism," early PRC leaders repealed most of the GMD's legal system including the Administrative Court. Instead, they established a comprehensive letters and visits system that was first designed to be a channel between the leaders and the mass. Since the formal judicial system was primarily focused on prosecuting the "enemies" of socialism, the letters and visits system soon became the most important means to address and solve less political disputes and complaints issuing from the people. The letters and visits system may have experienced its heaviest use during the relatively quiet times of the early 1950s and during the late 1970s, after the end of the Cultural Revolution.

The last chapter analyses complaint systems from 1982 to the present. As part of the wholesale reform policy, the Chinese Communist Party (CCP) began reforming the complaint systems. To uphold people's basic rights, it quietly restored the republican-style Administrative Court and publicized the *Regulations Regarding Letters and Visits* which had previously been informal and semi-secret. Yet, the "Bureaucratic Pragmatism" unleashed by the "open policy" and the slogan of "all looking forward (*yiqie xiangqiankan*)" have resulted in numerous complaints based on natural resistance. Among them, the Farmers' Burden, Rural Confiscation of Land, and Urban Relocation are the three biggest sources of complaints. To check the skyrocketing complaints, especially those to the capital, many local governments, with a green light from the center, have forcibly retrieved complainants from the capital and returned them to their home regions. As a result, the good intentions and reforms of the CCP regarding its complaint systems have not been fully realized.

In sum, this survey of complaint systems in Chinese history supports several conclusions with implications for the future. The idea that individuals and even groups that feel they have been wronged by local officials have a natural right to resist by complaining to higher authorities arose in fairly early times and resulted in an array of institutions that coexisted with more formal administrative and judicial bodies and practices and persisted over two millennia. To be sure, natural resistance had its limitations; complainants were expected in most periods to lodge their appeals progressively up the standard administrative hierarchy and those who dared to mount skipping complaints were usually subject to punishment even in cases where their complaints were found to be legitimate. But such limitations could be waived in times of great state insecurity or efforts at reform, and they were further attenuated during the early republican period when skipping complaints were fully legalized. The importance of the rich heritage of complaint systems was underlined when a full-blown variation was established in the People's Republic that claimed not only to listen to the people's grievances but to involve them with greater intensity than ever before in the actual process of formulating policies and governing. The formal apparatus for lodging complaints was set aside during the Maoist years of radical popular mobilization, but it returned with even greater force and articulation during the era of reform and opening under Deng and his successors. Given this history, it seems likely that some form of complaint system will continue to exist into the present century and may even survive the People's Republic. In the meantime it seems destined to help cushion the impact of some of the increasing demands of the Chinese state on the Chinese people in a highly competitive world and thus both to mitigate the worst abuses of that state as well as to prolong its life. Perhaps nothing more should be expected from any human institution functioning in the high-tension zone between state and society. It remains to be seen how the Chinese inheritance of complaint systems will interact with similar heritages in other societies to help shape statecraft in an increasingly integrated but conflict-prone world.

1 Hot potatoes

From early times to 1898[1]

The idea that aggrieved people who fail to get satisfaction from local officials should be able to register their complaints with higher levels of the administration including the highest authority in the land may have appeared as early as the Zhou dynasty (*c.* 1046–256 BCE). In the late Zhou, many important schools of thought began advocating key concepts such as heaven/nature, *minben*/people as the root, and heaven–human interaction that lay the foundations for natural resistance. These notions were further developed in the Han dynasty (202 BCE–220 CE), which seems also to have projected certain complaint institutions such as the Lung Stone (*feishi*), back into the Zhou. Han Confucians praised those institutions and variations on them appeared in subsequent dynasties such as the Jin (265–420), Northern Wei (386–584), Liang (502–557), and Sui (589–618). The Tang dynasty (618–907), which took both the Zhou and the Han as models and which embraced the Buddhist value of compassion, systematized the complaint systems even as it imposed restraints on natural resistance under the law. The Song dynasty (907–1279), which was inspired by renewed forms of Confucianism, modified the inherited complaint systems in line with its generally lenient policies toward officials and the scholar elite. The Mongol Yuan dynasty (1279–1368), which reunified China after centuries of civil war, went further to accept even illegal skipping complaints as a way to control various power-holders. The Ming dynasty (1368–1644), which was founded by a commoner who paid considerable attention to popular welfare, temporarily ended the practice of sending complaints back down to local officials to be resolved. The Qing (1644–1911), which was more oriented to elite interests, experimented with punishing illegal skipping complainants while also dealing with the merits of the cases they brought to the center's attention. Administrators may have accepted the institutions simply as safety valves to vent popular discontent and facilitate their control of the people while the people may have resorted to them for their own purposes to check the abuses of local officials. But both states and populace seem to have agreed that they were essential parts of governance, too hot to hold for long yet too valuable to drop entirely.

The origins of natural resistance

The long-lasting crucial notions such as heavenly principles, mandate of heaven, *minben*, heaven–human interaction, and parental rulers/officials that would justify people's natural resistance in Chinese history was initiated in the Eastern Zhou dynasty. For example, the concept of heaven, as historian Kung-chuan Hsiao notes, came from an early period when gods and spirits were honored.[2] In the Eastern Zhou, the *Book of Songs* had already adopted terms such as "heaven," "the mandate of heaven," and "the son of heaven." In one song, King Wen of the Zhou was said to have mandate from heaven; another song called the king the son of heaven. Heaven was regarded as formidable but loving of the people, an early form of heaven–human interaction.[3] The *Book of Songs* also for the first time used terms such as "parental rulers/officials." As one song stated: "[Those] virtuous and rulers/officials are people's parents."[4] A later Confucian text, the *Book of Documents* continued to believe that "heaven's way (*tiandao*)" was to punish the evil and bless the good. The *Book of Documents* also explicitly advocated the concept of *minben*, parental officials, and heaven's love of the people. As the book said, "people are the root of the state," "the son of heaven is both the parent of his people and the king of his state," and "heaven sees what people see." According to the *Book of Documents*, when Jie, the last king of the Xia dynasty (*c.*2070–1600 BCE) transgressed heaven's way, people complained to heaven. Heaven then punished the ruler by taking away his mandate to rule.[5]

Many late Zhou schools of thought such as Confucianism, Mohism, and Daoism continued to propagate these notions. Although Confucius "never claimed any positive knowledge of spiritual matters,"[6] he still respected heaven and feared the mandate of heaven.[7] Invoking the *Book of Documents*, Mencius reaffirmed that heaven "sees what people see." He also developed the old *minben* concept by arguing that people were more important than the ruler. In so doing, as Frederick Mote argues, Mencius "not only made the people the ultimate standard for judging government, but made man the standard for Heaven itself."[8]

Mo Zi advocated "universal love" and promoted the ideas of the will of heaven and heaven–human interaction. He argued that heaven was just and loved the people deeply. Only polities following the will of heaven were legitimate, and any killing of innocent persons would result in heaven's omen. He specifically stated that heaven would punish rulers who made false judgments on crimes and reward those who ruled justly.[9] While generally eschewing Confucian moralism, the semi-legendary Daoist patriarch Lao Zi opined that heaven's favor was "forever on the side of the good man."[10]

Contemporary historical works such as the *Commentary of Zuo* were also influenced profoundly by such notions as the mandate of heaven and *minben*/people as the root. For instance, when King Cheng of Chu commented on the fate of the fugitive Prince Chonger of Jin, he said: "When heaven intends to prosper a man, who can stop him? Violation of the will of heaven will draw serious punishment."[11] In 559 BCE, after the people of the state of Wei expelled their ruler, an official of the state of Jin named Shi Kuang, said that the exiled ruler of Wei had failed to nurture his people as children and to protect them like heaven.[12]

With the creation and influence of the concepts of heaven, the mandate of heaven, and *minben*/people as the root in this period, rulers would function both as the sons of a just, loving, and awe-inspring heaven and as the parents of their subjects. Due to a fear of the anger, punishment, and removal of their mandate by heaven and the inherent responsibility to look after their "children"—the people, many rulers were inclined to acknowledge people's natural right to complain. They were accordingly attentive to complainants' grievances. Complainants suffering from intolerable injustices had a firm faith in heaven's principles and their parental rulers who they thought had more concern about their grievances than other subjects and local officials. They regarded it as their natural right to complain to their "parents" and to heaven's sons or representative on earth—the rulers.

The early complaint systems and development of natural resistance

Unlike those concepts underlying natural resistance whose origin and development are relatively clear, the origin of Chinese complaint systems was rather murky because there is no archaeological or written evidence for complaint institutions in the Zhou period.

The first written evidence we have of the idea of a system of registering people's complaints at court comes from the Former Han dynasty (206 BCE–8 CE), founded by a commoner. In his *Shiji* (Historical Records), the great historian Sima Qian (135–90 BCE) quoted Han Wendi (r. 180–157 BCE) to the effect that the "ancient sage kings" had established at court a flag for whoever wished to submit good advice (*jinshan zhijing*) and a piece of wood for whoever wanted to criticize the rulers (*feibang zhimu*).[13]

Another Former Han-period text, the *Zhouli* (The Rites of the Zhou), an idealized description of the Zhou system, attributed two institutions for complaints to Yao and Shun, legendary sage rulers whom we now regard as symbols of early clans. The first was a drum erected outside the innermost palace gate under the charge of the Royal Groom (*dapu*), whose duties also included maintaining the royal throne, delivering the king's orders, and punishing wayward vassals. Complainants who were unable to gain satisfaction elsewhere were allowed to beat the drum. Whenever he heard the roll of the drum, the royal groom would immediately report the case to the king.[14] The other complaint institution was the Lung or Red Stone, which permitted even humble complainants to voice their grievances.[15] Later scholars attributed the wood, drum and stone to the Zhou dynasty and this view continues to be accepted by some scholars even today.[16] In any case, the idea that the wood, drum, and stone had existed in Zhou times was used to hold some Latter Han-dynasty rulers to account. For example, during the reign of Shundi (r. 125–144 CE) more than eighty people were arrested and were slated to be heavily punished according to the laws against criticism (*feibang*). Zhang Hao, the Minister of Works (*dasikong*), reminded the ruler that sage kings such as Yao and Shun had established the drum and the wood to welcome criticism. He warned Shundi that if he violated the liberal spirit behind those practices, no one under heaven (i.e., the known world) would dare to speak out.[17]

According to the Song historian Sima Guang, the earliest verified popular means of complaint was "going to the palace gate" (*yique*, the home and symbol of officials and the ruler).[18] In his view, that was an informal yet commonly practiced form of complaint as early as the Warring States period.[19] In 284 BCE, for example, Chuo Chi, the prime minister of the warring state of Qi accused his corrupt king, named Min, of ignoring the people who were voicing their grievances at the palace gate.[20] Another verified means of complaint was a short-lived regional petition canister created by Zhao Guanghan, the head of Yingchuan prefecture, in the Han Yuzhou region,[21] though no evidence shows that the petition canister had been used outside Yingchuan.

During the Han dynasty, the most important and widely used method of registering complaints was, as in the Zhou period, complaining to the palace gate.[22] In 167 BCE, in the reign of the humane ruler Wendi, a young woman named Ti Ying complained to the palace gate in Chang'an, the capital, when her father, a junior clerk, was about to be mutilated.[23] Her letter not only reached the hands of Wendi and saved her father's life but also helped persuade the ruler to abolish most punishments of bodily mutilation shortly thereafter.[24] In 127 CE, a low-ranking Recorder (*zhubo*) of Ningyang county, Shandong province, complained to the palace gate about grievances he had against the local magistrate that had been neglected for seven years. His complaint finally reached the ruler Shundi (r. 115–144 CE), although the result, unfortunately, is unknown.[25]

In the Han, not just officials of all ranks but also commoners could report directly to the rulers. In the Later Han, Xiang Kai, a commoner of Pingyuan county, Shandong province, wrote to Huandi (r. 146–167 CE) criticizing his execution of many innocent and upright officials and the blockage of loyal speech (*zhongyan*). "Since the beginning of the Han," Xiang Kai wrote, "we have not seen any reign that blocks criticism, kills upright officials, and implements harsh law like today's."[26] Although there was no reply from Huandi, the case suggests that commoners in the Later Han could complain directly to the throne about government policy and apparently, at least in this case, get away with it. Of course in this instance the declining authority of the state may have had something to do with the royal abuses, the commoner's criticism, and the critics ability to avoid punishment.

Officials and commoners also submitted complaints during the Han via public official carts (*gongche shangshu*) that were sent out by the court to bring students to the capital. In one case, a Later Han ruler became concerned when the driver of an official cart rejected one such complaint. According to Wang Fu, a scholar and critic, the Later Han ruler Mingdi (r. 57–75 CE) was surprised when a public cart refused to transmit a report because it had been submitted on a wrong day. Mingdi noted that "farmers stop working the land to go to the palace gate to complain." He asked: "How can it be the government's intention to reject their complaints simply because of the taboo date?" Mingdi thus abolished the practice of refusing to entertain complaints simply because they were submitted on the wrong days.[27]

How did Han complainants like Ti Ying and Xiang Kai dare to complain directly to the ruler without any fear of punishment? Why did Han rulers like

Wendi and Mingdi not only accept direct complaints but also order officials not to block them? One possibility is that the Han was founded by a commoner and early rulers may have followed a populist ideal.[28] Yet, more importantly, the notions of the mandate of heaven, heaven–human interaction, and *minben*, which originated in the Zhou times were solidified and systematized in the early Han. Lu Jia (240–170 BCE), a Confucian scholar and official, once warned Han rulers that they should correct their errors whenever natural catastrophes occurred.[29] Another Confucian scholar Jia Yi (200–168 BCE) sought to revive the *minben* concept in the Zhou. "I have heard that people are always the root in politics," Jia wrote, "[people] are the root of the state, of the ruler, and of the officials."[30] The most influential and renowned scholar in the Han was Dong Zhongshu (179–104 BCE). His systemization of the Zhou theory of heaven–human interaction and people as the root had a tremendous impact on later rulers and officials alike, which also enhanced the old *minben* concept. According to Dong, some natural events such as eclipses and earthquakes were warnings to the ruler that he was doing wrong (e.g., violating people's rights). If rulers ignored the admonition, a real catastrophe might well follow.[31]

Influenced by Dong's theory of heaven–human interaction, many scholars and rulers in the Han believed there existed certain correlations between people's grievances and natural disasters. For example, the Later Han historian Ban Gu wrote that any person who died while still harboring grievances would damage the harmony of heaven.[32] In 52 CE, during a severe drought, the Latter Han founder Guangwudi quickly sent emissaries to the prisons to review the grievances of the inmates. He pardoned some and released them from prison.[33] In this sense, rulers in the Han as well as in later periods tended to acknowledge people's natural right to complain to avoid grievances that could result in the anger and punishment from heaven.

Of course complainants in the Han, including even some of those cited above, were not always successful in having their complaints actually addressed let alone resolved to their satisfaction. The Latter Han Mingdi who had allowed complaints to be made on taboo days was blamed by the Minister of Education (*situ*) Bao Yu for arresting more than a thousand persons. Although we lack sufficient evidence to judge the guilt or innocence of these people, it seems likely that Mingdi was exercising in this case the highhandedness that stemmed from the relatively aristocratic nature of the Latter Han ruling class.[34]

Later Han scholar and critic Wang Fu argued that people found it difficult to complain about official abuse because most officials tended to protect each other.[35]

Thus even the Han, founded by commoners and receptive to commoners' complaints, ended up ignoring commoners' interests and being overthrown—by commoners.

The development of complaint systems based on early models

After the decline and fall of the Han in the early third century CE, subsequent states attempted to establish their legitimacy by following the Zhou and Han models in providing people with more methods of natural resistance.[36] The founder of the Jin dynasty, Wudi (r. 265–290 CE), who came from a Confucian background, formally established the Public Petition Drum (*dengwengu*, literally, "climb and listen drum"), based on that which had been described in the *Rites of Zhou*.[37] In 291 CE, shortly after the death of Jin Wudi, the Recorder of the Grand Guardian (*taibao zhubo*) Liu Yao beat the drum to protest the illegal killing of the Grand Guardian Wei Guan by Sima Wei, the king of the state of Chu. Although this was a case of official complaint about the handling of an inter-state incident and the result is not available, the point is that the drum for registering complaints at court was clearly in use.[38]

The Northern Wei (386–534 CE) inherited the drum from the Jin. Shortly after the founder Shizu's enthronement (r. 423–452), he placed a drum on the left side of the palace gate. People with grave grievances were allowed to beat it. The officials in charge of the drum were ordered to report any drum-beating to the ruler. In 436 CE, to check mounting official violations of the law and perhaps to strengthen central authority in a chaotic era, Shizu temporarily asked all officials and commoners to report on any illegal activities of the local officials serving in their areas. While mostly a short-term policy, this order was the first recorded invitation to the people to submit what would come to be called skipping complaints, or complaints over the heads of local officials who have engaged in putatively illegal activities.[39]

When Liang Wudi (502–549) ascended the throne, he followed classical models in ordering the placement of a slab of wood and a red stone accompanied by two boxes outside an office with the title of the Official Cart (*gongchefu*). He explained: "If aggrieved commoners have no other way to complain, they can write [their complaints] and throw [them] into the box beside the red stone."[40] Although the wood and red stone may have existed in earlier times as we have seen and in other parts of China during the sixth century, this is the first incontestable evidence I have of their actual existence and use. Of course, as would become clear in later ages, the presence of these institutions did not necessarily mean that they were always taken seriously or provided relief to the aggrieved common people of their afflictions. Liang Wudi was later criticized as being too harsh on commoners and too lenient toward the nobility and the powerful.[41]

Like Liang Wudi, Sui Wendi (r. 581–604) implemented several measures to make the legal system more humane. He codified the Ten Abominations (crimes considered so serious that they could not be amnestied), rooted out many cruel punishments, and evidently retained the inherited complaint system. But Wendi opposed skipping complaints that had recently been accepted by the Northern Wei. He decreed that all complainants should follow the regular or rightful steps up the administrative hierarchy, from township, to county, to prefecture, to province. Only if the provincial governor did not accept their cases could people complain to the palace gate. If still dissatisfied, he or she could beat the drum and the official in charge of it would report the case to the ruler. By outlawing the skipping complaints, the complaint systems in the Sui was gradually formalized and incorporated in the formal legal system. Moreover, like Liang Wudi,

Sui Wendi soon revealed the priority he placed on royal authority over due process by punishing people without complying with the law. He even instituted one of the harshest laws in Chinese history: that a person would be executed for stealing a dollar. Such harsh laws generated numerous grievances that had to be satisfied, if at all, by going through the many steps in the judicial system, not by direct complaints to the court.[42]

The complaint systems institutionalized

Incorporating the various institutions established separately during the Jin, Liang, Wei, and Sui, the Tang established a more articulated and comprehensive system than the Sui that served the interest of that much more expansive and enduring polity. For the first time in history, the Tang clearly distinguished among direct complaints, skipping complaints, and regular/gradual complaints. In a law code that has survived and influenced later polities, the Tang not only made the complaint system a part of the formal judicial system but also outlawed certain natural resistance such as skipping and direct complaints.[43]

Like the Sui, the Tang rulers usually required all people to complain up the required government hierarchy: first to local governments, and if dissatisfied, then to upper governments such as the Department of the State Affairs (*shangshusheng*), and finally to the central government (i.e., the three bureaus: the court, the Board of Punishments, and the Censorate). If all these complaints were unavailing, aggrieved people could complain to the palace gate or beat the drum to get their cases before the ruler.[44] Similarly, *The Tang Code with Commentaries* (*tanglu shuyi*) demanded that people complain step by step from the county, to the prefecture, to the province. This text, that reflected actual legal practice during the Tang, did not mention complaints to the central level.[45]

In addition to favoring regular complaints, The Tang Code illegalized skipping complaints by saying that government offices "must not accept them." Skipping complainants and officials who accepted skipping complainants would all be beaten with forty lashes of the whip respectively. If, on the other hand, officials wrongly refuse complaints that were legally mounted, they "will be punished with fifty lashes of the whip," a heavier punishment than that meted out to official who accepted skipping complaints.[46]

Despite these strict laws designed to enforce a kind of due process, many aggrieved people still at times ignored the law and made skipping complaints to the ruler—heaven's son. Indeed, on three occasions—in 722, 840, and 847—because of the mounting number of skipping complaints, several decrees were issued banning certain skipping complaints, especially civil-case complaints to the Petition Box (*guihan*) and the Censorate.[47]

Although the Tang prohibited skipping complaints, however unsuccessfully, it allowed direct complaints under certain circumstances such as people having grave grievances or complaints that had exhausted all legal means. The Tang Code permitted three main kinds of direct complaints: beating the drum, blocking the royal cart (*lanyujia*), and submitting to the court (*shangbiao*). But complainants taking advantage of these venues would be punished if their complaints proved to be without foundation. According to *The Tang Code with Commentaries*, direct complainants whose cases tuned out to be false would be beaten with "eighty blows of the bamboo."[48] The *Six Canons of the Tang* allowed people who had failed to get satisfaction through all other means to beat the drum, but this privilege was restricted only to people with important cases.[49]

Aside from the three main forms, there were other forms of direct complaint in the Tang. The fourth legitimate form was the red stone of classical provenance. The historian Liu Junwen argues that complaint drums were established outside the Forbidden Cities of both Western and Eastern capitals (Chang'an and Luoyang) along with the red stones. There were strict rules about the people who could complain via the red stone. Only very old and young persons or anyone who was mentally or physically incapable of making other forms of complaint could stand beside the red stone.[50] Shen Kuo, a prominent Song scholar and scientist, claimed to have discovered the Tang red stone that was eight to nine feet long and shaped like a human lung.[51]

A fifth form of direct complaint permitted during the Tang was going up to the palace gate—most likely, as we have seen, the oldest form of natural resistance in China that originated from the heaven–human interactions and the Confucian concept of *minben*/people as the root in the Zhou period. During the reign of the famously humane ruler Tang Taizong (r. 626–649), people could complain directly to the princes and the ruler.[52] Much later in the Tang, in 845, a commoner complained to the palace gate that his elder brother had been executed on the false charge of taking a bribe. The head of Jiangdu prefecture eventually succeeded in having the responsible local magistrate demoted for mishandling this case.[53]

The most novel, popular, and famous form of direct complaint in the Tang may have been the petition box initiated in 686 by Empress Wu Zetian (r. 690–705), which spread to Japan in the Tokugawa period.[54] At the outset, the box was big and had four sides. Each side was made for a different purpose. The satisfaction of grievances was only one of its purposes—it also accepted letters about criticism, extending mercy, and connecting to the occult. The petition box was managed by a Petition Box Office (*guishiyuan*). The chief official in charge was called the Commissioner of the Petition Box (*zhiguishi*). The Six Canons of the Tang noted that the Commissioner was supposed to "satisfy all grievances occurring under heaven."[55] Although the petition box was likely created by Empress Wu to receive secret reports against her enemies, it was later transformed to receive individual complaints.[56] Soon after Empress Wu's death in 705 CE, Tang Zhongzong (r. 705–710) ordered that both officials and commoners who had grievances or were wrongly punished could deposit their complaints in the petition box.[57]

The Tang system of the petition box continued to be modified over time. In 756, being afraid that important messages could be blocked by officials, Tang Suzong (r. 756–762) rejected the suggestion that all letters put into the box should be reviewed by the officials in charge of the box before being memorialized to the throne. He was afraid that these officials might block important messages coming from the people. Twenty-three years later, Cui Zao, Commissioner of the Petition Box, recommended that a regular complaint system should be enforced so that most "civil" cases would end up in the petition box only after they had been considered at all lower levels of the system. In the reign of Wenzong (r. 827–840), two further reforms were made. First, in 838, it was specified that all letters placed in the petition box were to go directly to the ruler without having been reviewed by censors and commissioners. Second, in 840, a decree reiterated that only people who wanted to criticize court policy, raised military and state issues, or had real grievances but had exhausted all legal methods could place their petitions in the box.[58]

The Tang created a complex and comprehensive complaint system as part of its effort to deliver good government on the Zhou and Han models and concepts such as the heaven–human interactions, hoping to manage a large realm and establish a durable order. Thus Tang Taizong compared himself with the Duke of Zhou and expressed shame that he had spent more money than Han Wendi.[59] During the reign of Empress Wu, the courageous official Chen Zi'ang, like the Han scholars Dong Zhongshu and Ban Gu, argued that the cries of people with grievances would upset the harmony of heaven and might well bring on disasters.[60] Similarly, the prominent poet and one-time director of the Board of Punishment Bai Juyi (772–846), connected floods and droughts to inmates' grievances in the prisons.[61]

While the Tang complaint procedures became an integral part of the formal legal system, and were more developed and comprehensive than those of previous polities, many complainants continued to find it difficult to obtain satisfaction. Some contemporary scholars and officials also criticized the Tang complaint systems for not effectively redressing many grievances. For example, although Empress Wu founded the petition box, grievances continued to be voiced during her reign and they were actually said to have increased. Chen Zi'ang, for example, criticized Empress Wu for allegedly turning a blind eye to extra-legal tortures and executions that caused enormous pain and resulted in many grievances.[62]

Even in 733, during the height of the Tang, some aggrieved people believed they had no effective way to voice their complaints but had to rely only on heaven and individual upright officials to satisfy their grievances. When Yuan Renjing, the supervisor of the Imperial Court (*daliqing*) whose duty was to handle complaints, suddenly died, many prisoners reportedly cried and chanted: "Why does heaven not show mercy on people with grievances? Why does [heaven] take away our beloved relative [Yuan]? We have reason but no place to complain. How sad!"[63] Had any part of the complaint system such as the petition box, the drum, the red stone, and the palace complaint been as effective as it claimed to be, those prisoners might not have cried out in those terms at the death of a single honest official. In the later Tang, the complaint system allegedly became even less effective. The contemporary poet Bai Juyi remarked that [late Tang] rulers were oblivious to complaints thrown into the box and the roll of the drum was no longer heard.[64]

Because their complaints were unavailing, some desperate subjects, having exhausted all legal and even illegal means of complaining, publically mutilated themselves in the capital in order to attract the attention of their parental rulers and sons of heaven. Thus even the relatively humane and concerned ruler Xuanzong issued a decree in 725 imposing forty blows of the bamboo on complainants who mutilated themselves, thereby unacceptably harming the bodies they inherited from their parents.[65]

The Five Dynasties (907–960) succeeding the Tang inherited most Tang institutions, including the petition box. In the late Five Dynasties, many people were reported to be "complaining to the court without passing through either the county or prefectural level." Those unlawful skipping complaints obviously enraged Zhou Taizu (r. 951–954) who followed the Sui and Tang practice and ordered that all such skipping complaints would be denied and the complainants "punished in accordance with the law."[66]

The management of the complaint systems

Learning a lesson from the Five Dynasties, the Song founder Taizu (r. 960–976) made several reforms in the legal and political systems. Because he had been a general in the Zhou state and had taken power from the son of his former ruler, he was keenly aware of the potential threat of powerful generals to the throne. He therefore created a centralized system of the rule by civil officials.[67] Although Taizu began by establishing strict laws, he was soon said to have enforced them quite leniently, "Whenever there was any small question about a case, he would reduce the punishment after the report."[68] Additionally, Taizu made it a family (dynastic) rule not to execute civil officials.[69] This leniency was continued by later Song rulers. According to Brian E. McKnight, the Song authorized the "fullest development" of the act of grace in Chinese history.[70]

In 963, the Song basically adopted the Tang law, "merely attaching new provisions to various sections."[71] It followed the Tang in formally banning skipping complaints but also informally accepting certain direct complaints.[72] The Song modified the Tang law governing self-mutilation, but only to punish that practice more harshly, probably in support of the Confucian value of bodily integrity and the Buddhist idea of respect for life.[73]

The Song retained the Tang drum and also maintained the Tang petition box. It developed the latter by setting up a Public Petitioners Review Office (*dengwen guyuan*) to manage it.[74] The second ruler Taizong (r. 976–997) created a Judicial Control Office (*shenxingyuan*) to accept complaints and transmit them to the Court of Judicial Review (*dalisi*), the board of punishment and the ruler for judgment.[75] In 997 the Song abolished the Complaint Review Office (*lijianyuan*) but under Renzong (r. 1022–1063), it reestablished it to clear the path for complaints and comments that had not been getting through to the throne.[76]

How well did this highly bureaucratized complaint system operate in the Song? In 996 Taizong decreed that all commoners should complain first to their local magistrates and fiscal commissions before going to the Drum Office (*gusi*) and the Public Petitioners Office (*dengwenyuan*). Later, Zhenzong reiterated the order. Unlike in the Tang, the Song made blocking the royal cart the highest level and not just one of regular complaints. Contemporaries regarded the Complaint Review Office in the Song as ineffective in dealing with complaints because after Renzong restored it, he ordered that any complaint unacceptable to it and to the Department of Drum could be delivered to the director of the office (*lijianshi*) for investigation.[77] If the Office had been effective there would have been no need to allow complainants to complain to the director. In both Tang and Song, the drum was by law reserved only for complainants with grave grievances (*qiyuan*) or crucial military and state affairs (*junguo dashi*). In the Song, however, the drum could on some occasions be beaten for lesser purposes. In the reign of Taizu, for example, Zhou Weijian, a state erudite (*guozi boshi*), beat the drum asking Taizu to appoint him as the Gentleman of the Interior of Forest (*yubu langzhong*).[78] This case shows that the drum in the Song was sometimes used irregularly by officials but also, at least in this case, somewhat effectively.

In the late Northern Song, Huizong (r. 1101–1125) modified the founder's strict prohibition of skipping complaints by allowing persons who had been beaten more heavily than the law stipulated to file skipping complaints to the Department of State Affairs.[79] His goal was to rein in harsh officials whose actions belied the ruler's reputation for "leniency" and threatened the very life of the dynasty as it faced powerful northern neighbors, the Jurchen.[80]

When the Song court was forced by the Jurchen Jin dynasty to move south from the central plain in 1127, it lost much political authority because of "emergent localism" and the "separation of the elite from the state."[81] Many local officials "went their own way and the degree of leniency or harshness of the punishments was controlled by persons [rather than by law]."[82] To regain its fading central power, the Southern Song (1127–1279) was perhaps forced to be more tolerant of natural resistance.[83] Some upright local officials in the Southern Song also considered it reasonable for complainants to make skipping complaints to the prefect because magistrates were biased in favor of clerks.[84] But, as under Huizong in the late Northern Song, in the Southern Song there were only a very limited number of instances of such natural resistance that could be made over the heads of local officials. All other categories of skipping complaints were to be punished.[85]

If Song Taizu had established the model of leniency toward officials, later Song rulers manifested a continuing belief in the concept of *minben* and demonstrated comparable leniency toward subjects. Ichisada Miyazaki brought to light a "most unusual judicial" case involving a female commoner who made a failed attempt to murder her husband in 1068. The supreme court and a prefect adopted different positions on this case that pitted filial piety against spousal loyalty, causing it to drag on for a year. This case reveals the care with which the Northern Song state weighed conflicting moral obligations and administered the death penalty.[86]

Despite the influence of Buddhism and Wang Anshi's rationalism, superstition, and Neo-Confucianism, Song rulers continued to believe in Zhou–Han notions of heaven–human interaction.[87] In particular, Song rulers believed that unsatisfied human grievances might cause natural disasters. In 992, for example, Song Taizong worried that judicial injustice might have been a cause of a long and ruinous rain. After a long drought in the Renzong reign, Renzong ordered officials to check all prisons in the realm to see if there were any grievances, and, if so, to correct them.[88]

In the standard view, the Song seems to have had more humane judicial policies and to have created a more expansive complaint system than its predecessors had done. During good times many people enjoyed the opportunity to complain to—or even speak with—the ruler without obstacles. Taizong, who often personally reviewed cases in the capital, claimed in 985 that in recent times officials had abided by the law and thus commoners were happy. He suggested that this offered a stark contrast to the lawlessness in the Five Dynasties when aggrieved commoners had had no place to complain.[89] Like Taizong, Southern Song rulers such as Xiaozong (r. 1163–1190) and Lizong (1225–1265) reportedly personally reviewed complaints in an effort to satisfy grievances.[90]

Nevertheless, even in the Song, this sort of royal concern for commoners' grievances had limited effects. As in almost all previous dynasties, many complaints remained unsatisfied in the Song. For instance, Song Zhenzong was reportedly shocked when he learned that 800 death sentences had been meted out in his name. He ordered the judicial department to review those death sentences to see if there were any reasons for grievances. But his order was never carried out because the department concluded that such a review would unduly delay the handling of other cases.[91] In the late Northern Song, government corruption apparently became more serious as most officials, if not all, "use public means to serve their private interests, kill innocent people ... and rob people publicly without any fear."[92] In the Southern Song, many magistrates reportedly never dealt with civil cases and rarely saw either clerks or commoners. Clerks, therefore, were able to decide the rights and wrongs of cases as well as the degrees of punishment, and many took bribes before making their judgments, resulting in numerous grievances.[93]

Although the Yuan dynasty was founded by the Mongols, a minority that conquered the Song in 1279, recent studies have argued that the Yuan made many contributions to the Chinese legal system. In the words of one specialist, it may have had "one of the most impressive and mature judicial systems that Imperial China had ever had for the administration of justice."[94] However exaggerated this argument may be, it at least shows that the Yuan was not a completely lawless regime and actually had a substantial judicial system. The Yuan also published legal documents and model petitions to teach people how to win their cases.[95] The complaint system in the Yuan generally followed that of the Song.[96] Even before Khubilai Khan (r. 1260–1294) reunified China after three centuries of division, he solicited the advice of Confucian scholars and established Chinese governmental institutions.[97] Chancellor Chia in the 1260s and 1270s used the petition box to encourage complainants to assist in curbing official misdeeds.[98]

In 1275 Khubilai instructed the Secretariat (*zhongshusheng*) to discuss the establishment of the drum so that persons who had failed to obtain justice after their close relatives were killed could come to court and beat the drum. But Khubilai discouraged people with frivolous cases (*xishi*) from beating the drum by stipulating punishments for doing so. Four years later when the Yuan prevailed over the Southern Song, Khubilai allowed subjects with grave grievances to complain to the Public Petitioners Drum Office if their cases were not justly dealt with at the provincial level. This order suggests that the Yuan adopted the drum office but not the other two parts of the Song complaint system (the two review offices). As in the Tang and Song, subjects in the Yuan could also lodge complaints with the Censorate. The Yuan went further, however, by recording all complaints against provincial and township officials and dismissing officials who incurred the highest number of complaints.[99]

Like its predecessors, the Yuan code required all subjects to complain through regular steps. All skipping complainants would be punished with fifty-seven lashes of the whip (slightly heavier than in the past). Only if the local government made a false judgment or repeatedly ignored complaints could aggrieved people complain to the upper levels. However, the Yuan made another seemingly small but actually very important modification of the system inherited from the Tang and Song. In both the Tang and the Song codes, not only had skipping complainants been punished but their cases had been rejected, whatever their merits. The Yuan code stipulated that skipping complainants should be punished for violating procedural regulations but their complaints should nonetheless be considered on their merits. This Yuan law giving skipping complainants more chances of success on the substance of their complaints was inherited by the Ming and Qing.

As in the late Northern and Southern Song, moreover, the late Yuan state during a time of political upheaval allowed subjects to make skipping complaints in some cases. "Any complaint against officials' taking bribes or acting unlawfully," the Yuan law stated, "could go straight to various responsible offices and would not be prosecuted as skipping complaints."[100] Once again a weakening state apparently tried to use the complaint system as a way to involve the people in curbing the abuses of its local personnel that threatened the very legitimacy of the regime.

The Mongol rulers and their Han Chinese advisors also shared the traditional concepts of the mandate of heaven, and the heaven–human interaction, both of which helped make Yuan rulers more attentive to people's natural right to complain. To cite one case, in 1324, upon the outbreak of some natural disasters, Yuan Taiding convoked his officials to discuss their meaning. One official traced the disasters to people's grievances and asked Taiding to rectify his policies to satisfy them.[101]

The vicissitudes of natural resistance in late imperial China

Despite the Yuan's considerable attention to the law, it lacked a complete and formal law code on the Tang model and it failed to enforce the laws very effectively, especially in its later years. The Ming founder Taizu (r. 1368–1398), a monk and commoner, rose to power believing that the Yuan had lost the mandate in part because of the laxity of its laws.[102] He therefore set about developing detailed statutes and enforcing them strictly to "ensure the survival of his dynasty."[103] Some observers have argued that Taizu's judicial policies were "unprecedentedly harsh."[104] In fact, Taizu was not as uniformly strict as some think. Although he adopted draconian measures against actual and potential political enemies, he often showed genuine leniency toward lawbreaking commoners.[105] In general, the Ming code was based on that of the Tang.[106] Even before he was formally enthroned, Taizu asked his Confucian advisors to teach him the Tang law every day.[107]

Like most of its predecessors, the Ming preserved the regular complaint system but also made some changes. For example, in 1378, Taizu established the Office of Transmission (*tongzheng shisi*) to clear the way for communications from the bottom of the bureaucracy to the top. In 1383, he transformed the Censorate (*yushitai*) into the Chief Surveillance Office (*duchayuan*, also called the Censorate). Thus in the legal/regular complaint system of the Ming, if the surveillance commissioner (*anchasi*) did not make a just decision, the complainant could lodge his or her grievance with the regional investigating censors (*xun'an jiancha yushi*). If the judgment was still unsatisfactory, the complainant could go to the Office of Transmission, which was responsible for passing the complaint on to the Chief Surveillance Office. If that office did not accept the complaint or made a judgment unacceptable to the complainant, the complainant could beat the drum to complain to the throne.[108]

While the Ming code continued to prohibit natural resistance, a practice dating back to the Sui, it initiated an important reform of no longer requiring skipping complaints to be sent back to the local governments for resolution. The upper courts were able and willing to adjudicate any cases coming to them including the illegally lodged skipping complaints.[109] In that regard, the Ming system may have been a more "populist" one than its predecessors had been at least back to Han times.

During the Ming, individual rulers' attitudes toward skipping complaints varied. Many adopted their own ad hoc policies. Believing that the Yuan had fallen because the path between the top and the bottom had been blocked by corrupt officials,[110] Ming Taizu allowed subjects to make skipping complaints against any corrupt and cruel officials, even though such complaints were nominally illegal.[111] Taizu followed this lenient policy toward skipping complainants for a couple of decades before he became exasperated at many skipping complaints that turned out to involve petty quarrels or false claims. In 1395, he ordered local governments to choose honest and capable village elders to decide local legal cases. Anyone who bypassed the elders and clerks and made complaints to regular government officials would be regarded as making an illegal skipping complaint.[112]

However, as in previous times, the Ming code and the founder's decree outlawing skipping complaints seem to have been ignored by many natural resisters who continued to bring complaints to the rulers—their "parents" and heaven's representatives. In the reign of Xuanzong (r. 1426–1435), for example, judicial officials pleaded for stricter sanctions against the increasingly allegedly false skipping complaints. As a result, Xuanzong modified the punishment of skipping complainants, whether their claims were true or false, to banishment, far more severe than the former fifty lashes in the early Ming. In 1433, Xuanzong found that this harsh law had its own problems. Although it had resulted in fewer skipping complaints, commoners' grievances continued to grow in number. Xuanzong thus instructed the judiciary that skipping complainants should be pardoned if their complaints proved valid and banished if their claims proved to be invalid.[113] This lenient ruling on skipping complaints may have been part of the reason for a surge in the number of such grievances in later reigns.

In the reigns of Xianzong (r. 1465–1487) and Xiaozong (r. 1488–1505), due to "rampant skipping complaints," both rulers once again imposed stricter controls on them. Even relatives of murder victims and people suffering from official corruption were not allowed to make direct complaints in the capital. Unable to satisfy their grievances legally, many natural resisters adopted extreme means such as shouting outside the Chang'an gate in Beijing, breaking into government compounds, and even taking officials hostage. In 1479 a decree banned all of those activities of natural resistance and stipulated that all violators and their instigators would be cangued (i.e., placed in mobile stocks) for one month or sent to the frontier. Other complainants, such as those whose whole families had been murdered or who had suffered from official corruption, should still complain step by step from the bottom up and the violators would be punished.[114] As a result, even complainants with grave grievances, who had been allowed to beat the drum in the capital in many periods, could no longer take their complaints to the capital. Early Ming populism was fading in the face of more bureaucratic authority.

As in the Song, the main methods of making direct complaints in the Ming were beating the drum, blocking the royal cart, and complaining to the palace gate. Ming law provided that any false complaint made by beating the drum and blocking the royal cart would be punished with 100 blows of the bamboo, twenty more than in the Tang.[115] The drum in the Ming may have undergone more changes than the others. In the first year of his reign, Taizu established a drum outside the Meridian Gate and ordered a censor to supervise it. Only for grave grievances and secret reports could subjects beat the drum. Later, the drum was moved to the right side outside Chang'an Gate where it was to be supervised in turn by the embroidered guards (*jinyiwei*) of all six departments.[116]

In 1378, to guard against false judgments and to limit the number of defendants condemned to death, Taizu ordered that relatives of criminals who had allegedly committed felonies should be allowed to beat the drum. Responsible officials should then seal the letter of complaint and report to the ruler at the time of the third review.[117] But, as in the Song, subjects in the Ming would sometimes beat the drum for seemingly minor causes.[118] In 1392, when the President of the Ministry of Personnel (*libu shangshu*) had neglected a clerk's plea for permission to retire after the death of his mother, the clerk beat the drum and Taizu ordered the high official to permit the clerk to show his final respects to his mother.[119]

As in the case of skipping complaints, some subjects abused the drum office by making frivolous complaints to it. Enraged, the late Ming ruler Shenzong (r. 1573–1620) in 1590 ordered that all people (including even princes) who beat the drum to report minor grievances should be severely punished. But under the inattentive Shenzong, this law was not strictly enforced and the ruler himself seems to have ignored it. Only four years later, Section Minister (*kechen*) Wang Jiamo hinted that "whenever there is a report [or a complaint]," the government accepted and reviewed it. He worried that "evil persons (*jiantu*)" would make ever more "annoying" complaints over minor matters.[120]

Another direct complaint—the Office of Transmission, designed to clear the way for communication between the top and the bottom of the polity, was created by Taizu in 1378.[121] Subjects with grievances could complain to the Office of Transmission, which was one level lower than beating the drum or blocking the royal cart.[122] In 1385, Taizu rejected as too harsh an official suggestion that subjects making false complaints to the Office of Transmission should be punished to the same degree as those who brought false charges to the drum or the royal cart. Instead, Taizu said the punishment should only be the same as for those making false complaints to other standard offices such as the Board of Punishment.[123]

The oldest direct form of complaint—made at the palace gate—continued to be mounted by both officials and commoners in the Ming. In 1628, near the end of the dynasty, when an upright prefect of Songjiang, Jiangsu province, was detained on a false charge of corruption, many commoners and degree holders complained to the palace gate for his release. Ming Yizong (r. 1628–1644) asked the judiciary to review the case and eventually the prefect was released and restored to his position.[124]

Despite challenges from the scholar Wang Fuzhi and other critics of the cosmology inherited from the Han period, Ming rulers and officials remained deeply concerned about heavenly warnings that might be related to people's grievances.[125] In 1392, Taizu dispatched judges and censors to check on prisoners all over the country to find out what possible grievances might be causing a prolonged drought. In 1511, Ming Wuzong (r. 1506–1521) believed the unusually hot weather to be caused by possible grievances among criminals convicted of both light and grave crimes.[126] A Ming local official Yan Junyan, stated his belief that the unjust death of a single commoner could cause frost to appear in July.[127] Undoubtedly, Ming rulers' persistent belief in heaven–human interaction allowed them to respect people's natural right to complain.

The Ming complaint systems had, like their predecessors, limited efficacy. After the clampdown on skipping complaints during the Xianzong and Xiaozong reigns, many potential complainants no doubt backed away from complaining. The Office of Transmission, which was supposed to receive and transmit people's grievances and suggestions, simply collected minor cases to report and neglected major ones.[128] During the reign of Wuzong the management of the prisons was said to be filled with abuses,[129] but the ruler reportedly forbade prisoners' relatives to beat the drum to complain.[130] In 1538, Shizong blamed judicial officials in the capital for not "using their hearts" in dealing with cases and protecting the local officials who were responsible for the original decisions.[131]

Some late Ming scholar–officials lodged equally sharp criticisms of the lack of communication between the top and the bottom. The prominent "upright official" Hai Rui (1514–1587) argued that "After [Shizong's] twenty years' absence from the court, the state legal system was breaking down."[132] Another late Ming and early Qing scholar, Gu Yanwu, criticized the general weakness of Ming local officials who failed to report the people's grievances to their superiors.

While the Qing founders and their successors tried to maintain their Manchu identity after the conquest of the Ming,[133] they adopted a legal code that was based heavily on those of the Tang through Ming.[134] According to Thomas Metzger, the Qing was also good at changing its laws to meet new situations.[135] The Qing carried over and modified the Ming complaints systems. Like its predecessors, the Qing required that all subjects submit their complaints gradually through legal steps, and minor ones (or civil cases), should go no higher than the prefecture.[136] Also, like its predecessors, the Qing generally tried to outlaw skipping complaints. Both Kangxi (r. 1661–1722) and Qianlong (r. 1735–1796), "the most sinified, Confucianized ruler,"[137] issued orders that prohibited skipping complaints.[138]

As in previous periods, the Qing faced the continuing practices of natural resistance, especially in the form of skipping complaints.[139] In some cases, it accommodated certain forms of those complaints for a certain length of time. In 1736 Qianlong allowed subjects who had been cheated or harmed by clerks (*fanyi*) of the capital gendarmerie to make skipping complaints to the Board of Punishment or to the Censorate.[140] But Qianlong himself soon restored the law against skipping complaints. In 1742, he warned that officials at any level would be punished if they accepted any skipping complaint.[141]

In the Qing, there was nonetheless an important category of cases that have been called capital complaints (*jingkong*, or capital appeals). They were lodged by complainants, who either, as required by law, had exhausted all judicial remedies at the provincial level, or, by ignoring the law, had skipped one or more levels of the required steps. They were addressed to such central organs as the Censorate and the Capital Gendarmerie.[142] Qing rulers, according to Jonathan Ocko, tended to be sympathetically predisposed to capital complaints because rulers "relied on them as a source of primary information about the empire's condition."[143]

The Board of Punishment and the Office of Transmission could also receive capital complaints (regular complaints or unlawful skipping complaints). Unlike in the Ming, most of the complaints to the capital were returned to the provincial governments for review and only a small number of them were reported to the ruler.[144] These practices caused a problem, especially in cases of complaints against the provincial officials. When such complaints were passed down to the very officials who were their targets, the officials were likely to escape punishment and the complainants were likely to suffer retaliation.[145] Hence, in 1819, an official asked Jiaqing (r. 1796–1820) to order that no capital complaints should be returned to the provincial officials. But Jiaqing rejected this proposal fearing that, if it were approved, he would have to resolve all the cases—including minor civil ones—that were directed to him.[146]

In 1784, Qianlong decreed that capital complaints made after exhausting all legal steps or that concerned cases that were particularly grave would be accepted but only if they proved to be true; those who complained about minor matters (whether valid or invalid) would be punished and their cases would be returned to the local governments.[147] This law failed to check the increasing number of complaints going to the capital, many of which had violated the law by skipping the required legal steps. In 1796, Qianlong endorsed with little revision a new proposal that central organs should refuse all complaints except those that had already been made at the provincial level. Complainants who lied that they had complained to the local government when they had not would be subject to one more degree of punishment than complainants who simply failed to complain first locally without lying about it.[148]

In 1796, facing growing official corruption and a spreading White Lotus rebellion,[149] Jiaqing modified his father's harsh attitude toward natural resisters. He instructed officials in the Censorate and the Capital Gendarmerie to accept skipping complaints from the people.[150] But Jiaqing's new lenient policy was short-lived, apparently because of the pressure of the large number of skipping complaints that had probably been inspired by his decree. In 1800, Jiaqing complained that every day was filled by skipping complaints and most of them were frivolous.[151] Complaints of all kinds and degrees of seriousness were simply being lodged over the head of local officials and directly to the capital. Jiaqing therefore ordered that any complainant who made a capital complaint without having gone first to the local level would be punished no matter whether his complaint was valid or false. Despite this return to Qianlong's strict outlawing of skipping complaints, Jiaqing, like his predecessors in the Yuan period, still allowed the content of the skipping complaints to be considered even after the complainants were punished for having made them.

By 1819, however, desperate natural resisters grew bolder, some of them going directly to the court and announcing that they would make their cases only in the presence of the ruler. Infuriated, Jiaqing ordered the Board of Punishment to punish such bold complainants more severely by one more degree than those who reported with sealed complaints.[152] However draconian the laws against skipping and false complaints, many natural resisters preferred to be beaten than to return to face the local officials without any support from the center. Such an embedded belief in the ruler—the "parent" and the son of heaven—was not unique to Chinese natural resisters in the Qing period. Many Italian and Russian complainants in the same period also trusted only the good prince or Czar and not his (or her) subordinate officials.[153] But the Chinese faith in the ruler was arguably older and more continuous than similar European convictions and therefore stronger and more difficult to shake.

Later Qing rulers generally followed Jiaqing's decree of 1801 against skipping complaints. In one case in 1875, having skipped the required provincial civil official, Sun Guoan, a farmer from Jiangsu province, mounted a skipping complaint to the Office of the Provincial Military Commander (*tidu yamen*) accusing a county secretary of having embezzled money donated by local people for dredging a river. The Board of Punishment decided that even if Sun had not lied [about skipping a level] he should still be punished according to the law against skipping complaints.[154] While the studies of Ocko and Buoye have correctly shown that the middle and late Qing state was lenient toward fabricated capital complaints and capital crimes (cases involving death penalty),[155] the above case shows that the leniency did not apply to skipping complaints.

Although skipping complaints were strictly prohibited after Jiaqing's decree, in the case of Sun Guoan the Board of Punishment still called all relevant parties to the capital and carefully interrogated them. Notwithstanding the heavy punishment for skipping complaints, aggrieved complainants from different backgrounds continued to ignore the law and to make them. By Qing times the cultural legitimacy of natural resistance and historical precedents for skipping complaints were so strong that state efforts to outlaw them proved largely ineffective.

Unlike in contemporary Tokugawa Japan where direct complaints to the actual head of state, the shogun, were illegal,[156] in the Qing, due mostly to wide and deep recognition of people's natural right to complain and light state's need for help in checking local officials, some direct complaints to the center were legal and others were illegal. Lawful direct complaints were defined similarly to those in the Ming. Complainants could beat the drum, block the royal cart, and complain to the palace gate. In 1644, a drum was established inside the Censorate and in 1657 it was moved to outside the Chang'an gate.[157] In the Qing, certain direct complaints reached the emperor,[158] but, in general making direct complaints was not easy. Only complaints regarding grave grievances, evil activities (*dajian*), national affairs, and those that followed all legally required steps were permitted.[159] Violators would not only be beaten with 100 blows of bamboo and sent to the border, but their complaints would also be rejected.[160] In 1726, Yongzheng ruled that any unlawful complainant at the palace gates would be cangued for a month if the complaint was valid and beaten with 100 blows of bamboo and sent to the army on the border if the complaint was false. In 1810, Jiaqing instructed that once their cases were decided, the complainants who continued to beat the drum or tried to commit suicide outside the Chang'an gate should be brought to the judiciary for punishment.[161]

Probably because legal direct complaints were so difficult, many desperate natural resisters, as in both the Tang and Ming, used illegal methods as a last effort to attract the attention of the son of heaven and the parent of the people. Shunzhi in 1661 was vexed that many troublesome complainants in the capital tried to cut their throats to attract court attention.[162] In 1741, a law stipulated that complainants who shouted loudly about grievances before the Meridian and Chang'an gates or knelt down in front of the palace gates would be punished regardless of whether their complaints were valid or invalid. In some extreme cases, natural resisters would attempt to climb over the wall of the Forbidden City or to commit suicide outside the palace gates or under the drum.[163]

As in previous times, Qing rulers and officials continued to embrace primordial notions such as the son of heaven, heavenly principles, parental rulers, and *minben*/people as the root. In 1740, Qianlong reminded his ministers that the people were their children as well as his.[164] In the late Qing, Guangxü, who directed the 1898 reform, instructed officials that the state "has always regarded people as the basis" and "all the state administration does is to serve our people."[165] Similarly, the mid-Qing governor Chen Hongmou believed that good officials should dedicate themselves to serving the people.[166] In this period, most rulers and officials continued to believe in the Zhou and Han cosmologies. In 1759, as the result of a long drought, Qianlong ordered officials to check the criminal dockets to ensure that there had been no miscarriage of justice.[167] Shortly after Guangxü ascended the throne, the court worried about an unexpectedly long downpour and ordered all prisons inspected because "unjust punishment would surely hurt the harmony of heaven and nature (*tianhe*)."[168] The heritage of *minben*/people as the root and cosmology provided a firm foundation for the Qing rulers' respect for people's natural right to complain.

In the Qing, as in previous dynasties, numerous grievances remained unsatisfied. After Fang Bao, a prominent scholar of Song learning, was imprisoned in the Kangxi reign—the beginning of the peaceful and prosperous High Qing period—he discovered first-hand how prison conditions could easily lead to many grievances. Rich or powerful prisoners could avoid the death penalty and beating by bribing the jailers, while poor prisoners were tortured and often died leaving behind many grievances.[169] Mark Elliot records that the grievances of some Han Chinese could not be satisfied in the Manchu city of Xi'an because of institutionalized Manchu privileges.[170] During a sorcery scare in 1768, some monks and beggars were beaten and even killed after being unfairly charged with collusion in sedition, one of the Ten Abominations. Such a crime by definition could never be amnestied, and the victims' grievances were unlikely ever to be satisfied due to the crackdown by the ruler.[171]

Even among the small percentage of complainants who successfully got their grievances before the central organs, including the ruler, many ended up unsatisfied. According to a report of a censor in 1876, for several decades no capital complaints had been rectified after they had been returned to the provincial governments. "Although some of them are false complaints by evil persons," a late Qing observer commented, "many of the others are real grievances."[172]

Many grievances were lodged against abuses that resulted from higher officials protecting lower ones, a condition that made the rectification of those abuses and the satisfaction of the grievances by lower officials highly unlikely. A memorial of 1883 pointed out that many prefects and governors either paid little attention to local officials' carelessness in handling people's complaints and/or tried to protect those local officials when grievances were lodged against them. One contemporary observer claimed that "only one or two out of every

100 [decisions made by local officials] were reversed [by upper-level governments]."[173] The corruption that became rampant in the late Qianlong reign undoubtedly caused many grievances among the people. Hong Liangji, an upright official in the late eighteenth century, wrote that, because of the widespread corruption and collusion among local officials, "only one or two out of a thousand lawsuits of 'Commoners vs. Officials' could win."[174]

Hong's argument is supported by the records of many complaints in the late Qing archives. To cite only one example, in 1876 Zhang Gui, a farmer from Jiangsu province, complained to the Board of Punishments against Xiong Jingshan, a local powerful person who had allegedly taken away a cow and a cart from Zhang's master whose identification is unknown. Zhang claimed that he was forced to make the skipping complaint to the Board because Xiong had bribed a local judicial official who had continually postponed dealing with the case.[175]

Conclusion

As we have seen, the crucial notions such as mandate of heaven, *minben*, parental rulers/officials, and heaven–human interactions that help legitimize natural resistance originated in the Zhou dynasty. Also in the Zhou, the idea of a complaint system to facilitate communication between the rulers and the commoners might have begun. The Han strengthened the link between the state and the common people with the ideology of the interaction of heaven and humans. The Tang fully institutionalized the complaint systems that had already seen new inventions such as the Public Petition Drum in the Northern and Southern Dynasties and the Sui. The Tang made the complaint system a part of the formal judiciary and distinguished among three kinds of complaints (regular, skipping, and direct). Dynasties after the Tang generally inherited the Tang complaint systems but made certain important modifications. For example, inspired by the Neo-Confucianism that took account of Buddhist ideas, the Song, especially the Southern Song, implemented lenient policies toward officials and natural resisters. The Yuan accepted even illegal skipping complaints as a way to control power-holders, while the Ming was sympathetic to complaints against elite and officials. The Ming, unlike previous states and the Qing, ended the practice of sending complaints back to the locations where they originated. Nevertheless, in all periods, despite seemingly sound systems and serious concern from the ruler, many complainants remained unsatisfied due to political corruption and bureaucratic connections.

After reviewing the history of Chinese complaint systems from the Zhou through the late Qing, we can see an institutional dilemma regarding the treatment of skipping complaints. Chinese rulers, imbued with Confucian doctrines such as the mandate of heaven, *minben*/people as the root, and parental officials combined with the interaction of nature with humans and an aim to gather information from the bottom, tended to regard complaining to the top as subjects' natural/heavenly rights, no matter how many illegal or trifling complaints arose to irritate them. In a few short periods, the rulers in the Southern Song and early Ming even lifted the longtime prohibition on skipping complaints. Similarly, by reading written materials or imbibing oral tales, natural resisters conceived of themselves as children of the rulers, whom they could naturally count on to satisfy their grievances. If the "parents" were not responsible for them, who else would be? Moreover, most natural resisters, like the rulers and officials, believed that the just and loving heaven might inflict immediate disaster on the rulers if their grievances were not redressed. In *Snow in the Summer*, a popular Yuan-period play, after Dou E, a young woman, was executed on the false charge of murder, snow fell in the summer as a sign of heaven's displeasure.[176] For many natural resisters, the serious injustices they suffer can become intolerable. In a natural response, they may adopt any means and pay any price (e.g., those who chose to jump in the moat or cut their own flesh) from the Tang to the Qing. Such people are determined to get justice no matter how futile or sometimes counterproductive their efforts might seem. In this sense, the complaint systems in pre-1898 China were Hot Potatoes: they frequently scorched the ruler's and the people's hands but were too valuable to drop.

2 Halfway revolutions

The late Qing period (1899–1911)[1]

In the late nineteenth century, both internal rebellions and external wars forcibly prompted the Qing rulers to conduct reforms in a variety of areas including the law. As a result, the late Qing state adopted a more tolerant attitude toward skipping and false complainants as well as collective complainants. It also attempted to establish a special Administrative Court expressly to deal with commoners' complaints against officials. In addition, the last years of the Qing witnessed a greatly enhanced role of public and private media in publicizing people's individual and collective complaints. All of these efforts, in theory or in practice, further expanded and strengthened subjects' natural right to complain. As the West moved into China and China became more aware of the rest of the world, Chinese at various levels of society turned to the West and Japan for institutions that could increase communication between the top and bottom of society. Opening the "word road (*yanlu*)" was a perennial Chinese ideal that seemed also to offer the prospect of wealth and power essential to compete with the foreign powers. Despite these reforms, the late Qing state was marked by rampant official corruption and breaches in the rule of law. As a result, complainants proliferated and many of them faced frustration in efforts to gain redress of their grievances. The late Qing reforms ultimately failed to achieve their primary goal of saving the dynasty. Inspired by new ideologies as well as old principles, they nonetheless had a tremendous impact on the succeeding polities that styled themselves republics.

Humaneness toward false and skipping complainants

As we saw in Chapter 1, with few exceptions the Tang and subsequent dynasties had generally criminalized skipping complaints lodged by people who firmly believed in natural resistance based on heavenly principles, parental rulers/sons of heaven, and *minben*/people as the root. The mid-Qing ruler Qianlong had imposed harsh punishments on both skipping and false complainants and had regularly sent all of them back to their own local governments where they seldom got satisfaction and were often abused. After initial experimentation with lenience, Jiaqing had soon made all skipping complaints, whether justifiable or not, punishable crimes. In that era, skipping complainants whose claims had turned out to be false had suffered one grade heavier punishment than those whose complaints had proved to be true.

Although the famous "Hundred Days Reform" designed to overhaul the entire Qing polity in 1898 ended abruptly, it indirectly resulted in important changes in the functioning of the Qing complaint systems. As shown in the cases of Sun Guoan and Zhang Gui in Chapter 1, before 1898 skipping complainants were regularly prosecuted and punished. Even in 1898, the very year of the reforms (unfortunately the month is unknown), a farmer named Xie Kailai lodged a skipping complaint to the Board of Punishment without going through the provincial government. Xie alleged that Fang Shan had murdered his father and evaded prosecution by bribing officials in the prefecture. Xie was harshly punished for making this skipping complaint even before the Board of Punishment investigate the case and determined that it lacked merit.[2] Thus the late Qing state persisted in enforcing the basic inherited law against skipping complaints even in the midst of contemplating other reforms.

In the very next year, however, the Board of Punishment adopted a new stance of lenience toward skipping complaints. In at least one case, it did so even when the complaint turned out to be unsubstantiated. Wang Qiyuan, a student from Henan province, mounted a capital complaint to the Board of Punishment accusing Yang Juncheng of killing his son. According to Wang Qiyuan, Yang Juncheng had deprived the Wang family of drinking water by some unspecified means. When Wang's son quarreled with Yang Juncheng over that issue, he was killed by Yang Juncheng and his brother. After the local officials refused to prosecute Yang Juncheng, Wang Qiyuan suspected that Yang had bribed the local officials. Wang therefore go to Beijing to charge the local officials with protecting the murderer Yang and attempting to extort money from him (Wang).

After a relatively detailed investigation, the Board of Punishment issued its report that the murdered man, Wang's son, had in fact committed adultery with the wife of Yang Juncheng's brother Yang Junqin. When Yang Juncheng had happened to find Wang's son and his (Yang's) sister-in-law in flagrante delicto, he had stabbed Wang to death in anger. The Board decided that Wang Qiyuan had mounted a skipping complaint based on "hearsay rather than the true story." The Board also noted that Wang had mounted a false skipping complaint out of anguish at the death of a son and that he had unknowingly misrepresented what had happened. The Board therefore ruled that Wang should be acquitted.[3] In this case, the late Qing post-reform state seems to have manifested a new, or at least renewed, spirit of lenience toward skipping complainants that had not been seen for decades or even centuries.

In 1900, one year before governors-general Zhang Zhidong's and Liu Kunyi's famous memorial calling for the elimination of corporal punishments[4] and about four years before the Qing court began taking concrete steps (in 1904) to abolish corporal punishments,[5] the Qing court decreed that corporal punishments such as beating by bamboo or whipping, the punishments that had usually been meted out to persons found guilty of making skipping complaints, should be abolished (a similar one was issued in 1904).[6] Although further research is necessary to locate the original edicts of 1900 and 1904 and determine their full contents, it appears from available documents that they made no specific mention of the offenses, such as skipping complaints, that were affected by this reform. Nor, so far as I know, did the edicts specify what punishments would replace beating and whipping (in fact, they were soon—in 1905—replaced by fines). With the abolition of these punishments, however, the late Qing state seems to have de facto adopted a more lenient posture toward persons lodging skipping complaints.

The developing situation was reflected in two additional cases involving skipping complaints in the midst of a proposed legal reform. In the first, in 1904, Zhu Zhaolian, a county student (*tongsheng*), from Shangcheng county, Henan province, presented a charge at the capital against Zhu Changrui for stealing his property. According to the student, thanks to the former magistrate Jiang, he had retrieved his land, but a new magistrate named Zheng, who was corrupt, had been persuaded by Zhu Changrui that he (the student) was a "bandit" and had sent runners to his home to confiscate his property and arrest five members of his family. The student had complained to the prefect to rein in the magistrate, but the magistrate, a supposed parent official, delayed any review of the case. The student had then complained to the governor. Meanwhile, Zhu Changrui, emboldened by the magistrate's support, attacked and wounded two of the student's brothers. The student, feeling his family was in danger, "begged his way 2000 li [over 600 miles]" to the capital where he charged the magistrate with "neglecting state law (*daxian*)."

Despite recent proposals from powerful reform-minded officials to prohibit skipping complaints and to punish the complainants harshly,[7] the Board of Punishment still instructed the governor of Henan to review the case. After a detailed investigation, the governor reported that the land of the student Zhu Zhaolian had actually been earmarked by his mother as the "family's burial land (*jitian*)." When the mother died in January 1901, Zhu Changrui and his brothers, who were relatives of the student, sold the burial land for 540,000 yuan to pay for her burial. The student's father opposed the sale of the family property and complained about Zhu Changrui to the magistrate. Another relative, who was also unhappy with Zhu Changrui's sale of the burial land, flooded his [Changrui's] land to prevent him from planting in it. It was at that point that Zhu Changrui accused the student and his uncle of colluding with local bandits to bring harm to his property. The magistrate sent armed men to put down the "uprising." According to the Board's inquiry, when the magistrate was investigating the case, someone else took the occasion to steal some of the student's property. When the student charged Zhu Changrui with the theft and the magistrate rejected the charge, the student had a complaint written out and taken to the Censorate in Beijing.

The governor concluded that the student had no connection to bandits and that his charges against the magistrate were partially correct. His principal crime, therefore, was mounting a skipping complaint on the basis of some false information and without waiting for the decision of the governor. According to the original Qing statutes, the student would have been subject to fifty lashes of the whip. Since this form of punishment was now abolished by the 1904 imperial edict, the same order as that of 1900, and no substitute had yet been provided for it, the governor recommended that the complainant be acquitted and allowed to return home without penalty.[8] In this case, the late Qing abolition of corporal punishment resulted in effective lenience toward a crime—a skipping complaint on false grounds—that had once been subject to that form of punishment.

In 1905 another skipping complaint from Henan resulted in a similar verdict. In this case, Pan Gaofeng, a national university student, went to the Capital Gendarmerie where he accused Pan Zhengrong of being responsible for his brother's death. According to Pan Gaofeng, Pan Zhengrong had tried to appropriate forty acres of his land by instigating Pan Shikai, one of Gaofeng's uncles, to steal the deed and change the title to Pan Zhengrong. After his uncle ignored the county official's decision to recover the land from Pan Zhengrong, the student's father complained to the prefecture. He also mounted several lawsuits against Pan Zhengrong. Annoyed by the lawsuits, Pan Zhengrong and his son assailed the student's younger brother who committed suicide. The student's mother then charged Pan Zhengrong and his son with the death of her younger son. To escape punishment, Pan Zhengong used personal connections and lied to the magistrate, resulting in a false judgment. When the student went to the prefecture and the province to lodge charges, Pan Zhengrong beat and robbed his son. Instead of waiting for the judgment from the provincial government as required by law, the student complained to the Capital Gendarmerie.

The Henan provincial report concluded that the student's charges were largely false. The student's idea that Pan Zhengrong had stolen the land was based on circumstantial evidence and the student's younger brother had actually committed suicide because of an internal family quarrel. The student's mother's attribution of her son's death to Pan Zhengrong was therefore also false, contrived merely to justify the filing of a capital complaint. According to the Qing law until very recently, the student should have been heavily beaten with eighty blows of the bamboo for filing a skipping complaint that proved to be false. But the Board of Punishment, citing the edict of 1904 abolishing all beating and whipping, decided not to punish Pan Gaofeng. As in the case of Zhu Zhaolian discussed above, the Board thereby extended the court's compassion expressed in abolishing corporal punishments to acquitting defendants charged with committing crimes to which those punishments had once applied. Indeed, in this instance, the Board spread its benevolence even further to cover a case that had emerged after the January 1, 1904 deadline mentioned in the edict. Probably because of the ongoing legal reform pushed by influential officials and the Qing's proclivity to a general leniency, what had once been exceptions, dependent upon the munificence of particular parental rulers, were now becoming the norms in a new and different judicial system.

In some other cases at this time, the Board of Punishment did not even cite any mitigating edict and simply acquitted skipping complainants, even those bearing false charges. For example, at the turn of 1904 and 1905, a farmer named Zhu Zhengwu went to the Capital Gendarmerie and accused a local runner of causing the death of his uncle. According to the official report, the runner in late 1903 had tried to collect a tax from a member of the Zhu descent group. Having no money, Zhu begged the runner to allow him to pay it later but the runner refused. Zhu's uncle happened to come by and quarreled with the runner. The quarrel turned into a fight during which the student's uncle kicked the runner's nephew to death. Accordingly, Zhu's uncle was sent to prison where he soon died. Although an official investigation concluded that the prisoner had died of disease, Zhu Zhengwu did not believe it. Being afraid that the actual case might be too minor to be accepted, however, Zhu embroidered it by claiming that the runner had frequently extorted money from him. When his companion in complaint fell ill and died, Zhu concocted a further story that he had been tortured to death by runners. "With a mixture of hatred and grief," Zhu made up his mind to complaint to the capital. In this case, too, it seemed that Zhu's capital complaint was not only skipping but also false. Yet, without citing any edict, the official at the Board of Punishment acquitted the complainant. The decision read,

> In this case, most of the capital complaint of Zhu Zhengwu and Zhu Genwu is not true. But as he admitted immediately when he came to the Capital Gendarmerie, he complained mainly because he had mistakenly trusted rumors. Thus he did not intend to misrepresent what happened, which distinguished him from those who fabricate false charges. Therefore, it is suggested that he should be acquitted...[9]

In 1906, a farmer named Yin Guangzhuo, from Sangzhi county, Hunan province, brought a charge to the Capital Gendarmerie against a local "thug" who had allegedly murdered his (Yin's) brother. According to Yin, he had complained to the local government, the prefect, and the governor before making this capital complaint. But all his local complaints had been returned to the magistrate and, up to the present, there had been no result. Yin accused the thug of bribing the local guard of the magistrate and lamented that he could not attain heavenly principles because "neither heaven nor earth answered when he shouted to them." Being at bay, he asked the central government to review his case directly lest it be returned again to the local magistrate and the law never be enforced. As in the case of many other capital complaints in the late Qing archives, capital judges investigated Yin's charge and deemed it not true. The official report noted that Yin's brother had actually committed suicide and had not been murdered. Yin's charge was mostly based on mere supposition. As Zhu Zhenwu had done, Yin had deliberately added the corruption of the guard to the charges and had written his own complaint. Rather than wait for the official results from the provincial government, Yin had made what could only be regarded as a skipping complaint. As in many other cases in this period, however, the Board of Punishment acquitted Yin without citing any edict, saying that he had admitted his fault as soon as the investigation started, making him different from those who persisted in lodging false complaints.[10] This case combined with others further demonstrates that leniency to skipping and false complainants had become regular after the 1904 edict abolishing corporal punishment. That was true even though leniency had originally been meant to apply only to cases that had arisen in the period before 1904 and there were no further edicts extending its provisions to the subsequent period.

Complainants who blocked the royal cart were treated less leniently than other kinds of skipping complainants in this period, but even those offenders were punished less harshly than before. Before 1898 the usual penalty for attempting to block the royal cart had been 200 blows of the bamboo and exile to the military frontier. After 1898 punishments were reduced to less heavy doses of beating and whipping and, in a few cases, offenders were let off without punishment on the basis of the 1904 edict abolishing corporal punishment.[11] In March 1904, for example, Zhao Shouyin, a farmer from Shandong, was arrested for attempting to block the royal cart. Under investigation, Zhao charged Zhao Zhongchao and Zhao Zhong'e with detaining his brother and robbing his family. When Zhao Shouyin had complained to the magistrate, he had claimed that Zhao Zhongchao and his brother had bribed local officials to bail out all detained robbers. After a number of unsuccessful complaints to higher levels of the government such as the prefecture and the province (both levels had simply returned the case to the county), Zhao Shouyin had come to Beijing and had attempted to block the cart of the parental ruler—heaven's son and his last hope. Although Cixi's two edicts of 1901 and 1904, issued in the name of Guangxü, could be and had been interpreted to justify acquitting skipping complainants, they were not often applied to complainants who blocked the royal cart. That was probably because that form of complaint posed at least a potential direct threat to the ruler's personal safety. If ignored, acquitted, or pardoned, such acts would only inspire more people to block the royal cart rather than to pursue the less dramatic course of simply complaining to higher officials. Accordingly, even though Zhao's charge was true, the Board of Punishment decided to punish him, but the punishment would be less than the original 100 strokes (if Zhao's complaint had been false, he would have been punished more heavily).[12]

In the same year of 1904, a monk tried to block the royal cart in Beijing in a complaint to the ruler to renovate a dilapidated temple in Guizhou. The Board of punishment decided to punish him with 100 blows of the bamboo.[13]

In 1905, as a result of the legal reform, the punishments previously stipulated for blocking the royal cart (beating and whipping) were explicitly replaced by fines as a result of the legal reform. In one case, Wu Changming, a farmer from Rehe, had bought land from Wei Buhe in 1904, which had angered a man named Wulizhan Jiabu, a Mongol. Wulizhan collaborated with Ma Fu to kidnap Wu and seize his property. After receiving a ransom, they released Wu. In early 1905, however, Wulizhan beat Wu's father and then accused Wu's father at the county office of beating him (Wulizhan). As a result Wu's father was detained. Seeing no chance to complain successfully on behalf of his father at the local level, Wu went to the Frontier Superintendency (*lifanyuan*) in the capital to complaint. There he was told to go home and complain to the county government. Fearing only retaliation at that level, Wu decided to try to block the royal cart. In addressing the case, the Board of Punishment cited the new law changing corporal punishments to fines and ordered that Wu be fined fifteen taels (ounces of silver) for his crime. In line with the new law, the Board asked the investigator to report on whether Wu had the means to pay the fine but it did not indicate what would happen if he did not.[14] In any case, fining with some attention to ability to pay was almost certainly a more lenient punishment than any number of blows with the bamboo let alone exile to the frontier.

The total number of recorded skipping complaints during the last decade of the Qing was limited. Moreover the handling of them was relatively unimportant in the effort to persuade the Western powers to end extraterritoriality perhaps because they were a category of litigation what was rather unfamiliar in the West. For these reasons, the late Qing lenience toward skipping complainants was manifested rather quietly in comparison with other reforms such as abolishing various forms of torture and capital punishment, drafting new criminal and civil codes, and building new prisons and police forces. After corporal punishments was replaced by fines in 1905, a reform that had its own roots deep in the past (e.g., in early Han times), lenience toward most forms of skipping complaints became only one part of a larger trend toward lenience on foreign and Chinese models.

Plans to establish an administrative court

One of the telling fruits of the late Qing reform movement was the idea of an Administrative Court (*xingzheng fayuan*) designed to protect people's "rights" (*quanli*) against governmental violations. Whenever a person believed that his or her legal rights had been infringed by any level of the government, that person would be able to complain to an Administrative Court for relief. Since almost all capital (or skipping) complaints involved government personnel either directly or indirectly, the Administrative Court promised to further enhance people's chance to protect their rights.

The origins of the Chinese idea of an administrative court have been found in Europe. The French republic separated constitutional, which provided for a judiciary, from administrative law, which provided for a check on the judiciary.[15] In the late nineteenth century, the German scholar Otto Mayer (1846–1924) claimed in the late nineteenth century that administrative law had developed in accord with the ideas of Friedrich Hegel who emphasized the need to provide citizens with protection against the state. In other words, administrative law allowed citizens to obtain redress after their rights had been violated by administrative decisions.[16]

Like much else from the West in this period, the notions of administrative law and the Administrative Court made their way to China through Japan.[17] As the Japanese historian Saneto Keishu and others have pointed out, many new words such as human rights (*renquan*), sovereignty (*zhuquan*), administration (*xingzheng*), democracy (*minzhu*), jurisprudence (*faxue*), freedom (*ziyou*), nationality (*minzu*), and constitution (*xianfa*) were first formed in the late nineteenth century in a complicated interaction among classical Chinese, Western, and Japanese writing systems.[18] In 1890, Meiji Japan passed a law on administrative judgments (*xingzheng caipanfa*), which soon came to the attention of the Qing. In 1905, the Japanese scholar Yoroshi Ota (1868–1945) composed the first part of a book titled *The Administrative Law of the Qing State* in which he described the administrative law that had been proposed in China. He explained the idea of administrative remedy (*xingzheng jiuji*) by means of which people might require the government to either withdraw a punishment or change it. The methods included: petition (*qingyuan*), request for review (*yiyi shenli*), and complaint (*suyuan*).[19]

Some Chinese scholars in the late Qing pointed to administrative law and court practice in Japan as models for establishing a constitution that could "save" China. In 1905, the same year the Qing court sent five officials abroad to inspect foreign constitutional systems, Xia Tongsu, a writer from Guizhou province, published his book entitled *Administrative Law*. In the preface, Xia claimed that his purpose in going to Japan was to study the origins of Japan's power and to see what measures could be adopted to strengthen China. Summarizing the thrust of many Japanese books, he noted that Japan had just defeated Russia because "Russia did not have a constitution and thus the top and the bottom were separated." Once Russia became a constitutional state, Xia warned, it too would become powerful. If China failed to establish a constitution, it would be the last centralized or authoritarian state in the world and it "would be the first to suffer" from the rise of Russia.[20] Xia argued that the ideas of the separation of powers, social contract, and the supremacy of the legislative power were the foundations of constitutional politics in which government "could not violate people's life, property, freedom, and body at will." Xia highlighted the study of administration as a prerequisite for the creation of a constitution. Only after Chinese officials were familiar with the study of administration could they "examine carefully the linchpins of state politics." Xia reiterated that if a constitutional government could be built up, China could be saved and it would be able to survive in a world characterized by the "survival of the fittest." Like Mayer, Xia also believed that the aim of administrative law was to protect people's "rights" from official infringement. If rights were violated, the victims would be able to complain to the administrative court to obtain compensation.[21]

As the debate over establishing a constitution mounted at the Qing court, more officials, scholars, and students went to Japan to study its legal system.[22] In 1907, Zhao Yongqing, who had visited Japan the previous year, published *A Summary of a Trip to the East*, which described Japanese administrative authority (*xingzhengquan*). In Zhao's view, administrative authority in Japan included not only relations between the state and one of its organs, but also relations among its organs and between those organs and the people. Zhao recorded that Japan had two types of courts: the Legal Court (*sifa shenpansuo*) and the Administrative Court (*xingzheng shenpansuo*). The Administrative Court dealt with "complaints regarding administrative violations of private rights (*siquan*), while the Legal Court made judgments on general civil and criminal cases (*minxingshi anjian*)." The Administrative Court provided people with an "active (*zhudong*)" means to complain against governmental violations of their rights, thereby "letting the top know the situation at the bottom." Because of this special function, foreign states gave the Administrative Court an independent status, although the precise nature of the administrative complaint varied among countries. Furthermore, Zhao added, the administrative complaint not only allowed people to protest governmental abuse of power but also endowed them with "the privilege to supervise the government." Although the emphasis on people's rights was not as strong in Japan as in Europe and America, Zhao concluded, the Japanese Administrative Court still allowed people to complain in compliance with the administrative law.[23]

Entertaining suggestions from many observers, the Qing court came to see the critical role of an Administrative Court in protecting people from official abuse, opening communication between the top and the bottom of society, and preparing the way for forming a constitutional government. In 1906, after the Qing announced a massive plan to revise the law and prepare a constitution to address both external and internal pressures, the institution of an Administrative Court became a high priority. Soon after the edict calling for a constitution, Shen Jiaben, the prominent legal scholar and official, enlisted the help of three Japanese scholars to draft the Organizing Law of the Court System (*fayuan bianzhifa*) that was finally approved in 1908.[24] Article 2 put the courts in charge of small (i.e., civil) and criminal cases but provided that "any other case pertaining to military law or administrative complaints" should be handled separately.[25]

Despite advice from many quarters, the Qing court never seriously considered transforming the Censorate into an Administrative Court. Unlike the Administrative Court that only handled people's complaints against official misbehaviors, the Censorate would deal with an administration/official's violation of either people's rights or state interest.[26] Accordingly, the Qing planned to maintain the Censorate and to create a separate Administrative Court. In 1909, the Qing promulgated the Draft of the Bureaucratic System of the Administrative Court (*xingzheng caipanyuan guanzhi caoan*). The prologue of the draft, which closely followed the 1890 Japanese administrative complaint law,[27] stated that the purpose of an Administrative Court was to protect people from official violations and to "satisfy all the grievances under heaven." The proposed court would coexist with the Censorate that had long played a somewhat similar role. The prologue stated that Germany, Austria, and Japan had the best administrative-court systems because they policed the boundaries between administrative and judicial authority and checked administrative authority on behalf of the people.

Article 1 of the draft noted that the Administrative Court was responsible for all charges against official abuses. Like most dynastic laws since the Tang, this draft law expressed a strong preference for complaints against officials to be handled step by step up the administrative hierarchy. It specified that

> Only complaints against ministries, governors, and governors-general will be allowed to be addressed directly to the court, [and] all other complaints should go to local governments. If [such complaints] are ignored or refused, complainants should complain to the next higher levels and eventually to the Administrative Court.

Perhaps surprisingly in light of the late Qing reformist tolerance of skipping complaints highlighted above, the draft law stipulated clearly: "No skipping complaint is allowed." In addition, the proposed Administrative Court would accept neither civil nor criminal cases. Although the head of the court would enjoy the first-grade (*yipin*) official position, one of the highest in the court system, the planned Administrative Court would not report directly to the ruler and all judges in the court would be considered to be normal government officials, i.e., under the authority of the ruler. Hence, this court would be unlikely to deal with charges against higher-ranking officials let alone the ruler him (or her) self.[28]

Although the Qing fell before it could actually establish an Administrative Court, the officials engaged in planning for it as well as the plans themselves persisted into the republican era.[29] In any case, the planning for a new Administrative Court revealed both the Chinese impulse for reform in a global context at the end of the Qing and the continuing power of Chinese ideas and practices developed during the millennium since the Tang.

Toleration of newspapers' reports of complaints

Newspapers too had roots in the Chinese past as well as models imported from abroad. To inform the public of state policies, the Han dynasty issued newssheets called *dibao* (literally, government reports).[30] During the Song, the first private newspapers appeared in print under the name *xiaobao* (literally, small reports).[31] In the Qing, there was a government gazette and late in the dynasty many private newspapers appeared. Private newspapers were first established in the treaty ports, where foreigners enjoyed extra-territorial privileges after 1844, and then in the interior in succeeding decades. At first the Qing tried to suppress the private newspapers that appeared under its jurisdiction.[32]

During the Sino-Japanese War an official named Chen Chi criticized the Qing ban on newspapers outside the treaty ports. In his words, "Despite the fact that the Qing government allows the foreigners to form newspapers, it prohibits the Chinese people from establishing them."[33] Zheng Guanying, a famous businessman and scholar, suggested that China should establish its own newspapers to compete with the foreign ones. At the same time, it should adopt the Western liberal principal of "freedom of the press" and allow newspapers to print articles critical of officials.[34] In 1896, with the support of the powerful official Zhang Zhidong, the scholars Wang Kangnian and Liang Qichao (1873–1929) established the *Chinese Progress* in Shanghai to advocate reform.[35] In the view of Liang Qichao's sense of Western imperialism, history, and revolution, and his understanding of China's political process had been profoundly shaped by Egypt's fate under the British imperialist rule and by prominent Japanese and European thinkers and revolutionaries such as Fukuzawa Yukichi (1835–1901), Johann K. Bluntschli (1808–1881), and Count Camillo di Cavour (1810–61). Liang remarked later that the press contained two essential meanings as it not only contributed to the progress of civilization by exercising intellectual freedom and guiding public opinion. It also spoke to the entire nation and hence helped create a national community.[36]

The Qing government soon accommodated itself to the idea of newspapers and, with its tacit support, newspapers quickly appeared in as many as eighteen provinces. During the 1898 reform period, a contemporary writer remarked in *China-Foreign Daily* (*zhongwai ribao*) that he was stunned by the sudden proliferation of newspapers in China. "In 4000 years," he wrote (with some hyperbole), "the recent prosperity of Chinese newspapers is unprecedented."[37]

After the suppression of the 1898 reform, the Empress Dowager Cixi tightened the press policy, explicitly banned newspapers in the hinterland, and officially denounced journalists as the dregs of the literati (*siwen bailei*). But before long, the repressive policy toward the press was replaced by a more supportive one as the Qing found that it was more reasonable to try to "shape and control the new press market."[38] In 1901 the high official Yuan Shikai, who had been instrumental in suppressing the 1898 reforms, proposed that the government should establish official newspapers operating under strict laws in all provinces. Their primary purpose would be to "enlighten the people" (*kaiminzhi*) so as to insure their "livelihood" and prevent costly "assaults on churches" (*jiao'an*). In addition, official newspapers would resist the influence of foreign newspapers.[39] In the following legal reform and especially during the constitutional movement, private newspapers thrived. In 1908, in reaction against increasing criticism from independent private newspapers, the Qing once again authorized closer official surveillance of those newspapers.[40]

Despite the vicissitudes of official policy toward the press in the late Qing, newspapers provided complainants in China with a new venue for voicing their grievances and gaining public support for their demands for redress. As early as 1872 the Shanghai based foreign-owned *Shenbao* (*Shanghai Daily*) had played an important role in influencing Qing judicial handling of a case in which a wife (Xiao Baicai) was falsely charged with killing her husband to have an affair with a student (Yang Naiwu).[41] Studies show that *Shenbao* paid close attention to it from the beginning to the end and played an important role in obtaining final satisfaction of both Yang's and Xiao's grievances.[42] As the legal scholar William P. Alford argues, "The paper (*Shenbao*) not only accused officials of colluding with each other and breaking the law, but also called into question the very soundness of certain aspects of the formal criminal justice process."[43]

In the first decade of the twentieth century as Qing authority declined, the role of the public media in helping people publicize their grievances and obtain satisfaction increased. The range of grievances stretched from individuals and small groups to cities, provinces, or even the whole country. After the revolutionary activist Xu Xilin assassinated the Anhui governor in 1907, the Qing executed Qiu Jin, a prominent woman scholar in Zhejiang, on the grounds that she was Xu's accomplice.[44] Some newspapers, including *Shenbao*, and *The Vernacular Journal* (*baihua bao*) in Hangzhou, Zhejiang that had revolutionary connections, openly challenged the government's case on Qiu Jin. On July 23, 1907, *Shenbao* editorialized that there was no evidence that Qiu was involved in Xu's assassination and that officials had executed her as a "shortcut to get promotions."[45] Another newspaper *Shibao* (*The Times*), in the words of Joan Judge "the most influential reform organ of the day,"[46] compared Qiu's execution to that of the patriotic general Yue Fei in the Northern Song, arguing that both were convicted and executed on fabricated charges.[47] Even bolder than *Shenbao*, *Shibao* charged Qing "remonstrating officials" with ineffectively conveying people's sufferings. The newspaper claimed that journalists were able to "relay information to and from the people more swiftly and accurately than any imperial censorial institutions could."[48]

In the face of increasing challenges from the newspapers, the Qing court sometimes responded with harsh retaliation. In 1903 Zou Rong published a book titled *The Revolutionary Army*, which called for the overthrow of the Qing dynasty. This led to Qing efforts to suppress the revolutionary newspaper *Subao*, which was published in the foreign concession of Shanghai. Under Qing pressure, the Shanghai authorities arrested six journalists of the newspaper and the Shanghai Mixed Court sentenced Zou Rong and Zhang Binglin to two and three years of prison respectively. Zou Rong died in prison.[49]

A few years before the end of the Qing, radical newspapers like *Minhubao* (literally, "the people's shout"), *Minyubao* (literally, "the people's call"), and *Minlibao* (literally, "the people stand up") also wanted to become "representatives of the people." Located in Shanghai, these newspapers vigorously publicized people's grievances, public discontents, and mass calls for establishing a constitution.[50] On June 8, 1909, for example, *Minhubao* reported a demonstration of a group of small businessmen in Tianjin. The demonstration was kindled by an increase in the amount of a fee levied by the police from which small businesses had usually been exempt. According to the report, the businessmen planned to complain to the city council first, asking for an exemption from the fee. If the complaint failed, they threatened to boycott the market by closing their doors. In the same year, *Minhubao* reported many cases involving demonstrations in favor of reclaiming authority over railroads and mines that had been conceded to foreign investors by the Qing government in 1899. For example, on June 8, *Minhubao* reported a protest of thousands of Henan local elite and people against the Henan government's contract with a British company that allowed it to exploit the coalmines of Henan. During the constitutional movement, *Minlibao* reported numerous demonstrations in an extended series of general protests against the state. As some desperate natural resisters did in the dynasties, many demonstrators used self-mutilation to draw government attention. For instance, in late 1910, *Minlibao* reported some Tianjin students who demonstrated for a quick opening of the parliament by writing requests with their own blood or cutting off pieces of their flesh.[51] While those newspaper reports, however forceful, might not by themselves have forced the Qing emperor to step up his pace in establishing a parliament, they certainly raised the popular political consciousness and prompted more people to join the constitutional movement. In addition, those reports also raise the much-debated issue of the emergence of what the German theorist Jürgen Habermas called "civil society and public sphere" in this period.[52]

Collective complaints and public demonstrations

Although states in China, like states anywhere, hardly encouraged collective complaints, much less public demonstrations, there was a long history in China of literati expressions of open dissent from—and even manifestations against—corrupt and ineffectual regimes. They included recurrent student demonstrations about the occasion of civil service examinations at all levels and major scholar–student movements at the ends of the Han and of the Ming dynasties.[53] The Qing, like pre-Revolutionary France or Tokugawa Japan,[54] was probably less tolerant of collective complaints and public demonstrations than the Ming had been. It became even more sensitive about popular grievances as its authority declined under internal and external assaults in the late nineteenth century.[55] Such sensitivity often resulted in repression. For example, after the Qing dismissed soldiers who had been conscripted for the Sino-Japanese War (1894–1895) but did not pay them fully as promised, the soldiers sent 500 representatives to the provincial governor's office to complain. The governor immediately denounced this collective complaint as a "rebellion" and ordered the arrest of its leaders.[56]

Other public complaints could not be so easily suppressed. One of the most famous collective complaints in the late Qing was the Public Cart Complaint in 1895, a practice that could be traced back to the Han dynasty. When the news of signing the Treaty of Shimonoseki arrived in Beijing, Kang Youwei (1858–1927), the future leader of the 1898 reform, and thousands of other provincial graduates (*juren*), who had come to the capital to take the metropolitan examination, decided to encourage the Qing court not to sign the treaty that imposed harsh terms on China. They elected Kang to draft a complaint letter in which Kang proposed a plan to continue fighting with Japan. This mass complaint was weakened when most of the graduates declined to put their names on the complaint letter for fear of subsequent reprisals.[57] In the end, the report was not even delivered to the Censorate, which was supposed to turn in all such complaints to the throne. Despite these failures, this collective complaint garnered 1300 signatures and marked a beginning of a wave of intellectual complaints and demonstrations against government policies and state authority.

A second major collective complaint resulted in the 100 Days of Reform of 1898. After the failure of that reform due to divisions at court, Liang Qichao commented that,

> Public demonstrations and [independent] social organizations are always prohibited by the state. Kang Youwei's Society for the Study of [Self-] Strengthening (*qiangxuehui*) and the Society to Defend the Country (*baoguohui*) as well as the Southern Study Society (*nanxuehui*) founded by Hunan patriots have all been required to close.[58]

Liang's conclusion was premature, however, for the situation changed again with the new policies after 1901. The government consistently suppressed "secret society" activities as well as overt "revolutionary" movements.[59] But it was forced to live with rural resistance to reforms effected in the name of "modernization" as well as with urban demonstrations for constitutional reforms including the early opening of a "responsible parliament." As recounted by both Roxann Prazniak and Kristin Stapleton, some of the collective complaints against taxes turned to rebellions.[60]

As the Qing neared its end, more and more people availed themselves of the strategy of "first-complain-then-demonstrate." For example, in October 1910 fifteen officials in Sichuan complained to the Censorate in Beijing about alleged corruption in the management of the Sichuan railway company that had been formed by local officials and members of the elite and the people.[61] A month later more than 100 members of the local elite and business community in Sichuan, speaking on behalf of the people of the province, complained to the Regent regarding the same issue. They expressed the hope that "the Regent would be concerned about the 'little people' and would help them protect their hard-earned investments." When some of the complainants tried to block the Regent's cart at the Di'an Gate in Beijing, they were detained. They were soon bailed out by Sichuanese who were serving in the capital, an informal and irregular—but long-standing and increasingly common—form of collective action. At this point the complainants were given the classic runaround by the central bureaucracy. After two weeks, the case was transferred to the Supreme Court of Justice (*daliyuan*). When the head of the railroad refused to come to the court and used his influence to sway the judges, the case was passed to the Ministry of Posts and Communications. The Ministry also denied any responsibility and told the complainants to complain to the Censorate. When they went to the Censorate, they were told that they should wait as the case was under investigation by the Ministry of Posts and Communications.[62] In this case the solidarity among officials, elite, merchants, and the people of a province enabled them to challenge the corruption of a local powerful person by taking their case to the capital. Although they were ultimately not successful in regaining control over the Sichuan railway, they persisted in their collective action and did not suffer unduly from it if only because the state was becoming too weak to retaliate. Indeed, the Sichuan railway case was an important step toward the overthrow of the Qing in 1911, opening the way for decades of even less effective government and more assertive collective action.[63]

Halfway revolutions

The late Qing reform might have been impossible had the rulers not been under immense pressures from both within and without. Since it lost the first Opium War, the Qing rulers had largely been constrained by the notion "Chinese learning as the essence, Western learning as the tool" coined by Feng Guifeng, a reform-minded official and a disciple of the Imperial Commissioner Lin Zexu whose order to destroy foreign opium in 1838 precipitated the First Opium War. Equally influential in this time was the famous argument of scholarly official Wei Yuan (1794–1857) that it was good to study foreign technologies so as to outwit the foreigners (*shiyi changji yi zhiyi*).[64]

After the Qing lost the Sino-Japanese war in 1895, despite roughly equal military and scientific knowledge,[65] many people including scholarly officials became highly critical of the Qing policies of stressing only Western technologies and resisting calls for political reforms. For instance, infuriated by the seemingly insatiable demands of the foreign powers and patronizing toward the failed policies of the Qing court, Zheng Guanying stated that the basis of power and prosperity "consists not at all of strong warships and cannons, but of a top-to-bottom unity and a parliament."[66] Likewise, Kang Youwei claimed in his first memorial to the Guangxü emperor that China's "biggest disease (*dabing*)" was the blockage of communication between the top and the bottom and not the relative weakness of its warships and cannons. He argued that with the exception of a few high-ranking officials, most officials could not see the ruler and, with the exception of a few complainants, the people at the base could not get their grievances to the top. Thus, Kang concluded that connections between the ruler and ministers, high-ranking officials and lower-ranking officials, and officials and the people were all obstructed. The best solution was to establish a parliament to which even the emperor would be subject.[67]

With the assistance of Kang Youwei and his followers like Liang Qichao, the young Emperor Guangxü launched the1898 reform, a more moderate reform than the one outlined three years later but one that nonetheless portended change in the status quo. But, due to an internal struggle over power between the Empress Dowager Cixi and her nephew Guangxü,[68] the reform lasted for only 103 days. It was followed by two disastrous years during which the Qing used anti-foreign Boxers to oppose foreign encroachment only to have the Boxers put down by another foreign invasion, this time of eight foreign powers.[69] The failure of the Boxer movement persuaded most Chinese of the need to revise the "old laws."[70] In its 1901 reform decree, the Qing finally called for a comprehensive reform on the basis of Western learning as the "essence" and not just as "hair and skin." The ensuing late Qing reforms went far beyond the 1898 ones by covering all fields from political to legal systems, from police to the new army, and from new schools to model prisons.

In hindsight, the late Qing reform of its complaint systems involved four improvements that were, in some senses, "revolutionary." The humane treatment of skipping and false complainants was a radical change from pre-1898 Qing policies of harsh punishments, which greatly enhanced people's natural right to complain. The Administrative Court was so far merely a plan or proposal and it shared certain features with the long-standing Censorate. But it went well beyond the Censorate because its primary purpose was to protect people's rights, while the Censorate's was to serve the ruler. Through directly entertaining commoners' complaints against the misbehavior of local officials, the Administrative Court could at least potentially offer restitution to the aggrieved.[71] Late-Qing newspapers took unprecedentedly bold steps in publicizing commoners' complaints and in challenging official accounts of events. Whether out of fear and weakness or in response to past and foreign models, the late Qing state also showed a higher level of tolerance of collective complaints and even collective action than had been the case for most of its existence since the seventeenth century.

The late Qing reforms, while potentially "revolutionary," were hardly unprecedented. As the late Qing reformers were often aware, many earlier rulers had shown various kinds of lenience in the legal process. Shen Jiaben praised Han Wendi (r. 179–157 BCE) and Han Jingdi (r. 156–141 BCE) for their "lenient hearts" in abolishing mutilation and reducing corporal punishment, making their reigns famous as times of "civility and peace (*wenjing zhizhi*)."[72] In addition, I could cite as evidence of earlier humane practices: Liang Wudi's (502–549) extreme lenience toward a usurper;[73] the Sui code's amelioration of many severe punishments;[74] Tang Taizong's (r. 627–649) abolition of remaining mutilations, his restrictions on the death penalty, and his reduction of judicial torture and corporal punishment; and the Song dynasty's numerous general amnesties. Even commoners, such as Ti Yin in the reign of Han Wendi, had complained directly to the ruler without fear of punishment.[75] Also, in the reigns of Song Huizong and some Southern Song rulers, the ban on skipping complaints was lifted as we have seen.[76]

The legal historian Chen Guyuan has pointed out that in most times and places, including most of the world even today, administrative law has not been clearly distinguished from constitutional law. In that sense, as one Japanese legal scholar has pointed out, Zhou China probably had the world's earliest administrative law, and every dynasty since then has had extensive rules and regulations pertaining to the administration.[77] The most important aim of the administrative court—protecting people's rights against officials' violation—seems to have been envisioned much earlier. As we saw in Chapter 1, commoners in the Zhou and Han dynasty could complain directly to the palace gate without fear of being punished. The establishment of the Red Stone and the Public Petition Drum by Liang Wudi and Jin Wudi respectively were most likely to prevent official abuse of the people.

Although there was no legal provision for it, complainants often banded together and lodged collective complaints in Chinese history. The earliest recorded case took place in the Former Han, and people continued to make collective complaints in later periods.[78] During the Ming dynasty, several large-scale collective complaints eventually reached the ruler and were successful in obtaining their goals.[79] In these cases, it seems the Ming was less likely than the Qing to charge collective complainants with committing "banditry."

Many of the harshest punishments that were outlawed in the late Qing had relatively recent origins or had been imposed only informally or intermittently in the past. As Shen Jiaben noted,[80] the law sanctioning (but also regulating) the buying and selling of slaves had appeared only the late Zhou period. The practice was at its worst in the Qin and Han when slaves were regarded as property, and it was greatly attenuated and ameliorated in the Qing when slaves were treated more like hired workers.[81] The punishment of cutting up the corpse had first appeared in the Qin period, but it was not until the late Ming (1579) that it became law, and even then it was reserved for those who killed their parents or grandparents. It was only in the Qing that quartering was extended to criminals executed for robbery. Beheading was adopted by the Qin and Han for particularly egregious crimes such as the killing of all members of a family (*zuzhu*), but it was abolished by the Sui and renewed only in the Ming and Qing. The particularly painful method of execution known as slicing appeared for the first time only in the Liao dynasty. It was formally adopted by the Song but only for certain egregious crimes, and it was generally restricted to such crimes by later dynasties. Thus, in abolishing these harsh punishments, the late Qing state was building on the more humane impulses of many earlier polities.

The late Qing legal reforms nonetheless differed from earlier reforms in certain ways. For example, the reformers were driven in part by the desire to satisfy foreign expectations and demands so that the foreign powers could be persuaded to give up the extraterritorial privileges that infringed on Chinese sovereignty. Although the Chinese had many times before undertaken reforms in an effort to resist foreign domination, they had never before made their punishments of convicts more humane to that end, especially toward complainants who blocked the royal cart. In addition, the late Qing legal reforms were more comprehensive and thorough than any previous such reforms. They went beyond Han Wendi to abolish all mutilations, not just some, and beyond Liang Wudi to extend lenience to commoners as well as to nobles. The late Qing reforms abolished all corporal punishment, including beating with whips and bamboo, and they outlawed all forms of torture, whether in the course of investigations or as part of the process of punishment. Third, the late Qing legal reforms were consciously based on a new ideology of "equality" and new terminologies of "humaneness" that owed something to contemporary Western civilization as mediated by Japan. The reforms abolished the very social category of slave, allowed marriage between hired workers and other commoners, and emphasized "protecting human rights (*baohu renquan*)"[82] or "respect for human dignity" (*zunzhong renge*).[83] Meanwhile, the new wave of reform arising from below was largely built on ideas such as people's rights (*minquan*), constitutionalism, and democracy that arrived from the West and Japan and that had only partial foundations in Chinese thought and history.[84] For the first time, the new Western concepts endowed upon people's natural right to complain are different from the traditional Confucian doctrines, mandate of heaven, and the heaven–human interactions. As we will see in the following chapters, both traditional and Western concepts worked concertedly in shaping the complaint systems in the republican periods.

Second, those "revolutions" in the late Qing were not complete because they failed to solve the old problems such as official corruption and the internal problems inside the Qing complaint systems that had caused numerous grievances in the past. On the contrary, the complaint systems deteriorated in the late Qing due to political disruption and new reforms that resulted in new grievances.

For example, despite its leniency toward skipping and false complainants, the Qing court was reluctant to reverse decisions of the provincial governments,[85] and most complaints to the capital continued to be turned down after 1898 as they had been before.[86] Middle levels of the bureaucracy similarly continued to respond to complaints against lower levels by sending the complaints back to the lower levels that often ended with no satisfaction or worse. To give one example, in 1904 Deng Guozheng, a farmer from Henan, whose wife had been raped and killed by a local bully and who had failed to get justice at the county level, complained to the provincial level only to have his case sent back to the county.[87] The problem, some felt, was not any lack of good laws but the failure to enforce them. In 1905, the reform-minded official Zhao Erxun argued that there were many good laws, such as those providing for lenient punishment, but "the people who have enforced them are few..."[88]

Since official corruption remained uncurbed in the late Qing, the New Policies (*xinzheng*) opened up in 1901 solved some problems but led to others such as more greedy local officials and heavier new taxes. Even the court acknowledged in 1903 that only a few local officials were "really giving the people heartfelt service (*jinxin minshi*)."[89] In 1909 a metropolitan graduate from Jiangxi asked the ruler to control the use of fines. He pointed out that after the punishment by whip and bamboo had been replaced by fines in 1905, venal local officials were taking advantage of the new law to make money. They imposed fines all out of proportion to the seriousness of the crimes and "used force to squeeze money" from even the poorest of litigants.[90] New taxes for education, police, and Confucian temples, that benefited the elite more than the commoners who paid most of them were notoriously unpopular and caused more complaints. When desperate people in Laiyang, Shandong province, complained to the government and were repeatedly ignored, they often ended up supporting violent uprisings.[91]

Although the court was more attuned to collective complaints than in the recent past, it was not strong enough to deal with powerful officials like Qiao Shuzhan, the corrupt head of the Sichuan railroad, who refused to show up at the Supreme Court and was therefore never prosecuted for his corruption and violations of people's rights.[92] Because of the existence of a new judicial system, governors were neglecting to forward undecided cases to the Censorate. In 1908, seeing the possibility that many complainants would die in prison without any concerned words from the investigators, the Censorial officials felt like crying "hard for the powerless little people."[93] In the fall of 1911, shortly before the demise of the Qing, the head of the newly elected national assembly, in reproaching the throne for the sham of establishing a constitution, warned of a dangerous situation consisting of cruel officials, unfair judgments, incomplete reforms, and unprotected people's property and lives.[94]

Many late Qing scholars and officials lashed out at the Qing complaint systems and some critics like Kang Youwei and Liang Qichao went so far to argue that aggrieved people had "no way to complain."[95] Likewise, in 1904, the Empress Dowager Cixi complained that officials, whose salaries ultimately came from the people, showed little sympathy toward them. She demanded to know "How can such officials feel secure at night when they know that commoners have nowhere to complain?"[96] In 1907, the censor Lu Baozhong noted that the reason the Chinese people could find nowhere to lodge their complaints was not simply the appointment of bad officials but the blockage inside the administration.[97] Although those scholars, officials, and even Cixi failed to notice the improvements in the late Qing, their criticism may have been shared by many contemporary complainants like Zhao Shouyin.

Thus, for these two reasons, the late Qing reform of its complaint systems, regardless of its many revolutionary elements, was at most a halfway revolution.

Conclusion

Under tremendous internal and external pressures and inspired by domestic and foreign models, the Qing government moved in its final years to reform its inherited complaint systems and took firm steps toward expanding and improving people's natural right to complain. After abolishing the corporal punishment that had long been meted out to skipping and false complainants, it adopted a lenient attitude toward those kinds of complaints and soon substituted the more humane punishment of fines. To offer another recourse to people who felt they were mistreated by local officials, the Qing planned the establishment of an Administrative Court that was eventually realized by the succeeding republican regime. The late Qing also overcame its early aversion to private newspapers, which often amplified popular dissatisfaction with state policies and it allowed such media to proliferate and become yet another venue for popular complaints. Additionally, the late Qing allowed for collective complaints and even collective action, hoping that tolerance in that sphere would avoid violent confrontations that would threaten the existence of the state. In the end, the late Qing reforms were too little and too late to save that particular polity, but they contributed to a heritage of reform that would continue to inform subsequent complaint systems under the republics.

3 A golden age

The early republic (1912–1927)

The Qing dynasty confronted a major uprising on October 10, 1911, and was replaced by a new kind of state, the Republic of China on January 1, 1912. In contrast to the Qing and previous monarchs who might have claimed to rule on behalf of the people and to regard the people as the root of the state (*minben*), the republic (literally, joint rule, *gonghe guo*) would be based on the principle that the people were actually in charge of a people's state (*minguo*). In this view, the new state would certainly protect the rights of the people more effectively because it would be governed not just *for* but *by* the people. To cite but one of many examples, the republican governor of Jiangxi province, Li Liejun (1882–1946) claimed that sovereignty in a republican state lay with the people.[1] Sun Yat-sen, the interim president of the newborn republic, attempted to link the inherited idea of the mandate of heaven and nature to the new state by declaring in his inaugural speech that the "heavenly endowed freedom (*tianfu ziyou*) had long been cherished by the Chinese."[2] In a later speech, Sun argued that in an empire there was only one emperor while in the republic all the Chinese people would be emperors.[3] In the interest of continuity and stability, the new government adopted most of the laws enacted in the late Qing.[4] It abolished torture, which it deemed a violation of the sacred human rights (*renquan shensheng*) and banned references to officials as "big masters" (*dalaoye*), a title at odds with their rightful function as public servants of the people.[5] In addition, the republica adopted many cultural and social reforms such as cutting queues, ending the *ketou* (kowtow), and giving up Chinese-style clothes, signaling radical changes to come.[6]

Under the new democratic ideology that the people were not just the base of the state but its hosts or masters, the republican government overhauled the inherited legal systems so as to further accommodate people's natural right to complain. To be sure, some long-standing and dramatic institutions such as the public petition drum and blocking the royal cart were allowed to fade away, but they had always been risky and therefore rare and they may not have been much missed. More importantly, persistent and common practices such as skipping and false complaints that had been punishable crimes in most eras after the Sui dynasty were now not just left unprosecuted or acquitted (albeit the law still required complainants to follow legal steps), as they had been in the late Qing, but were no longer regarded as crimes subject to punishment. The republic also developed a more articulated court system, clearly distinguishing between civil and criminal offenses, and passed a new *Complaint Law* (*suyuanfa*) that allowed citizens to seek redress for injuries sustained from inappropriate (*budang*, unjust but not illicit) as well as illegal (*bufa*, violating the law) measures. To handle complaints not resolved at lower levels, the republic established two new central apparatuses, an Administrative Court (literally, ministry of just governance, *pingzhengyuan*) that would accept lawsuits against official misgovernment and the Department for Disciplining Government (*suzhengting*, hereinafter the Discipline Department) that would inspect the adjudication of the Administrative Court and accept people's direct complaints (not lawsuits) against government misconducts. In the republic, other central government organs, such as the Interior Ministry (*neiwubu*) and the Congress, could also accept people's complaints about official abuses (which we might see as an elaboration of the inherited *yique* system).

Despite all the improvements made in this period and the new justifications of people's natural right to complain, the original principles of what I am calling natural resistance (the mandate of heaven, heavenly principles, parental rulers, people as the root) remained in people's minds and influenced their actions. In his attempt to become a constitutional son of heaven in late 1915, Yuan Shikai claimed to have "the mandate of heaven" and his followers called for popular support of "our holy (*shensheng*) emperor."[7] On December 21, 1915, Yuan Shikai also invoked the Confucian concept of *minben*/people as the root by instructing his subordinates to love the people as if they were their children.[8] As we shall see, many complainants visible in the archives during this period continued to practice natural resistance by ignoring the new *Complaint Law*, which required the lodging of complaints through the standard hierarchy and yet avoided prosecution for violators (skipping complainants).

After the death of Yuan Shikai in 1916, China suffered serious political disintegration as powerful warlords controlled their own territories and expressed little respect for the central government in Beijing. The subject of warlordsim has been studied by a number of scholars such as James Sheridan, Gavan McCormack, and Ernest Young. According to Sheridan's pioneering study of warlord Feng Yuxiang, the modern warlordism in China appeared in the 1890s in the wake of the Chinese loss in the Sino-Japanese War (1894–1895), which prompted the Qing court to move toward military modernization.[9] In the following decade, not only was a military career no longer despised but a martial spirit was also kindled as foreign powers scrambled to partition China or create a sphere of influence there. The abolition of the civil examination in 1905 also helped make the military a promising career to power in the eyes of many Chinese. The warlord period lasted from 1916 to 1928 when Zhang Xueliang, the son of Zhang Zuolin, a main warlord and "the final and main enemy of the revolutionary armies,"[10] agreed to put Manchuria under the rule of Chiang Kai-shek's Guomindang. During the decade-long warlord era, warlords waged numerous wars against each other and the central government in Beijing existed mostly in name. Chinese people whose rights were violated by officials at the local level were rarely to have their grievances actively considered at the center let alone redressed there. Political disorder, official corruption, judicial flaws, and other factors combined to undermine the efficacy of the early republican complaint systems in practice.

The judicial complaint systems

The formation of the Administrative Court and the Discipline Department

During the early republic, the new government established a court and a department that took on the character of what I may call judicial complaint systems. Although the idea of establishing an Administrative Court to protect people from governmental abuse had been proposed in the late Qing, the dynasty fell before such a court could be created. Shortly after the 1911 revolution, the liberal revolutionary Song Jiaoren drafted The E'zhou (Hubei) Constitution of the Republic of China (*zhonghua minguo Ezhou yuefa*) that stated that people could complain to an Administrative Court about any alleged official violation of their rights.[11] In the Draft Organization Law of the Republic of China Interim Government (*zhonghua minguo linshi zhengfu zuzhifa caoan*), also drafted by Song, Article 14 reiterated that people could complain to the Administrative Court when they believed their rights had been violated by the government. The term "Pingzhengyuan" for an Administrative Court first appeared in this draft.[12] On March 11, 1912, President Sun Yat-sen signed this draft into law as part of the Provisional Constitution of the Republic of China (*zhonghua minguo linshi yuefa*). Article 10 stated that people "had the right to complain to the Administrative Court against official infringement [of their rights]." Article 49 of the same constitution clearly distinguished between the role of the general court system and that of the Administrative Court. "The general court system (*putong fayuan*) makes judgments concerning civil and criminal lawsuits, while the Administrative Court decides administrative and other special lawsuits according to different laws [administrative litigation law]."[13]

However, partly because the republic was in its formative period marked by chaos and political struggles, the Administrative Court was not actually inaugurated until two years later. After President Yuan Shikai suppressed the Second Revolution (*er'ci geming*) launched by former revolutionaries against his growing autocratic power in late 1913, he secured his control over the country and began taking steps toward institutionalizing his supremacy. On May 1, 1914, he promulgated the Constitution of the Republic of China (*zhonghua minguo yuefa*) as a replacement of the previous provisional constitution. Although these steps were highly irregular and severely undercut due process of law in the new republic, the Administrative Court emerged relatively unscathed: citizens continued to have the "natural" rights to complain to the court when faced with what they considered to be official abuses and violations of their rights.[14] The Yuan administration may have retained the Administrative Court and the Discipline Department to deal with the corruption that was rampant among its many unqualified officials. On May 22, 1914, Yuan complained publically that with the exception of a few capable magistrates, most local officials in the country were ignorant and unqualified. Indeed, in Yuan's view, such officials were responsible for the contemporary chaos and mounting violence in the society. Yuan warned that if unqualified officials continued to be appointed, people's living conditions would continue to worsen. "All local officials who bear the responsibility for the local [people]," Yuan remarked, "should both stabilize the roots of the state and protect commoners. How dare they only serve their friends and relatives and do harm to innocent [people]?[15] To address and check such official corruption, the Yuan administration established a new organ—the Discipline Department—separate from the Administrative Court. The new office was established inside the Administrative Court but was intended to function independently. One of its principal missions was to supervise and punish officials who committed crimes such as violating the constitution, offering and accepting bribes, abusing power, and ignoring people's grievances.[16]

The organization and function of the Administrative Court and the Discipline Department

In May 1914, the republican Congress enacted the Draft Organization Law of the Administrative Court (*pingzhengyuan bianzhifa caoan*). This law divided the Administrative Court into two levels: the Local [provincial] and the Central Administrative Courts. The Local Court dealt with complaints from parties who contested decisions by local governments (*defang zhengfu*), disputes between provincial government heads, and disputes among local-level [non-governmental] organizations (*difang tuanti*). For complainants who refused to accept the decision of the highest local (i.e., provincial) government and lodged lawsuits against local (i.e., county and prefectural) government officials at the Local Administrative Court, the court's first judgment would be the final one and there was no way for complainants to complain further. For complainants who were not satisfied with the adjudication of the Local [provincial] Court,[17] they could move on to bring their complaints to the Central Court in Beijing. The Central Court was responsible for cases in which complainants refused to accept the decisions made by a central government unit. The Central Administrative Court had the final say in the following three cases: when complainants did not agree with the decisions of the Local Court; when complainants did not agree with the decisions made by a central government office; when the heads of two central government officers or units were in dispute.[18]

The law also established a supervisory department (*jianchating*) as a subordinate unit of the court. The supervisors had the authority to prosecute any governmental activity found by them to be in violation of people's rights and to supervise the implementation of the [Courts'] adjudications.

To ensure the independence of the Administrative Court from interest groups, the law prohibited any person who was affiliated with a political party, a lawyer, a businessman, or a member of either a local parliament or a political council from becoming the judge of the Administrative Court. Once appointed, those judges held their terms for life and could not be dismissed for any reason.[19] But the law did not indicate who would appoint those judges and whether the judges, after appointed, could be dismissed in case of malfeasance.

A revised version of the law, the Organizing Regulation of the Administrative Court (*pingzhengyuan bianzhiling*), highlighted the functions of both the Administrative Court and the Discipline Department to supervise other officials. While it preserved most of the draft version of the law, it eliminated the Local Administrative Court most likely due to the ongoing serious financial problems. It also replaced the Supervisory Department of the Administrative Court with a separate Discipline Department that was given a similar function and authority.[20] In addition, the law made an effort to protect judicial independence while ensuring responsibility by stipulating that only if judges of the Administrative Court and the Discipline Department could be moved only if they committed crimes and were convicted by the regular judicial system [civil and criminal courts].[21]

Within a few months, the legislature that had established the Administrative Court and the Discipline Department promulgated several more laws and regulations regarding their operation. The Acting Regulations of the Administrative Court and the Discipline Department (*pingzhengyuan suzhengting chuwu guize*) first stated that any person complaining to the Discipline Department would be asked to turn in concrete evidence or have the endorsement from an official of his hometown (*tongxiangguan*).[22] Another law, the Regulations on Complaints to the Discipline Department (*suzhengting gaosu gaofa zhangcheng*), gave all people the right to complain directly to the department.[23] Complainants were required to go to the department in person and fill out a special form. Moreover, probably to discourage false complaints, the regulations required all complainants to have their complaint forms signed by either the managers of hotels where they were staying in the capital or by officials from their home provinces (who were not, obviously, the targets of their complaints).[24] On June 8, 1914, the Regulations to Enforce the Adjudications of the Administrative Court (*pingzhengyuan caijue zhixing tiaoli*) stated that if any government official ignored the adjudication of the Administrative Court, the judges of the Discipline Department could bring this official up for possible discipline [by the head of the state]. This regulation was revised in 1919 to beef up the enforcing power of the Administrative Court. As the new regulation put it:

> If any government [official] did not follow the decision of the Administrative Court, the head of the Administrative Court could urge that official to comply with its decision within a certain period of time. In the meantime, the court head could report the case to the president.[25]

The Administrative Court and the Discipline Department were two halves of the same walnut. Both of them were designed to protect people from official violations of their rights. The main difference between them was that the Discipline Department was able to accept direct complaints of any kind made by people against officials while the Administrative Court could accept only formal lawsuits against officials. As a republican legal scholar, Feng Zhen, argued, the Administrative Court was in effect a court and the Discipline Department was like a prosecutor.[26] In addition, however, according to legal historian Nie Xin, the Discipline Department could function independently and supervise the Administrative Court in order to make sure it followed the law,[27] something prosecutors in Western judicial systems were unable to do.

While people were allowed to file lawsuits against alleged official violations of their rights, they could not just complain directly to the Administrative Court at will. On July 20, 1914, the legislature passed an Administrative Litigation Law, a Complaint Law, and the Regulations for Correcting and Impeaching Officials (*jiutan tiaoli*). This legislation strictly stipulated the conditions under which cases could be accepted by the Administrative Court. If people felt that their rights had been violated by a local official, they could complain to the upper levels of governments step by step. Only after their failed to get a hearing or satisfaction at the highest local [i.e., provincial] level and at other central organs could they file lawsuits at the Administrative Court. In this respect and to this degree the early republican state returned to the practice of the periods of the Sui through Tang of outlawing skipping complaints.

According to the Complaint Law, people were able to lodge complaints in two sorts of cases: first, their rights had been violated by allegedly illegal decisions (*bufa chufen*) of either the central or local government; second, their rights were infringed by allegedly inappropriate decisions (*budang*) of either the central or local government. Under either circumstance, people were asked to follow regular steps and should not skip required levels. In cases of allegedly illegal government decisions, people could file lawsuits at the Administrative Court only after they had exhausted the required process of complaining to the highest central or local government. But in the case of allegedly inappropriate central/local government decisions, the decision of the highest central/local official government would be final and people were not allowed to complain to the Administrative Court. The Complaint Law also permitted collective complaints but it also tried to confine them. The law stated that if many people wished to complain together, they should elect three representatives to carry the complaint forward to the authority.

Like the Complaint Law, the Administrative Litigation Law stipulated that, if people wanted to file lawsuits at the Administrative Court, they should do so within sixty days of the promulgation of the allegedly illegal government decision. In case of an unexpected problem or change, they could ask the Administrative Court for an extension of the deadline. Once again, the decision of the Administrative Court would be final and no further complaint (e.g., to the head of state) was to be allowed.[28]

The operation of the Administrative Court and the Discipline Department

In theory, the early republic followed the Western practice of separation of power. Unlike in the Qing and earlier times, all civil and criminal legal cases were to be handled by the judiciary not the regular administration. In fact, because of a chronic lack of funds, most counties in China were unable to establish independent courts during the republican period. Complaints thus had to be made to local officials just as they had been in the period before 1911.[29] Complainants who could not get satisfaction at the lower levels of the administration could take their cases to higher levels and eventually to the Administrative Court. Dissatisfied commoners could also complain about officials directly to the Discipline Department in the capital. The Department could decide whether a case should be rejected or passed to the Administrative Court for adjudication.

In one case, some businessmen in 1915 lodged a collective complaint to the Administrative Court charging the prefect of Huaiyang, Henan, with infringing people's rights. According to the businessmen, the prefect not only levied high taxes and took enormous bribes but also raped women and collected profits through gambling. "Because of those unbearable crimes," the businessmen decided to complain to the Administrative Court. As the Administrative Court was not set up to accept direct complaints, however, it refused to consider the complaint and told the businessmen that, if what they said was true, they should take the case to the Discipline Department.[30]

The Discipline Department

We do know that the Discipline Department rejected some cases on the basis of logical reasoning, but conducted in-depth investigations of others before deciding whether to reject or accept them. For example, in May 1916, farmer Chen Hongru from Qinyang county, Henan, accused the local magistrate of violating the law. According to the Discipline Department investigation, Chen's land had been occupied by Chen Huaishan and San Guiming. For five years, Chen lodged suits at the local court against these two men but in vain. The current county magistrate had studied the case for six months but had yet to make any progress in solving it. Thus, Chen blamed him for ignoring the long-standing complaint and for not making a serious investigation. The Discipline Department finally rejected this complaint on the grounds that it was a civil matter (*minshi*) that should be made to the prefectural level. Meanwhile, the complainant should inform the local court of what he was doing.[31]

In another case, the Discipline Department conducted an investigation before rejecting the complaint. A commoner, Ma Chaolun from Jincheng county, Shanxi, accused the local magistrate of extortion by levying excessive taxes and fines. The Discipline Department investigated the charge by collecting much evidence and conducting numerous interviews. It finally decided that most of Ma's charges were groundless. For example, Ma alleged that the magistrate had repeatedly raised taxes on his own authority since he had taken office, but the record showed that all the increased taxes had been approved by the financial department of the prefecture. Another charge of Ma was that the magistrate had extorted money from several local companies. But again the Discipline Department ruled that there had been no "extortion" because all the money levied by the magistrate had been turned over by the magistrate to the state. The report questioned Ma's accusations that the magistrate judged cases based on the amount of bribes he received and that his personal runners meddled in public affairs (*gongshi*). The report further provided much evidence that the magistrate was, contrary to the charges, a good and capable official who had several times been praised by his superiors. As a result, the report charged the complainant with filing a false complaint. As in the late Qing, however, the report said nothing about any need to punish the complainant.[32]

When the Discipline Department found that a complaint against an official for unlawful activities was true, it would report the case directly to the president of the republic in compliance with the Correcting and Impeaching Law. The president might then order the Administrative Court to examine the case. For example, in 1914, shortly after the establishment of the Administrative Court, President Yuan Shikai was informed by the Discipline Department about an allegedly corrupt prefect of Shuntian prefecture in Hebei. Yuan asked the Administrative Court to decide whether this case should be handled by a criminal court or by the Disciplinary Committee for Civil Officials (*wenguan chengjie weiyuanhui*), a committee similar to the Censorate the primary duty of which was to supervise all civil officials in the republic, or a criminal court. According to the Court's report, the prefect, named Wang Zhixin, had committed four crimes: openly selling government posts thus becoming infamous throughout the country; collecting heavy taxes and asking for excessive donations; obstructing an investigation into his alleged involvement in an opium case (including inciting his subordinates to destroy evidence); and embezzling public funds (and returning the money in an effort to avoid punishment). The court stated that all charges were true, but the case should be sent to the criminal courts for judgment because it involved charges of criminal wrongdoing.[33]

The Administrative Court

Unlike that of the Discipline Department, the primary mission of the Administrative Court was to deal with lawsuits of common citizens against officials. The court would usually accept direct accusations against the highest local and central officials and lawsuits lodged by complainants who had exhausted all legal means of complaint based on the *Complaint Law*. When the Administrative Court received a complaint, it would decide whether to accept it. If it accepted the case, the court would, as many cases showed, conduct careful investigations before making final judgments. In general, the court would report to the president about its final decision on a case and the president was supposed to sign an order instructing the indicted official to comply with the decision.

For example, in the summer of 1914, a Zhejiang businessman Shi Fengxiang filed a lawsuit with the Administrative Court against the Interior Ministry, charging it with making an illegal decision. According to the Court report, a Manchu named Zhi Sen had inherited a famous pharmaceutical shop only to have it confiscated by the Zhejiang Military Government during the wave of anti-Manchu sentiment that accompanied the revolution in 1911. The government then auctioned off the shop so as to be able to pay hundreds of thousands of soldiers and civilians who had been disbanded or retired. Shi Fengxiang, a businessman, won the bid for 200,100 yuan and was given an official license to run the shop. Zhi Sen was furious at what he deemed to be the illegal confiscation of his shop. He complained to the State Department (*guowuyuan*) and the Interior Ministry, requesting the return of his property. The Interior Ministry on March 6, 1914 ordered that the shop be returned to Zhi Sen and that all profits earned by the shop should be evenly divided between Zhi and Shi. Unsatisfied, Shi complained to the Administrative Court to nullify what he considered to be the illegal order of the Interior Ministry depriving him of half of his recently acquired property. After a detailed survey, the court found that neither the former Zhejiang Military Government's confiscation of the shop from Zhi Sen nor the Interior Ministry's recovery of half of the shop from Shi for Zhi Sen was lawful. According to the Treatment of Minorities such as Manchu, Mongol, Muslim, and Tibetan (*manmeng huizang daiyu tiaojian*), an agreement made in February 1912 between the new republic and the Qing court to protect ethnic minorities, Zhi Sen had the right to keep (or now to regain ownership of) his entire shop. In addition, after the military government had illegally taken Zhi's shop, it sold it publicly. Thus Shi's purchase of the shop was legal. The report blamed the Interior Ministry for failing to pressure the Zhejiang local government to return the money it got from Shi to him. In the end, the Court decided that the Zhejiang regional supervisor should return the shop to its original owner Zhi and the money used to purchase the shop to the original buyer Shi.

In this case, the Administrative Court made a rational and lawful judgment. The court cited appropriate legislation to repudiate the deal proposed by the Interior Ministry and it complied with the *Administrative Law* by enlisting the president in enforcing the decision. In the process it served the interests of both citizens even when it was at the expense of the state.[34] In this case, the new republicanism seems to have approximated.

In September 1916, a little more than two years after its establishment, the Discipline Department was terminated due largely to a lack of funds.[35] Its function of receiving direct complaints was transferred to the Administrative Court. The Court was now responsible for accepting or rejecting such complaints, or referring them to a civil or military court.

In October 1916, a former magistrate named Wang Kunnan of Jinxi county, Jiangxi, complained to the Administrative Court that he had been falsely incarcerated in 1913 by the Jiangxi Police Department for allegedly "communicating with rebels." The new head of the Jiangxi Provincial Political and Civilian Department appointed by Yuan Shikai, Qi Yang, had set up an interim military court to deal with Wang's case. At first the court, which was controlled by Qi, had sentenced Wang to two years imprisonment by issuing an "announcement." Later it had revised the judgment to a life sentence, which, Wang argued, was illegal. Asserting that there was no way to obtain justice when the "dictator Yuan Shikai was in power," Wang escaped from jail the following year. But Qi sent soldiers to Wang's home and confiscated his property, and tortured Wang's brother to death. Aware that false complainants had been punished in the Qing, Wang swore that all he said was true, and he declared: "If there is anything false, I am willing to suffer the death penalty." Wang, as natural resisters in the past who had unshaken faith in heavenly principles, implored the Administrative Court to punish Qi on the basis of "heavenly principles" and the state law.

Despite the seriousness of this complaint by an ex-official against a superior official, the Administrative Court decided not to accept it because it involved a criminal charge and not just an administrative one.[36] This case shows the limitation on direct complaints to the Administrative Court because the Court could avoid handling serious charges against unlawful government decisions (its responsibility) by characterizing them as criminal cases and referring them to the regular courts.

In the early republic, the Administrative Court seemed more likely to accept collective complaints against corrupt or abusive officials. In August 1919, thirty-nine people of Yongjia county, Zhejiang, sent the Administrative Court a letter accusing a local prefect of neglecting his duty and engaging in corruption. The letter listed charges such as violating provincial and central orders, protecting evil subordinates, and extorting money from common citizens. The complainants asked the head of the Administrative Court to pass the complaint letter to the president, hoping the president would conduct an investigation and dismiss the prefect. This collective complaint was not about any violation of the complainants' rights. The complainants only wanted to remove the prefect in the public interest. With this purpose in mind, they perceived the best place to complain was the Administrative Court which, they knew, was under the direct control of the president. The Administrative Court obviously accepted the complaint as five judges signed their names after they read it, but unfortunately the outcome is not available.

While the republic promised that the people were the masters of China, many complainants, like their dynastic counterparts and even President Yuan Shikai, continued to think in terms of heavenly principles, parental rulers, and *minben*/people as the root. The ex-official Wang Kunan, for instance, invoked heavenly principles to justify his complaint to the Administrative Court (skipped the provincial governor). In another case, Ma Shangong, a representative elected by people from Shaoxing, Zhejiang, complained to the Discipline Department against law-breaking governor Wang Jinfa and judge Xu Weisan. In his accusation, Ma claimed that Wang and Xu violated both law and heavenly [principles] (*lifa*). Manifesting an unwavering faith in the concepts of *minben*/people as the root and parental rulers/officials, Ma praised the officials at the Discipline Department for "loving people as their own sons." As most Chinese had for millennia, Ma regarded the republican leaders as heaven's representative (sons of heaven) and asked the "heavenly [ruler]" to dispatch high-ranking officials to Shaoxing to investigate the case.[37]

An assessment of the Administrative Court

Even during the republican period, some legal scholars argued that the Administrative Court was not effective. For example, the legal scholar Ruan Yicheng commented in the early 1930s: "Since 1914, the Administrative Court made judgments on no more than twenty cases. The cases that [it] had actively investigated were merely twenty-three. All the other [cases] were decided under the influence of the superior officials."[38] In the PRC period too, some legal scholars have also criticized the early republican Administrative Court. Guo Shu, a lecturer in law at Beijing Normal University, writes that the early republican Administrative Court was in general "a failure" because it accepted so few cases.[39]

However, numerous materials from both contemporary publications and archives suggest that even though the situation in the early republic was tumultuous, the record of the Administrative Court was not as bad as some scholars have argued. In fact, it had actually accepted and solved a good number of cases, questioned the authority of the prime minister in an effort to defend its independence, and pursued cases against top government officials.

From the beginning, the Administrative Court was supposed to report each month the number of cases it had accepted, decided, and sent to the president. For example, on March 11, 1916, the Administrative Court reported to the secretary of state (*guowuqing*) that in January of that year it had accepted a total number of thirty-seven new and old cases. By March, it had solved twenty-four of those cases and the rest (thirteen) were still in process.[40] In June 1916, the court reported to the president that it had accepted nineteen cases in May. It had decided eleven of them and was working on the other eight.[41] Data from 1917 and 1918 are missing, but on March 17, 1920, Xia Shoukang, the head of the court, reported to the president that a total of 275 cases had been accepted among which 237 had been decided in 1919.[42]

Although these statistics are very incomplete, they are sufficient to suggest that the Administrative Court, contrary to its critics, accepted a respectable number of cases and decided most of those they reviewed.

The independence of judiciary from other branches of government was stipulated in the 1912 *Provisional Constitution of the Republic of China* and reiterated in the 1914 *Constitution of the Republic of China*. As a judicial organ, the Administrative Court also enjoyed and practiced its independence at times. Since the Administrative Court was responsible only to the president of the republic, it had the authority to discipline all high-ranking officials including the prime minister. On February 18, 1917, the Administrative Court raised doubts about an order issued by the prime minister. The order said that the Administrative Court should accept only complaints against unlawful government punishments made to it in accordance with the Administrative Litigation Law. Cases made to and accepted by other government units pursuant to special orders from the president would be beyond the authority of the Administrative Court. The Administrative Court, however, argued in a report to the president that the prime minister's order implied that the president was not an administrative organ (*xingzheng zhuguan guanshu*). If so, whatever cases the president approved for consideration by other administrative bodies would be outside the purview of the Administrative Court because they would not be administrative decisions. Under the guise of this order, the court contended, all the decisions made by various government bodies would automatically risk becoming the decisions of the president. The Court worried that all government bodies would take advantage of this order to prevent people from complaining against illegal decisions because once a government body's request was endorsed by the president it would be hard for people to file lawsuits against them. If this happened, the Court noted that it would "extremely restrict (*jiduan xianzhi*) people's constitutional rights to complain."[43]

The Administrative Court not only tangled with the prime minister to defend its jurisdictional authority; it also entertained lawsuits against the prime minister. In 1924, a senior official working in the Bureau of the Legal System (*fazhijü*),[44] driven by grievance and inspired by republicanism, accused a former prime minister of firing him without giving any reason. According to the official, named Liu Jian, he had started working in the bureau in 1912 and had been promoted in 1918. Yet, on November 24, 1924, he was fired by Prime Minister Gao Lingwei on the basis of a report that Liu had left his post in Beijing for two years. Liu argued in his complaint that he had never missed a day since he came to work at the bureau. Liu cited the *Protective Law of Civil Officials* (*wenguan baohufa*) that forbade the dismissal of any civil official who was not convicted of a crime or punished according to the disciplinary law. Therefore, Liu complained that the prime minister had dismissed him illegally on the basis of a false report and concluded that "nothing could be a more serious violation of the law."

When the Administrative Court received Liu's complaint, it discussed whether to accept it. One of the four judges raised the question "Can the prime minister be a defendant?" The question appeared to be rhetorical with an implied answer of "no." Another judge stated that the Administrative Court was responsible directly to the president and all the heads of the ministries in the State Department were treated as state staff. Accordingly, the appointment and dismissal of all officials inside the State Department should follow the same rules. As a result, "being the head of the State Department, the prime minister does not have the authority to dismiss a subordinate [without following proper procedures]," and Gao had not followed those correct procedures. This view was finally shared by the other three judges and they reached a consensus to accept the complaint against the prime minister.[45]

By challenging the order of the prime minister and accepting a complaint against the prime minister, the Administrative Court acted quite independently of the executive branch and strongly reaffirmed people's natural resistance to wrongful state action. Although it could not—or at least did not—challenge the authority of the president, the prime minister and therefore all other government officials were considered fair game. Such had been rarely the case in previous periods of Chinese history and it was to become quite inconceivable in the later years of the republic and in the subsequent period of the People's Republic.[46]

That the Administrative Court functioned relatively independently and stuck to the existing laws in its handling of citizens' complaints against officials can be further illustrated by another case in which a famous writer Lu Xun (1881–1936, aka Zhou Shuren) filed a lawsuit against the Minister of Education.

In the summer of 1925, students[47] from Beijing Women's Normal University, a public institution, protested against Yang Yinyu, the conservative president of that school who allegedly ran it as a "dictator." The tinderbox was kindled when three students from Zhejiang were dismissed by President Yang after their return to school was delayed by a war between the militarists of Zhejiang and Jiangsu. The students became incensed and sent delegates to the Ministry of Education demanding Yang's dismissal. This request was rejected by Zhang Shizhao, the Minister of Education. One of the supporters of the students was Lu Xun, then an official in the Ministry of Education. Lu Xun published several articles against Yang Yinyu. This angered Zhang Shizhao who, on August 12, asked Duan Qirui, the president of the interim republican government, for permission to fire Lu Xun from his position in the Ministry of Education on the ground that Lu Xun at the same time was a member of the board of Beijing Women's Normal University. This request was approved by Duan. A week later, Lu Xun, as a firebrand of the New Cultural Movement in the 1910s, decided to lodge a lawsuit against Zhang's order in the Administrative Court, the natural right of the "masters" under republicanism.

On September 12, a month after Zhang's order, the Administrative Court decided to investigate the case. In his complaint, Lu Xun argued that he had become a committee member of the school one day after Zhang's order to dismiss him. Thus Zhang's accusation that Lu Xun had taken two posts at the same time was not true. Like Liu Jian in his complaint against the prime minister, Lu Xun cited the *Regulations of Disciplining Civil Officials* and the *Protective Law of Civil Officials*, charging Zhang with violating those laws and abusing his power. Instead of mentioning the two laws that Lu Xun cited, Zhang quoted another law, the *Order of Official Service* (*guanli fuwuling*), as saying that all government staff should obey the orders of their superiors. If a member of the staff violated an order, the head had the authority to warn or punish him or her.

On March 17, 1926, the court decided in favor of Lu Xun and against Zhang. It found that Zhang could not prove that Lu Xun had violated the ministry order by having a second position outside the ministry. Even if Zhang could substantiate it, the judgment said, the case was subject to the *Regulation of Disciplining Civil Officials* and should have been sent to the committee for disciplining civil officials for discussion. However, Zhang had not followed the lawful procedures but instead had simply sought the president's permission to dismiss Lu Xun. The court concluded that this action "is certainly not in compliance with the current laws and regulations." The court ordered Zhang to cancel his previous order firing Lu Xun and asked the prime minister to enforce the decision. On March 31, the prime minister issued an order to Zhang that the original ministry order dismissing Lu Xun should be rescinded. On the same day, the Ministry of Education invited Lu Xun to come back to the ministry to resume his job.[48]

In the case of Lu Xun vs. Zhang Shizhao, the Administrative Court acted independently and made its judgment solely on the basis of a meticulous reading and balancing of the contemporary laws and regulations. It did not make a decision favoring Zhang because of his superior position but rather decided against him despite that position. Nor did it decide in favor of Lu Xun because of his fame and popular support but because he had the law on his side. Most important, one current political leader, the prime minister, approved the court decision and ordered the Ministry of Education to comply with it.

In a recent preliminary study, Huang Yuansheng, a legal historian, has examined the practice of the early republican Administrative Court through an analysis of 186 cases from 1915 to 1928. Among them, 160, or about 86 percent were cases related to property disputes such as administrative fines, special taxes and fees, mining, forced confiscation and closure, intellectual property, etc.

In Table 3.1, although the number of cases accepted and decided by the Administrative Court is still far from certain,[49] the available statistics suggest that the percentage of complaints against government officials that were satisfied or partially satisfied by the court was about 46 percent, almost half of the total number of complaints. Based on the table, Huang says that it is hard to argue that the Administrative Court obviously leaned toward the government side. The data suggest that the president was also likely to respect the court decisions due to the high satisfaction rate. Huang concludes, "It is unfair to say that it [the Administrative Court] was totally ineffective."[50]

To be sure, Huang's data are insufficient to weigh the effectiveness of the Administrative Court in the early republic. But, besides Huang's data, when the court rejected Zhang Shizhao's dismissal of Lu Xun on the basis of existing laws and regulations, it demonstrated that it could act independently and not bend to executive power. When the court accepted a complaint against the prime minister and made a decision ordering the head of the Ministry of Education to withdraw his dismissal of a staff member, it might be regarded as almost unprecedented in Chinese judicial history.

Why was the early republican Administrative Court able to challenge powerful officials and make its own decisions based on the laws? I would suggest several reasons.

First, when members of the Revolutionary Alliance (*tongmenghui*, founded in 1905) joined together in 1905 to work to topple the Qing, they held a firm belief in the republican system as a superior form of government.[51] In that year, Sun Yat-sen claimed that one purpose of the revolution was people's rights (*minquan*).[52] Wu Tingfang who became the first Minister of Justice in the republic asserted that he had cherished the thought of people's rights from a young age.[53] After the 1911 revolution, some of the founders of the new government

Table 3.1 Administrative cases collected by Huang Yuansheng

Year	*Number of cases*	*Rejected complaints (number)*	*Rejected complaints (%)*	*Reversed official decisions (number)*	*Corrected official decisions (%)*	*Modified official decisions and punishments (number)*	*Modified official decisions and punishments (%)*
1915	18	11	61.1	3	16.7	4	22.2
1916	18	11	61.6	3	16.7	4	22.2
1917	11	8	72.7	2	18.1	1	9.2
1918	23	13	56.5	5	38.4	5	5.1
1919	15	9	60	2	13.3	4	26.7
1920	30	18	60	9	30	3	10
1921	18	9	50	4	22.2	5	27.8
1922	6	4	66.6	1	16.6	1	16.8
1923	16	4	25	7	43.7	5	31.3
1924	10	6	60	3	30	1	10
1925	7	2	28.6	3	42.9	2	28.5
1926	7	2	28.6	3	42.9	2	28.5
1927	4	2	50	1	25	1	25
1928	3	2	66.7	0	0	1	33.3
Totals	*186*	*101*	*54*	*46*	*24*	*39*	*22*

Source: Huang Yuansheng, "Minguo diyi ge xingzheng susong shenpan jiguan," 2002: 189–215.

endeavored to realize their republican dreams. Song Jiaoren, the founder and head of the Nationalist Party (*guomindang*, GMD, or KMT), centered his attention on congressional politics and tried hard to form a strong cabinet to govern the state. But Song died because his political plan challenged the power of President Yuan Shikai.[54] As a lawyer and minister, Wu Tingfang devoted his energy to safeguarding both people's rights and the defense of judicial independence, two related republican principles.

In one case, shortly after the establishment of the republic, a magistrate named Yao Rongze of Shanyang county, Jiangsu, was accused of having executed two revolutionaries. Chen Qimei, then the Shanghai military head (*hujun dudu*), asked President Sun to send Yao to a military court that would punish him more severely than a civil court would. Minister of Justice Wu Tingfang, however, insisted on the need to "show respect for the law" in judging all cases and that Yao should be judged according to the regular legal procedures.[55] Otherwise, Wu warned President Sun in a telegram, the republic would suffer the same fate as the Qing and would forfeit the good feelings that friendly foreign states were so far manifesting towards it. If that happened, the republic's hope to regain control over justice in the treaty ports would be impossible. As Wu put it, "this [argument] is not for Yao alone, but it is for the future of the republic." In another letter to Chen, Wu wrote that the reason he had allowed Yao to hire a lawyer was that foreigners had long labeled China as a state without law. When Chen tried again to meddle in the judicial process, Wu wrote him another letter demanding to know: "If [you] interfere in everything, will the judicial department not exist in name only?" Wu resisted Chen's effort to politicize the judiciary, stating that he [Wu] knew "only how to follow the law and nothing else."[56]

Wu's example of protecting people's rights and judicial independence was followed by his successors. Justice Minister Xu Shiying in late 1912 stressed that judicial independence was both the main element of a constitutional state and the principal spirit of a rule-of-law state (*fazhiguo*). He argued that only when China actually respected judicial independence would it be able to retrieve the sovereignty over its territory that continued to be infringed by the foreign powers.[57] In early 1913, after the liberal Prime Minister Song Jiaoren was assassinated, President Yuan Shikai (who was actually behind the killing) proposed to form a special court to investigate the case so that he could control the process. Xu Shiying, however, insisted that the case should be judged by a regular [criminal] court (*putong sifa jiguan*). It has been recently acknowledged recently that in the early republic, both the Ministry of Justice and the Supreme Court (*daliyuan*) defended their judicial independence.[58] With staunch defenders of judicial independence in charge of the Ministry of Justice, it was easier for judges working in the Administrative Court to assert their authority and challenge powerful officials.

Second, many of the judges in the early republic had earned their law degrees overseas and imbibed Western judicial principles such as making judgment according to the law. According to Mei Huaquan, a professor of Dongwu University in Suzhou, Jiangsu, in the early republic, among the forty-three current judges at the Supreme Court in the early republic, forty had studied law in Japan and two in Europe or America. Only one of them had studied Chinese law in China. In 1922, Mei observed: "the foreign influence on Chinese law is very strong."[59] In a more recent study, the legal scholar Zhang Sheng has found that, from 1912 to 1927, of seventy-nine judges in the Supreme Court, fifty-two had studied abroad.[60] The percentage of judges in the Administrative Court who had studied abroad was not as high as that in the Supreme Court. Still, according to Huang Yuansheng, eleven out of the twenty-four judges, or nearly 50 percent, of the Administrative Court judges whose records are known had experience of foreign study.[61] Having lived or at least visited abroad, those judges would be more likely to follow the legal principles and practices (e.g., judicial independence and due process of law) espoused in some foreign countries.[62]

Third, both the *Regulations for Enforcing the Adjudications of the Administrative Court* and the *Regulations for Correcting and Impeaching Officials* authorized the Administrative Court and the Discipline Department to ask the president of the republic to enforce their decisions.[63] This authority cleared the path for them to bring charges against all government officials including the prime minister. In the case of Lu Xun vs. Zhang Shizhao, when the Administrative Court had the support of the prime minister, it was able to have its judgment carried out by a ministry even when the president was unsympathetic.

Non-judicial complaint systems

In the early republic, complaining to the government was the natural right of every republican "master." Besides the Administrative Court and the short-lived Discipline Department, the legislature was authorized to accept complaints. Both Article 7 of the *Provisional Constitution of the Republic of China* and Article 6 of the *Constitution of the Republic of China* gave people the right to *complain* to the legislature,[64] albeit the word "*complain*" here is *qingyuan* in Chinese, which normally refers to political petitions or demands such as demanding more political freedom. *Qingyuan* is different from more common complaints such as *suyuan, gaosu* or *konggao* as appeared in the republican Complaint Law and archives that usually involve legal accusations against alleged criminals or corrupt officials who have violated people's rights.

In 1912, in one case, the Senate in Beijing received a complaint from the provincial parliament of Jilin. Senator Jin Dingzhu said that the Senate should pass the complaint letter to the government in accord with the regulations on the Administrative Court. The chairman of the Senate, however, argued that the complaint did not come directly from the people. In any case, he argued, "all complaints [to the Senate] should be turned in to the Complaining Committee of the Senate [before they could be processed]." This case demonstrates that some complaints were accepted by a special committee in the senate.[65]

The Interior Ministry and natural resistance

The Interior Ministry was one of the most important central venues where people could complain. The ministry founded a special department called "the Department of the People's Rule [*minzhiting*, literally, people govern hall]" to deal with people's complaints. Similar to the Administrative Court, the Interior Ministry received both individual and collective complaints against official corruption and unlawful government policies at the *provincial* level. But other complaints (i.e., complaints against local officials) would be turned down or transmitted to other government organs. Desperate complainants who were unable to gain access to civil and criminal courts might also complain to the Interior Ministry.

Like their ancestors who had skipped the legally authorized venues and complained at the palace gate or blocked the royal cart, many natural resisters in the early republic also disregarded the Complaint Law that required legal steps and sent letters of complaint directly to the president or asked the Interior Ministry to transmit their complaints to the president. To this extent, long-standing institutions for lodging complaints that had seemed to fade away in the early republic were reincarnated as time went along. They persisted in practice along with new institutions designed to achieve similar goals.

In December 1919, a group of Anhui local elite, including businessmen, and scholars, headed by Ma Jicai, made a direct complaint to the president and all ministers asking for the dismissal of the Anhui governor. Their letter was later referred to the Interior Ministry for review. According to the complaint, the governor had done nothing positive since taking office. He had a spoiled son whom was said to have regularly beaten people and threatened them "with a gun." Although the provincial parliament had impeached the governor, he had refused to resign. Unlike dynastic natural resisters who held beliefs only in *minben* and parental rulers, the rhetoric of the complaint reflected a mixture of republican and Confucian concept of *minben*/people as the root. Arguing first that people were the masters of the republic, the complainants later simply begged the state leaders to do justice by firing the governor. When the complaint was transferred to the Interior Ministry, the minister rejected it saying the dismissal and appointment of officials could not be decided by the people.[66] If that was the end of the case, it suggests both the possibility of complaining directly to the head of state and the limited effectiveness of such complaints. The case also reveals that natural resisters who felt they had been wronged had no compunctions about lodging their complaints with the highest authorities in the republic just as their predecessors had done under earlier polities, very possibly with equally limited results.

In another case of what can only be described as a skipping complaint, a widow named Wang Lengshi from Yichang, Hubei, complained in 1925 to the Interior Ministry against an allegedly corrupt local judge and a lawbreaking officer. According to her complaint, a local security officer (*baodong*) named Zhang Lanting had cheated her seventy-year-old aunt and tried to inherit part of her (Wang's aunt) deceased husband's land. Widow Wang had first filed a criminal charge against Zhang at a local court, but the local judge rejected her complaint because he deemed the case a civil and not a criminal one. Unsatisfied, widow Wang complained to the Hubei High Court three times. Widow Wang was unsuccessful in getting redress of her grievances and impoverished by having to pay legal fees. Losing faith in the established judicial system, she complained directly to the Interior Ministry, a violation of the required legal procedure addressed by the Complaint Law. Not surprisingly, the ministry refused to consider the case and ruled that she should retrace her steps and complain at the prefectural level. Widow Wang's efforts, like those of her pre-republican predecessors, were ultimately all in vain. Her only consolation was that she was not prosecuted for lodging the skipping complaints.[67]

If people's complaints to the Interior Ministry involved another ministry, the Interior Ministry would typically accept them and transfer them to the relevant ministry. In 1921, Yi Yanyun, a local financial officer from Altai, a border region between China and Russia in Xinjiang, accused his superior named Zhang Qingtong of absconding with a large amount of borrowed money. According to the officer, when Zhang Qingtong was in the capital, he asked Yi to lend him some money to pay for salaries of soldiers and civil staff in Xinjiang. He promised that he would reimburse Yi with the money as soon as he came back from Beijing. With that promise, Yi borrowed the needed money from local businessmen in Altai and gave it to Zhang. When Zhang came back from Beijing, he he took the money Yi had borrowed from the businessmen for himself and absconded with the money. Yi was now accosted by his creditors. After becoming insolvent and losing his family, Yi went to the Interior Ministry to complain. The Interior Ministry accepted the case and, because it was related to finance, transferred it to the Financial Ministry. It hoped that the Financial Ministry would ask the local court in Shanghai, Zhang's home, to determine the extent of Zhang's family property. The Interior Ministry also copied the decision to the governor of Xinjiang.[68] Although the outcome of the case was not available, we can see that common citizens could avail themselves of venues other than the Administrative Court to get redress of their grievances.

In sum, the above cases lucidly show that aggrieved people could take various measures, legal and illegal, to complain about what they considered to be official violations of their rights. Some natural resisters like Widow Wang saw the Interior Ministry and the state leaders as the last recourse when they were unable to get justice through the legal steps and could not afford to file further lawsuits. The Interior Ministry, however, seemed to be more interested in coping with cases involving unlawful government policies or minor official misconducts. As we shall see, it would be less likely to accept people's complaints about corrupt judges.

Collective complaints and media

The freedom of press and the right to demonstrate were both protected by the early republican constitutions.[69] Criticisms of the government were largely permitted if only because successive regimes were too ephemeral and weak to suppress them.[70] More often than in the late Qing, people in the early republic protested in the streets or sent letters complaining about the government to major newspapers. During the course of 1919, *Shenbao* reported some sixty-nine public political complaints including writing letters and telegrams, sending delegates to the capital, and delivering speeches.[71]

People with particular individual or collective complaints often vented their anger at state malfeasance in the public media. In 1919, for example, a group of farmers in Shanghai wrote a letter to *Shenbao* complaining about an order of the local government. They claimed that in 1742 the Qing Ministry of Public Works (*gongbu*) had allowed farmers to plant on the newly formed and unworked coastline without having to pay any tax. For almost 200 years, the policy had not changed. But recently the local government had tried to sell the farmland without informing the farmers who had come to consider it their private land. The farmers did not complain to the upper-level government that would only back up the local government, but they complained to *Shenbao* so that the public could know their situation, put pressure on the officials, and ward off retribution from the local officials.[72] According to Susan Glosser's study, distraught young people also wrote letters to newspapers and popular magazines like *Family Research* (*jiating yanjiu*) complaining about arranged marriages and other family issues.[73]

In certain fields there was no specific target but a general system of oppression. In such cases, some people complained to the newspapers for help. For example, in 1928, an apprentice at a Shanghai pawnshop wrote to the publication *Life Weekly* (*shenghuo zhoukan*) about his predicament and asked for help. In the words of the young man, the business of pawnbroking was inherently hierarchical and oppressive. Apprentices, for example, lived in a prison-like situation and any minor mistake would lead to harsh punishment by the managers and threats of dismissal. To preserve their jobs, the apprentices had to bear much maltreatment. "We are suffering a life sentence in a prison," complained the young man, "we are deeply aggrieved. We do not know when we will be liberated so that we can get rid of such a solitary life (*yushi gejue*)." He warned the leaders of the pawn-broking business to reform their enterprises quickly before all the pent-up workers' grievances burst out.[74]

During the almost constant civil wars of this period, citizens often complained through newspapers to the public on behalf of the country. On January 16, 1919, for example, *Shenbao* published a letter of a number of Anhui people (*minzhong*) asking both northern and southern congressmen to hold peace talks and stop the civil war.[75]

The freedom allotted to the press in principle and often in practice, allowed newspapers and magazines to develop rapidly in the early republic, providing aggrieved people with another venue to complain. With its wide coverage and free access, many people with different aims liked to complain to the public media. Although some of them like the coastal farmers in Shanghai could by law have filed a complaint to an upper-level government, they chose instead to complain to a famous newspaper. The young pawnbroker apprentice, seeing no specific government office to complain to, turned to the newspaper. By working through the media, complainants hoped to make their grievances known to the public, appeal to the public conscience, and to encourage public pressure on the local government or leaders in relevant fields.

An assessment of the non-judicial complaint system

Without question, the non-judicial complaint system in the early republic witnessed a major shift from most previous periods. Under the influence of republican principles such as "people are state masters" and "heavenly given freedom," not only were prior natural resistances such as skipping and direct complainants no longer punished, but certain laws and regulations openly recognized people's right to complain including by skipping certain levels of the hierarchy and going directly to the top. Despite those promising developments, both judicial and non-judicial complaint systems in this period were under attack by contemporary political leaders and scholars for various reasons.

In July 1913, Yuan Shikai declared martial law and used force to attack defiant provincial governors in an effort to strengthen central authority.[76] Within a year, his regime executed thousands of people, including members of parliament for sedition without following the law.[77]

On December 31, 1913, Minister of Justice Liang Qichao complained that, since the 1911 revolution, the number of lawsuits had sharply increased, yet few provinces reported cases to the Ministry of Justice for review.

> The process of lawsuits has actually been terminated. I do not know how many innocent people are falsely charged [by the court], how many cases are wrongly decided but fail to be corrected. How many people in our society have grievances but with no place to complain? This is the reason why judicial corruption has been criticized by the people.[78]

In 1919, a newspaper columnist stated that there had been no law in China since the formation of the republic. That was an extreme claim, but he had good reason to accuse many powerful men in China of committing countless acts in violation of the laws.[79]

Some of these arguments were made during the May Fourth Movement when many Chinese, disgusted by domestic oppression and foreign exploitation, held their own inherited civilization responsible for many contemporary problems. They do not appear to have taken much account of vital traditions such as the complex of ideas around natural resistance and of contemporary achievements such as the brelatively independent and fair judgment of the Administrative Court. Yet, these sharp criticisms reflected certain impressions of many contemporary complainants and observers that we must take into consideration in evaluating the complaint systems of this period.

In 1914, Ma Shanggong from Zhejiang, charged a former judge and current head of the Zhejiang Opium Suppression Bureau (*zhejiang jinyan zongju*) with mass nepotism and corruption. Attracted by the ideals of republicanism, Ma complained that official power was still unchecked in the republican period. "What is the difference between the republican and the dynastic period?" Ma asked. He told the Discipline Department that his life was in danger after making his complaint. As in the case of Ma Jicai in Anhui, the central government remained the last hope of many complainants, but it did not in fact give many people much help, partly because of its weakness in the face of powerful local militarists who routinely ignored central orders. Without an effective central check, local officials in Anhui and Zhejiang had good reason to think they could violate people's rights with impunity.[80]

Like the commoner complainant Ma Shanggong, some scholars in this period believed that the political corruption in the early republic was very serious and rendered the regime no better than that in the Qing. In 1917, for instance, Chen Duxiu, the radical editor of the *New Youth* magazine (*xinqingnian*) and later a founder of the CCP, stated that although Yuan Shikai had died, Yuan's authoritarian thought (*zhuanzhi sixiang*) was still alive as even those who had opposed Yuan had not actually opposed the monarchical system.[81] In 1923, Zhang Dongsun, a philosopher and later a leader of the Chinese Democratic League, also argued that China continued to be ill despite the dozens of cures that had been tried since the late Qing.[82]

Why did so many complainants, officials, and scholars bombard the political and complaint systems in the early republic? Why were many complainants still unable to redress their grievances in the so-called republic? I would argue that there are several particular circumstances in this period that may have caused those bad impressions and experiences.

First, as I have pointed before, the political situation in most of the early republican period was chaotic and in many instances the law was difficult to implement, especially when the violator was a powerful military or civil official. At the beginning of the republic, there was, in warlord Wu Peifu's words, a short period of prosperity under the rule of Yuan Shikai.[83] But it was Yuan Shikai whose plans to strengthen central power and his ambition to restore imperial authority that most likely precipitated many of the following social and political disorders and scuttled China's best chance so far to practice democracy.[84] In 1913 Yuan was behind the assassination of the liberal Prime Minister Song Jiaoren. Next year, he complained that the administrative power was too small and the political knowledge of Chinese people was in its infancy.[85] In late 1915, with the support of American legal scholars such as Wellington B. Willoughby and Frank J. Goodnow who argued that what China needed in the stage of democratic creation was an authoritarian power,[86] Yuan restored the emperorship and to rule as the Hongxian (literally, broad constitutional) emperor.[87] Yuan's action angered many republican founders. Although they had lost their war against Yuan in 1914, they regrouped in 1916 and successfully forced Yuan to step down before he suddenly died.

In the post-Yuan era, China was even more divided than before and political struggles persisted inside the Beijing government and between the southern and northern militarists.[88] In the Beijing government alone, from 1912 to 1928, thirty-two cabinets were formed and fifty-nine full or temporary prime ministers were appointed.[89] The central power was even less respected than before. The historian Zhang Yufa observes that after Zhang Xun's 1917 effort to restore the Qing was crushed, provincial governors took advantage of a weak central government and grasped all civil, political, military, and financial powers.[90] Accordingly, in a period full of civil wars and internal disorders, local governments enjoyed more freedom than before.

In such a turbulent period, people sometimes did not know whom they could trust and count on. According to one political observer writing in 1922, the general rule of the early republican polity was that the seeming "protectors" of people's rights soon turned out to be "dishonest powers" that people tried to get rid of.[91]

With a loose central power unable to enforce the laws, many officials at both central and local levels and especially the militarists among them, ignored the laws and regulations.[92] For example, as shown in the case of Ma Jicai vs. the Anhui governor, the governor's son beat people at will and frequently threatened to kill people. The governor had spoiled his son and did nothing to punish him. When Ma complained to the Interior Ministry, probably the best place to complain, the Interior Ministry rejected the complaint for the very un-republican reason that common people had no say in the dismissal and appointment of officials.

In the early 1920s, the warlord Wu Peifu argued that there was no law in most of the republic because of the south and north division and the wars between them.[93] Wu's argument may find support from some of today's Western scholars. According to Thomas B. Stephens, for example, the military commanders and court in Shanghai promptly executed criminals "as they pleased irrespective of any legal restraints."[94] The historian Xiaoqun Xu argues that the republican government routinely executed people they labeled "bandits" without due process.[95]

Because of a weak central government and a turbulent political situation, the Administrative Court and the Interior Ministry in Beijing would have had no means of dealing with unlawful officials in the militarist-controlled areas even if they had attempted to. It is thus certain that in the chaotic early republic, many complainants did not have their grievances heard or satisfied when their rights were violated by militarists or local officials.

Second, the judicial reform per se in the early republic was criticized by many contemporary legal scholars for being filled with flaws, which resulted in many unsolved grievances. In 1922 Zhang Yipeng, law professor at Dongwu University in Suzhou, Jiangsu, criticized the legal reform initiated in the late Qing as having "yet to attain one tenth of the perfect level (*wanshan*)."[96] Likewise, Mei Huaquan, a colleague of Zhang's, argued that the judicial system in the republican period was unsatisfactory. "Without a separation between the judiciary and the administration, the reform of the legal system is simply an empty word," Mei wrote. "Only after the arrival of judicial independence and the selection of upright judges will [the reform] be effective."[97] Although these professional opinions may not be wholly accurate representations of the actual judicial system in China and in Western countries, they offer a general impression of the Chinese legal system and of continuing abuses of power by the republican administration.

Third, although the idea of judicial independence was written into the republican constitutions, at the local level most magistrates still had to deal with legal cases because of a shortage of courts and judges. As in the past, many complainants in the early republic who had grievances against the local government would find it difficult to gain satisfaction at the county level.

Finally, even the Administrative Court itself had its own limitations that left many grievances unaddressed. Because there was only one Administrative Court and it was located in the capital, people who wanted to file lawsuits had to go to Beijing, which was not only time-consuming but costly. The relatively high fee to lodge complains at the Administrative Court was another high hurdle for many poor complainants. When Lu Xun accused Zhang Shizhao at the Administrative Court, he had to pay a fee of 30 yuan.[98] But in 1920, average workers in Shanghai earned only 0.30 yuan a day, nine yuan a month.[99] Therefore, an average worker would have to spend three to four months wages to pay the fees to lodge a complaint at the Administrative Court. Worse, before 1925, the Administrative Court required only the loser to pay the fee. But on January 29, 1925, the Court stipulated that the plaintiff should always pay the fee no matter whether he or she won or lost the complaint.[100] No matter how serious their grievances and how confident they were in winning their cases, poor people would have been deterred by the high fees from filing a lawsuit with the Administrative Court.

Conclusion

Inheriting the basic ideas of natural resistance and borrowing the ideals of republicanism from the West, the early republic continued the late Qing reforms of the complaint systems and realized most of them. It established an Administrative Court and briefly a Discipline Department and passed relevant laws that made those institutions separate from the rest of the judicial system. Some top officials believed firmly in the republican ideal of judicial independence from the other branches of the government. This enabled the Administrative Court to function quite independently and to accept and rule positively on people's complaints against even the highest officials. In these respects, the early republic may be viewed as a kind of golden age in the history of Chinese complaint systems. Complainants with the required resources and with strong cases could mount what were effectively legal complaints that were heard by the Administrative Court. But, despite the impact of republicanism, many republican leaders and complainants continued to firmly believe in traditional concepts such as heavenly principles, mandate of heaven, and *minben*/people as the root. Some complainants still practiced natural resistance by lodging illegal skipping complaints.

In theory, at least, republicanism reinforced the Chinese people's natural resistance to misrule. The weakness of the central government in Beijing and the strength of local militarists plus the distance and expense involved in complaining in person in the capital nonetheless constituted major barriers to the redress of commoners' grievances against officials during this period. As a result, the early republic may have been a golden age in theory for a small minority more than in practice for the vast majority of the Chinese people.

4 A mixed picture

The later republic (1928–1949)

In 1924, with the support from the Soviet Union and cooperating with the newborn Communist Party, Sun Yat-sen reorganized the Guomindang (GMD or KMT) and formed a powerful army.[1] Within four years, Sun's followers conducted a successful Northern Expedition that at least nominally unified most of China for the first time in a decade. During its two-decade rule, while continuing to be plagued by internal wars and external invasions, the GMD managed to establish a kind of central administration. It was based on Sun Yat-sen's theories of the Three Stages of Government (*sanzheng*), the Three People's Principles (*sanmin zhuyi*), and the Five-Power Constitution (*wuquan xianfa*).[2] Although the later republic was in some ways more authoritarian than the early republic, it is not true that it had no complaint system worthy of the name.[3] In fact, the later republic with its capital at Nanjing (and in Chongqing during wartime) largely inherited the main complaint systems of the early republic. Indeed, some complainants in this period continued to see a certain improvement of their rights. The GMD made several revisions in its complaint systems that, at least in theory, provided complainants with more opportunities and less monetary cost to air their grievances. Data in archives of the central government (Nanjing), Shanghai, and Hubei province palpably indicate that many aggrieved people remained strong believers in embedded concepts such as "heavenly principles," parental rulers/officials, *minben*/people as the root, and the relatively new republicanism. Many complainants in this period continued to have faith in the leader and rested their last hope for justice on generalissimo Chiang Kai-shek, whom they regarded as "heaven's representative" and who himself expressed belief in the concept of *minben.* This inspired some to mount skipping complaints even though they continued to be illegal. The general picture of the complaint system in the later republic is nonetheless bleak. A combination of endless wars, the particization of the judiciary, the corruption of officials, and the internal problems of the complaint system often resulted in the frustration of efforts to get justice. In sum, the later republic presents a mixed picture of an improved formal structure and an impaired actual process in handling complaints against government abuses.

The judicial complaint systems

Formation

As in the early republic, the Administrative Court and the regular administration constituted the primary judicial complaint systems of the later republic. Both legal experts and high-ranking officials stressed that the Administrative Court was to protect people from governmental violations of their rights. For example, Zhang Yuanruo, a law professor at the Central University, observed in 1933 that effective methods should be adopted in cases where officials infringed people's rights.[4] Similarly, in an explanation of a newly drafted constitution, a committee of the Legislative Yuan stated in 1940 that people should be allowed to complain to the government when their rights were infringed by illegal or inappropriate official decisions. If people's private rights were violated, they should be allowed to seek protection and remedy from a court.[5] Zhang Zhiben, the head of the Department of the Judicial Administration (*sifa xingzhengbu*), gave a clear justification for providing such administrative remedy,

> If a government official contravenes the law while implementing the law, what [punishment] should be administered? To settle this problem, there exists a sort of administrative remedy. Both complaints [to administrations] and administrative litigation offer the most important administrative reliefs.[6]

Shortly before it had nominally unified most of China in 1928 the GMD passed the Organizing Law of the National Government in which it declared the establishment of the Republic of China was based on Sun Yat-sen's theories. Sun had envisioned political development in three stages: military rule (*junzheng*) to unify China; political tutelage (*xunzheng*) to train the Chinese people in self-government; and constitutional government (*xianzheng*) through which the people would govern themselves.[7] The newly established Nanjing government now claimed to be entering the period of political tutelage in which "power must stem from the 'foreknowers' (*xianzhi xianjuezhe*)."[8] It proceeded to establish five Yuans (ministries) designed to train the Chinese people in self-government so that they would be able to establish a constitutional regime. Article 33 of the new law provided that the Judicial Yuan would be the supreme judiciary administration, managing legal adjudication as well as judicial administration, official discipline, and administrative adjudication (*xingzheng shenpan*).[9] In this era, the Administrative Court was no longer responsible to the president as it had been in the early republic but now reported to the Judicial Yuan instead. This change tended to reduce the authority of the court.

In the article providing for "The Five Yuans in the Political-Tutelage Period," Weng Jingtang, a renowned judge and the head of Shanghai branch of the Supreme Court, argued in 1938 that Administrative Adjudication was akin to the Administrative Court in the early republic. Because the number of administrative cases coming before the Administrative Court was limited, Weng pointed out that there was no need to appoint additional members for that body. Instead, administrative cases might be decided by judges in both civil and criminal courts.[10]

Most likely due to the subsequent internal power struggles among different GMD factions such as Jiang [Chiang Kai-shek], Gui [Li Zongren], Feng [Feng Yuxiang], and Yan [Yan Xishan], the Administrative Court proposed by the two laws was not immediately established. It was not until late 1931, when the perceived threats from the Japanese invasion of the northeast and the Communist alternative republic in the southeast helped to unify the GMD leadership, that an Administrative Court was finally established as part of the Judicial Yuan. In an updated Organizing Law of the National Government, Article 36 stated that the Judicial Yuan was composed of a Supreme Court, an Administrative Court, and a newly established Committee for Disciplining Civil Servants.[11]

During this period, the GMD promulgated several crucial laws regarding complaints and administrative litigation. On March 24, 1930, the Legislative Yuan passed a Complaint Law, which generally preserved the principles of the 1914 complaint law but also added some more detailed regulations. For example, the 1914 complaint law had simply stated that victims of allegedly illegal and inappropriate punishment could complain to the next higher level of the government above the one that had imposed the punishment. If dissatisfied with the decision, complainants could file further complaints to even higher levels of the government. The new law went further to classify five different types of complaint corresponding to different situations. For example, if a party dissatisfied with a decision of a county or municipal government should first complain to the appropriate provincial department, then to the provincial governor. People who refused to accept the decision of a provincial department, could then complain to the provincial government and then the responsible department in the central government and the responsible ministry. Those who refused to accept the decision of a department in a city directly controlled by the Administrative Yuan could first complain to the municipal government and then to the responsible department in the central government. Finally, if complainants refused to accept a decision of a municipal government directly controlled by the Administrative Yuan, they could first complain to the responsible central department and then to the relevant central ministry.[12]

A revision of the complaint law in 1937 added two more situations in which people could complaint. First, if a complainant refused to accept the decision of a department in the central government, he or she could first complain to the original department that might have violated his/her rights and, if unsatisfied, then to the relevant central ministry. Second, if a complainant refused to accept the decision of a ministry in the central government or a department that was directly under the control of the National Government, he or she should complain to the original ministry or department that had allegedly violated his/her rights.[13]

The biggest change in the system inherited from the early republic came in a newly drafted Administrative Litigation Law of 1932. This law continued the old law's provisions that a party must lodge two complaints [to responsible governments] before complaining to the Administrative Court and that the decision of the Court was final, permitting no further complaint. The new law went on to make three major improvements.

First of all, the 1914 law had not accepted requests for compensation, but the 1932 law allowed complainants to seek reparations from government officials who had allegedly violated their rights. Second, while the 1914 law permitted the Administrative Court to make judgments regarding the requests of the plaintiff and the defendant whenever it wished to do so, it did not give the court clear authority to make judgments when the government refused to send an agent or file a defense (*dabianshu*). The new law mended that loophole by stating that if a government defendant refused to send an agent or file a bill of defense, the Administrative Court could pressure it with a more formal request. If the government defendant again refused to respond, the court could conduct its own investigation and make its own judgment. Third, the old law provided that the Administrative Court would ask the president to implement court decisions. Under the new law, the Administrative Court would ask the Judicial Yuan to report to the National Government for the implementation of court decisions.[14] In theory, because the National Government was supposedly a collective organ serving the people, no one, including the president, could be exempted from the Administrative Court investigation if he violated people's rights. The new law thus attempted to enhance the authority of the Administrative Court.

In addition, on May 6, 1933 the National Government took an important step to enhance people's right to complain by relieving complainants of the obligation to pay certain fees associated with their cases. This was a far cry from the early republic when many complainants refrained from complaining because of mounting fees, especially after 1925 when they had to pay the fees even when they had won their cases.[15]

The operation of the Administrative Court

Unlike its predecessor in the early republic, the Administrative Court of the later republic dealt mainly with relatively minor alleged official violations of people's rights. The court did not accept people's direct complaints against official corruption or cases involving criminal charges. In this respect, the Administrative Court seems to have played a less important role than its counterpart in the early republic.

Another difference between the Administrative Courts in the early and later republics lay in the process of accepting cases. In the early republic, complainants whose rights had allegedly been infringed by the highest local or central government bodies could complain directly to the Administrative Court without having to file complaints at lower level organs first. The law gave the Administrative Court the power to conduct investigations of such cases. In the later republic, however, the 1932 law stipulated that all complainants had to make two complaints [to responsible governments] before complaining to the Administrative

Court.[16] Thus, the Administrative Court was limited to making judgments only after such second complaints (*zaisuyuan*).

Before rendering its decisions, the Administrative Court would first listen to the main bills of depositions of both defendant and plaintiff. It would then make its own judgment to fully support, partially endorse, or completely reject the claim of the complainant/plaintiff by carefully citing certain laws, regulations, or legal principles.

In one case, for example, Zhu Haiting, a landlord living in Bishan county, Sichuan province, lodged a lawsuit in 1939 to the Administrative Court against the Financial Ministry (*caizhengbu*). The official report of the Administrative Court shows that in 1933 Zhu Haiting had allowed Zhu Zelin to rent his land. In their contract, both parties agreed that Zhu Zelin would first pay the annual crop tax (32.6 yuan) and other required fees (totaling five yuan). But Zhu Haiting would later reimburse Zhu Zelin for the payment. Zhu Zelin, however, did not cultivate the land himself. Instead, he hired He Zefu to do the work and pay the tax and fees. In 1936, having failed to get reimbursed by Zhu Haiting for his payment of the tax and fees, Zhu Zelin complained to the Bishan county government. The magistrate there, like hundreds of other magistrates in the later republic, also served as a judge.[17] That government, however, ordered Zhu Haiting to pay the 32.6 yuan and He Zefu to pay half of the five-yuan fees. Both Zhu Haiting and He Zefu refused to accept the decision and complained to the Sichuan Provincial Government to reverse it. The provincial government modified the Bishan county decision and decided that it was Zhu Zelin who should pay all 37.6 yuan of the tax. Angered, Zhu Zelin submitted another complaint, this time to the Financial Ministry. That ministry favored Zhu Zelin by rejecting the decision of the Sichuan Provincial Government. Zhu Haiting refused to accept this decision and filed a lawsuit with the Administrative Court against the Financial Ministry.

Zhu Haiting argued in court that, according to an interim regulation passed in 1936 by the Sichuan provincial government, any tenant who did not cultivate his own rented land but instead leased it to another person would be considered as a big tenant (*dadian*). If the tenant took more than half of the income from his rented land, he was supposed to pay for all related taxes and fees. If and when he decided to discontinue the lease with his landlord, he could not ask the landlord for any compensation for those tax payments. Since this regulation had long been implemented during hard times in Sichuan, Zhu Haiting claimed that Zhu Zelin, the big tenant in this case, should pay all the taxes and fees.

The Financial Ministry, on the other hand, contended that since this case was a civil one, it should be judged by a common court (*putong fating*) and not the Administrative Court. In the contract signed by Zhu Haiting and Zhu Zelin, Zhu Haiting had promised that he would pay the annual taxes and fees. This meant both parties had no dispute on this issue. The government was only supposed to collect taxes from taxpayers and not supposed to have power to interfere with people's contracts. The Sichuan interim regulation should not be regarded as a law because the Sichuan provincial government failed to obtain endorsement of it from the ministry.

Having heard both parties' bills of defense, the Administrative Court, made its own adjudication. Apparently accepting the rationale of the Financial Ministry, the court report stated that people's contracts belonged to private law (*sifa*) and disputes over them should be decided by a common court in compliance with civil procedures; no administrative organ had any jurisdiction in such matters. In this case, Zhu Haiting and Zhu Zelin had made clear in their contract that Zhu Haiting would pay the annual taxes and fees. When the Bishan county government made its decision against Zhu Haiting in accordance with the civil law and procedure, Zhu Haiting should have complained to the upper court. Instead, considering the county judgment as an administrative decision, Zhu Haiting had complained to the Sichuan provincial government, which had reversed the county decision. The Administrative Court argued that as the Sichuan interim regulation was not a law, the decision based on it was incorrect. In the end, the court said that the Financial Ministry's decision that the landlord Zhu Haiting should pay the taxes was correct. In this case, the court, in supporting the principle of private law, backed the Financial Ministry and rejected the complaint of the plaintiff (Zhu Haiting).[18]

In another case, the Administrative Court, acting in compliance with the law, sanctioned the stance of some plaintiffs against government defendants.

In 1946, a group of fish-teeth (*yuya*; aquarium) managers took the Fuzhou Tax Bureau to the Administrative Court. According to the court report, in 1938, the inspecting unit (*chajishi*) of the Fujian Financial Department suspected that many fish-teeth firms were evading taxation. The unit and the Fuzhou Tax Bureau sent inspectors to check on those firms. They found that the businesses had indeed failed to pay their taxes and had neglected to show the prices of their products to the customers. According to the Fujian butcher-tax (*tuzaishui*) regulation, the Fuzhou Tax Bureau fined some firms five times the amount of tax that they had evaded. In addition, the bureau calculated the value of goods for which some firms such as *Gongmao* (literally, public trade) and *Hengchang* (literally, everlasting prosperity) had failed to list prices to the customers. The bureau punished the firms by confiscating goods of comparable estimated value and turned the resulting windfall over to the state as a defense tax (*guofangjuan*). Refusing to accept this decision, the managers complained to the Fujian Financial Department and the Fujian provincial government. When both government organs rejected the complaints, the plaintiffs filed a lawsuit with the Administrative Court in accordance with the Complaint Law.

In the court, the fish-teeth managers argued that the Fuzhou Tax Bureau's collection of fines merely on the basis of the inspecting unit's estimation and not of the actual facts was unreasonable and unlawful. Even in the course of the managers' second complaint to the Fujian Financial Department, the department had acknowledged that it had been inappropriate for the Fuzhou tax bureau to fine the businessmen five times what they had failed to pay in taxes according to the Fujian butcher-tax regulation. Additionally, if there was any fraud in the sale of fish-teeth, those managers stated, it would have been the fish-teeth manufacturers who directly stole customers' money, not the managers who were mere intermediaries. This had been testified to by one customer, Tang Ruiqing. But the Fujian Financial Department disregarded Tang's testimony and insisted on contributing the proceeds of the fines to the state's defense fund. The plaintiffs' charge was also rejected by the Fuzhou Tax Bureau. The bureau argued that it had ascertained that those firms had evaded taxation. The fine complied with the provisions of the Fujian butcher tax. The collection of the money from the firms and its allocation to the state defense donation had been approved by the provincial government.

The Administrative Court made a final decision based on two flaws in the government defendant's bill of defense. First, although the Fujian Financial Department had found that it was not right for the Fuzhou Tax Bureau to fine fish-teeth firms on the basis of the Fujian butcher tax, it had not revoked the decision but instead had rejected the plaintiffs' complaint. In this case, no matter whether the firms had committed fraud or not, the court decided the Fuzhou Tax Bureau had no legal foundation to earmark the amount of money derived from taxes on the firms' goods for the state defense donation. In this regard, the court affirmed the stance of the plaintiffs and cancelled the decisions of both the Fujian Financial Department and the Fuzhou Tax Bureau should be rescinded.[19]

The above cases indicate that the Administrative Court in the later republic would sometimes make adjudications in accordance with the law or legal principles. Although it sometimes rejected the plaintiffs' complaints, it did so according to its reading of the law and not simply because the power and connections of the defendants.

An assessment of the Administrative Court

Like the Administrative Court in the early republic, the Administrative Court in the later republic came under fire in both the republican and the PRC periods. In 1932, after the passages of the Administrative Litigation Law and the Complaint Law, Yang Zhaolong, the chief procurator of the Supreme Court (who would eventually be labeled a "rightist" in the early PRC), found a few fundamental errors in the new laws. Yang highlighted Article 1 of the Administrative Litigation Law which stated that if people's rights were illegally violated by central or local governments, they could lodge lawsuits at the Administrative Court, but only after they had sought and been dissatisfied with the decisions on their second complaints or had awaited in vain an official decisions for more than thirty days. In fact, Yang argued, inappropriate (*budang*) official decisions could harm people's rights just as well as illegal (*bufa*) ones. And complaining and waiting for government decisions on complaints could waste valuable time before people could even complain to the Administrative Court. To protect people's rights, Yang argued that it would be better if complainants were able to complain directly to the Administrative Court, thus saving themselves time and money now being lost in complaining to other bodies. He also believed that measures should be found to prevent officials from protecting each other and retaliating against complainants.[20] Although Yang's proposals had merit, they were not adopted by the later republican state.

In 1933, law professor Zhang Yuanruo questioned the relationship between the Administrative Court and the Judicial Yuan. He wrote that if the Judicial Yuan controlled the court, the independence of the administrative power would be compromised and as a result the running of the state administration (*guojia xingzheng*) would be blocked. Therefore, Zhang proposed that the Administrative Court should be under the direct control of the National Government and not the Judicial Yuan so that it would have greater authority in adjudicating illegal and inappropriate official activities.[21]

PRC legal scholars, of course, later subjected the republican complaint systems to even more trenchant criticism. Yang Haikun, law professor at Suzhou University, acknowledged in 1992 that the GMD passed the Administrative Litigation Law, but he argued that "semi-colonial and semi-feudal social system" (*ban zhimindi ban fengjian shehui zhidu*) and the presumed absence of any "indigenous root for a real democratic legal system," "[the Administrative Court in the early republic] was largely ephemeral or decorative (*zhuangshipin*)." Yang Yuqing, a former judge of the later republican Administrative Court and an advisor to the State Council in the PRC, asserted that the administrative adjudicating system (*xingzheng shenpan jigou*) in the late republic "merely tried to cheat people with a people's signboard (*renmin de zhaopai*)." Therefore, "the history of administrative litigation (*xingzheng susong*) [in the later republic] is almost zero."[22]

Although these charges may have been hyperbolic, another feature may have undermined the autonomy of the Administrative Court in the later republic. Unlike in the early republic, its judges were all required to be GMD party members.[23] That requirement was a byproduct of the Leninist party-state introduced from the Soviet Union in 1924.[24] Such court personnel would find it difficult to challenge party leaders and accordingly the judicial independence suffered significantly. Xiaoqun Xu aptly points out the particization of judiciary in the late republic, "the further development of a modern Chinese judiciary under he GMD became almost a party affair, and the system was politicized as much as possible."[25]

Despite the criticisms, most of which were justified, administrative litigation in the later republic could rightfully claim some achievements. For instance, as we have seen, the Administrative Court lowered fees for making complaints, judged even official defendants who refused to come to the court, and permitted complainants to request compensation. More important, the court sometimes upheld the laws and invoked legal principles in making judgments. According to *A Collection of the Administrative Court Judgments* produced by the court, a total of eighty-four cases were decided by the court between 1933 and 1947. Among them were a substantial number of people-against-official cases that were successful.[26]

As shown in Table 4.1, thirty-one out of eighty-four, or 37 percent, of the original government decisions were either partially or fully reversed by the

Table 4.1 Analysis of the cases contained in *A Collection of the Administrative Court Judgments*

	Total	*Reversed decision*	*Partly reversed decision*	*Complainants and complaints rejected*
Substantive content of complaints (*shiti bufen*)				
Land	4	2	1	1
Water project	3	0	1	2
Storage	1	0	1	0
Tax	22	2	4	16
Customs	3	1	0	2
Salt	1	1	0	0
Mining	6	0	0	6
Business	5	3	1	1
Trademark	22	4	0	18
Education	3	1	0	2
Transportation	1	0	0	1
Inspection	1	0	0	1
Others	3	2	0	1
Procedural part (*chengxu bufen*)				
Administrative Court complaints	4	4	0	0
Non-judicial complaints (*suyuan*)	5	3	0	2
Totals	84	23	8	53

Source: author's analysis of data taken from Xingzheng fayuan ed., *Xingzheng fayuan panjue huibian 1933–1947*, 1948.

Administrative Court. Although the percentage was arguably dwarfed by that in the early republic (46 percent, see Chapter 3), it is an exaggeration to claim that the court was "largely decorative" or "its history is almost zero."[27]

In addition, contrary to Yang Zhaolong's claim, in some cases in the *Collection of Administrative Court Judgments*, some government officials did not protect each other. In the case of Zhu Haiting, the Financial Ministry reversed the decision of the Sichuan provincial government and the Sichuan provincial government itself reversed the decision of the Bishan county government. Also, Yang's view that government decisions on complaints were largely unlawful is incorrect. Many cases in the book showed different levels of government making decisions about complaints on the basis of specific contemporary laws, regulations, or legal principles.

The non-judicial complaint system

Like previous constitutions, both the 1931 Political Tutelage Constitution of the Republic of China and the 1946 Constitution of the Republic of China reiterated that people had the right to complain.[28] In 1947, a revision of the constitution made by congressman Hu Kuisheng noted that citizens had the right to complain when administrative organs violated their rights.[29] However, the right to complain does not mean that aggrieved people could complain at will. As the Complaint Law explicitly stated, it was required that all complaints had to follow the regular and legal steps. Although some people did complain legally, many other complainants, as natural resisters in the past, continued to ignore the law and to lodge unlawful complaints in this period.

In the early republic, the Provisional Constitution of the Republic of China had allowed people to complain directly to the Congress and the Constitution of the Republic of China had permitted people to complaint (*qingyuan*) directly to the Legislative Yuan.[30] In the later republic, the three constitutions of 1931, 1936, and 1947 stated simply that people had the right to complain (*qingyuan*) and did not indicate where.[31] Whatever the motivations behind this constitutional omission of specific places that would entertain complaints (it may have been to discourage complaints), it seems likely to have expanded rather than restricted the number and variety of places where complaints were legally lodged in the late republic. Not only had almost all central organs including the National Government (i.e., Chiang Kai-shek and his immediate aides) and the Five Yuans accepted complaints, but local congresses and even some non-government organizations had also accepted people's complaints. Moreover, since the Administrative Court in this period was not designed to accept complaints against official corruption or official infringement of the law, those tasks were transferred to numerous other organs of both central and local governments and to both governmental and non-governmental bodies. Consequently, the number of places where people could lawfully complain was greater than in the early republic.

Despite the increasing venues and no punishment on many natural resisters who had firm beliefs in the parental rulers in the late republic, the central organs, according to the archival cases I have studied, did not accept complaints against officials below the provincial level. For any complaints against local officials, the central organs would ask them to complain to the provincial government.

As the most powerful organ in the later republic, the National Government (i.e., the president) was one of the central venues to which many complainants would take their grievances. While the National Government, like the Qianlong and Jiaqing rulers in the Qing period, issued a proclamation on August 10, 1929 prohibiting skipping and direct complaints to itself,[32] that order did not last long. Six years later, Chiang Kai-shek, in an effort to crack down on government corruption, briefly allowed both commoners and elites to report any corrupt official directly to himself.[33]

In September 1947, a military veteran named Cai Guangzu complained to the National Government about local officials' handling of a powerful local thug who had allegedly abducted his (Cai's) wife. Driven by the unbearable grievance, Cai begged "big officials (*zhangguan*)" to transfer his complaint letter to President Chiang Kai-shek or General Xue Yue so that his grievances could be heard by the leaders.[34]

As part of the GMD efforts to nourish the local self-government and implement constitutional government,[35] the Shanghai Congress was elected by the Shanghai citizens and was supposed to represent the people of the city. Citizens of Shanghai complained to the Congress about the malfeasance of officials, the unjust treatment of citizens, and the problems they faced in their everyday lives. For example, in 1948, Zhang Yunshan, a small landlord whose living depended on renting out his rooms, complained to the Congress that an officer at the Shanghai garrison headquarters had forcibly occupied his house. The Congress investigated and found that the officer had come to the Congress in person to explain the incident. The officer assured the Congress that he had already canceled his rent contract with Zhang and withdrawn from the house.[36] Further information on this case is not available, but it suggests that at least some aggrieved citizens regarded the Congress as a potential check on military abuses.

Also in the later republic, certain non-governmental organizations played some role in helping people with their complaints. In 1936, eight widows complained to the Shanghai Pudong Fellows Society (*pudong tongxianghui*) about the death of their husbands in a car accident. The aggrieved widows claimed that the accident had been caused by the poor road conditions and that the Bureau of Industrial Works (*gongbujü*) should take responsibility. They thus entreated the society to help them obtain the compensation from the Bureau. Upon receiving the complaint, the society agreed to ask the head of its special legal committee to deal with the case.[37] Again, I could not learn anything about the upshot, but this case shows that some people would complain to a non-government organization and might receive some help from it.

The existence of more central and local places accepting complaints did not mean that people in the later republic could complain to whichever organs or in whatever way they wanted. Organs that received complaints that they deemed wrongly directed would transfer them to other organs and tell the complainants that they should wait for the response from those other organs. As so often in the past, people lodging skipping complaints to government organs would be told to follow legal steps.

Case studies of natural resistance

In the late republic, many complaints were lodged according to the required steps as stipulated in the Complaint Law. To cite just two cases, in August 1939, a student complained through the regular hierarchy to the Hubei provincial government that the former magistrate of Nanzhang county had allegedly killed innocent people and plundered people's treasures. Two months later, having received no response, the student continued to complain to the provincial government. The provincial government replied that the case was under investigation by the official of the Fifth District (prefecture) and the student should wait for the result.[38] A decade later, in 1948, an organization called Saving the Township (*jiuxiang yundong*) mounted a collective complaint to the Legislative Yuan against Li Pinxian, the governor of Anhui province, for his misgovernment. As the Legislative Yuan thought the case was more closely related to the Administrative Yuan, it sent a copy of the complaint letter to the Administrative Yuan.[39]

However, as in the past, many complainants made skipping complaints that were deemed illegal and therefore refused.

In 1947, a desperate farmer named Yang Zhenhua from northern Hubei province complained via telegrams to several central organs such as the National Government, the Defense Ministry, the Five Yuans, and the Supreme Court. In his complaint, Yang charged several powerful local headmen (*baozhang*) with forcibly selling the land that belonged to him without giving him any compensation. "Because of the tremendous power and wealth of the local headmen," Yang said that he seemed to be living in hell and "dared only to feel angry but not to speak." Assuming that those local headmen had bribed the local officials (i.e., magistrate), Yang decided to "take the risk" and "fight to the death" in hopes of compelling official behavior in line with "heavenly principles." Unlike natural resisters who were unaware of the law, Yang knew that it was illegal to make skipping complaints to the central government bodies. At the end of his complaint letter, Yang called himself "a criminal person (*zuimin*)." Yang's personal efforts failed to generate any favorable results. The only response came from the Hubei provincial government that flatly rejected Yang's complaint not because of his skipping levels but because there was no seal on his complaint letter. Yang could not put a seal on a telegram and the provincial government did not accept telegrammed complaints.[40]

In another case, a farmer named Wang Huichen in September 1948, barely a year before the CCP took power in Mainland China, represented his village in Fengyang county, Anhui province, by filing a skipping complaint to the Legislative Yuan in which he accused the county magistrate of levying unlawful taxes. In his letter, Wang invoked both new republican laws and old values to make his case. "At the inception of the constitutional government," Wang wrote, "the magistrate dares to violate the law and to neglect the people's livelihood by imposing illicit taxes never before seen in history." Despite the egregious pains and legal logic in the complaint, the Legislative Yuan turned down the complaint on the grounds that it had been illegally set forth. The Yuan told Wang that he should first complain to the Anhui provincial government.[41]

In this period, many complainants continued to trust heaven's representative and the parental ruler, now believing that the generalissimo Chiang Kai-shek was their best and last hope to satisfy grievances on earth. In 1947, three farmers wrote a complaint letter to Chiang Kai-shek against Fu Liangju, the magistrate of Xiangyang county in Hubei province. According to the Complaint Law, the farmers should have complained first to the Hubei provincial government, but they chose to neglect that law and brought their complaint directly to Chiang Kai-shek. The farmers charged Fu with five crimes, including embezzling [public] grains and money, collaborating with bandit leaders, selling official positions, committing jobbery, and stealing and selling public properties. Staunchly believing in the Confucian concept of *minben*/people as the root, the farmers argued that the "heavenly duty" of parental rulers/officials was to protect the people. They flattered Chiang Kai-shek as being like a "loving mother" who "always treated people as his own children." In conclusion, the farmers wished that Chiang would not forget his people who were living in "an extremely dire situation" in northern Hubei province. Although the upshot of the case is not available, the archives show that Chiang Kai-shek did receive the complaint letter and sent all relevant materials to the Hubei provincial government for further investigation.[42]

The skipping complaint of Liu Haixu vs. Zeng Peiyuan

While working in the Hubei Provincial Archives, I fortunately came across one file of a complaint case that was quite complete and well preserved. It contained not only the original letters of complaint but also official responses and investigative reports on the case. On December 13, 1945, less than four months after Japan surrendered to the allies, Liu Haixu, a high-school student who lived in Jingmen county, Hubei, lodged a skipping complaint to Chiang Kai-shek on behalf of his family and friends. In the complaint he accused two township heads, Zeng Peiyuan and Ai Junlong, with corruption and abuse. He concluded that no person in the republic could redress such a serious grievance except President Chiang Kai-shek. Knowing that his complaint was against the law, Liu begged Chiang to forgive his unlawful action.

In the complaint, Liu argued that the two township heads had intensified the local people's burden after the end of the war with Japan by raising taxes. Both Zeng and Ai were also said to have come from low social positions and to have willfully done all kinds of evil. When the local people complained to the magistrate, the county government "did not accept the complaint but instead assisted the evildoers (Zeng and Ai) by transferring the complaint letter back to the township government (i.e., Zeng and Ai)." Under protection from the county government,

Zeng and Ai had become even bolder and more violent. As a result, "all local people were afraid that they could suffer persecution anytime." Living under such grim conditions, Liu's father hoped that Liu could complain to the provincial government. Yet, "because it is extremely questionable" whether the [Hubei] provincial government would pay serious attention to a few voices of complaint, Liu presumed that the provincial government would very likely pass his complaint back to the county and township governments. "If that happens," Liu worried, "[the situation] will be even worse." Therefore, Liu repeated his firm belief that only Chiang Kai-shek, whom he praised as the highest wise leader (*xianming lingxiu*), was able to save the local people and eliminate the local misgovernment.

Upon receiving Liu Haixu's skipping complaint letter, the National Government that was responsible for receiving complaint letters for Chiang Kai-shek did not reject the complaint, probably because of the ongoing competition with the CCP and the need to gain people's support. It instead ordered the governor of the Hubei provincial government to investigate whether Liu's complaint was true. Fearing that the provincial government would, as usual, simply transfer the complaint back down to the county magistrate, the National Government emphasized that the governor should dispatch a provincial official to deal with the case personally.

Under the direct order of the National Government, the governor asked an official from the Civil and Political Department (*minzhengting*) to conduct a meticulous and empirical investigation of the case. On March 15, 1946, about three months after Liu Haixu's complaint to Chiang Kai-shek, the official completed a very detailed report of the investigation. One by one, the report tried to provide answers to all of Liu's accusations. For the complaint that Zeng and Ai had increased people's burden, the report listed ten major burdens of the local people such as army provisions, grains for county and township officials, funds and provisions for the county militia, and the like. All the added burdens were necessary to "exterminate the bandits (the CCP army)." The report admitted that the problem was virtually a common one in most Hubei counties and not just in Jingmen county. The report warned the governor: if the problem was not resolved quickly, not only would people's living become direr but officials at the levels of township and county would also feel the pains of seeing a declining income.

With regard to Liu's criticism that both Zeng and Ai came from a low social position and did all kinds of evil, the report expressed its sympathy and verified that Zeng was an opium addict and Ai was mentally unstable. However, since the new magistrate of Jingmen had dismissed Zeng and Ai in November 1945 and reshuffled the internal personnel in the township, the public attitudes toward the local township government had gradually improved. The most in-depth and complex study in the official investigation was of Liu's charge that the county government clandestinely forwarded local people's complaints to Zeng and Ai. According to the report, although the charge was plausible, the problem was that there was no hard evidence. When the official of the Civil and Political Department went to Liu's home and asked his father and brother for the details of the case, he was told that it was the former county secretary Jiang Zhenmin and other two county officials who had given Zeng and Ai the complaint letter after receiving a bribe totaling 180,000 yuan. But unfortunately, there was no witness. Worse, the person who had related the story had died last winter and there was no way to corroborate his account. The provincial official then conducted a secret investigation among the local people and had gone back to the county government asking the magistrate for the original materials of the case. But all his (the official's) efforts had been in vain. In conclusion, the official report argued that, had the case been coped with quickly at first or had the new magistrate chosen to continue the investigation and not tired to resolve it privately, the suspicion that the county government had passed the complaint onto the township would not have arisen.[43] While the official investigation failed to satisfy Liu Haixu's grievances, it acknowledged most of the issues raised in the complaints. It also proposed that the government should reduce the burdens on the local people that had sparked Liu's complaint.

However uncommon both in content and form, the case of Liu Haixu vs. Zeng and Ai demonstrates that Chiang Kai-shek and the National Government could sometimes directly and seriously respond to certain grave, even if illegally filed, complaints, especially those coming from regions close to where the CCP was strong, if only in an effort to regain the trust and support of the local people. Such positive and direct responses to people's skipping complaints, which were illegal, would confirm people's reliance on the center to address their grievances, and important element in what I am calling natural resistance. The continuing absence in this period of any punishment for lodging such complaints in an illegal fashion probably only further strengthened people's belief in this form of resistance.

Other means of complaint

Besides writing or visiting various levels of government, congresses, or societies, complainants in the later republic availed themselves of other opportunities to lodge their grievances. In a study of the republican legal reform, Xiaoqun Xu has shown that many people confronting allegedly unjust local court decisions, official corruption, and abuses of power would complain to provincial-level courts. Some complaints about the alleged misconduct of individual judicial personnel could usually be addressed by such judicial authorities.[44] As in the late Qing and early republic, newspapers continued to be an important venue by which complainants would voice their grievances and hope to generate public compassion or pressure. The public media acquired phenomenal power in the late republic. In the mid-1930s there were some 910 newspapers and around 900 magazines, some with circulation as large as 150,000.[45]

In one famous case, Shi Jianqiao assassinated Sun Chuanfang after that former warlord had killed her father. Although such personal revenge was not generally sanctioned by Chinese laws, the public media depicted Shi as a heroine. Partly because of such "overwhelming public support," the GMD quickly pardoned Shi.[46] Once again, an extreme form of natural resistance seemed to be validated. In a very different case, after the GMD launched a campaign against superstitions in the 1930s, numerous Buddhist monks bombarded the GMD with complaints. Some monks circulated complaints about the political campaign to major official newspapers such as the *Central Daily News* and private ones like the *Shanghai Daily*.[47]

In other cases, certain influential newspapers actively reported people's complaints to stimulate public concern and sell more newspapers.

On December 20, 1934, for instance, *Da Gong Bao*, one of the most influential newspapers in northern China, reported that a group of people had complained to the ongoing GMD party's plenary session. According to the newspaper, the complainants came from Chongqing county, Sichuan province. Because heavy rains in the summer had caused devastating flooding in Chongqing, the complainants had suffered a great loss in properties. The local magistrate named Zhu Ying, however, not only failed to report the disaster to provincial authorities, but also collected even more taxes from the residents who could not afford to pay them. Living in the distant west, the complainants said that they had no way to protect their livelihood or to resist the cruel magistrate. Fortunately, the GMD was meeting in plenary session in Nanjing at this moment. They therefore sent a complaint telegram to the plenary session asking it to the rescue of the some 5000 people affected by the official injustice. The GMD response, if any, was not recorded, but I may surmise that the newspaper report assisted the complainants in their efforts and enhanced the popularity of this form of public agitation and natural resistance.[48]

An assessment of the informal complaint system

As we have seen, both lawful and natural resisters in the later republic had more government and non-government organs to complain to than before. Some of those organs, including the National Government (i.e., Chiang Kai-shek), took positive steps toward addressing citizens' complaints. Still, many complainants in this period might well have concluded that their rate of success in satisfying their grievances was no better, if not worse, than their predecessors in former periods. First, the total number of complaints I have found so far in both the national and provincial archives was small. They almost certainly constituted only a tiny fraction of all the complaints that were made. Second, many aggrieved persons surely chose not to complain publically because they lacked resources, including money and literacy. Some must have simply swallowed their grievances for fear of possible revenge, or out of caution about the perils and pains of travel to provincial and national capitals. Third, some complaints that were filed might not even have reached any government organ.

As in the past, the most serious violations of people's rights were perpetrated by corrupt officials acting unlawfully. Complaints against such violations, however, were often not redressed or were simply ignored by the many government organs that were supposed to take care of them. This must have emboldened many official violators of people's rights and resulted in more grievances than would otherwise have been the case in the later republic. Wu Chaoshu, a member of the GMD Central Executive Committee, once admitted in a letter to Sun Ke, the head of the Legislative Yuan, that

> People's freedom has been violated at will and [many people] have been detained without any reason or following any legal procedure. After they are detained, the investigation period is endless and no one knows when they will be set free. [Many suspects] are confined to jail and have nowhere to complain.[49]

What was behind those official infringements of people's rights? Why were so many grievances never addressed let alone satisfied? I would argue that the mixture of a single-party state and the rise of Confucian fascism in the late republic exacerbated the already rampant official corruption and misconduct,[50] resulting in most of the grievances. Other causes of complaints include such recurrent ones as the internal problems of the judiciary and complaint systems. In addition, the adverse circumstances accompanying civil and international wars also generated numerous grievances in this period.

Party-state and violations from the top

When Sun Yat-sen and his comrades struggled to establish a constitutional republic, they tried to follow Western models,[51] especially that of the United States despite obvious social problems including the mal-distribution of wealth.[52] In 1924, The GMD adopted a new policy cooperating with the Soviet Union and the CCP, and announced that China would go beyond Western liberal democracy in which only the capitalists or bourgeoisie had rights and would establish a form of democracy in which every commoner would have rights.[53] On February 7, 1928, the GMD proclaimed that Sun Yat-sen's "Three-peoples' Principles" were the "highest guiding principles of the great harmony (*datong*)," the ideal society that would encompass the whole world.[54]

To realize the Three-people's Principles under conditions of pervasive political chaos and limited rights consciousness and in the absence of Western recognition of his government, Sun eventually adopted the Leninist party-state system that seemed to have carried out a successful revolution in the Soviet Union.[55] Because only the GMD, the "first Leninist party in China,"[56] could fulfill the three principles of the people, the party had the responsibility to maintain its power until the Chinese people were able to govern themselves. Sun shared the misconception of many other Chinese as well as Westerners, that the Chinese people were accustomed to being slaves and had no idea how to govern themselves.[57] He pointed to the examples of Zhuge Liang, the presumably capable prime minister of the Shu-Han state during the Three Kingdoms (220–280 CE), and Liu Adou, the allegedly stupid heir to Liu Bei as ruler of the state of Shu-Han. In Sun's view, the GMD was the Zhuge Liang while the Chinese people were the Liu Adou of the era who were unable to govern themselves. Sun argued that today's Liu Adou would be wise to allow today's Zhuge Liang to decide everything.[58]

Like Sun Yat-sen, Chiang Kai-shek in the late 1930s argued that the Chinese people were comparable to Tai Jia, a young ruler of the Shang dynasty (*c.* 1675–1029 BCE) while the GMD was the equivalent of Yi Yin, an upright minister and regent in the Shang who disciplined Tai Jia. During the phase of political tutelage, Chiang stated, the GMD should first teach, discipline, and cultivate the Chinese people, the future masters of China, and eventually turn authority over to them.[59] On another occasion, Chiang described GMD officials as the parents of the people, echoing a crucial element drawn from Confucian paternalism and the *minben* concept.[60]

With such ideologies as the party-state, regents, and the concept of *minben* in mind, the GMD naturally sought to concentrate authority in its own hands. The 1931 Provisional Constitution of the Republic of China during the Political Tutelage granted the president of the GMD the power to appoint and dismiss the ministers of the five major Yuans, thereby making the president the de facto supreme authority over the Republic of China.[61] Moreover, during the period of political tutelage, even the judiciary whose independence had been stressed by many republican founding fathers was under the control of the party. As early as 1926, the first GMD Central Executive Committee stipulated that all government officials, including judges, had to be party members.[62] In 1934, Chiang Kai-shek was pleased to claim that almost all government organs, including the judiciary in several "revolutionary provinces," could be counted on to follow the orders of the central government.[63]

According to the principle of democratic centralism, both Sun Yat-sen and Chiang Kai-shek demanded that all members of the GMD strictly follow the leaders of the party. Believing that loose discipline in previous parties had caused many failures, Sun stated that strict organization and discipline were required if the GMD hoped to take control of China and implement the Three-people's Principles.[64] Similarly, Chiang in 1926 also talked about the importance of party discipline: "once a person joins the GMD, his life will belong to the party and no longer to himself. He will scrap all of his personal freedom and equality [to the party]."[65] With Chiang's blessings, fascist organizations such as the *Lixingshe* and the Blue Shirts were created. They were loyal only to Chiang and tried by all means to oppose Chiang's enemies inside and outside of the party.[66]

To make sure that China could stick to the path of the GMD, the party tried to outlaw any opposition party that opposed the Three-people's Principles.[67] In 1929, the third GMD congress announced that all Chinese people must support the principles of the GMD before they could hope to enjoy the people's rights in the Republic of China.[68]

Under these guidelines, the GMD unleashed waves of unlawful crackdowns on citizens who dared to challenge it. They included illegal arrests, torture, and assassination throughout the later republic.[69] As most of these political crimes were conducted by the GMD, few perpetrators were ever punished, leaving behind numerous grievances. In 1932, one year after the Japanese invasion of northeast China, General Feng Yuxiang, a former warlord now nominally part of the Nanjing government, sharply criticized the GMD for its lack of democracy and excess of crimes,

> [Today's GMD] simply represses people's movements, suppresses people's freedom, and distorts people's opinions in the name of rule-by-the-party.... Most lawbreakers manage to avoid punishment. The Supervisory Yuan can punish only magistrates and heads of some bureaus, but not powerful persons[70]

In 1935, the GMD itself admitted at its fifth National Congress that local politics was "dominated by corrupt thugs and local tyrants" and the "old cruel politics was worsening today," making people's lives more difficult than before.[71]

During the second civil war that started in 1946, corruption became unbridled and was among the top features that people hated.[72] In a speech to the GMD, Chiang Kai-shek admitted that government corruption and impotence had become so serious as to humiliate the party. Chiang noted that the GMD needed to discipline itself and root out corruption.[73]

Indeed, such reform is always easier said than done. Although Chiang swore that he would check political corruption, he himself was behind numerous political assassinations and opium production and allegedly protected his corrupt protégés from punishment. It was under Chiang's direct order that the GMD secret police assassinated CCP members and renowned liberals such as Yang Xinfo and Shi Liangcai.[74] Liu Jianqun, a member of the fascist *Lixingshe*, accused GMD leaders of ignoring the violations of the law by their loyal followers.[75] With protection from the top, many officials became bolder in violating the law and people's rights.

Scholars such as Ruan Yicheng, a law professor at the Central University in Nanjing, also complained in 1933 about the lawlessness in contemporary China. He argued that too many government organs had power to make judgments about people's guilt or innocence, and every year countless people were killed without judgments from the courts. In addition, it was very common that the administration meddled in the judiciary.[76]

As shown in the complaints against corrupt officials such as Anhui governor Li Pinxian and Xiangyang magistrate Fu Liangju, republican citizens who might have more direct contacts with local officials expressed similar views on political corruption. In 1946, four college students, having become disillusioned by the rampant official corruption, filed a direct complaint to Chiang Kai-shek arguing that China would become hopeless if only President Chiang was upright. They lamented that Chiang's decades of sincere efforts to check corruption were useless as Chinese society and politics continued to be very dark.[77] Unlike some complainants in the past and present whose personal or family rights had been wronged, those college students had no personal reasons to complain. But, like citizens of the new republic, they believed that they had a natural right to complain to the president about the current woes of the state.

Closely related to political corruption were numerous violations of the law by powerful officials that resulted in many unresolved grievances.[78] In the early 1930s, although Ruan Yicheng believed that China had promulgated enough good laws since the late Qing, he regarded the republican government as the biggest obstacle to the rule of law. As Ruan wrote: "The government is accustomed to use its power and authority (*weixin*) and not to follow the law."[79] Similarly in 1941, Qiu Hanping, a law professor at Dongwu University, argued that it was officials and the elite and not the ordinary people who routinely violated the law.[80] Indeed, as various sources have showed, many powerful people, including President Chiang Kai-shek, violated the law, resulting in numerous grievances.

In his memoir, Shen Zui, a former lieutenant of Dai Li, exposed lots of violations of the law perpetrated by powerful officials and government organs. When Shen was the head of Juntong branch in Changde, Hunan province, he had been the most powerful person around. If his subordinates violated the law, Shen admitted, he would simply look the other way. In Sichuan, during the 1940s, the GMD built a prison for arrested Communists, causing many people to lose their homes and lives. But Shen asked, who would care?[81]

Endless wars

The second cause of many grievances in the later republic was the seemingly endless warfare and "in almost no year in this period was China at peace."[82] The continual wars had a considerable impact on GMD policies and gave rise to many grievances. In general, the wars were used by the GMD to justify postponement of the process of constitutional government. In 1929 the GMD declared that the political tutelage had begun and would last for six years. However, by 1935, the year that the planned political tutelage should end, the GMD had not even completed the work of preparing for local self-government, let alone established a constitutional government. In the end, the GMD could only announce that it "regretted" the failure.[83] Chiang Kai-shek also acknowledged in the mid-1930s that, because of the unification wars (with the CCP), "the GMD has finished neither the work of the political tutelage, nor even some work [i.e., unification] that needed to be done during the period of the military government."[84] With a constantly prolonged period of political tutelage, government officials had more leeway to evade legal punishment if they violated people's rights or interests. On May 20, 1944, Chiang Kai-shek admitted that, owing to numerous military actions, it was hard for the government to supervise all officials. Hence, many people in the country would have their rights violated by officials who were neglectful or who exceeded their authority.[85]

In addition, during most of the later republic, the GMD continued to regard the Chinese Communists as its biggest enemy. Chiang Kai-shek had always treated the CCP as a "disease of the heart" that posed more lethal threat to the GMD as opposed to the Japanese who were a "disease of the skin." Even during the deadly Sino-Japanese war, the GMD continued to try to crush the Communist army.[86] To crack down on possible communist sabotage in the GMD controlled areas, the GMD resorted to extra-legal measures. On July 26, 1929, the National Government ordered that, before the implementation of the jury system to deal with counterrevolutionaries (i.e., Communists) the Judicial Yuan and all levels of courts should not stress the need for evidence when they dealt with cases involving Communists.[87] In late 1929, the GMD passed the Interim Jury Law for Counterrevolutionary Cases (*fan geming anjian peishen zanxingfa*), which noted that when any court was adjudicating such a case, it had to have a six-member jury composed only of GMD party members. That jury had the power to decide whether the suspect was guilty or innocent, or of undetermined status due to a lack of evidence.[88] In 1932, another law indicated that the handling of any allegedly counterrevolutionary case would not be confined by or subject to either civil or criminal laws.[89]

Two years later, dissatisfied with the tardiness of court decisions on alleged counterrevolutionaries, the GMD transferred communist cases to the military court. In 1948, the GMD once again transferred communist cases to a special criminal court to speed up its suppression of communists.[90] In 1949, shortly before the end of the GMD rule on the mainland, a Shanghai government order restored collective punishment in efforts to check the expansion of CCP influence in the city.[91] Under the above laws, military and political officials could and did ignore other laws arbitrarily, punishing CCP suspects at will. As a result, no one knows the number of grievances that innocent victims would have had.[92]

Incomplete judicial independence

The third cause of many unsatisfied grievances in this period was the incomplete nature of judicial independence and reform. Admittedly, the late republic generally inherited the judicial system of the early republic and preserved its independent spirit. In 1937, the legal scholar Xia Zhenmin praised the republican legislation for placing more emphasis on human rights than in the past.[93] The historian Philip C. C. Huang also points out that GMD jurists "tended on the whole to be quite legalistic in their approach to law and justice."[94] Many judicial officials such as Ju Zheng (1876–1951), the minister of the Judicial Yuan from 1932 to 1948, tried to defend judicial independence. For example, to help safeguard judicial independence, Ju Zheng, in 1941, realized his goal of having the central government pay all judicial bills, which might lessen the interference of local governments in adjudication through the financial lever.[95]

The later-republican courts maintained judicial independence in some circumstances by resisting orders from the top. According to Lin Houqi, a long-term republican judge and head of many provincial courts, after the end of the Sino-Japanese war, the alleged traitor Zhou Fohai, who had served in the reformed republican regime in Nanjing under the Japanese, was convicted and sentenced by the Supreme Court to a death penalty. Chiang Kai-shek, however, sent his personal order to the court asking it to change its judgment because Zhou had provided the republic in Chongqing with useful information during the war. The Supreme Court, however, decided to reject the president's order to maintain its independence. The court argued that it had made the judgment in accordance with the legal procedure and could not change it. If Chiang believed that the defendant had worked for the country, he should set him free by a special amnesty.[96]

Despite such small victories, the situation of the judiciary in the later republic remained unsatisfactory. Despite its supposed independence, the judiciary was unable to punish powerful people. Although Ju Zheng managed to get the central government to pay the judges like other civil servants, the funding provided was always far from enough. In 1948, to solve their financial problems, many local courts had to rely on local governments, which surely weakened their independence. In one case, two government organs in Sichuan, the land and crop office (*tianliangshu*) of Leshan and the Sichuan Financial Department, quarreled over the matter of a bankrupt factory. Both parties wanted to control the factory and sued in the local court. As the court was financially dependent on both departments, it dared not favor either party. As a result, the court simply kept delaying the final judgment.[97] Thus, local courts dependent on governments for funds were unlikely to be able to prosecute those governments according to the law when they violated people's rights.

Additionally, the Judicial Yuan in 1929 unveiled its ambitious six-year plan to establish thousands of courts, model prisons, and detaining custodies in the country,[98] but in 1936, magistrates in over 1400 counties still functioned as judges owing to a paucity of funding and professional judges.[99] In that year, the legal critic Yang Peng pointed out that many magistrates lacked the proper training and often failed to follow the law in their judgments, leading to a tremendous number of grievances.[100] Even professional judges sometimes failed to follow due process in handling cases. In 1933, after a landlord in Shehong, Sichuan, was killed, his relatives accused two neighbors of committing the crime. The county judge reportedly decided to execute the two persons without conducting any investigation.[101]

Procedural obstacles

The final reason for the inability of complainants in the later republic to redress their grievances was the existence of procedural obstacles such as numerous fees imposed on anyone filing a lawsuit.[102] And then there was the need to fill out all forms. Republican judge Lin Houqi noted that the republican court was to some extent worse than those that had preceded it. "In the feudal period, complainants could beat the drum or block the royal cart to voice their grievances [orally]," Lin said, "in the republican period, however, people could not complain to the court because they were illiterate and therefore unable to fill out the required forms." To be sure, there were exceptions. For instance, Shanghai Nanshi District Court set up a bell, similar to the Public Petition Drum in early times, for non-literate complainants to ring if they wanted to complain. But this institution did not last long.[103] Further research would be necessary to determine whether other less "developed" places in China had more or fewer such institutions designed to give voice to people who were unable to read and write.

Conclusion

The complaint systems in the late republic offer a mixed picture. On the one hand, the late republican government took solid steps to improve citizens' chances of success in exercising their natural right to complain. Although it largely inherited the institutions of the early republic, including the Administrative Court and the Complaint Law, the late republic made certain important modifications including allowing complainers to ask for compensation, granting the court the authority to make direct decisions, and repealing the application fee of the early republic that might have forced many complainers to back off. In addition, the Administrative Court could deal with people's complaints in accordance with the laws. More important, complainants in this period would find more sites, both governmental and non-governmental, for registering their complaints and seeking help and some natural resisters continued to make skipping complaints that were illegal. In its response to natural resistance such as Liu Haixu's complaints against local township heads, the National Government (i.e., Chiang Kai-shek) could undertake meticulous and exhaustive investigations on the basis of an illicit skipping complaint.

On the other hand, during a time of single-party rule, civil wars, and foreign invasion, violations of the law or people's rights by officials, especially top officials, resulted in many grievances that were never made public let alone addressed and resolved by the state. The combination of official abuses and restrictions on people's rightful resistance kept the theory and practice of natural resistance very much alive in this period.

5 Revolutionary idealism

The early People's Republic (1949–1982)

From its founding in 1921, the CCP (Chinese Communist Party) espoused the Marxist theory of history and claimed that its ultimate goal was to eradicate the system of private property and gradually attain the goal of Communism.[1]

Taking advantage of Soviet Union's assistance,[2] responding to the invasion from Japan, benefiting from the internal divisions in the Guomindang (GMD), and developing a populist ideology, the CCP eventually grew into a major political force supported by a powerful army. In 1949, the CCP successfully toppled the GMD on the mainland and founded the People's Republic of China (PRC). From 1949 to 1976, the CCP launched repeated campaigns such as the Three-Anti and Five-Anti movement (*sanfan wufan yundong* 1952), the Anti-Rightists movement (*fanyou yundong* 1957), the Four Clean-ups (*siqing yundong* 1962), and the Great Proletarian Cultural Revolution (1966–1976) in efforts to root out "capitalist remnants" and consolidate the foundations of socialism, the preparatory stage of communism.[3]

As part of its effort to create a "New China," the CCP abolished almost all the GMD state institutions including its administrative court and complaint systems. It nonetheless maintained its own form of one-party rule and soon established its own informal systems of eliciting public opinion. Indeed, it considered the new systems to be one of the cornerstones of the people's democratic centralization government (*renmin minzhu zhuanzheng*) in which the masses were the "real" PRC masters. As part of a renewed ethos of populism not seen since the early Ming dynasty,[4] the new state greatly expanded people's natural right to complain by establishing letters and visits offices on all levels of the government. The new government encouraged people to make suggestions about public policy and, incidentally, to lodge any complaints they might have about official misconduct at the local level and all the way up to the top. Moreover, from its very beginning, the letters and visits system was, unlike its previous counterparts since the Tang, quite separate from the formal legal system.

Despite its secular nature, the CCP's more populist republicanism was a continuing assumption if not a conscious belief in heavenly principles, parental rulers, and people as the root of the state. These ideas which I have associated with a cultural style of natural resistance remained strong among many CCP officials including Mao Zedong, the paramount leader and ultimately, in some people's eyes, a kind of "living god" in the last years of this period. Populist republicanism founded on natural resistance nonetheless remained largely an ideal. Under the national and global circumstances of the era, it failed to brighten the generally bleak picture of the complaint systems of the past. Mao Zedong's revolutionary idealism combined with his "emperor thought" and "unchallengeable power"—in the words of some of his critics—resulted in numerous and sometimes violent political campaigns that almost certainly left behind uncounted number of grievances.[5]

The development of the complaint systems in the early PRC

The early PRC developed its complaint systems to meet changing political requirements. From the dawn of the base areas (1927) to the early 1980s, the systems developed through four phrases.

Origins (1927–1949)

According to Diao Jiecheng, an official who worked at the Letters and Visits Bureau of the General Office of the CCP (*zhonggong zhongyang bangongting*), the earliest CCP complaint system may date back to 1921, the year when the CCP was founded. In that year, two workers from the coalmines of Anyuan, in Anhui province, complained to Mao, then a low-profile CCP figure, about their poor working conditions. Mao paid serious attention to the complaint and went to the mine to talk to the workers.[6] In the early 1930s, Ilpyong Kim argues that the Chinese Soviet government of Xingguo county, Jiangxi, established a Workers' and Peasants' Inspection Committee (*jiancha weiyuanhui*), which was an independent "complaint bureau" charged with receiving the complaints and grievances of the people. The committee also set up a "complaint box," reminiscent of empress Wu Zetian's "petition box" in the Tang, giving all people the right to complain about government malfeasance.[7] In 1941, the border government of Shanxi, Gansu, and Ningxia allowed people to complain against its judges if they were dissatisfied with their judgments.[8] The 1946 Constitutional Principles (*xianfa yuanze*) of the base governments stated: "With respect to all governments, people have the right to supervise, complain, and raise suggestions at will." In the section on the "judiciary," the law reaffirmed the historical right of people to complain, stating that "People have the right to accuse by all means any public workers of their misconduct."[9]

In the base period, most probably to woo more support from the people when it was still relatively weak compared with the GMD, the CCP initiated a policy of the "mass line"[10] that in theory gave people almost unlimited rights to complain. A former head of a letters and visits office in a major city confirmed the general view that the people felt so close to the CCP leaders in this period that many people called Mao "old Mao (*lao Mao*)," using a term of respect and endearment.[11] The leaders were widely said to be willing and able to satisfy people's grievances. During the Sino-Japanese war (1937–1945), for example, the

CCP central guards once confiscated the land of some farmers for their own use. When the farmers complained directly to Mao, Mao immediately announced that the government should not take a single *mu* (one-sixth of an acre) of land from the people. If the state really needed land, it should negotiate an arrangement with the farmers. He ordered the central guards to return the land to the farmers and to make an apology.[12]

Nonetheless, even during the base period, when the relations between the CCP and the masses were supposedly better than they later became in the PRC,[13] many political grievances went unaddressed. In the Jiangxi Soviet period (1927–1934), Mao approved the suppression of the so-called AB faction resulting in cases of torture and thousands of deaths.[14] In 1942, Wang Shiwei, a special researcher and translator at the Central Research Institute (*zhongyang yanjiuyuan*), charged CCP officials with enjoying a higher standard of living (e.g., in food and clothes) than the masses. Wang also called on the masses to criticize the "big figures (*darenwu*)." During the 1942 "rectification movement," Mao denounced Wang and four of his "collaborators" and labeled them a "Trotskyite Five-Member Anti-Party Gang." The base government eventually beheaded Wang and his case was not reevaluated until 1991.[15]

The framing of the systems (1949–1957)

Very likely influenced by Lenin's view that a political authority representing farmers and workers "does not recognize any other political authority and law; does not recognize the institutions made by any other persons,"[16] the First Plenary of the Chinese People's Political Consultative Assembly, on September 29, 1949, shortly before the establishment of the PRC, passed the Common Principles (or *Gongtong gangling*), an interim constitution that replaced most of the GMD legal system. As in the Republic of China, the CCP, the self-claimed representative of the Chinese people, continued to grant both individuals and groups the right to complain to the people's procuratorates or to the people's judiciaries regarding any "illegal activities" of any state organ or official.[17]

Although the PRC initially denounced the GMD's political and judicial systems including its administrative court and complaint system,[18] it actually preserved part of the GMD's complaint system and gradually expanded it into a more comprehensive and all-purpose institution.

The General Office of the CCP was the first central organ to invite people to send letters and pay visits to express their complaints and suggestions.[19] As early as March 1949, the Central Secretariat (*zhongyang shujichu*) appointed special persons to be in charge of people's letters to Mao and the central government. In August, an organ called the Political Secretary Unit of the Central Secretariat (*zhongyang shujichu zhengzhi mishushi*) was formally established mainly to deal with people's letters and visits. Thus, "the Political Secretary Unit was the earliest special complaint organ in the history of the CCP."[20] The unit became the secretary unit of the General Office in early 1950. In addition, people could also complain and report to the State Council (*zhengwuyuan*) that had accepted people's letters from its founding in October 1949. In March 1951, the Secretariat (*mishuting*) of the State Council established the "Unit for Letters from the Masses (*qunzhong xinjianzu*)" to accept people's letters and visits on a variety of topics such as socialist construction, veterans and military martyrs affairs, counterrevolutionaries, and official corruption.

Because people's letters and visits raised a wide variety of problems, the General Office and the State Council began dividing their duties. The General Office would deal with suggestions to and complaints about the CCP and letters sent directly to Mao. The State Council would share responsibility for letters and visits regarding economic construction, employment, and the like.[21]

In the early years of the PRC, both central and local governments received a skyrocketing number of people's letters and visits. For instance, in 1949, the General Office received only 4457 people's letters and visits. The number rose sharply to 26,219 the next year, and to 346,865 in 1951.[22] Similarly, the number of letters and visits received by the Tianjin government also rose dramatically from 17,529 in 1951 to 167,390 in 1954.[23] Unable to solve all those complaints and suggestions, Liu Shaoqi, then the vice chairman of the PRC, proposed on February 28, 1951 that all levels of the people's government should establish "special and capable" organs to cope with people's requests, to answer people's letters, and to receive people's visits.[24]

Liu's proposal was apparently not followed well by many local governments. Annoyed by the slow process of responding to people's letters, Mao on May 16, 1951 sharply criticized bureaucratism,

> [Government officials] must treat [people's letters] as a means to strengthen the relationship between people and the people's government. Do not neglect [people's letters] and practice bureaucratism. – Any person (or government) who ignores [people's letters] should recognize and correct his (or its) wrong attitude.[25]

In response to Mao's criticism, the State Council issued an order on June 7, 1951 that all governments should be sympathetic to people's letters and visits. The order also required all government units to have special units and personnel to deal with people's letters and visits and to try their best to solve people's problems. Any retaliation against accusers was strictly prohibited. If people wrote letters criticizing government officials that got published in the newspapers, the superior officials should conduct studies and the officials charged should issue replies or, if they were guilty, offer self-criticisms to be published in the newspapers.[26] Once again, people's natural right to complain was endorsed by the CCP leaders on the basis of populism and republicanism.

Due to an unclear division of labor among local governments, many local officials refused to accept complaint cases passed down from the State Council. To solve this problem, both the General Office and the State Council determined that the General Office would ask Mao to decide where to transfer those cases involving national problems. The State Council would entertain letters or visits from intellectuals. Complaints against the corruption of local governments would be transferred to local Party committees. Complaints regarding civil and criminal cases should be sent to the court, regarding Party members to responsible Party committees, and regarding military personnel to the military committees (*junwei*). All other cases should go to relevant organs in the central government.

In 1952, the mounting number of people's letters and visits prompted the State Council and most provincial governments to expand existing complaint offices or establish new ones. Most counties at this time, however, still had no complaint office. Therefore, like their counterparts in the past, early PRC complainants had to skip levels and send complaints directly to the provincial or central government. Being fully aware of this problem, the State Council urged all county governments to establish complaint offices, to put a vice magistrate in charge, and to appoint special staff. According to Diao Jiecheng, after 1952 most counties established complaint offices with special staff.[27] In many counties, magistrates and Party secretaries also set aside time to meet with complainants.[28] The establishment of complaint offices at the local levels aimed to prevent direct complaints to the center. But many natural resisters continued to skip levels in lodging complaints in Beijing to leaders of the CCP—still treated as parental rulers and the ultimate authorities on earth.

From 1952 to 1957 the number of individual letters and visits rose steadily. The majority of them were about personal problems relating to work and study. Collective visits and letters and complaints directly to the center also increased in both number and scale.[29] Yang Shangkun, the head of the General Office of the CCP, complained in May 1957 about the mounting number of visits in Beijing. He wrote "At the gates of the Zhongnanhai, where many CCP leaders were living, and at the State Council, numerous people gather almost every day hoping to visit. Some of the groups have dozens of persons."[30]

Under the pressure of the soaring number of letters and visits, the General Office and the State Council jointly convoked the First State-wide Letter and Visit Conference. The conference reviewed problems with the complaint systems such as increasing numbers of letters and visits and bureaucratic disregard for people's problems. In his speech, Yang warned local officials about serious consequences if they continued to neglect people's complaints. The conference in the end reiterated that sending letters and paying visits were both democratic rights of the people and methods for people to supervise the CCP and the government. Given the secularist nature of the new government's ideology, it did not invoke any spiritual dimensions of the people's right to complain. But it seems highly likely that it took those dimensions into account in treating people's complaints with some seriousness. The bottom line was the government must investigate and resolve people's complaints. To avoid official retaliation against complainants, the conference stipulated that all charges and criticisms of officials should be transferred to the targets' superiors and not to the targets themselves.[31]

Apart from various policies made in response to the ever-changing complaint situation, the PRC created a system to supervise the management of people's letters and visits. On April 25, 1955, the annual major work plan of the Shanghai Supervisory Bureau (*Shanghai jianchajü*) stated that the bureau should not just deal carefully with people's accusations against lawbreaking officials, but also continue its work of "supervising the government's acceptance of citizens' letters and visits."[32] The bureau should oppose all government misconduct, such as arrogance, coercive orders, suppression of critics, retaliation against complaints, and unwillingness to listen to citizens' opinions and to respect citizens' rights, all violations of the law that would isolate the government from the masses.[33] In the early years of the PRC, the supervisory system relied heavily on people's complaints. According to Diao Jiecheng, 70 percent of the cases received by the people's supervisory system came from people's letters and visits.[34]

Why did the CCP establish a complaint system that differed from that of the GMD? What were the major motives underlying the CCP reform of its complaint systems? What was behind the increasing complaints after 1949?

I would argue that the primary purpose of the CCP to form a "new" complaint system was its revolutionary idealism based on the Marxist theory. According to Marxist theory, class struggle has persisted throughout human history. In the capitalist system, the class struggle is between the working class and the capitalists. When the working class, led by its vanguard of communists, takes over political power, it must overhaul the old capitalist system.[35] Since Marx developed his theory in the context of nineteenth-century English society, it was not immediately applicable to the Chinese situation in the twentieth century. In China, about 90 percent of the population was still living in the countryside. Accordingly, the Chinese communists drew on Lenin and others and adapted Marxist theory to Chinese conditions.[36] CCP leaders, many of them coming from the countryside, may have also inherited notions of social equality, *minben*, and monarchical thought (*diwang sixiang*) similar to that of earlier farmer rebels such as Chen Sheng (?–208 BCE) at the end of the Qin, Zhu Yuanzhang at the end of the Yuan, and Li Zicheng (1606–1645), at the end of the Ming. The great attention paid in PRC historiography to "peasant uprisings" in Chinese history would indicate as much.[37]

After the fall of the GMD on the mainland, the CCP, with broad popular support, moved to realize its ideal of establishing a New Democracy or a people's socialist state,[38] which would be superior to the previous Old Democratic or capitalist one. Unlike in the late republic, the master in the socialist PRC would be a coalition between the workers and farmers.[39] The 9CCP's commitment to the socialist ideology was akin to that of the GMD to Sun Yat-sen's Three-people's Principles. In the fall of 1956, Supreme Court justice Dong Biwu claimed that the people's democratic system in the PRC was the most democratic form of socialism in the world.[40]

To establish a socialist society, the CCP followed the Soviet model by creating agricultural cooperatives and reconstructing heavy industry.[41] To some extent, these socialist policies were consistent with deep-seated ideas of Confucian collectivism and monarchical paternalism. In a way, the Chinese people were supposed to become once again a big family with the CCP acting as the "parents" who would take care of their children, the common people. When people had problems, they tended to complain to their "parental rulers/officials" for help. For example, in the words of the governor of Anhui province in 1958, once the agricultural cooperatives were established, the farmers expected them to solve all of their problems.[42]

Although the CCP believed that the "fundamental interests" of the Party and of the masses were almost identical, it was inevitable that problems would occur between the leaders and the led. According to Mao's theory, contradictions among the people were normally non-antagonistic, unlike contradictions with the enemy (e.g., the GMD or its foreign supporters), which were typically antagonistic. In early 1957, facing increasing numbers of people's letters and visits, Mao called on the CCP to listen to people's complaints. He wrote: "if they (people) don't argue with us (the CCP) when they have grievances, whom can they argue with?"[43] This view was similar to the long-lived Confucian *minben* concept that people—the children—had the natural right to complain to their ruler—the self-claimed parent and representative of heaven and nature.[44]

In Mao's view the legal system was designed to exercise democratic centralism and to insure the dominance of the ruling class, in this case the alliance of workers, farmers, and intellectuals, over the rest of the population.[45] To address contradictions among the people, the CCP gradually developed a comprehensive and all-purpose complaint system. As Yang Shangkun remarked in 1957, 90 percent of people's letters and visits reflected internal contradictions among the people.[46] The reports of the Tianjin letters and visits conference in this period stated that the task of receiving people was crucial to settling such contradictions and would ultimately strengthen the tie between the Party and people.[47]

If the implementation of socialist institutions such as cooperatives (*hezuoshe*) stimulated many letters and visits, so too did the establishment of the legal system of the PRC. First, the CCP allowed people to complain to the Supreme Court if they were dissatisfied with local court decisions. Justice Dong Biwu noted that, in the first quarter of 1955, 90 percent of the complaints to the Supreme Court were related to the legal system and among them 60 percent were in opposition to court decisions.[48] Second, after the repudiation of most of the republican administrative court and complaint system, people in the PRC who thought their rights had been violated by officials had to complain to those same officials, in a way similar to that of many complainants in the past when officials had acted as judges and there had been no independent judiciary. This situation might also have contributed to the surging number of letters and visits to the government. Third, people with civil cases sometimes preferred to complain to the letters and visits offices rather than to sue through the courts, although the legal system did accept both civil and criminal cases.[49] In 1956, for example, two brothers in Zhuoxian, Hebei province, had their dispute over a piece of land settled by the county complaint office.[50]

As in preceding polities, the most popular means for people to voice their views were writing and visiting. People's letters could be reports and suggestions as well as complaints, but almost all visitors lodged complaints. According to Yang Shangkun, many complainants would first follow regular steps and write letters to the appropriate office. If no response was heard, some would "act" by complaining to the local government while others would, as natural resisters in the past, make skipping-level or direct complaints to the central government, especially the State Council and Zhongnanhai (i.e., the residence of the top leaders).[51] In Tianjin alone, 830 direct complaints were made to the central government in 1954, a much higher number than in 1953.[52]

Like many predecessors who believed in the paternal responsibility of the ruler, some PRC complainants wrote letters directly to Mao. Elizabeth Perry reports that in 1952 some aggrieved workers from Shanghai's Dadong Tobacco Factory complained directly to Beijing [Mao] after the factory's operation was suspended due to insufficient business. It was mostly because of Mao's intervention that Dadong factory soon reopened and the complainants resumed their jobs.[53] In May 1955, Tan Shiying, Mao's classmate in primary school, complained directly to Mao that his citizenship had been revoked simply because he had worked five years in the GMD government at Shaoyang city, Hunan province. Upon receiving this letter, Mao wrote the Party committee of Xiangxiang special district regarding Tan's issue. Most likely because of Mao's letter, the committee reported to Mao within twenty days, but it insisted that Tan's punishment had been correct. Mao then wrote to Tan giving his personal endorsement of the ruling by the Xiangxiang Party committee. Although Mao showed little sympathy for his old classmate, his inquiry quite possibly accelerated the investigation.[54]

After an enormous demobilization of military veterans in the 1950s that was said to be "unprecedented in Chinese history," many veterans also lodged complaints with the government. As Neil J. Diamant has shown, many of them either went to Beijing or wrote directly to Mao asking to be allowed to stay in the big cities rather than being sent to their original homes in the countryside.[55] In such cases, confidence in their natural right to resist government policies at odds with their welfare took precedence over any natural tendency to gravitate to their old hometowns (*laojia*), the loci of their ancestral spirits.

The newspapers in the early years of the PRC lacked independence, but seemed to have played a more important role reporting people's grievances than their predecessors had during the republic.[56] One possible reason is that there was no relatively independent administrative court or the opportunity for public protest against the government in the early period of the PRC. In 1951 the State Council ordered all government officials to respond to people's criticisms published in the newspapers and it also encouraged people to write to newspapers concerning their complaints.[57] To deal with people's complaints and inform Party leaders about popular opinion, many newspapers created Mass Work Departments, which in Ben Liebman's words, served as official ombudsman.[58] As a result, influential newspapers like the *China Youth Daily* created a column of "Readers' Letters" where people could voice their grievances against local officials among other things. The papers reported complaints originating in "lingering feudal thinking (*fengjian canyu sixiang*)" and charges against officials who allegedly broke the law.[59]

In a few cases, newspaper reports were actually fairly effective in pressuring local government officials to take actions. On March 31, 1953, the *China Youth Daily* published a letter of complaint about a torture case. After a primary school teacher named Han Xijie in Nong'an county, Jilin, had criticized Liu Chang'an, a former head of the school education department, during the Three-Antis movement in May 1952, Liu took revenge by encouraging some students to charge Han with raping a student. Liu also detained and interrogated Han without any legal authority, allegedly holding him in a dark room for forty-five days. Although the county court found that the student who had allegedly been raped by Han had committed perjury, the county education department still fired Han and the county youth league deprived Han of his membership. The letter of complaint ended up with a strong demand that the government renew the investigation of this case and apologize. The upshot of this case was not available, but the press role in airing it was clear.[60]

From 1949 to 1956, the CCP gradually developed full-scale and complicated complaint systems in line with its revolutionary idealism and efforts to maintain a close relationship with the people. Undoubtedly, many people found their grievances addressed in this period. According to a later Tianjin government report, between 1953 and 1955, more than 90 percent of the complaint cases had been "solved."[61] Another government report from Huangxian county, Shandong, shows that from 1953 to 1957, its magistrate met people twice a month and clearly expressed his opinion on each case he dealt with. In three years, the county had made eighty-four receptions to complaints and the total number of complainants was 2658. Among those complaints, 1590 had reportedly been solved. The percentage of supposedly solved cases was almost sixty. Although we lack information on the full meaning of "solved" in these cases, this percentage would suggest a fairly high level of effectiveness at least from the government's viewpoint.[62]

However, as in the base period, the political campaigns in the early 1950s also caused many innocent people to suffer. Scholars' accounts in both China and the West estimate that millions of persons were reportedly executed in the Land-Reform and Counter-Revolutionary movements and at least several hundred thousand lives were lost in the Three-and-Five-Antis movements.[63] Among them, many, if not most, were innocent or at least were killed without benefit of fair trials. To the extent that the judicial system was used at all, it was flawed. By one account, it was the worst among socialist countries.[64] The system itself therefore resulted in numerous grievances. Supreme Court justice Dong Biwu in an internal report admitted in 1953 that the problems of false arrests, detainments, judgments, executions, and torture were very serious and prevalent. Some 350,000 cases had failed to be resolved. Two years later, Dong acknowledged that the problem of torture was still quite serious.[65]

The era of political turbulence (1957–1976)

From 1957 to 1976 Mao and his supporters led the People's Republic into a turbulent period. Driven by the fever of revolutionary idealism and the theory of permanent revolution,[66] Mao launched several major movements such as the Great Leap Forward, the Four Clean-ups, and especially the Cultural Revolution in an effort to clear the path to socialism.[67] Due to different political goals at different times, the complaint system saw big ups and downs in this period.

After the 1957 crackdown on the "rightists," the number of letters and visits received by the central government sharply declined.[68] But the number of anonymous letters increased, especially at the local level. Diao Jiecheng explains that the main causes of these sometimes conflicting data include: first, almost all county government established special complaint offices after 1957 so that people could lodge their complaints locally; second, many local governments set up social welfare units to help people solve their basic problems, thus reducing the number of grievances taken to the capital; third, many local leaders during the Great Leap Forward prohibited people from taking complaints to the capital; fourth, people were scared by the suppression of the rightists, many of whom had criticized the CCP in a sincere effort to improve its governance; finally, some local governments were indifferent to people's complaints, making efforts to voice them seem futile if not counterproductive.[69] Among these causes of fewer complaints, the Anti-Rightist movement seems to have been the most important. According to Li Rui, Mao's former secretary, some 500,000 people, nearly one-tenth of the estimated five million intellectuals in China, had been labeled rightists in 1957 merely because of their verbal criticisms or non-socialist opinions. Many of them had been sent to work in the labor brigades (*laodongdui*), which, in the words of Gu Zhun, a famous intellectual in the PRC who was labeled as a rightist at this time, were virtual concentration camps (*jizhongying*).[70] As most letters and visits were more or less related to the government, or were at least easily deemed to be so, people became very careful because voicing even a slight criticism risked incurring the label anti-socialist and being sent to a labor camp.

In one case, when the higher administration passed down to a county government an anonymous letter that disclosed that many of the county's residents had died because of a shortage of food, the Party committee of the county immediately ordered the police to find out who the writer was. The police investigated 300 persons before it finally found a woman working in a bank. The county Party secretary then instructed the police to punish the woman in the same way as they did counterrevolutionaries.[71] If an anonymous letter could cause so serious a consequence, how would people dare to write public letters of complaint using their real names or pay visits to the government? The result was often "political diglossia," in which people would pay lipservice to the official rhetoric in public while concealing their complaints until the time appeared to be more propitious for outbursts.[72]

Assuming that the decline in the number of people's letters and visits was caused by local bureaucratism, the State Council issued an order on November 19, 1957 that any official negligence in dealing with people's letters was incompatible with the spirit of the ongoing Rectification Movement (*zhengfeng yundong*). The order demanded that all levels of the government have a leader whose principal task was receiving people's letters and visits. In some cases, the relevant Party leader should personally address people's letters, receive people's visits, and even settle their cases.[73]

In February 1961, President Liu Shaoqi warned against official retaliation against complainants. One year later, Premier Zhou Enlai criticized some local governments for having paid little attention to people's criticisms and suggestions conveyed through letters and visits and for having shown insufficient respect for people's democratic rights. Probably because of such top-level criticisms of official misconduct in the lower ranks, the number of people's letters and especially visits started to climb again at both central and local levels.[74]

To ensure that central government organs took people's visits seriously, on August 10, 1963 both the General Office and the State Council promulgated several regulations. They stipulated that all central government organs should accept and expedite action on people's problems transferred to them by the General Office, the State Council, and the general office of the People's Congress. The regulations also classified people's problems into ten categories, each of which was specifically assigned to a different organ.[75] At about the same time, the State Council stipulated work methods for archiving people's letters and visits regarding eleven major issues. Thus, on paper at least, the PRC complaint system became more systematic.[76] A month later, both Liu Shaoqi and Zhou Enlai ordered all central and provincial governments to designate one leader charged with passing people's complaints along to the relevant organs to deal with. In general, provincial governments should solve more cases themselves and pass fewer down to subordinates. Since 80 percent of letters and visits were about local (sub-county) problems, county governments were ordered to solve most of them.[77]

Pursuant to the announcement, the State Council on October 5, 1963 promulgated its most significant regulation in this period, the Working Regulations for State Organs to Deal with People's Letters and Visits. In the preamble, the document justified people's right to complain as one of their democratic rights that enabled them to join in the political process and to supervise state organs. The regulations stated that all government organs should listen carefully to people's voices, correct people's mistakes, help them solve problems, and peacefully resolve their internal contradictions. Only after following all these measures, the regulation pointed out, could the CCP spark people's ardor, strengthen people's democratic central authority, and achieve both socialist revolution and development. The regulations required all provincial governments to establish a complaint office and all county level governments to establish a complaint office or appoint specific staff to deal with complaints. In a section called "solutions" the regulations indicated that both central and provincial governments should directly resolve problems passed down from their superiors or sent up by their inferiors. The county government, however, should in general directly solve problems shown in people's letters and visits and not pass them down to the communes.[78] Though these regulations failed to become a formal law, they laid the foundation for future complaint regulations after the Cultural Revolution.

In March 1966, the central government issued an order reiterating that county government officials should regularly meet people in the subordinate communes and make such visits a regular institution. Although the order stated that its purpose was to make complaining more convenient for farmers and to demonstrate that government officials were the people's actual servants, its more important goal was probably to reduce the number of farmers complaining to the upper-levels of government.[79]

During the Cultural Revolution, no more laws regulating complaints were promulgated. But, contrary to some accounts,[80] the system remained in place and people continued to make complaints throughout this turbulent period.[81] The number of people's letters and visits to the State Council declined to less than 10,000 a month between 1967 and the fall of 1971 when Lin Biao, the vice chairman and heir apparent to Mao, was in power. After Lin attempted to assassinate Mao and died in a plane crash while trying to flee China, the number of complaints climbed sharply again. The ranks of complainants were swelled by those who had been attacked by Lin Biao and his followers and who now saw a chance of having their grievances heard. In 1971 the number of letters and visits reached 130,000 and from 1972 to 1975, the number received by the State Council alone was more than 280,000. Among them, most were related to grievances caused by political movements such as the 1962 Four Clean-ups and the Cultural Revolution.[82]

Shortly after the beginning of the Cultural Revolution (1966–1976), many leaders of mass organizations sent letters directly to Zhou Enlai. Being dissatisfied with the slow speed in managing those letters, Zhou demanded a better solution. In 1968 the State Council, formed the "Unit to Manage Letters to the Premier (*zongli qinqixin xiaozu*)." It was charged with dealing correctly and secretly with politically charged letters. The unit, which lasted until 1972, annually received more than 10,000 letters.[83]

In this period of turbulence between 1957 and 1976, the most popular means of registering complaints were still letters and visits. But some complainants, as desperate natural resisters had often done in the past, resorted to unlawful methods such as blocking the vehicles of Party leaders or lofting their complaints high outside government offices.[84] Despite the heightened political tensions of the Cultural Revoltion, collective complaints continued to be practiced by many complainants. On April 15, 1974, two years before Mao's death and the end of the Cultrual Revoltuion, more than eighty former military veterans working for the Wuhan Steel Company flocked to the Labor Bureau of the Hubei Revolutionary Committee (*Hubeisheng Geming weiyuanhui laodongjü*), demanding the return of their additional wages (*fujia gongzi*) between 1968 and 1971. After the committee rejected their demands, those complainants began using force to attack officials of the committee and threatened that they would come back if their requests could not be satisfied.[85]

A big change from the early years of the PRC was in newspaper reports. Unlike in the years before 1957, newspapers in this period lost their limited power to help redress people's grievances. Particularly in the Cultural Revolution, major newspapers were under tighter control by the Cultural Revolution Small Group that dominated the Party Central and their content consisted mainly of political propaganda.

The complaint systems per se, however, also became a weapon in the political struggles of the Cultural Revolution. The group later named the "Gang of Four" (Jiang Qing, Yao Wenyuan, Zhang Chunqiao, and Wang Hongwen) and their followers used a variation on the complaint system for their own political purposes. At the inception of the Cultural Revolution, the Shanghai worker Wang Hongwen, opposed the factory managers for their allegedly loose grasp of class struggle, their practice of Soviet-style revisionism, and their ignoring of mass opinions. Wang soon led his fellow workers of Shanghai's No. 17 Textile Mill, along with other followers, to "venture north to plead their case directly to the Party Central."[86] The "Gang of Four" were also subsequently accused of secretly establishing complaint offices and meddling with the work of the General Office in an attempt to "control people's letters to Mao and the Party Central."[87] In addition, the "Gang of Four" attacked the existing complaint office as "a base for capitalists" and encouraged their own followers to write "black letters" against certain Party leaders who were at odds with Mao.[88]

The period between 1957 and 1976 was the peak of revolutionary idealism, which saw millions of people, including numerous innocent ones, arbitrarily arrested, tortured, sent to the labor camps, or killed.[89] Some people were attacked or tortured to death simply because they had said something "wrong,"[90] while others were killed after complaining to Mao against corrupt local Party heads.[91] In the Cultural Revolution, according to Mao's secretary Li Rui, "grievances existed everywhere. From the President of the state to marshals, no one could be exempted."[92] If even the current President Liu could not protect himself, who else could?

It seems that, between 1957 and 1976, many complainants continued to regard Mao as a "living god" and ruling elites as parental officials, but the largely secular and ideologically charged CCP, unlike many if not most previous rulers, no longer feared that unredressed grievances would result in any punishments from heaven and nature. Absent this crucial belief that had long underlain natural resistance, the complaint systems in this period became even more than ever before tools of the dominant, albeit severely fractured, leadership. The CCP continued to allow complaints on certain issues, but the satisfaction of such complainants and the redress of grievances during political campaigns were increasingly subject to arbitrary decisions of shifting wielders of power.

In a talk in 1978, Hu Yaobang, head of the CCP Organization Department (*zuzhibu*), listed several big grievances in the Cultural Revolution. For example, in Qiuxian county, Hebei, the total population was 120,000. But after someone charged the county with the creation of a "new GMD," thousands of people were labeled as GMD members. In the ensuing warfare, dozens died, thousands were injured and jailed, and over 10,000 were driven from the county.[93] Dai Huang, a senior reporter of the Xinhua news agency and a critic of the Cultural Revolution, gave a daunting figure for the total number of people assaulted in the

Cultural Revolution. "How many people were wronged in the Cultural Revolution?" Dai asked. His answer was: "people labeled landlords, rich farmers, counterrevolutionaries, bad persons, and rightists were about 30 million. If their relatives and friends are counted, the number would be at least 200 million."[94]

As in the early 1950s, the judiciary itself created many grievances before it was abandoned in the Cultural Revolution.[95] At the beginning of the Hundred Flowers Movement in 1957, legal scholars and "rightists" Yang Zhaolong and Wang Zaoshi claimed that, in a period roughly between 1950 and 1957, the percentage of criminal cases that involved false arrests, detainments, and judgments was as high as 34 percent.[96]

To be sure, despite this generally bleak picture, the period between 1957 and 1976 also witnessed some cases of efficacy in the functioning of the complaint systems. For example, in 1973, Li Qinglin, a farmer in Putian, Fujian, like former natural resisters, sent a complaint letter directly to Mao, the contemporary Red Sun comparable to earlier "sons of heaven" in the dynasties. Li complained that his eldest son, a sent-down youth, could not find a job and had to rely on his father for support. Shortly after Mao received Li's letter, he sent him 300 yuan along with a personal letter. More importantly, Mao ordered the politburo to respond quickly to provide sent-down youth in the countryside with financial relief.[97]

Some government organs in this period also seriously settled people's grievances. According to a report of the Party committee of Mingshui county, Heilongjiang, after a new Party committee was established in 1970, it emphasized people's letters and visits by creating an office and selecting four able cadres to work there. The complaint system was also reportedly effective in a commune called Shuren. In 1970, for instance, the commune received 232 visits and twenty-three letters and resolved almost all of them, According to a report, only five farmers in the commune remained unsatisfied and complained to the county government.[98] Although a Tianjin government report claimed that many complainants were attacked or forbidden to lodge complaints in the Cultural Revolution, the city in 1975 managed to solve 329 out of 385 complaint cases, which, if true, was quite high.[99]

The post-Cultural-Revolution period (1977–1982)

After the Cultural Revolution and specifically in 1978, many of the returned or new top leaders, such as Deng Xiaoping, Hu Yaobang, and Peng Zhen who had been assailed in the Cultural Revolution, repudiated Mao's revolutionary idealism that had brought chaos to the country and hardship to themselves. Leaders like Deng Xiaoping, a pragmatist, were determined to restore political stability and focus on economic development in China. Despite his hesitation to discredit Mao, Deng was highly critical of Mao's policies that were responsible for "the most severe setback and the heaviest losses suffered by the party, the state, and the people since the founding of the PRC."[100] Under the new policies, both central and local governments saw a surge of complaints.[101] Although few regulations or orders about the complaint system were passed, the government made many concrete efforts to redress complainants' grievances.

Seeing a prospect of satisfying the grievances caused by political movements, tens of millions of people, including many former leaders, wrote letters to or visited both central and local governments instead of resorting to the formal legal system that was considered to be an improper venue for political rehabilitation. The State Council alone received 130,000 letters in 1976, 510,000 in 1978, and 570,000 in 1979, which was a historical record. Local governments such as Shandong in 1978 and Tianjin in 1979 also received a record number of complaints, five or six times as many as in 1977.[102] According to Party Secretary Hu Yaobang, 70 percent of those letters and visits asked for rehabilitation of personal grievances and false punishments caused by the "Gang of Four" and other political movements, 20 percent were against official violations of the law, and the remaining 10 percent were suggestions on policy. Hu praised the increase of the letters and visits and argued that it reflected "a new height of people's consciousness and the recovery of the normal democratic life of the CCP."[103] Hu then launched a massive rehabilitation campaign to review and correct about 20 million cases of those who had been persecuted, convicted, and penalized in the past decades. Eventually, millions of them were in fact rehabilitated.[104]

To strengthen their authority in the wake of the arrest of the "Gang of Four," the new leaders endeavored to win public support. They not only allowed but also encouraged people to complain against personnel and policies inherited from the Cultural Revolution. Hua Guofeng, Mao's hand-picked successor, emphasized in early 1978 that the government should pay serious attention to people's letters and visits, never suppress people's opinions, and never take revenge on people who made criticisms.[105] Minister of the Public Security Ministry Zhao Cangbi also stated that both the constitution and the CCP charter gave people the right to make direct complaints to as high as Chairman Hua and the Party Central.[106]

At the end of 1978, a political earthquake took place at the top. Deng Xiaoping and his followers condemned Hua Guofeng's policies of "Two Whatevers" (*liangge fanshi*) (whatever Mao's directives, whatever Mao's policies) in the Third Plenary Session of 1978 and hammered out the Open policy. This historical conference also had a tremendous impact on the legal system. As Albert H. Y. Chen remarks, many law-related subjects which had been "forbidden zones" could now be freely discussed and debated.[107] Although the Third Plenary did not mention the rule of law, it focused on the need to construct a socialist legal system and to recognize the equality of all before the law.[108] Since 1978, numerous laws had been enacted or restored.

Similarly, the complaint systems also underwent telling changes after the Third Plenary. In the interest of reform, the Third Plenary further strengthened people's right to complain by encouraging people to make direct complaints to superiors against official misbehavior. In 1982, an official document blamed Hua's wrong political line of the "Two Whatevers" for hindering the solution of people's complaints.[109] The result was a flood of complaints that threatened to overwhelm the existing complaint systems. On January 26, 1979, the Central Disciplinary Committee (*zhongyang jilü jiancha weiyuanhui*) instructed all levels of government to speed up the processing of people's complaints. It ordered leaders at all levels to heed important letters and visits, to protect complainants from retribution, and to punish officials who retaliated against their accusers.[110]

The next day, a *People's Daily* editorial reiterated that attentively resolving people's letters and visits was one of the CCP's critical tasks, providing all levels of governments with an important way to communicate with the people. It argued that the skyrocketing number of complaints was mainly in reaction against the abuses of the "Gang of Four," but it also acknowledged that the irresponsibility of some current government leaders also precipitated some of the complaints. Regarding the mounting direct complaints to the central government, the editorial stated that the relevant officials should never reject them outright but should, on the contrary, patiently listen to their grievances. Invoking the old model Judge Bao (*Baogong*) of the Song dynasty, the editorial called on both capital officials and local officials to become the people's "Blue Sky" (*qingtian*), the Confucian term meaning honest officials.[111] Right after the publication of the central order and especially of the editorial, the number of complaints soared. According to Diao Jiecheng, in 1979 there were three "climaxes" of complaints, each lasting about one month during which 1200 complainants arrived in Beijing everyday.[112]

Obviously, neither the order nor the editorial improved the situation very much, because in late August 1979 the central government sent more than 1000 cadres selected from various central organs to supervise the complaint work at the local level. The new unit, soon known as the "Investigating Organization of One Thousand Cadres" worked for five months and reportedly handled many cases so well as to "put a stop to the mass skipping complaints." According to statistics drawn from ten provinces, the organization had successfully resolved 820,000 cases, 78 percent of the total number.[113]

Realizing that it was impossible to satisfy all the grievances caused by decades of political movements, the *People's Daily* editorialized on October 22, 1979 that many problems left over from history would have to wait for future resolution. But the editorial demanded that all levels of government deal strictly with current officials whose actions were resulting in new grievances. At the same time, the editorial asked all levels of government to explain "patiently" to complainants that current "economic difficulties" might impede quick solutions in some cases.[114]

Most complainants in this period announced their grievances in letters and visits to official organs. Some, however, like their counterparts before 1957, wrote letters of complaint to national newspapers. Renowned newspapers such as the *People's Daily* and the *China Youth Daily* restored the popular columns of "Readers' Letters" used in the early 1950s for people to complain.[115] By publicizing citizens' grievances, major newspapers could also exert some pressure on officials who violated people's rights, particularly at the lower levels.

On April 24, 1979, for instance, farmer Yang Chunting wrote a letter of complaint to the *People's Daily*. In 1978, after a drought had damaged most of the cotton in their fields, farmers in Jiaxiang county, Shandong, tried to recover their losses by planting 400 *mu* of sesames. But a local official named Liu Changcai said that the planting of sesame on that land had reduced the production of cotton. Liu ordered the farmers to cut down all the sesame plants. As the farmers refused to do so, Liu asked some students to cut the sesames down, resulting in a loss of 20,000 *yuan* for the farmers. Although enraged, farmers acknowledged to Liu that "we can do nothing because you have the power." Liu retorted arrogantly: "I know you can do nothing. You can complain to the upper-level government. But wherever you complain, I am not afraid." The Jining prefectural Party committee, superior to Jiaxiang, ordered the county government to severely punish Liu. But "owing to the protection of some officials in Jiaxiang," Liu never made any self-criticism to the farmers. Indeed, what made the farmers even angrier was that Liu even got a promotion at this time.

The editor of the *People's Daily* remarked that the content of the letter of complaint had been verified by the local government. Very likely because the *People's Daily* was the most influential daily in the PRC, the Party committee of Jiaxiang responded quickly to the daily's inquiry regarding the complaint. The committee admitted that Yang Chunting's complaint was generally correct. But, according to the committee, the case had already been resolved the previous year when Liu had received a "disciplinary punishment within the Party." Even if true, this light punishment might have been insufficient for the victims. But, the letter of complaint at least brought the case of official abuse to public notice and served as a warning to other petty officials tempted to abuse the common people.[116]

Despite some successful complaints, many other letters of complaint to the newspapers in this period elicited neither the editor's comments nor any official action. On June 7, 1979, a person from Xishui county, Hubei province who was working in the army complained to the *China Youth Daily* about two officials who had forced his sister to commit suicide. In this case, one official named Yan Heli reportedly put pressure on the complainant's sister, Zhan Xiaohong, to marry his son. After she refused his request, Yan joined with another official to try to coerce Zhan into giving in. In response, Zhan killed herself. In this case, there was no follow-up report by the editor or any official response to the news.[117]

There is no denying that, with some pragmatic leaders at the top, many people in the first several years after the fall of the "Gang of Four" had their grievances, mostly caused by the past political movements, satisfied. According to a document of the Third State-wide Complaint Conference held in February 1982, in the fall of 1979 both central and local governments had set up a "Letters and Visits Leadership Organizations (*xinfang lingdao xiaozu*)," aiming to improve the complaint systems. Between 1979 and 1981, the government had reportedly solved about eight million complaints. As a result, the complaints received by the Party Central and the State Council dropped 20 percent and 50 percent respectively from 1979 to 1981.[118] In Tianjin, it was said to be unprecedented that all the Party organs had collectively dealt with people's complaints and had solved most old and fresh complaints by early 1980.[119]

However promising the situation for some complainants, many other people found their grievances unaddressed. In 1978 Wang Dongxing, head of the State Council, conceived it as "very serious" and "totally the style of the Guomindang" that many officials had taken revenge on complainants and, in some cases, had caused deaths. In the beginning, the central government simply attributed official negligence regarding people's grievances to the influence of the "Gang of Four."[120] After the Third Plenary confirmed the new leadership of the Party, however, the complaint system still made little progress in effectively addressing cases. Although the One Thousand Cadres investigation sent by the central government in 1979 had satisfied many grievances, complaints to the central organs increased soon afterwards and numerous historical grievances still existed.[121] Only then did the leaders begin to realize that the obstacles to settling complaints were rooted in the political system and would not disappear along with the leadership of the "Gang of Four." In 1982, the new General Secretary Hu Yaobang warned fellow Party members that, historical grievances that remained unresolved for more than five years after the fall of the "Gang of Four," would cause people to shift their dissatisfaction from the "Gang of Four" to the current Party leadership.[122]

Even as an enormous number of historical grievances remained unaddressed, some officials in this period were busy creating many new grievances. Some of them were publicized in the newspaper columns "Readers' Letters." Others were reported in the major newspapers working on their own. For example, in January 1979, *The People's Daily* published a case in which a city Party secretary carelessly wrote "eight" instead of "seven" in a court decision meting out a criminal's years of sentence. When the court pointed out the mistake to the secretary, he said "I cannot correct what I have written, let's just sentence him for eight years." Because the decision had been made by the highest official in the city, there was little chance for the victim to rectify the injustice.[123]

In this period, the role of major newspapers in helping people satisfy their grievances was also limited. Not only was the number of published complaints quite small, but complaints against higher-ranking officials, from the provincial level on up, were almost non-existent. Reporters in charge of encouraging and managing the "Readers' Letters" were "sometimes harassed, slandered, or even beaten in the process of carrying out their duties to investigate." Such conditions intimidated many reporters and reduced the significance of their columns.[124] Some published letters of complaint failed to gain government attention. To cite one report, on November 24, 1979, an official working in the propaganda department of Shaoyang city, Hunan, wrote to *The People's Daily* complaining that most readers' letters had not drawn much attention from the government organs that were responsible. "Most readers' letters fail to be heeded by certain units, except those reprimanding letters that focus specifically on certain government organs," the official argued, "Some of our government [officials] still pay no attention to people's criticisms in the newspapers."[125]

Revolutionary idealism unraveled

In reviewing the history of complaints from 1950 to the early 1980s, a tumultuous era, we have found that, while numerous complaints were successfully addressed, many more grievances resulting from political campaigns, arbitrary judges, and irresponsible officials were never resolved. As in previous periods, there were several fundamental reasons for the limited success of the existing complaint system.

Revolutionary idealism

Without doubt, Mao and some other top CCP leaders were the driving forces behind the revolutionary idealism that produced perhaps millions of grievances in the early PRC. Driven by his idealism, romanticism, charisma, power, despotism, and possibly his neurasthenia,[126] as well as by the domestic and foreign political conditions, Mao and his cohorts repeatedly adopted radical measures to realize socialism in China and fought fiercely to smash any obstructions in their path. In 1950, in the context of the GMD survival on Taiwan as a result of the Korean War, Mao led the Party in launching a crackdown on counterrevolutionaries. Although Mao ordered his subordinates to avoid any wrongful arrests and killings,[127] many officials at lower levels apparently neglected the order. Consequently, many people were wrongly punished or even killed. In the spring of 1957, in the context of public opposition to socialist states in China and in Eastern Europe, Mao encouraged scholars and people to criticize the mistakes of the CCP. When criticism touched on the basic legitimacy of the PRC, however, Mao and other party leaders changed course and mounted a campaign against rightists who were depicted as enemies of socialism. Consequently, about half a million people were labeled as "rightists" and many of them were sent to labor camps and died with their grievances unaddressed.[128]

After the Great Leap Forward (1958) suffered a serious setback, Liu Shaoqi and Deng Xiaoping moved to the front, attempting to reform the economy by providing farmers with some monetary stimulation that inevitably caused social inequality. Mao, however, fearing a revival of capitalism in China, insisted on launching the Four Clean-ups in 1962, which was in fact an educational movement to maintain socialism in the countryside. As in former movements, the Four Clean-ups falsely punished many innocent people including officials opposed simply to Mao's approach to attaining socialism.[129]

Believing that Liu Shaoqi was determined to follow the capitalist road, Mao in 1966, supported by defense minister Lin Biao and the so-called "Gang of Four," initiated the Cultural Revolution. Scholars in China and abroad today concur that Mao's motives in launching the Cultural Revolution included the prevention of revisionism as well as a quest for a power, among other things.[130] Whatever the multiple causes of the violence of the Cultural Revolution, which included efforts to deal with the American war in Vietnam and a Russian military build-up on the northern frontier, millions of civilians were attacked and many of them died along with their grievances.[131]

CCP's violations of the law

Another reason behind the limited efficacy of the early PRC complaint systems stemmed from the nature of the CCP itself. As in the late republican period, many CCP leaders in both central and local governments routinely violated the law and undermined the fledgling independent judicial system inherited from the early republic. The root of this problem arguably lay in the Leninist party-state tradition that endowed many Party leaders with nearly absolute power.[132] One Western scholar even argues that Mao's China was governed by decrees and regulations rather than by laws.[133] Although Mao himself was said not to like different ideas,[134] he seemed to have been aware of this problem. In 1962, he blamed some leaders for being unwilling to listen to different opinions and to accept criticism.[135] Nevertheless, from Wang Shiwei to Gu Zhun, from Peng Dehuai to Liu Shaoqi, scholars and even top officials who were assailed under Mao's regime generally died without satisfying their grievances.[136] In this period and in the case of such prominent people, the general concern to avoid having people die without having their grievances addressed seems to have been largely attenuated.

Following Mao's example, many lower-ranked cadres of the PRC regularly violated the law without giving it much thought. In 1954, Peng Zhen, the head of the Central Political and Legal Unit (*zhongyang zhengfa xiaozu*), denounced some officials' views that "big figures" and "big officials" did not need to follow the law.[137] One year later, Supreme Court justice Dong Biwu also accused some officials of disregarding both state laws and regulations.[138]

Several years after the end of the Cultural Revolution, many die-hard leaders continued to ignore the law, making it difficult to address old grievances and creating new ones. In September 1979, acknowledging that it was shameful to see so many complainants three years after the downfall of the "Gang of Four," *The People's Daily* harshly denounced some upper-level leaders for their unwillingness to address—let alone satisfy—people's grievances.[139] Once again, we would need to know more about the political context of these charges to understand their historical significance. But the common urge to avoid the consequences of people dying without having their grievances addressed seems to remain in evidence.

Bureaucratism

A third reason for the limited value of the complaint system was bureaucratism, a long-standing problem and a variant of government corruption in China and elsewhere. Before it took power in 1949, the CCP was generally in harmony with the masses in the base areas because it needed people's support. The situation changed soon after the establishment of the PRC. Under the rule of one party that controlled the state and the military, the CCP enjoyed a high degree of centralized authority. Many, if not most, officials thought that they no longer needed to woo mass support. As Xi Zhongxun, the head of the secretariat of the

State Council, remarked in 1957, after their living and working conditions had changed since the revolutionary victory, many CCP leaders had distanced themselves from the masses and cared less about people's complaints.[140]

In April 1951, a man surnamed Han from Shandong province skipped the regular levels and complained directly to the State Council, saying that a group of bad people had taken his family property and tortured him because he insisted on the "right principles." The State Council immediately passed the case down to the county where Han lived. After two months, no one had investigated the case. It was only after the State Council urged the county government three more times to act that it turned the case over to the county court. But the court judged that the defender (an allegedly bad person by Han) was innocent. Han had to complaint again to the State Council. It was not until September 1952 that the Shandong provincial government, under direct pressure from the State Council, finally ruled that Han's complaint was valid. Although Han finally satisfied his grievances, it had taken him fifteen months, four laborious complaints to Beijing, and no less than fifteen interventions with the county government and court to succeed.[141] The resolution of grievances could come at a very high price.

In this case, the bureaucratic irresponsibility and possible corruption combined to make Han suffer physically, psychologically, and monetarily. Clearly, without intolerable grievances and a firm belief in the central organ and natural principles, Han would not have complained so long and so strenuously. His experience was actually no less painful than those complainants in the post-Tang dynasties who had cut their flesh or jumped into the moat in the capital. Even so, Han was still lucky if compared with those earlier complainants who obtained no central backing and had to endure punishment for their natural resistance.

Bureaucratism was ostensibly one of the major targets of the Cultural Revolution.[142] But after Mao's death, bureaucratism and the attendant routine neglect of people's complaints persisted and became worse. In September 1978, Zhao Cangbi, Minister of Public Security, condemned some government leaders who had adopted a bureaucratic attitude toward people's letters and had expressed little concern for people's grievances.[143] Three months later, *The People's Daily* in an editorial talked about a case in which a victim failed to solve his or her problem after having gone to a dozen places and filled out more than 100 complaint forms.[144]

Bureaucratism was largely inherited from the past but aspects of the new government's ideology also inhibited any radical solution to the problem. On February 27, 1957, Mao argued that bureaucratism of some officials should be treated as an internal contradiction among the people and thus should be addressed in a democratic and not forceful way.[145] This justification although theoretically defensible actually made the reduction of bureaucratism more difficult to achieve.

After Deng and his followers regained power after the fall of the "Gang of Four," they took steps to reverse the harsh Maoist policies toward cadres including those who had manifested bureaucratism before and during the Cultural Revolution. On February 7, 1981, a *China Youth Daily* article denied the existence of a "bureaucratic class" in contemporary China. While the article admitted that it was legitimate to oppose bureaucratism due to the corruption of some officials, it recalled the history of the Cultural Revolution, arguing that many good officials had been severely punished under the charge of belonging to a bureaucratic class.[146] In this case, as in some others, a strong reaction against the abuses of the Cultural Revolution was used to justify an end to some of its more democratic impulses.

With such persisting protection from the top, many officials would feel bolder to commit bureacratism and to ignore people's grievances.

Judicial problems

The judicial system in the early PRC was separate from the letters and visits system.[147] Unlike the letters and visits system that was first designed to deal with the non-antagonistic contradictions between the people and the CCP, the PRC judicial system was a powerful weapon of the dominant class (the proletariat and farmers) against antagonistic class enemies (capitalists). With greater power and distance from the population, it was even more liable to becoming a major source of people's grievances.

Shortly after its birth, the PRC began overhauling the judicial system inherited from the republic. As early as in March 1949, Supreme Court justice Dong Biwu denounced all "anti-people" laws of the GMD. He called on all officials and particularly judicial workers to learn the legal thought of Marx, Lenin, and Mao Zedong and infuse a revolutionary spirit [into the law].[148] In September 1951, Dong stressed that the courts should be used to protect the people's democratic centralization.[149] During the Anti-Rightist movement, Wei Ming, a judge of the Shanghai court, remarked that the law should only serve the CCP and the proletariat. Those people who were punished because they advocated views at odds with socialism had no right to ask for legal protection.[150]

Despite this assault on the old republican judicial system, the early PRC actually relied at first on many former republican judicial personnel who strongly believed in the ideal of judicial independence and valued judicial expertise.[151] In 1952, when some of those judges were not strict enough in dealing with counterrevolutionaries, Dong Biwu decided to remove them from the legal system. He replaced them with progressive workers, farmers, and veterans, most of whom had little training in—or knowledge about—the law.[152] The criterion for selecting judges was henceforth to be unabashedly political. As Shi Liang, the head of the Judiciary Ministry, argued in 1952, any person who proved to be politically steadfast during the ongoing Three-Antis-and-Five-Antis movement could become judges.[153]

While ideas such as judicial independence were condemned in the early 1950s, the PRC judiciary still demanded that judges make their decisions based on the law. For example, The Interim Procedure for People's Courts to Deal with Cases, which was promulgated by the Fuzhou people's court in 1952, required all judges to make decisions based on hard evidence and not on confessions or assumptions.[154]

During the course of the Anti-Rightist movement, however, the residual independence of the judicial system from politics faded away. In October 1957, Peng Zhen, head of the Central Secretariat who supported equality before the law but also subordination of the law to CCP policies,[155] ordered all courts to report to the Party secretary before making final judgments.[156]

As a tool of the ruling Party, the judiciary would rarely challenge the government, especially in politically charged cases. In late 1957, a county court judge issued opinions on nine death-penalty cases. Among them, he felt confident about the guilt in only two cases, felt rather unsure about five, and was completely unsure about two others. When he sent the nine cases to the county party secretary for review, however, the secretary promptly pronounced all nine guilty and sentenced them all to execution. The judge did not argue with the secretary and simply followed the order. The result was at least two and probably seven cases of injustice, leaving behind seven families with grievances.[157]

In the Cultural Revolution, the legal situation became arguably worse as many police, courts, and procuratorates, imperfect as they were, were completely disbanded. Many people, from party leaders (i.e., Liu Shaoqi) to citizens were labeled as enemies of socialism and were arrested, tortured, and executed without trial. Whoever dared challenge the order of the Party secretary in power would be labeled as "leaning to the right (*youqing*)" or as a counterrevolutionary, two scary titles that resulted in numerous deaths.[158]

After the fall of the "Gang of Four" in 1976, the legal situation failed to improve much. While leaders such as Peng Zhen and Wan Li, the vice premier, called for following the principles of the rule of law,[159] the low quality and irresponsible behavior of judges continued. In 1979, *The People's Daily* reported a case in which Xiong Yifu, an army veteran, committed suicide after mounting scores of unsuccessful complaints about his grievances to the local courts and officials. The daily severely condemned bureaucratism and charged that some local judges and officials who "paid little attention to people's grievances" had driven Xiong Yifu to suicide.[160] In such a case we may suspect that the newspaper's sharing of the common assumption of the legitimacy of natural resistance lay behind its decision to publicize the case in the teeth of local power holders.

Other reasons

Some other factors that were not necessarily new made the complaint system less effective in the early PRC. For example, the complaint systems were far from universal or complete. In 1978, Minister of Public Security Zhao Cangbi admitted that many places, especially at the local level, did not have sufficient qualified personnel to serve as complaint officers.[161] Similarly, in July 1979, complaint officers in the central and populous province of Henan complained that they had insufficient manpower to deal with a 40 percent increase in complaints since 1976.[162]

The high cost of lodging complaints was another obstacle faced by many complainants, specifically farmers. In 1957, a farmer complainant had to buy a stamp of 0.15 *yuan* to mail a letter of complaint to Beijing. The cost of the stamp was equivalent to that man's daily expenses for food. Zhao Cangbi noted in 1978 that many complainants spent all their savings and some of them even sold their houses in order to fund their travel in efforts to satisfy their grievances.[163] Like their counterparts in the dynasties (e.g., Zhu Zhaolian in the late Qing), many grievance-driven complainants in the PRC continued to pay heavy prices, physically and financially, to complain (e.g., Han in 1951). Some of them ended up swallowing their grievances due to their inability to fund the costly complaint trips.

Conclusion

Under the banner of revolutionary idealism, the CCP regarded the republican judicial systems including its Administrative Court and Complaint Laws as serving only the capitalist ruling class and abolished most of them. To ensure that the people were the real masters of the PRC, the CCP created the letters and visits system, which was not only more comprehensive than any other complaint systems in Chinese history but also rationalized and updated the long-standing people's natural right to complain. Since the 1960s, the complaint offices were required to be established in all government organs in the capital and down to county-level government. With no Administrative Court and the letters and visits offices functioning mostly as an extra-legal apparatus, the status of the complaint systems in the early PRC was different from that in post-Sui dynasties and the republic of China. Additionally, the mixture of CCP's populism, republicanism, Mao's image as a "living god," and the commune system that was consistent with the inherited *minben* concept helped encourage many aggrieved people to practice natural resistance in this period. Yet, because of the revolutionary idealism, numerous political movements particularly the Anti-Rightist movement and the Cultural Revolution, may have led to more grievances than in most, if not all, other relatively peaceful times. Moreover, the communist secularism freed PRC officials from heaven's punishments, one of the key elements of natural resistance, and made it less possible for many complainants to redress their grievances. Therefore, the complaint systems in this period increasingly became a pawn of the ruling Party. It was not until 1978 that some of those grievances had a chance to be redressed while some other grievances, caused by fundamental flaws in the political and judicial systems, remained unaddressed.

6 Bureaucratic pragmatism

The reform period (after 1982)

Assuming that Mao's revolutionary idealism had resulted in the "lawless" Cultural Revolution, the new primary leader Deng Xiaoping, who had been attacked during the Cultural Revolution, called for legal reforms in 1979.[1] At the Third Plenary Session held in late 1978, Ye Jianying, the president of the National People's Congress (NPC), claimed that since the establishment of the PRC, China had never had a decent legal system. In his view, that was the main reason the "Gang of Four" had been able to destroy the socialist legal system, causing numerous deaths of innocent people. Ye concluded that "all nations should have a legal system with stability, continuity, and immense authority."[2] Peng Zhen, the chair of the NPC Legal System Committee, also emphasized the role of law and seemed to challenge Party dominance when he said that law was more important than the CCP central committee.[3]

Indeed, the full-scale legal reform marked a momentous period in lawmaking activities since 1978.[4] In 1978, the new leaders restored the Procuratorate (abolished in 1975) and in 1979 they reinstated the Ministry of the Judiciary (canceled in 1959). Also in 1979, both Beijing and Shanghai allowed the reestablishment of Lawyer Associations. In the same year and in 1986, the NPC passed the Criminal Law and the General Principles of Civil Law. In 1982, a revised Constitution stipulated that no one person or organization "has authority exceeding that of the Constitution and the law."[5] Like almost all previous constitutions since the Late Qing, the new constitution once again acknowledged citizens' right to complain.[6]

In the 1990s, and especially after the Fourteenth Congress of the CCP (in 1992) proposed the establishment of the socialist market economy, the legal reforms accelerated. Some scholars argued that the market economy required the rule-of-law.[7] The law would play a vital role when the Chinese economy merged with the world economy.[8] Consequently, both the NPC and local congresses have enacted thousands of laws. Many important laws such as the Judge Law, the Procurator Law, and the Criminal Procedure Law were revised in the 1990s. The height of the legal reform discourse as opposed to actual operation was in 1997 when President Jiang Zemin formally announced at the Fifteenth Congress that the PRC would "use law to rule the nation."[9]

Since the 1980s, the PRC has tried to increase people's legal consciousness. In 1985, Deng Liqun, the propaganda minister, launched a plan to "popularize the law."[10] Since then, the PRC had attempted to create more newspapers and TV programs focused on the law to enhance both official and popular legal consciousness. Major newspapers like the *China Youth Daily*, the most popular newspaper in a 1985 urban poll, created new columns such as "Legal Society" and "Life Special" in the early 1990s devoted to publish articles on the law.[11] The Chinese Central Television (CCTV) initiated the popular "Focus Interview (*jiaodian fangtan*)" in 1994 and the "Online Rule-of-Law (*fazhi zaixian*)" in 2003 to promote legal consciousness. These efforts had a great impact on many people living in both urban and rural areas.[12] In 2003, I interviewed a young migrant worker from Anhui who pointed out that he learned the law mostly by reading newspapers and watching TV.[13] But, as we shall see, the increase in complaints in the 1990s stemmed from something more (or less) than growing rights consciousness.

Accompanying the comprehensive legal reform was a significant change in the PRC complaint systems, which became more open and institutionalized, albeit still largely extra-legal. Many political scientists and legal scholars around the world have done serious studies of the recent overhaul of the complaint systems. For example, in their examination of administrative litigation in rural China, Kevin O'Brien and Lianjiang Li discuss the flaws of the Administrative Court and argue that farmers need to mobilize other support from higher courts, sympathetic leaders, interested media, and people's congresses if they are to win their lawsuits.[14] Carl Minzner's in-depth research on the "paternalistic" letters and visits system shows that it overlaps the formal legal system and partially invalidates the Administrative Court.[15] Looking at costs and benefits, Yongshun Cai asks why some collective resistance succeeds and some fails.[16] After reviewing the record of the letters and visits system from 1949 to the mid-1990s, Laura Luehrmann argues that it is "toothless" in controlling official abuse but effective in discouraging most complainants from defying the Party.[17] Ben Liebman argues that the "mass work departments" in most media function as official ombudsmen in the West.[18]

In the absence of access to archival sources, this chapter functions more as a critical review of our existing knowledge of contemporary Chinese complaint systems. First, it will examine both the judicial (administrative litigation) and non-judicial (letters and visits) complaint systems and both collective and individual complaints. It will then provide a detailed account of two major reforms in this period: enacting and publicizing the first Regulation Regarding Letters and Visits (*xinfang tiaoli*); and restoring an administrative litigation law that existed in the early and late republic but was abolished in the early PRC. The chapter will argue that Confucian notions, such as natural principles, parental rulers, people as the root, combined with republican ideas, such as popular sovereignty and natural rights, to support natural resistance in the face of a strong state. While the new policies of reform and opening promised domestic political change and receptivity to foreign ideas, the accompanying bureaucratic pragmatism after 1989 fueled numerous grievances. Increasing numbers of complainants skipped ranks in the administrative hierarchy and complained directly to central organs thought to be more responsive to popular needs. Given the secular amorality of the state commited to wealth and power and the limited effectiveness of rightful resistance under conditions of growing social, political, and economic inequality, the scale and scope of natural resistance reached unprecedented highs in this period.

Two major reforms in the complaint systems

In 1982, as part of an effort to "modernize" the PRC legal system, the CCP revised the 1963 Regulation Regarding People's Letters and Visits. This revised regulation continued to be an informal and semi-secret rule drafted by the State Council and passed out only to local governments. Its official, bureaucratic nature was clear in its first sentence: "Correctly dealing with people's letters and visits is a regular political mission of all levels of Party secretaries and government unit."[19] The regulation reaffirmed the old notion that writing letters and paying visits to the government were people's democratic rights and a way for people to supervise the government. But the revised regulation also made two noticeable changes. First, it repudiated the old regulation's claim that the complaint system was to enhance the socialist revolution and construction (read consolidation of revolution).[20] Instead, the new regulation argued that the purpose of rightly dealing with people's letters and visits was to advance China's socialist modernization (read economic reform). Second, the new regulation ordered all local governments and Party organs to establish a comprehensive complaint system.[21] Based on the new regulation, state-run companies, universities, and townships where there previously had been no complaint offices would now have to establish them and appoint certain officers to take charge of them.

The 1982 regulation lasted for thirteen years until late 1995 when a second, more drastic wave of legal reform occurred. On October 28, 1995, a major reform in the complaint system took place. Arguably a by-product of the ongoing campaign for the rule of law, major newspapers such as *The People's Daily* for the first time were allowed to publish the latest revised Regulation Regarding Letters and Visits.[22] Since then, the regulation has no longer been semi-secret that communicated only internally "from one part of the government to another part of the government." Instead, in the best legalist tradition, the regulation became publicly known and complainants could use it as a legal basis of their right to complain. The regulations were designed as a sword of Damocles to be hung over the heads of officials who were unresponsive to people's complaints and/or who took revenge against complainants. Whether they would actually function that way remained to be seen.

At the same time, the new regulation imposed more restrictions on people's right to complain than former regulations had done. For example, it stated that all complaints should be valid and lodged step by step; complaints pertaining to courts, people's congresses, and procuratorates should be made only to those organs; complainants who were visiting should go only to specifically designated places; collective complainants could not exceed five in number; the attacking of government organs and intercepting of public vehicles (*gongwuche*) were prohibited. The new regulation, like previous ones, outlawed official suppression of complainants and revenge against them, yet it failed to say what punishment official violators of that ban would face. On the bright side, the regulation required all levels of government to resolve complaints within a limited period: thirty days if the government body was directly responsible for coping with the complaint and ninety days if the government body was only indirectly responsible. The regulation had the additional positive feature of forbidding officials from passing a complaint against local officials back down to its original target where it was almost certain to be ignored and where retribution could easily be taken.

Practitioners of rightful resistance could use these new regulations as a firmer base for their actions, but they were also limited by the regulations in what they could rightfully do. People who continued to believe in the principles of heaven and nature, in parental rulers, and in *minben*/people as the root, could use these regulations when they were to their advantage but ignore them when they seemed contrary to their basic principles, whether consciously articulated or simply tacitly assumed. Such people, for example, could continue to skip the ranks in the bureaucracy and appeal directly to the center in Beijing.

The 1995 regulation resembled the republican Complaint Laws in its transparency and in its emphasis on due process. Unlike the republican Complaint Law, the 1995 regulation maintained, however weakly and hypocritically, the Maoist idea that the CCP should listen to people's voices, accept people's supervision, and work hard to promote the people's welfare.[23]

We should also note the immediate context of the 1995 regulation. It was promulgated three years after the CCP announced the establishment of the "socialist market economy," suggesting that it was devised to achieve that end. It was promulgated on the heels of two years of sometimes violent protests against local officials who were often charged with engaging in corrupt practices and with imposing heavy tax burdens on the population. This suggests that the regulation was designed to check the abuses of local officials as well as to control the activities of complainants. Despite the legalistic language, the 1995 regulation seems to have tacitly accepted the basic principles of natural resistance: that people have a natural right to push back against bad governance. To be sure, two years later President Jiang Zemin called openly for the rule of law, implying that natural resistance should be carried out within the parameters of the law. Thus the state seemed intent on balancing the claims of due process against those of moral rectitude both of which could be used by it or against it just as they could be deployed by the population in its own interest or to limit that interest.

The second major reform in this period was the Administrative Litigation Law which resembled that of the republic and reappeared after a hiatus of forty years. This law had many imperfections, which limited its value as a foundation for effective popular challenges to misgovernment.[24] It nonetheless demonstrated again the CCP's good intention to reform its legal system and provide people with more protection against administrative abuses.[25] Article 1 stated that the law was enacted in accordance with the constitution to protect the lawful interests of citizens, legal persons (*faren*, usually corporate bosses), and other organizations, and to supervise administrative organs' exercise of their authority. Articles 2 and 3 allow any citizen, judicial person, or organization to accuse an administrative organ whose activities violate their legal rights, and promises that the court will make its judgment independently, free of any outside interference. Article 37 stipulates that people can appeal only to an administrative organ immediately above the one they are targeting as prescribed by the law, or they can avail themselves of regulations for reconsideration (*fuyi*) or bring a suit directly before a people's court.[26]

Like its republican predecessor, the PRC administrative law aims to protect the people against unlawful government activities. But there are several key differences between them. First, unlike in the republic, the PRC does not have a single, central, and more or less independent Administrative Court. Instead, it has set up special Administrative Adjudicating Departments (*xingzheng shenpanting*) in all existing courts. Second, while the republican administrative court was responsible to the president (in the early republic) or the National Government (in the later republic), the administrative adjudicating department in the PRC is responsible to neither the president nor the National People's Congress but instead to regular Party organs such as the Central and provincial Party Committees. This will make it difficult for the department to go after powerful officials let alone enforce its judgments against them. Third, the republican Administrative Litigation Law required all complainants whose rights had been infringed by the central or local governments to complain to upper-level government bodies before bringing their suits to the administrative court. The PRC has given complainants more options: to apply for administrative reconsideration (*xingzheng fuyi*), in which case the complaint would be addressed by an administrative body or to bring their suits directly to the administrative court, which would then take up the case.[27]

The passage of the Administrative Reconsideration Law, another big step in the legal reform to protect people from state abuses, came one year after the Administrative Litigation Law. The Reconsideration Law was akin to the Complaint Law in the republic because its main purpose was to correct both illicit and unjust administrative activities.[28] Unlike the republican Complaint Law, however, the Administrative Reconsideration Law stipulated far more specific circumstances under which people were allowed to apply for administrative reconsideration. For instance, if citizens, legal persons, or other organizations are dissatisfied with an administration's forceful (*qiangzhi*) decisions such as warnings, fines, confiscations of illegal property, detainment, restriction of personal freedom, and so forth, they can apply for reconsideration. The law also allows people to apply for administrative reconsideration against administrative organs' illegally raising funds, collecting money or things of value, apportioning expenses or illegally requiring them to perform other duties. If dissatisfied with the decisions of the administrative reconsideration, they can bring suits to the administrative adjudicating department.[29]

Although the PRC's move toward "modernizing" its legal system turned out to be more or less a revival, if not a replication, of republican complaint laws and administrative litigation laws, on paper at least it gave citizens more legal protection to complain about official misconduct than they had had for decades. Furthermore, the Regulation Regarding Letters and Visits formalized the non-judicial complaint system, which had been largely informal and unprotected in the republican period.

The judicial complaint system

Long before the Administrative Litigation Law went into effect in 1990, special administrative courts (separate from the civil and criminal courts) had been granted the power to hear complaints against administrative decisions. And between 1983 and 1990, more than 27,000 cases were tried by such special administrative courts.[30] From the late 1980s and particularly after the passage of the Administrative Litigation Law in 1989 to the early 2000s, the total number of first-instance administrative cases accepted and settled fluctuated. As shown in Table 6.1, between 1993 and 1999 the number generally saw an upward turn, though the number became more volatile after 1999.[31]

In 1990, the Supreme Court justice Ren Jianxin claimed that more than 2400 local courts had set up administrative adjudicating departments to deal with administrative cases. Throughout China, 9934 first-instance administrative cases had been decided in 1989, which was 15.8 percent more than in 1988.[32] Ma Huaide, a law professor at Chinese University of Politics and Law, argues that in 1995, there were 3224 administrative adjudicating departments and 12,215 administrative judges. Among the 141,949 administrative cases accepted between 1990 and 1995, about 30 percent of the plaintiffs won their suits against administrators.[33] This figure, however, is at odds with the table above which shows merely 11.7 percent to 21.3 percent of cases had been successful.[34]

Therefore, despite the CCP's initiative to launch legal reform and its good intention to pass administrative laws to protect the people, the success rate of administrative lawsuits has been phenomenally low in comparison to the reportedly 33 percent success rate in the late republic. In addition, the total number of annual administrative complaints accepted was minimal when compared to the millions of civil and criminal cases handled by the courts.[35] In 2002, Wu Yuanxing, the head of the administrative division in the Sichuan High Court, admitted that, for the eighty million people of Sichuan, the 3000 administrative cases per annum were a mere drop in the bucket.[36] Worse, the number of abandoned cases is about half of the accepted cases. Why has the success rate of the administrative suits been so low? O'Brien and Li have done a profound study of the difficulties at each stage of the process of administrative litigation in rural China. "The toughest battle of most litigants," they argue, "is persuading a court to accept a case."[37] One of the biggest obstacles to getting an administrative case accepted is that all Party secretaries and city-level government officials are actually exempt from prosecution.[38]

Table 6.1 Administrative cases dealt with between 1989 and 2003

	Cases accepted	*Cases settled*	*Official decisions upheld*	*Official decisions rescinded*	*% of winning suits*	*Lawsuits withdrawn*	*% of withdrawn cases*
1988	8573	8029	–	–	–	–	–
1989	9934	–	–	–	–	–	–
1990	13,006	12,040	4337	2012	16.7	4346	7.9
1991	25,667	25,202	7969	4762	18.9	9317	10.2
1992	27,125	27,116	7628	5780	21.3	10,261	37.8
1993	27,911	27,958	6587	5270	18.8	11,550	41.0
1994	35,083	34,567	7128	6547	18.9	15,317	43.0
1995	52,596	51,370	8903	7733	15.1	25,990	49.0
1996	79,966	79,537	11,549	11,831	14.9	42,915	53.0
1997	90,557	88,542	11,230	12,279	13.6	50,735	67.0
1998	98,350	98,390	13,036	15,214	15.4	47,817	48.6
1999	97,569	98,759	14,672	15,251	15.0	44,395	45.0
2000	85,760	86,614	13,431	13,635	15.8	31,822	37.1
2001	100,921	95,984	15,941	12,943	12.8	31,083	30.7
2002	80,728	84,943	15,520	11,042	13.6	26,052	32.2
2003	87,919	88,050	16,356	10,337	11.7	27,811	31.6

In March 1999, for instance, sixty-one private businessmen filed a collective complaint against four government organs including the municipal government of Germu county in Qinghai province. According to a *China Youth Daily* report, in 1991 those businessmen went to Germu to establish a shop to sell second-hand products. But the Germu municipal government in February 1998 suddenly ordered the destruction of the shop and in March began razing the rest of the businessmen's properties. The destroyed properties were worth about 640,000 yuan. Two days after the businessmen accused the Germu government of unlawful actions, the court told them that the city government was not involved in the incident and thus could not be the defender. The court rejected all of the businessmen's charges against the Germu government. As a result, the businessmen lost their administrative suit.[39]

In this case, the sixty-one businessmen showed strong legal consciousness and courage in their accusation of the Germu government. They lost their case because of the pitfalls of the administrative litigation system. Jiang Ming'an, a law professor at Beijing University, remarked that the Administrative Litigation Law clearly forbids courts to accept suits against abstract (*chouxiang xingwei*; e.g., administrative regulations or documents) and internal administrative activities, national activities, and final activities (*zhongjü*; e.g., cases whose final decisions have been made). Because of those restrictions, people would find it very difficult to satisfy their grievances.[40]

Once a court accepts a People-Accuse-Officials (*min'gaoguan*) case, "some officials [will] go so far as to employ illicit means to encourage complainants to drop the accusations."[41] O'Brien and Li mentioned a case in Gongyi county, Henan, in which a villager filed a suit against some local police who had mistreated him. To force the villager to drop his accusation, the local police jailed him, tortured him for forty-eight hours, and charged him with raping his ex-girlfriend.[42] Being afraid of such official retaliation and pressure, nearly half the plaintiffs in administrative suits dropped their complaints shortly after their suits were accepted by the court.[43]

When an administrative court starts to investigate a case, complainants usually find it hard to hire a lawyer. Few lawyers want to risk their careers and personal freedoms by confronting officials in the court. *The Southern Weekend*, a newspaper renowned for its audacity in criticizing government officials, reported a tragic story of a lawyer who had helped defend complainants against various officials including those from the Financial Ministry. In 1998 the lawyer Li Jinsong helped a worker accuse the Guangdong Committee for Collecting Donations (*Guangdong mujuan weiyuanhui*) of wrongfully denying that it had sold the worker a winning lottery ticket. The head of Li's law firm informed Li that someone in the government had censured him for his temerity in suing the government. Li did not back off and insisted on representing the worker. His law firm was intimidated, however, and Li was forced to resign from the firm. He was unable to find a position at another law firm, but he continued to work for the complainant on his own until they finally lost the case two years later. The head of a law firm based in Foshan city, Guangdong, commented on Li's situation: "while [Foshan] has forty to fifty law firms and hundreds of lawyers, only Li Jinsong dares repeatedly to accuse the local government." That lawyer told a reporter of *The Southern Weekend* that there was an informal rule among law firms that lawyers had better not lodge administrative suits in their own cities because of "countless ties among [local] administrators." The reporter later recorded that lawyer Li had lost all the suits he had brought against administrators.[44]

Even if a complainant succeeds in hiring a brave lawyer, s/he might well face another problem: the official defendant will refuse to appear in the court.[45] A municipal court report in Jiangxi revealed that from 1989 to 2000, 95 percent of official defendants failed to appear in court on occasions when they were required to be present.[46] The Nanjing-based *Yangtze Evening News* gave a more comprehensive figure on the number of government defendants who attended administrative adjudication sessions. It claimed in 2003 that less than one in a thousand official defendants had appeared in People-Accuse-Official cases.[47]

In the absence of the official defendants, some courts might still make their decisions. In some cases they even decide in favor of the plaintiffs and against the officials. In such cases, however, the plaintiffs still have the problems of getting the courts to enforce their decisions and of avoiding the official defendants' retaliation. As court judges were inferior in rank to many county officials and court budgets were controlled by local governments, it was very hard for many courts, if not most, to oppose local officials or impose their adjudicatory decisions on them.[48] Accordingly, *Legal Encyclopedia*, a national legal magazine, stated that, although many government officials had lost their cases, the courts found it difficult to enforce their decisions. Some official defendants utilized their power to play with the law, while others took revenge on the plaintiffs.[49]

Common people faced other obstacles in accusing officials, including long waits and high costs. In one case, a Yunnan villager sued a township for illegally confiscating his TV set but ended up having to spend ten times the cost of a TV on the necessary marathon litigation.[50] Even people who finally won their lawsuits against abusive and corrupt officials would find their compensation not commensurate to their physical, psychological, and monetary sacrifices. That was initially because there was no law requiring state compensation (*guojia peichangfa*) of the victim. Even after the State Compensation Law was passed in 1994, many victims of abusive officials were unable to get reasonable state compensation.[51]

In sum, however sincere the CCP might have been in trying to provide people with more protection from officials, however beautiful the words in the Administrative Litigation Law and the Administrative Reconsideration, and however effective some administrative suits were in checking official arbitrariness,[52] the administrative litigation in the PRC has been largely a beautiful pillow with grass in it. The relatively limited number of administrative suits, the low success rates, and the nearly 50 percent of cases withdrawn best reveal its general ineffectiveness. As Minzner and Cai have remarked, one result has been that people have continued to complain less in "rightful" and more in "natural" ways.[53]

Economy-driven complaints in the 1980s

Since the late 1970s, under Deng Xiaoping's aphorism that "to get rich is glorious," capitalism reappeared in China after decades of being under attack. In the name of decentralization and privatization,[54] the government allowed urban people to create their own companies and stores, thus becoming a new generation of private entrepreneurs. In the countryside farmers were able to plant crops in contracted lots and sell extra produce in the market. The popular slogan of "Looking ahead" morphed into the more critical homophonous slogan "Looking to money," causing at least one member of the National People's Congress to state in 1983 that it was wrong for people to substitute capitalist for socialist material principles.[55] In this period, the complaint system began to reflect problems and grievances brought on by the policies of reform and opening. In cities such as Shanghai and Tianjin, people now complained about their cramped living quarters, backward public transportation, and growing air pollution.[56] Many farmers complained about the birth-control policy that had begun to be strictly enforced in the late 1970s, about economic disputes, and about political corruption.[57] In 1979, dissatisfied with their poverty and injustice, thousands of farmers from depressed rural areas, like their predecessors many times in the past, came to Beijing to complain directly to the central government.[58]

During the 1986 state-wide Letters and Visits Conference, Zhou Jie, vice head of the CCP General Office, noted that the percentage of cases left over in history had diminished from 80 percent of all cases in 1982 to 30 percent of all cases in 1986. Nevertheless, Zhou said that the total number of complaints did not decline but on the contrary rose by 35.8 percent in 1986. Many of the new complaints were related to the reform and open policies.[59] In a similar report, the Tianjin government in 1988 said that 99 percent complaints were about "current issues." The number of collective complaints also climbed sharply.[60]

As in the early 1950s and late 1970s, major newspapers in the 1980s provided a venue for people with grievances to complain about local officials. To cite one case, on July 3, 1984, *The China Youth Daily* published farmer Chang Xiaoquan's complaint letter in which he charged some village officials with robbery. In 1983, after the village officials in Tanghe county, Henan, asked Chang to raise saplings, Chang decided to sign a contract to undertake the work and was successful in doing so. Seeing that Chang would make lots of money, some village officials became jealous. They first ordered Chang to yield most of his flourishing saplings to the village. When Chang refused, some village officials reportedly stole those saplings. Chang complained to the Party Secretary of Henan who ordered the township government to investigate. But the township official was attacked by village officials and Chang's grievance remained unredressed. In despair, Chang wrote to *The China Youth Daily* saying: "I entreat upper-level governments to support us specialist households (*zhuanyehu*) and to protect our lawful rights."[61] In this case, Chang Xiaoquan was one of the pioneering complainants regarding abuses stemming from the economic reform.

Aside from such incipient reform-related complaints, many old problems such as government corruption and abuse of power, "feudal" marriages and family abuse, and damages from the Cultural Revolution continued to be targeted.

In 1979, Yang Xiaomin who was the son of the vice head of the Qinghai provincial Party office, deliberately killed Wang Qiang, who had accidentally splashed some water on Yang's clothes. This seemingly "simple and clear" case took six years to settle. After a district court in Xining, the capital of Qinghai, sentenced Yang to death, the provincial high court, which by law could review the judgments made by lower-level courts, reversed its decision, saying Yang killed Wang during a fight.[62] The head of the provincial high court, Yang Shufang, allegedly revised the Xining court decision of "deliberate killing" to "killing," which paved the way for future revision of Yang's "death sentence" to a "life sentence." Wang's aggrieved mother and sister complained to the Qinghai provincial government where they got no sympathy for their grievance. With firm belief in heavenly or natural principles and in the parental function of the central government, both mother and sister went all the way to Beijing to complain. It was not until the Party Secretary Hu Yaobang intervened in the case in 1985 that Wang's grievance was finally satisfied.[63] In this case the state's failure to provide justice triggered natural resistance that was ultimately successful.

In his book, *The Complaint Story of Dahe Immigrants*, Ying Xing, a law professor at Chinese University of Politics and Law in Beijing, recounted a series of farmers' complaints in Chongqing, Sichuan, in the 1980s. In 1986, when the regional government's food aid to Shanyang county was behind schedule, ten local complaint leaders collected donations from the farmers of three townships to skip the intervening levels and lodge collective complaints in Beijing. They visited many central organs such as the Water and Electronic Ministry, Public Security Ministry, and the Central TV Station but no one accepted their complaints. Disappointed but energized by what they felt was their natural right to seek satisfaction of grievances, the complainants boldly spread copies of their complaint letters outside the backdoor of Zhongnanhai, the office and home of many CCP leaders. This time, they succeeded in forcing an official to come out and accept their complaints. But their grievances remained unredressed.[64]

Other "old issues" like domestic violence and "feudal marriages" remained among the major complaints of women in the early 1980s. On May 10, 1983, a female worker in Shaowu county, Fujian, wrote to *The China Youth Daily*, accusing her husband, a judicial official, of abusing her for a long time after she gave birth to a girl and not a boy. Believing in heavenly principles, the afflicted female worker wrote: "I cannot bear it anymore! I want to accuse! He is a CCP member and judicial official; he understands the law but violates it, losing all his heavenly/natural good character (*tianliang*)."[65]

One of the last "historically-left-over (*lishi yiliu*)" form of complaints in the 1980s was made by the youth sent down to the countryside during the Cultural Revolution. Since the late 1970s, many of them had believed that they had the right to return to the cities. As local officials often opposed their leaving, they complained to Beijing with the hope that CCP leaders would redress their grievances. In the mid-1980s, thousands of representative sent-down youths, like their desperate predecessors through the ages, launched a number of complaint marches and hunger strikes in Beijing.[66] Probably because of the daunting number of the demonstrators as well as the fading of any ideological justification for their rustication, the central government finally agreed to let them return to the cities.[67]

In the 1980s, overall, the number of complaints remained quite small and most of them related to old issues.[68] This was partly because the legal consciousness of most people was still low, and farmers in particular remained cautious about accusing officials.[69] The first few complaints about the consequences of reform and opening appeared, as we have seen, but they still constituted only a small minority of cases in this period. This situation would change in the 1990s, however, particularly and ironically after the passage of the Regulation Regarding Letters and Visits in 1995.

A rising tide of natural resistance after 1990

When the CCP in 1989 repressed the Tiananmen demonstrations for more democracy, many people predicted that it would slow down the policies of reform and opening. In fact the CCP on one hand buried all the "reasonable elements of revolution and socialism" and on the other hand proceeded further into the market economy combined with state violence and monopolization.[70] Deng Xiaoping's 1992 visit to Shenzhen, one of the first and most prosperous special economic zones, accelerated the reform in almost all of its social aspects and opened the economy wider to the world.[71] Five years later, in the Fifteenth CCP congress, Jiang Zemin promised that the government would not only permit but also encourage the private sectors of the economy. He called for faster reform of the putatively decrepit state-run companies. In addition, he vowed to establish a Chinese-style rule-of-law system led by the Party.[72]

To boost the economic reform, the CCP sped up the pace of decentralization that had started in the early 1980s.[73] In 1994, the central government allowed local governments to make decisions on taxation, investment, foreign trade, and the distribution of resources.[74] At the same time, the state left intact a system in which official careers depended more on satisfying the demands of superiors than on meeting the needs of the people. Many officials, if not most, moved to maximize profits by any possible means so as to become "new capitalists" themselves.[75] As a result, Maurice Meisner argues, a kind of "state bourgeoisie," reviled in the Maoist era, revived in the Deng Xiaoping era. "Deng Xiaoping's institutionalization of bureaucratic power and his introduction of a market economy," Meisner writes, "soon combined to produce a bureaucratic capitalist regime that seemed to hark back to economic practices common during the imperial and Guomindang eras."[76] The latest round of what we are calling "Bureaucratic Pragmatism" started in the early 1990s. It soon entailed much official misconduct and the violation of many people's rights under the constitution.

People soon responded with skyrocketing skipping and collective complaints that were also in violation of the law. It was this basic structural confrontation, even more than deficiencies in the administrative litigation system and a growth in rights consciousness, that resulted in a new high tide of natural resistance across China.[77]

On December 15, 1998, Zhou Zhanshun, the head of the Letters and Visits Bureau of the State Council and the Central Office, pointed out that the number of collective complaints the bureau had received in that year jumped 79.1 percent over the previous year, the highest single-year jump in recorded history.[78] The situation at the local level was the same, if not worse. In the same year, an official in Henan commented that from 1992 to 1997 the average increasing rate of complaints, especially illegal collective complaints, in Henan was 30 percent, and the highest yearly increasing rate reached 69.7 percent. He added that many irregular collective complaints were more violent than ever before and had "clear signs of an inclination toward an uprising."[79] Likewise, a head of a township letters and visits office in northern China said that complaints, especially rebellious collective ones, began to rise after 1995 and more illegal skipping complaints were seen in 1997.[80]

Complaints continued to climb in the early 2000s. The complaints received by all China's courts increased from 5,277,241 in 1990 to 10,691,048 in 1999.[81] In the first three quarters of 2002, the collective complaints in the whole country again climbed sharply. Some collective complaints had as many as 10,000 complainants, several orders of magnitude above the legal limit of five representatives.[82] From July 1 to August 20 in 2003, about 19,000 people had complained to the Party Secretary of Beijing and the number of collective complaints was 347. The Central Disciplinary Committee had received over 10,000 complaints and 453 collective ones, both numbers unseen since the late 1970s.[83] Among the top causes of mounting natural resistance have been the Farmers' Burden, Rural Land Confiscation, and Urban Relocation.

The Farmers' Burden was an "old problem" that reappeared in official newspapers in the 1980s. On November 1, 1985, the central government admitted that most farmers were still facing heavy burdens despite years of central orders to reduce them.[84] The problem only intensified in the 1990s as bureaucratic pragmatism and political corruption worsened.[85] In 1990, a farmer from Hebei complained directly in a letter to Prime Minister Li Peng about his heavy burden. Although the annual individual income in his township was only 606 yuan, the local government asked his family to pay 434.16 yuan as a contract fee (*chengbaofei*).[86] The *Xinhua News Agency* reported that in 1992 a farmer in Hunan committed suicide because she could not afford the government fees.[87] Unable and unwilling to pay the ever-increasing fees, many farmers began filing skipping or direct complaints to central organs.

In October 1997, a farmer from Lingbi county, Anhui, pressured by the unbearable burden, begged his way to complain in Beijing—his last hope under heaven—thus violating the regulation that required taking regular steps. After two unsuccessful capital complaints, he suffered an asthma attack that is still troubling him today.[88] This farmer's action resembles that of Zhu Zhaolian in the late Qing who begged his way over 2000 li to complain in Beijing. It shows that in the populist PRC, no less than in the elitist Qing, people pushed to the edge by unjust burdens will take extreme action in violation of the niceties of the rule of law but in accord with the principles of natural resistance. While individual complainants may fail, a group of complainants using the tactics of "issue linkage" would more likely be successful in forcing local officials to reduce taxes.[89]

Rural Confiscation of Lands is another major cause of mass complaints. The problem here is that local officials strive to produce "visible achievements" that are required to gain bureaucratic promotions. Such officials can also become personally wealthy by selling confiscated lands to commercial developers. According to one report, nearly 10,000 square miles of farmland was lost to development in 2003 alone. One third of China's 3837 development zones and industrial parks are technically illegal, lacking the required approval.[90] Most complaints against land confiscation were made because of relatively low compensation of—and official violence against—the victims. In May 2002, for example, the local government of Qihe county, Shandong province, sold the land of four villages to a developer for building villas. The compensation was merely 200 yuan per *mu*, about one-fifteenth of the market price. Despite farmers' opposition, bulldozers went in and destroyed all crops on the land. The villagers had no choice but to send representatives to complain in Beijing in hopes that the paternalistic central authorities would protect their rights.[91] Yet, after complaining for one whole year, the farmers lost hope and no longer believed that the "leaders will even see their complaint letters."[92]

The seriousness of the relocation issue in rural areas also drew attention from some Western media. In 1994, the *New York Times* reported a case in which local officials in Yülin, Shaanxi, confiscated farmers' land for a development zone. The compensation was just $60 per *mu*. When infuriated farmers heard that the land was leased to developers for fifty times that amount, they lambasted the local officials for "pocketing all the money for themselves." When one farmer threatened to complain to Beijing, an official warned him: "So you dirt-poor trash think you can oppose the city government? You don't have a chance in hell." Two old farmers did make an illegal complaint directly to Beijing and tried to present a letter to the head of the Ministry of Land Resources, but a guard instructed them to send the complaint by express mail. Either way, the farmers' complaint would be ignored on grounds that it had not been mounted according to the required steps. The upshot was a mass protest in the town that was quickly suppressed by the local government.[93]

Unlike the farmers' burden and the confiscation of land, urban relocation touches both urban and rural dwellers and has sparked numerous complaints, many of which are in the mode of natural resistance. In fact, urban relocation is a double-edged sword. On the one hand, urban relocation has not only transformed the appearance of many cities but also greatly improved many people's living standards. According to a report, in 2003 Shanghai had built 150 million square meters of apartments since the late 1980s. The average individual living space expanded from five square meters to 13.1 square meters in 2002.[94] In addition, many urban citizens are now proud of their beautiful cities. A government official of Xuzhou, Jiangsu, apparently unaware of many complaints generated by relocation policy, noted that Xuzhou's appearance had become much better in recent years.[95] On the other hand, urban relocation has created a huge number of tragedies and resulted in numerous complaints. Between January and July 1995, the complaints regarding urban relocation in Beijing alone accounted for 43.2 percent of the complaints in that city.[96] In August 2003, a Shanghai official acknowledged that the problem of urban relocation was becoming the top issue in collective complaints—most of which entailed natural resistance surpassing the limits of the law.[97]

Complaints regarding urban relocation have turned out to be more convoluted than those regarding the farmers' burden and the confiscation of land. Many urban complainants have recently begun to adopt methods that their rural counterparts have not used or at least have not used much. Besides the conventional tactics of skipping or direct complaints to Beijing, some urban complainants have tried to complain to foreign media or to Chinese non-government organizations through the internet. Some have been "forcing local governments [to accept their demands] through foreign pressure."[98]

The principal cause of most complaints is that many relocation companies take whatever means are necessary, legal or illegal, to force people to move out of their homes. Many people do not want to yield because of the low level of compensation.[99] Pi Shufeng, a Beijing resident who had eleven private rooms and a yard of 500 square meters was asked in 2001 to sell up and move out by a relocation company which had local government backing. As both parties were at odds over the price, Pi refused to move. On February 2, 2002, a group of "unidentified" persons arrived with bulldozers and destroyed two of Pi's rooms without her permission. Pi called the police but no one came. Although Pi complained repeatedly to the Dongcheng district government, it was all in vain. She then made a skipping complaint directly to the CCP leaders, asking: "In the era of exhorting the 'rule of law…,' is there anybody who is going to stop these outrageous violations of the law?" Like many other urban residents who have been forced to relocate in this period by governments and companies, Pi resorted to illegal action in the name of natural resistance but was still unable to get satisfaction.[100]

With government support, relocation companies were almost fearless. In September 2003, the *Xinhua News Comment*, a mouthpiece of the CCP, sharply criticized some local governments for backing relocation companies and neglecting residents' property rights. Being a much weaker party in most cases, many residents could not negotiate effectively with relocation companies. Alluding to an ancient form of illegitimate monopoly power, some people asked rhetorically: facing "hegemonic agreements (*bawang xieyi*)," "can residents' rights be protected?"[101] In the absence of state support, the answer was clearly "no."

Given the failure of the usual legal and illegal forms of complaint, some complainants against forced relocations sought other ways to voice their grievances.

In September 2003, a desperate man in Nanjing burned himself alive in front of a local relocation company. That extreme action prompted the government to temporarily stop all relocation projects.[102] In Hongzhou, Zhejiang, after hundreds of complaints against the relocation of their homes proved ineffective, a dozen senior teachers donned white robes with big-character words such as "Everyone Should Protect the Constitution" and "Citizens' Homes Should not be Infringed." They then ignored the law requiring pre-registration for demonstrations and confronted a meeting of a district people's congress. Although their collective complaint was peaceful, they were quickly arrested and their leader was sentenced within ten days. When he accused the police of the detainment to the court, the court backed the police.[103]

In addition to the Farmers' Burden, Rural Land Confiscation, and Urban Relocation, there were other forms of official misconduct that precipitated complaints. O'Brien and Li discuss farmers' "rightful" complaints against unfair village elections in the 1990s.[104] Ching Kwan Lee studies labor complaints and protests on issues ranging from corruption to unpaid wages and pensions in Guangdong and Liaoning in the early 2000s.[105] Dorothy Solinger shows that many "peasant migrants" could find nowhere to complain against police abuses and attacks by local bullies in league with the authorities.[106]

In this period, entrenched "old problems" such as government corruption and other abuses of power remained one of the major targets of natural resistance. For instance, in Hubei in 1995, farmer Hu Yuanjin's grandson fought with his neighbor, and the neighbor then allegedly killed Hu's wife and severely wounded Hu by axing his head. As the neighbor was a sworn brother of the township police chief, Hu could get no justice at the local level. Starting in early 1996, therefore, Hu ignored the state regulations and began a series of arduous skipping complaints to various central organs that extended over eight years. Although none of these initiatives was successful, Hu vowed that he would continue to complain until his grievances were satisfied.[107]

Many people who resort to skipping complaints in violation of the law are commoners with no special talent or training in speaking truth to power. A few, however, have some special skills and higher education that should enhance their chances of success. One such person in this period was Wang Peirong, associate professor at Chinese Mining University in Xuzhou, Jiangsu. According to Wang, in the late 1990s a local ruffian named Yan Jiaxun built many public apartments for college professors. Yet, within a year, many of the residents found that their anti-theft doors were of poor quality. Wang gathered thousands of signatures and presented a collective complaint to the local government. Yan Jiaxun secured the cover of the local police and threatened to kill Wang. Wang then sent letters directly to the central government pointing out the corruption of the local police. In a serious official violation of the 1995 Regulation Regarding Letters and Visits, some of those letters ended up in the hands of the local police. In October 2002, seeing little sense in complaints even to the center, Wang filed an administrative suit against the local police, but he lost. After repeated pressure from the public media and the provincial and central governments, Wang's situation took a turn for the better after the appointment of a new mayor. In early 2005, the Xuzhou police arrested Yan and the government returned all the money to residents who had bought Yan's bogus anti-theft doors.

In this case, Wang partially succeeded after four years of hardships in lodging complaints and suits.[108] His success is partly explicable by his academic status which he shared with many of his co-complainants. It also owed something to the growth in the power of the new media, the internet. Finally, Wang benefited from the sympathy of officials who, after all, had more authority than the police or a local strongman if they were willing to use it. In other cases where the officials were complicit or unsympathetic, even such small victories would be more difficult to achieve.[109]

One such case was that of Guo Guangyun, an honest official in Hebei province. In 1995 Guo wrote a letter to the central government accusing Cheng Weigao, the former Party secretary of Hebei, of collaborating with a corrupt official who was vice head of the Hebei Construction Committee. Contrary to the regulations, the letter fell into Cheng's hands. In November 1995 Cheng, now serving as governor of Hebei, had Guo detained. Guo was put in jail where he was questioned and tortured on a daily basis. In January 1996 he was released but immediately consigned to a labor camp for two more years on grounds of having vilified provincial leaders. Deeply aggrieved, Guo wrote more letters to the central government complaining about Cheng. He also used connections to get word of his case to Wei Jianxing, one of the highest-ranking CCP leaders. Wei made two interventions regarding Guo's case, but neither of them was heeded by the Hebei provincial government. It was not until 2003 when Cheng retired from all his provincial posts and power that Guo finally obtained redress of his grievance.

Guo was hardly a typical commoner; he was rather an official who enjoyed contacts with a very high official. He nonetheless endured years of hardship for having lodged a reasonable charge against a higher official. Indeed, his experience made him feel like a simple commoner. In his words, "How small, isolated, and helpless an ordinary person like me feels when he confronts [the government's] arrogance, inefficiency, and negligence!"[110] Indeed, that is how many commoners feel as they try to blow the whistle on official corruption and abuse of power.

As in previous times, many common citizens resisted local misgovernment by complaining directly to the central government. In 2003, I met a couple from Tangshan, Hebei, in Beijing who were making a complaint to the Central Disciplinary Committee. According to them, the husband had lost his left leg in late 2002 when he was hit by a truck. The local police first arrested the truck driver but they soon released him secretly without obtaining any compensation for the victim. Suspecting that the police had taken bribes from the driver, the couple complained to the local police but they were quickly dismissed. They then chose to mount a skipping complaint in Beijing without visiting other levels of the administration in Hebei. The wife said that it was common for farmers in their village to lodge direct complaints of this kind. When asked what to do if the central organs did not satisfy their grievance, the wife said they would come again until it was solved.[111]

Like aggrieved people in earlier ages, many complainants in this contemporary period expressed deep-rooted faith in heavenly/natural principles, heaven–human interactions, parental rulers/officials, and *minben*/people as the root. In Luonan county, Shannxi, the magistrate Ma Baoquan was famous for taking care of the local people and for resolving many complaints. In 1998 the local people were said to have described him as the "parental official who loves people (*aimin fumuguan*)," terms very familiar in both dynastic and republican periods.[112] In October 2008, Jiao Jitang, a commoner from Lingtai, Gansu, complained to leaders in Beijing that the local police harbored a suspect who had kidnapped his sister who was disabled with psychosis. Profoundly believing in a righteous heaven and retribution, Jiao denounced those local officials who had ignored his repeated complaints and he expressed the wish that they would soon be punished by heaven (*tianqian*) for their offenses against heavenly/natural principles.[113] On April 13, 2010, hundreds of people in Zhuanhe city, Liaoning, like subjects in the dynasties, kowtowed in front of the city government hoping that the mayor—the parental official—would take action against village corruption. But the mayor refused to meet the complainants.[114]

Collective complaints grew in number and importance in this period. We have already seen them in response to the farmers' burden and relocation. Many scholars have recently studied such major strategies as "rightful resistance," "justice from below," "issue linkage" and "disruptive tactics" used in collective actions in China.[115] Although the Regulation Regarding Letters and Visits restricts collective complainants to only five delegates to present their complaints, many collective complainants largely ignore this part of the law. During a visit to the Shanghai letters and visits office in 2003, I found hundreds of complainants filling the waiting hall. A businessman from Fujian said his group included more than 100 people who had invested in a textile market in Qibao, Shanghai, in the last year. But recently the market owner had fled, taking all their investments with him. Because the market had been endorsed by the Qibao township government, the investors had complained to the Qibao township and district governments but without any effect. The investors thus had come to the city government to complain. Although the law forbade collective complaints of more than five people, the businessman believed that hundreds of complainants would be a pressure big enough to force the Shanghai government to take action.[116] The result of this case is unknown, but the strategy of using large numbers of complainants to persuade officials to respond has been adopted by other collective complainants.[117]

An assessment of the complaint systems

The CCP is aware of the seriousness of the complaint problem. On the one hand, it recognizes people's right to seek legal support and to complain about official misconduct. It has passed important guidelines such as the Regulation Regarding

Letters and Visits and several administrative laws to regularize the complaint process. On the other hand, it wants to restrict collective complaints which could easily get out of hand and challenge the authority of the state. In 2003, as more people took collective complaints to the capital, the CCP began to consider the number of complaints coming from a locality as evidence of the effectiveness of local officials. According to an official in a northern county, the National Bureau of Letters and Visits (*guojia xinfangjü*) secretly stipulated that any magistrate confronted with a collective complaint of more than fifty people should resign and the official in charge of the letters and visit office should be fired. Another confidential central order prevented any county sending collective complaints to Beijing from being considered an "advanced county," thus depriving the magistrate of any chance to be promoted.[118]

Although the state has not publicized these central orders to avoid enhancing the power of complainants, many local officials who are aware of them have become quite fearful of complaints, especially collective ones. One vice township head in 2003 reported to me that whenever farmers complained to the upper-level governments, local officials' posts would be in danger. Consequently, local officials would rather spend money "bribing complainants" than allow them to proceed to the capital.[119] No matter what efforts the CCP and local governments have made to increase the effectiveness of the general complaint system, the system has come under heavy criticism from contemporary scholars and reporters.

Between December 14 and 19, 2001, an investigation of the *Xinhua News Agency* on forty complainants at the letters and visits office in Dalian, Liaoning, found that only two of them had had their grievances redressed there. Some complainants said that complaints were even harder to register at lower levels of the government. They had come to Dalian only because they had found no one at a lower level willing to entertain their complaints.[120] Similarly, a reporter of the *New York Times* argued in March 2004 that the Chinese complaint system "which involves filing formal complaints with certain agencies, is largely considered a futile exercise."[121]

So far, the most authoritative investigation on China's general complaint system is one made by Yu Jianrong, a researcher at the Chinese Academy of Social Science. According to Yu's recent statistics of 632 farmer complaints in Beijing, merely 0.2 percent of them had satisfied their grievances through complaints.[122]

To be sure, the above gloomy figures and reports have their limitations. They may underestimate the effectiveness of the complaint system. Based on my interviews and study of documents, I find different complaints may have different chances of effectiveness. For example, as we might expect, complaints against lower-ranked individual officials and policemen are more likely to be satisfied than those against higher-ranked or well-connected officials or policemen. Moreover, as other scholars have found, some collective complaints have a better chance of success than some individual ones.[123] The extremely low (0.2 percent) success rate of complaints in Beijing may be much lower than success rates at the local level because, as Ethan Michelson argues, many local heads are willing to redress people's grievances.[124]

In this period, one of the biggest causes of skyrocketing natural resistance is the predatory policy resulting from bureaucratic pragmatism at both state and local levels. In the words of Douglass C. North, a "predatory state" will maximize the revenue of the group in power at the expense of the rest of society.[125] The Farmers Burden, Rural Land Confiscation, and Urban Relocation have to different degrees severely violated people's rights. In the 1990s, rural complainants launched numerous efforts at rightful and natural resistance against the ever-increasing burdens. Yet the root of the problem was in central government policy, so their burdens did not diminish at first. Only in 2000, when the farmers' natural resistance threatened to develop into open rebellions did the central government finally change its policies and reduce local taxes. Complaints against government confiscation of land and urban relocation have been less successful. In major cities such as Beijing, Tianjin, and Shanghai, the lives and properties of many legal residents have been threatened by local governments or government-backed companies without redress. Citizens like Pi Shufeng, the Nanjing man who immolated himself, and the senior teachers in Zhejiang, were unable to redress their grievances through police, courts, and governments at both local and central levels.

While the CCP promulgated laws to allow people to complain—the "natural" right of the "masters" of the PRC, it also followed the later dynasties (but not the republic) in banning skipping complaints and authorizing both central and local officials to discourage them.[126] In 2002, for example, the Heilongjiang government made a regulation that allowed police to detain any complainant who insisted on "unreasonable requests" instead of what could be settled through legal means. The same year, an old woman was detained for seventy-five days simply because she had filed numerous skipping complaints in Beijing over a long period of time. Almost one year later, the woman, who was continuing her complaints in Beijing, lived in fear that police from Heilongjiang would find and detain her.[127]

Like local governments, police in Beijing could also detain people who made illicit skipping or direct complaints to Beijing.[128] The detention centers themselves may have been designed to discourage skipping complaints. Wang Xueping, a complaint leader who was detained by the Beijing police in the 1980s told a researcher that he would never allow himself to be detained in Beijing again as the conditions were simply too terrible.[129]

To contain the surging complaints, many local governments or state-run companies pursued other means. In 2003, an electric company in Fengcheng city, Jiangxi, threatened to fine any workers who lodged complaints to the government about the company's latest dismissal plan.[130] Many local governments use organized crime members to attack complainants and take revenge on them. According to a *China Youth Daily* report, about 53.6 percent of polled complainants had been attacked by criminal gangs connected with local officials.[131] Aggrieved people who try to complain through the internet are sometimes severely punished as part of the government effort to curb rising complaints. According to a report of Human Rights in China, in 2004, Ma Yalian, a complainant who had posted articles on the internet exposing the dark side of China's complaint system, was sentenced to one and half years of Reeducation Through Labor (RTL, *laogai*).[132]

As in most periods of Chinese history, corrupt officials, especially powerful government heads, not only caused countless grievances but also made it more difficult for them to be satisfied.[133] In Guo Guangyun's fight with the Hebei governor, it took him eight years to attain some measure of relief. In cases such as the land confiscation in Qihe, Shandong, and Pi Shufeng in Beijing, many local officials took advantage of decentralization to act more independently and to show less care for people's rights.

Political protection and nepotism had existed under Mao Zedong, but they became worse under the more paternalistic and market-oriented regimes of Deng Xiaoping and Jiang Zemin. Despite Jiang Zemin's repeated cliché that the Chinese people were the masters of the PRC, he also noted that the CCP should be the leader and "educate" the people.[134] This statement in essence is reminiscent of the Confucian *minben* concept and is akin to Sun Yat-sen, Chiang Kai-shek, and Mao Zedong's *minben*-like arguments. Hence, the Chinese people, as in the past, have little means and power in checking the state and its corrupt officials. With protection from the top, stress of loyalty, and bureaucratic pragmatism,[135] government officials in this period have come to exercise nearly unchecked power. Some utilize their power to recruit their relatives and friends to government posts, and others make profits from selling official posts. These efforts create a powerful and closely connected official net, generating more complaints and making it more difficult for people to complain against certain officials. In 2003, the Party secretary of Xiangfan, Hubei, and many of his subordinates, were arrested and charged with corruption. Yu Zhengsheng, the Party secretary of Hubei province, acknowledged that many of those officials had acquired their posts through bribes in a climate in which the "buying and selling official posts have become a market behavior."[136] Nepotism and commercialization together create a powerful integrated network that both generates more complaints and impedes efforts to obtain justice. We have seen this network in action in the cases of Yang Xiaomin, Hu Yuanjin, and Wang Peirong.

During the 1980s and 1990s, Deng Xiaoping and Jiang Zemin repeatedly called for ruling according to law and for establishing judicial independence. But in 1997 Jiang reaffirmed that the law was the tool of the Party.[137] In 2003, a Supreme Court justice stated that all courts should follow the Party.[138] Under Party rule, power generally surpasses the law, which obviously contradicts standard Marxist principles that the judiciary should be independent.[139] A famous judge complained in 2003 that it was very hard to be a judge in China because "the law is the condiment (*tiaoweipin*) of the ruler" which he uses in his own interest.[140] Accordingly, in this period, when people file complaints to the Administrative Court against official violations of their rights, most of them would find that the court could do little to redress their grievances.

Even when courts arrived at just conclusions about a case, there was no guarantee that their decisions would be implemented. In 2003, the head of the Intermediate Court in Xuzhou, Jiangsu, argued that the toughest thing under heaven was enforcing court judgments.[141] In April 1996, one year before Jiang Zemin's call for ruling by law, a policeman in Kaili county, Guizhou, was suddenly dismissed for no legitimate reason. He complained to the local labor mediation committee, whose main duty was dealing with disputes between employees and employers. After four years of investigation, the committee decided that the police bureau's dismissal was unlawful. It demanded that the police bureau reimburse the policeman for his four years of lost salary. When the police bureau stalled, a local court issued several orders asking it to follow the committee's decision. For more than a year, the police bureau continued to ignore all such orders, even those coming from provincial leaders.[142] The policeman's complaint has yet to succeed. If a police department can treat one of its own members in such an arbitrary and unlawful fashion, one can easily imagine how it could disregard the rights of common citizens.

Despite reforms after 1982, the extra-legal complaint system has continued to suffer from some internal problems. For example, owing to a lack of political will and enough personnel, both central and provincial letters and visits offices generally have to pass complaints down to the lower levels for resolution. Consequently, contrary to the explicit provisions of the regulations, complaints will often fall into the hands of the very persons who are being charged. In such cases, complainants become highly vulnerable to retaliation and their complaints risk being buried. We may recall here the cases of Wang Peirong and Guo Guangyun whose complaints to the central government eventually fell into the hands of their local opponents greatly complicating the redress of their grievances. In the words of an article published by the *China Youth Daily* in 1986, "Those [officials] who ignore both state law and Party regulations share one common notion: wherever [complainants] complain, [their complaints] have to be settled by them [the original officials]." As a result, those officials are less afraid of skipping or direct complaints than they might otherwise be.[143]

As in the early PRC, the letters and visits offices continue to be the most popular places for people to register their complaints.[144] But in many cases the offices are unwilling to accept people's complaints. Even in cases they accept, they usually find it hard to impose their judgments on officials who have the "real" power to satisfy or reject people's grievances.[145] To give but one example, in 2001 a farmer in Hunan complained to the county government about the destruction of her house by the local officials with insufficient compensation. No one accepted her complaint. In the city letters and visits office, an official told her that the office could do nothing if the county government did not act. The woman visited the provincial letters and visits office, which wrote a letter to the county on her behalf. But a county official told her that such letters were useless. The woman had to complain to the provincial letters and visits office where she was repeatedly told that the office could not solve her problem unless the county government acted. In April 2002, after a year of such exhausting activity, the woman gave up and returned to her hometown. In this respect, she was different from many complainants both past and present who persist in bringing their complaints to the central government despite repreated setbacks, but she may be more representative than they in reconciling herself to the limits of the existing system.[146]

While there are millions of complaints annually, no complainants, especially those going to the capital, can continue to complain regardless of the costs, hardship, and even dangers. Many complainants who cannot endure these difficulties eventually have to back down. Although satisfying grievances in the court system is more expensive, complaining to letters and visits offices is also not cheap. Like many complainants in the past (e.g., Zhu Zhaolian in the late Qing), some complainants in the PRC also have to beg their way to the cities to complain.[147] Some lose their lives in the process of complaining against powerful government organs. In early 2002, a businessman named He Haisheng in Hainan became involved in a court case that may have cost him his life. His mother had established a company that was transferred to another party by a local court. She appealed to a higher court but that court endorsed the lower court's decision. Suspecting that there was a network within the Hainan court system, He Haisheng complained to the Central Disciplinary Committee in Beijing. In taking this step, he apparently believed that the central government remained heaven's representative on earth, a paternalistic authority of last resort that would mete out justice when lower government bodies did not. He Haisheng's bold complaints resulted in numerous threats to his life. On June 25, 2002, he suddenly died without any explanation. His mysterious death abruptly ended the investigation because others who had promised He to testify left China for fear of future retribution.[148]

Conclusion

Since 1978, as part of the comprehensive reform toward "modernity", the PRC has implemented measures to protect and channel people's constitutional rights to complain about official abuses. It has formalized the system of letters and visits offices, revised the regulations regarding letters and visits, and established the Administrative Courts against misgovernment. Some of these reforms hark back to the system in place during the republican period and some involve improvements on past practices. Meanwhile, the ongoing socioeconomic reform, decentralization, and especially the practice of "bureaucratic pragmatism" in the 1990s resulted in more official violations of people's rights than before. Some complainants respond with "rightful resistance" in which they cite existing laws as bases for pushing back against violations of their rights. Many others go beyond the laws to lodge skipping and direct complaints justified by what I would call the ideology and practice of "natural resistance." Collective complaints by large groups greatly exceeding the statutory limit of five representatives are on the rise, threatening in some cases to turn into civil disobedience or even open rebellion. Until the PRC adopts more effective political reforms separating the Party from the state, making both subordinate to the law, and addressing growing inequities in the socioeconomic system, such natural resistance, rooted in Chinese culture and history and refreshed by influences from outside, seems likely to increase.

Conclusion

Natural resistance in three periods

We may divide the development of natural resistance and various complaint systems in Chinese history into three basic periods.

During the first (see Chapter 1), some crucial and long-lasting ideas such as heavenly principles, the mandate of heaven, *minben*/people as the root, the paternalism of rulers, and heaven–human interactions were initiated by a variety of important schools of thought and they were later shared by both the rulers and the subjects. Together those notions helped lay the foundation of natural resistance—the heavenly/natural right of people to complain against governmental abuses. Governments from the semi-legendary ages of the sage kings such as Yao and Shun through the more fully historical Zhou, Qin, and Han tended to be in relatively close touch with the population. Commoners as well as officials felt comfortable complaining to the central administration when local officials abused their power. Although our sources are limited, it appears that there were no formal or institutionalized systems for registering complaints in this period and even the idea of such systems was inserted into ancient texts by later generations of scholars.

During the second period (see Chapter 1), from the Jin through most of the Qing, as the central states became more powerful and bureaucratized, rulers and officials recognized the need to establish specific central mechanisms, such as the petition drum of the Jin, and formal institutions, such as the Public Petitioners' Drum Office of the Song and the Chief Surveillance Office of the Ming, for the reception and handling of people's complaints. Such states, each in its own way, also regularized the complaint process as part of the judicial system. Thus the Tang encouraged complaints initiated at the local level and outlawed complaints that did not follow the regular steps. In addition, the Tang law prohibited officials from accepting illegal complaints regardless of whether or not such complaints had merit. The Southern Song and the early Ming, on the other hand, as part of their efforts to strengthen the central administration, briefly allowed and even encouraged people to make such nominally illegal "skipping complaints." To manage the increase in skipping complaints, the Yuan, Ming, and Qing mostly followed the Tang by punishing skipping complainants. But in some short periods, they followed the Southern Song by temporarily encouraging such complaints, by addressing the issues, and even occasionally by redressing the wrongs for such practical reasons as consolidating the central power or checking local corruption. Hence, although the commoners' natural right to complain was still respected in the second period as in the first period, certain avenues of complaint, such as skipping and direct complaints, were now restricted or even punished in most of the successive polities. Despite the harsh laws, however, many aggrieved persons, retaining firm belief in heavenly principles, *minben*/people as the root, and the parental ruler–heaven's representative (son) on earth, continued to make skipping or direct complaints that were mostly prohibited by the law. Some natural resisters, after their last hopes were dashed in the capital, would take extreme measures such as cutting their flesh or killing themselves. During this period, complaint systems, for better and for worse, became integral parts of the judicial systems that were themselves integral parts of the successive Chinese states.

From the late nineteenth century through the present (Chapters 2 to 6), Chinese governments have supplemented inherited informal and formal mechanisms with new institutions designed to accommodate people's complaints against officials and to enhance people's involvement in government. Inspired by republican and democratic principles and contemporary practices in Europe, the Qing court proposed the establishment of an Administrative Court with special responsibility for handling complaints against officials. The early republic inaugurated this court and made it separate from the rest of the judicial system that was itself expected to be independent of the executive and legislative branches of the state. Drawing on the long Chinese tradition of complaining and on the new republican idea that people should be the master of the state, both early and later republican regimes adopted various methods to justify and enhance people's right to complain. For instance, the early republic created a Department for Disciplining Government and opened the doors of various central government agencies, such as the Interior Ministry, to receive people's complaints, while the later republic retained the Administrative Court and expanded the number of government organs authorized to accept people's complaints. Although the republican laws, as in the post-Sui period, required complainants to follow the legal steps, many natural resisters continued to invoke traditional notions such as heavenly principles, *minben*/people as the root, and parental rulers as well as the new republicanism to justify their skipping or direct complaints to central organs or the ruler. Unlike their counterparts in the dynasties after the Sui, natural resisters in the republic did not face punishment. As shown in the case of Liu Haixu vs. Zeng Peiyuan (Chapter 4), President Chiang Kai-shek would sometimes respond to skipping or direct complaints.

After the CCP took power in 1949, it immediately abolished much of the republican judicial system, including the Administrative Court. Influenced by what I may call revolutionary idealism, however, it also established a comprehensive system of letters and visits that made popular participation in governance legally and politically legitimate. As it happened, after an initial burst of popular participation in politics and policy making, people increasingly used these new offices to register complaints against local officials. As I have shown in Chapter 5, numerous natural resisters continued to complain directly to the Party central including Mao. Under the reforms after 1978, the PRC restored the Administrative Court and moved to make the judicial system more autonomous. It also preserved the letters and visits system, which retained political as well as judicial functions. Like the Complaint Law in the republic, the new regulations of the letters and visits system prohibited skipping and direct complaints. However, as predatory bureaucratic pragmatism gained momentum after 1990, natural resistance, especially collective natural resistance, witnessed a renewed surge in both number and scale of instances.

Despite the varieties of and changes in Chinese complaint systems over time, there are two elements that have persisted to the present. First, the practice of complaining to the palace gate, the oldest form of complaint, continues to be frequently practiced by complainants in China today. Second, the notion of natural right to complain, based initially on unbearable grievances, heavenly principles, the Confucian *minben* concept, parental rulers, and heaven–human interactions, and bolstered in more recent times by republicanism, has persisted in the minds and to some extent in the practices of Chinese rulers and people.

Fundamental problems and pseudo-*minben*/people as the root

While we may conclude that successive Chinese polities have persistently acknowledged people's natural right to complain, we must also recognize that many grievances in most periods remained unsatisfied. This was true even during the reigns of so-called good or effective rulers such as Tang Xuanzong and Ming Taizu. Many complaints continued to be made and ignored even during the republic in which the people were supposed to have become masters of the country. In the People's Republic, the CCP, the self-proclaimed representative of the people, revived the administrative court and created the most comprehensive complaint system in history to address people's complaints, but the number and intensity of complaints, especially natural resistance, have continued to increase. The inadequacies of various complaint systems are partly to blame for the mounting number of complaints and for the high percentage of unsatisfied grievances. As we have seen, grievances during each period of Chinese history have their particular causes, including civil wars, one-party rule in the republic, political movements in the early PRC, and bureaucratic pragmatism in contemporary China. Yet, if we consider Chinese history as a whole, it will be clear that some fundamental problems intrinsic or related to the complaint systems and natural resistance either persist throughout all periods or recur from one period to another.

Aside from problems such as the paucity of judicial independence and internal dysfunctions of the complaint systems that may have resulted in numerous unsatisfied grievances, I would argue that the biggest problems hampering redress of those grievances and fueling countless instances of natural resistance have been political corruption and bureaucratic protection. These fundamental problems have appeared in most historical periods and polities.

Why have both fundamental problems lasted in most historical periods? Why were Chinese polities, including dynasties and republics unable to solve those problems? The most fundamental problem, I submit, was the existence of what I may call pseudo-*minben.*

The Confucian concept of *minben* or people as the root of a state aims to provide a potentially strong foundation for a more responsible political system. But it also all too easily serves as a cover for political corruption and bureaucratic protection. As an important Confucian doctrine, the concept of *minben* frequently appeared in the discussions and edicts of Chinese rulers over the ages. After the introduction of republicanism in the early twentieth century, leaders from Yuan Shikai to Chiang Kai-shek continued to use the *minben* concept to justify their authoritarian rule (see Chapter 4). In the PRC, despite Mao's revolutionary rhetoric that the people would govern the state and that the CCP should serve the people whole-heartedly,[1] he insisted that the CCP should be the real power holder and the leading core (*lingdao hexin*) of the Chinese people. During the Cultural Revolution, Mao became nearly a "living god" in many people's eyes, a concept that was more consistent with the Chinese notion of cosmic authority as well as the Western concept of divine right than with democracy.

Even today, the rule by one paternalistic political party offers the Chinese people little opportunity to challenge the state when it fails to fulfill its rightful functions. China's current ruler, Hu Jintao, argues for "building a Party that serves the interests of the public and governs for the people.[2] This statement is similar to that of the Guangxü emperor who remarked in the late Qing that his court was dedicated to serving the people. Like their leaders, many PRC officials have interpreted the concept of *minben* as a paternalistic call for good—but not necessarily democratic—rule. For example, a Hebei magistrate said he wanted to be the "blue sky" for the people, an image that required him to be an honest parental official without opening the door to popular participation in government.[3] The Party secretary of Chongqing, Bo Xilai, insisted that "parental officials" should have genuine affection for the people and should really do something for the people, but he did not say what he thought the people's role should be.[4]

From this we can see that the *minben* practice by most Chinese rulers in history differed in many respects from the original concept of *minben.* As one of the classics, *The Book of Documents* clearly stated, the "people are the base of the state" and "heaven hears as the people hear, heaven sees as the people see."[5] The most radical definition of the *minben* concept was made by Mencius. Mencius cherished an ideal state governed by an enlightened and humane ruler, and some of his arguments were close in theory to those of what has come to be understood as democracy.[6] For instance, Mencius believed that the ruler should take care of people's livelihood. His most famous argument was, "the people are the most important element in a state, next are the gods and grain, least is the ruler himself." A ruler who committed mistakes and refused to correct them should be removed. Mencius also justified people's right to rebel against a ruler who became a tyrant.[7]

If compared with the idea of *minben* in such classics, the *minben* concept that has been understood and practiced by most rulers from the past to the present has not been a "real" *minben* but a pseudo one. Although most rulers have loved to say that people are the base or even the masters of a state, in most cases they have actually made the ruling class or Party the most important player in the state.[8] Most rulers, like the Ming founder, have not believed that the people should ever have the right to rebel against them and they ardently embraced Confucian paternalism, patriarchy, and hierarchy. While patriarchal rulers are inclined to show fatherly love to their "children"—the people—they at the same time and for the same reason tend to treat the people as powerless and needing their guidance and governance. In a pseudo-*minben* state, officials are not elected by the people but are selected by their own superiors. When appointing officials, paternalistic/parental rulers do not typically bother to ask the people for advice, which explains why few officials have been elected directly by the people since the founding of the republic in 1911.

Since his power comes from his superiors, an official is more likely to answer to his superior than to the people he governs. Officials in a pseudo-*minben* state, be it a dynastic family state or a republican party state, have been less attentive to the people, who are their "children," than to their superiors, who are their actual masters. The power of many appointed officials depends not on their capacities but on their loyalty to their superiors. Chiang Kai-shek was said to have the habit of "handing out posts for political reasons or as rewards for loyalty, rather than as a recognition of ability."[9] The CCP has been no better in this respect than the GMD. According to the research of one careful scholar, only the Center has absolute power. All officials are vulnerable to those above them because their superiors often have extraordinary leverage over them in terms of career advancement, housing placement, and even marriage and divorce.[10] Even a recent CCP magazine admits that, thirty years after the reform, the appointment of major Party cadres continues to be dominated by a few persons.[11] In the 1990s, as China became more decentralized, subordinate officials seems to have more opportunities to pursue corrupt policies of extraction from the people than to assert their independence from the top leadership. Accordingly, to keep their power and to achieve promotions, PRC officials have every practical incentive to follow their superiors closely. In return, when they face troubles or even commit crimes, their superiors are very likely to protect them.

Given such "good connections" between upper- and lower-level officials, corruption and bureaucratic protection are almost inevitable. With the protection from above, many officials, have become so bold that they have little to fear by infringing people's rights.[12] In the Song dynasty, some magistrates openly encouraged clerks to transgress people's rights.[13] Qing magistrates were also reported to love clerks who saw people as no different from powerless grass or wood.[14] In the later republic, the head of the Yunnan provincial garrison reportedly blamed his chauffeur for swerving to avoid hitting a pedestrian, thus inconveniencing the passenger. With his great power, the military officer was not afraid of committing the manslaughter of an innocent person.[15] In the PRC period, a magistrate in northern Hebei province confidentially described many officials as "official masters" who enjoyed enormous privileges rather than as "servants of the people".[16] In the case of professor Wang Peirong, the Xuzhou policeman abused his authority without qualms because he enjoyed protection from his superiors.

Although political corruption and bureaucratic protection have emboldened officials to violate people's rights, forced aggrieved people to take the method of natural resistance, and have rendered the PRC letters and visits system more ritual than substance,[17] such practices sometimes also backfire, especially in dealing with collective natural resistance. That is because many desperate complainants can turn to rebellion if they have no way to satisfy their collective grievances. In the late eighteenth century, the leading scholar-official Hong Liangji (1746–1809) warned emperor Qianlong: "When people know that they cannot redress their grievances through complaints to the upper levels, they will rebel."[18] Examples of this were the 1871 and 1910 tax rebellions, both of which originated as collective complaints that were strictly banned.[19] More recently in the PRC, local official's failure to deal with popular but unsanctioned collective natural resistance about a suicide case in Weng'an county, Guizhou, resulted in popular riots against the state.[20] Desperate individual natural resisters, of course, have less power to initiate a local disturbance. The most they can do is to continue their unsuccessful complaints to embarrass the government or take extreme measures such as hurting or killing themselves as a last resort to draw attention to their complaints and perhaps bring down heavenly retribution against their tormentors. If the grievances of individual natural resisters accumulate, however, they may at least weaken the legitimacy of the government. During a crisis, such people may at best fold their arms and not offer resistance to rebels and at worst join in the opposition against the government.

With the belief and practice of natural resistance on the one side and political corruption and bureaucratic protection on the other, Chinese complainants confront an unpromising fate. In the absence of more fundamental reform, what the Chinese dissident Guo Luoji ironically calls the "Chinese grandeur" of millions of complainants flooding various central and local governments will not disappear anytime soon.[21]

Two likely models

As both the Tang emperor Taizong and the Song scholar-official Sima Guang argued, history is a mirror through which we can learn lessons from the past. Through careful study and analysis, we may know better what may have caused those recurrent fundamental problems in the long history of Chinese complaint systems and what policies the Chinese state may have to adopt today to make the complaint systems more effective and fair. In particular, two periods in Chinese history might provide models for today's reformers. During the early period, thinkers such as Confucius and Mencius developed ideas of the people as the root of the state that had presumably inspired earlier rulers such as Zhou Wenwang and would inspire later rulers such as Han Wendi. During this period, even the imperious Han Wudi was quite attentive to people's complaints so that even some commoners felt free to lodge direct complaints to the ruler (see Chapter 1). Similarly, during the early republic, inspired by Western ideals of the rule of law and judicial independence, judges of the administrative court entertained complaints from the general public against even the highest authorities, arguably producing another kind of golden age in the complaint system at least in Beijing and nearby regions (see Chapter 3).

Despite its continuing nominal respect for people's right to complain, the People's Republic may not be willing any time soon to retain and improve its complaint systems to enhance the rule of law, advance the cause of both legal and natural justice, or increase the level of democracy. But it may ultimately find it necessary to do so to increase the chances of political and social stability.[22] If many people have forgotten the Qing scholar-official Hong Liangji's warning that the failure to redress people's grievances could result in rebellions, most people cannot ignore the more recent case in Weng'an, Guizhou, where the failure of a collective complaint resulted in a popular uprising. Even unsatisfied individual grievances, however often relatively hidden, may be quietly eroding the legitimacy of the governing party. Once enough of them accumulate they may break out like a prairie fire. In this regard, in the long run persistent individual grievances may prove to be more hazardous to the Chinese government than periodic collective complaints.

Epilogue

Chinese complaint systems after 2005

The 2004 national debate about the complaint system that I discuss in the Introduction of this book ended with the promulgation of the new *Regulations Regarding Letters and Visits* in 2005. Many officials and newspapers immediately expressed optimism. They hailed the new regulations as being able to "improve the letters and visits offices' capacity to tackle problems and resolve social contradictions better and faster."[1] Zhu Jingwen, a law professor at the Chinese People's University, believed the new regulations reflected "the spirit of the rule of law" and were useful in protecting "people's rights." An official working in the National Bureau of Letters and Visits said the new regulations would provide complainants with greater "protection of their rights."[2]

Several years after the promulgation of the new regulations, however, evidence coming from various sources such as my own interviews, the research of Human Rights Watch, and reports of both Chinese and Western newspapers shows that old habits die hard. The millennial pattern of the natural right to complain continues to coexist with fundamental problems like political corruption and bureaucratic protection.

For example, the new letters and visits regulations continues to allow people to complain. Like all former regulations, the new regulations are supposedly designed to maintain close relations between the government and the masses. They stipulate that all levels of government should clear the path for submitting complaints and expedite the process of redressing grievances. To better protect complainants, the new regulations for the first time require all government heads above the township to deal with important letters and visits and make clear that any official who has violated the rights of or taken revenge on complainants will be subject to punishment. At the same time, the new regulations, like the 1995 regulations and previous laws from the Tang through the Republic of China, outlaw all skipping complaints and collective complaints brought by more than five people. Extreme measures of complaint, such as besieging or assaulting state organs, stopping public vehicles, and blocking means of transportation, are strictly forbidden. To be sure, unlike dynastic laws after the Tang, the new regulations do not make such actions punishable crimes,[3] but many skipping complaints are punished by local officials with tacit if not open central permission.

Unyieldingly believing in their natural right to complain, numerous aggrieved citizens have continued to skip required levels and lodge jumping or direct complaints to both local and central governments every year since 2005. According to a report in the respected *Southern Weekend*, the situation of recent letters and visits remains as serious as it was in the past. The Chinese Academy of Social Science claims that contemporary China has developed a so-called "Complaint Culture" as many complainants swamp central organs and come back again after the government sends them back home. Thousands of them choose not to leave Beijing but to stay in the "complaint village, a ghetto created by aggrieved complainants outside Beijing."[4] A spokesman of the National Bureau of Letters and Visits acknowledged in 2007 that most of the current complaints concentrated on five fields: land confiscation; urban relocation; environmental protection; reorganization and bankruptcy of certain enterprises; and disagreement over court decisions.[5] Among them, most are recurring problems.

In the summer of 2005, three months after the announcement of the new letters and visits regulations, I met a natural resister named Gao Chunyuan from Linzhang county, Hebei province, who had six times filed skipping complaints to central agencies in Beijing. According to Gao's account, he had signed a fifty-year contract in 1995 for planting pear trees. But in 2004, He Rixin, an envious village official, wanted to terminate the contract with Gao. When Gao refused, He allegedly destroyed Gao's trees. Deeply aggrieved, Gao began his skipping complaints to Beijing. Gao argued that the new regulations were "useless" because local officials refused to follow the orders of the letters and visits offices of the central government, which he had in his possession. Since then, Gao had continued making trips to Beijing and had visited the letters and visits offices of various central organs such as the People's Congress, the State Council, the Ministry of Public Security, and the Ministry of Inspection. Like natural resisters in the past, Gao invoked both heavenly principles and the concept of *minben* and wished that there were "blue sky" [upright] officials in Beijing who could punish the criminal (He Rixin) on behalf of heaven. In March 2006, ten months after the new regulations, Gao, like natural resisters in the past who trusted parental rulers, staunchly believed in the CCP leaders. As he said, the local officials did not take his case seriously and simply kicked him back and forth among different local government agencies, but the top [leaders] were good. He said he would continue to complain to Beijing despite a debt of 20,000 yuan, which he already owed to his relatives for their support for his efforts to complain.[6]

Despite Gao's continuing faith that complaining to Beijing will eventually pay off, his experience strongly suggests that the new letters and visits regulations have failed to improve the situation and this view is shared by overseas observers. In late 2005, Human Rights Watch, a non-governmental organization based in New York City, issued a report based on interviews with dozens of petitioners regarding their experience in China. The report argued that while the new regulations adopted on May 1, 2005 promised more protection to complainants and specifically prohibited official retaliation, "petitioners report that security personnel have continued to attack and detain them since that date." One complainant, surnamed Ming, a teacher from Shanxi, told researchers that after three members of his family were beaten to death by a group of thugs allegedly under the order of the village secretary he called the police, but they conducted no serious investigation. In the next eight months, he had gone to all levels of the government, including those in Beijing, seeking justice. Although the letters and visit offices in Beijing sent letters to the local government ordering it to deal with the case, no one took them seriously. The director of the local letters and visits office told Ming: "We'll drag it out till you're dead. Once you die, the problem will be solved."[7]

In 2008, just days before the grand opening ceremonies for the Beijing Olympics, many complainants were reportedly detained by police for fear that they could "smear" the image of China. In 2006, after their homes in Beijing's Qianmen district had been demolished by the government to make way for a modern commercial site, Zhang Wei and Ma Xiulan had complained to the local court. The had got no help, perhaps in part because the judges were all appointed by the CCP. Later they tried the more irregular path of complaining to foreign reporters who they said were the only people who would report what had happened to them. This time they were detained by police. The arrests came just two days before the Olympic Games started, clearly an effort to avoid embarrassment during the Games.[8]

As in most previous eras after the Sui dynasty, desperate natural resisters would continue to bring skipping or direct complaints to the central agencies, their last hopes and the ultimate authority under heaven. Some of them, driven by perceived violations of heavenly principles, violated the law by blocking leaders' cars or trying to break into leaders' houses. According to one report, a female complainant from Xuzhou, Jiangsu, disagreed with the final decision of a local court over her divorce. She went to Beijing and insisted on complaining to the central government to retrieve heavenly principles. This was, of course, already a violation of the new regulations. After many unsuccessful attempts in Beijing, she accepted a more extreme measure. Like complainant Zhao Shouyin in the late Qing who had attempted to block the royal cart to attain justice, this complainant attempted to break in through the Xinhua Gate to the compound where many CCP leaders live and work. She was immediately detained and sent home where she was held for ten-day custody.[9] Such "troublemaking," in Xi Chen's words, usually incurs only moderate punishments from the government because of their "credibility, justifiability, significance, and urgency."[10]

In the light of the defects of the letters and visits system, scholars such as Yu Jianrong have argued that the system should be terminated to clear the way for constructing the rule of law in China (see Introduction).[11] Other scholars and officials oppose Yu's view. They contend that the passage of the *Regulations Regarding Letters and Visits* per se is a step toward the rule of law. This is because the new regulations require both complainants and officials who deal with letters and visits to abide by the regulations.[12] However, both arguments seem to be problematic. On the one hand, as I have commented in the Introduction, Yu Jianrong seems to be unaware of the existence of various complaint systems in countries that claim to have sophisticated versions of the rule of law. Moreover, the letters and visits system may provide complainants with certain forms of assistance that the formal judicial system may not be able to do. For example, some minor problems can be solved more quickly and with less cost by the letters and visits system than they would be in the regular court system.[13]

On the other hand, the scholars and officials who oppose Yu and want to preserve the system tend to ignore the fact that requiring officials of the letters and visits system and complainants to obey the law makes only a small contribution to the general rule of law in China. Indeed, Carl Minzner has aptly argued that Chinese leaders only want to strengthen the letters and visits system to avoid undertaking "more sweeping political and legal reforms."[14] In other words, without more substantial political and legal reform, CCP's efforts to improve the letters and visits system will bear little fruit. As this whole study has shown, most complaints, especially those based on natural resistance, have been and are being triggered by official misbehavior. Therefore, it is imperative to develop the rule of law in China in general and not merely in the letters and visits system. As long as the CCP remains above the law and a pseudo-*minben* still dominates Chinese politics, government abuses of people's rights will not diminish. Also, until the CCP takes real and concrete steps toward the rule of law, those notions that have fostered the long-lived natural resistance, including heavenly principles, parental rulers, *minben*/people as the root, and republicanism, will surely persist.

Glossary

aimin fumuguan	爱民父母官
anchasi	按察司
ban zhimindi banfengjian shehui zhidu	半殖民地半封建社会制度
baodong	保董
Baogong	包公
baoguohui	保国会
baohu renquan	保护人权
baozhang	保长
bawang xieyi	霸王协议
bengu bangning	本固邦宁
budang	不当
bufa	不法
bufa chufen	不法处分
caizhengbu	财政部
chajishi	查稽室
chengbaofei	承包费
chengxu bufen	程序部分
chouxiang xingwei	抽象行为
chushen faguan	初审法官
dabianshu	答辩书
dabing	大病
dadian	大典
dajian	大奸
dalaoye	大老爷
daliqing	大理卿
dalisi	大理司
daliyuan	大理院
dangjiade	当家的
dapu	大仆
darenwu	大人物
dasikong	大司空
datong	大同
daxian	大宪

defang zhengfu	德方政府
dengwen guyuan	登闻鼓院
dengwengu	登闻鼓
denwenyuan	登闻院
dibao	邸报
difang tuanti	地方团体
diwang sixiang	帝王思想
dongfang zazhi	东方杂志
duchayuan	都察院
er'ci geming	二次革命
fan geming anjian peishen zanxingfa	反革命案件陪审暂行法
fanyi	番役
fanyou yundong	反右运动
faren	法人
faxue	法学
fayuan bianzhifa	法院编制法
fazhi	法治
fazhi zaixian	法治在线
fazhiguo	法治国
fazhijü	法制局
feibang	诽谤
feibang zhimu	诽谤之木
feishi	肺石
fengjian canyu sixiang	封建残余思想
fujia gongzi	附加工资
fumuguan	父母官
fuyi	复议
gaosu	告诉
gongbu	工部
gongbujü	工部局
gongche shangshu	公车上书
gongchefu	公车府
gonghe guo	共和国
gongshi	公事
Gongtong gangling	共同纲领
gongwuche	公务车
Guangdong mujuan weiyuanhui	广东募捐委员会
guanli fuwuling	官吏服务令
guihan	匦函
guishiyuan	匦使院
guofangjuan	国防捐
guojia	国家
guojia peichangfa	国家赔偿法
guojia xinfangjü	国家信访局
guojia xingzheng	国家行政

guomin zhengfu	国民政府
guomindang	国民党
guowuqing	国务卿
guowuyuan	国务院
guozi boshi	国子博士
gusi	鼓司
hezuoshe	合作社
hujun dudu	沪军都督
jiancha weiyuanhui	监察委员会
jianchating	监察厅
jianli	奸吏
jiantu	奸徒
jiao'an	教案
jiaodian fangtan	焦点访谈
jiating yanjiu	家庭研究
jiduan xianzhi	极端限制
jingbao	京报
jingfang	京访
jingkong	京控
jingqiaoqiao de geming	静悄悄的革命
jinshan zhijing	荆善之旌
jinxin minshi	尽心民事
jinyiwei	锦衣卫
jitian	祭田
jiutan tiaoli	纠弹条例
jiuxiang yundong	救乡运动
jizhongying	集中营
junguo dashi	军国大事
junwei	军委
junzheng	军政
juren	举人
kaihuanglü	开皇律
kaiminzhi	开民智
kechen	科臣
ketou	磕头
konggao	控告
lanyujia	拦御驾
lao Mao	老毛
laodongdui	劳动队
laogai	劳改
laojia	老家
liangge fanshi	两个凡是
libu shangshu	吏部尚书
lifa	理法
lifanyuan	理藩院

lijianshi	理检使
lijianyuan	理检院
lingdao hexin	领导核心
lishi yiliu	历史遗留
lixingshe	力行社
lizhi	礼制
manmeng huizang daiyu tiaojian	满蒙回藏待遇条件
minben	民本
mingaoguan	民告官
mingui junqing	民贵君轻
minguo	民国
minquan	民权
minshi	民事
minxingshi anjian	民刑事案件
minzhengting	民政厅
minzhiting	民治厅
minzhong	民众
minzhu	民主
minzu	民族
mishuting	秘书厅
mu	亩
Nanjing linshi zhengfu	南京临时政府
nanxuehui	南学会
neiwubu	内务部
pingzhengyuan	平政院
pingzhengyuan bianzhifa caoan	平政院编制法草案
pingzhengyuan bianzhiling	平政院编制令
pingzhengyuan caijue zhixing tiaoli	平政院裁决执行条例
pingzhengyuan suzhengting chuwu guize	平政院肃政厅处务规则
pudong tongxianghui	浦东同乡会
putong fating	普通法庭
putong fayuan	普通法院
putong sifa jiguan	普通司法机关
qiangxuehui	强学会
qiangzhi	强制
qingtian	青天
qingyuan	请愿
qiyuan	奇冤
quanli	权利
qunzhong xinjianzu	群众信件组
renmin de zhaopai	人民的招牌
renmin minzhu zhuanzheng	人民民主专政
renquan	人权
renquan shensheng	人权神圣
renzhi chuantong	人治传统

sanfan wufan yundong	三反五反运动
sangang wuchang	三纲五常
sanmin zhuyi	三民主义
sanzheng	三政
shangbiao	上表
Shanghai jianchajü	上海监察局
shangshusheng	尚书省
shenbao	申报
shenghuo zhoukan	生活周刊
shensheng	神圣
shenxingyuan	审刑院
shibao	时报
shiti bufen	实体部分
shiyi changji yi zhiyi	师夷长技以制夷
sifa	私法
sifa shenpansuo	司法审判所
sifa xingzhengbu	司法行政部
siqing yundong	四清运动
siquan	私权
situ	司徒
siwen bailei	斯文败类
suyuan	诉愿
suyuanfa	诉愿法
suzhengting	肃政厅
suzhengting gaosu gaofa zhangcheng	肃政厅告诉告发章程
taibao zhubo	太保主薄
tiandao	天道
tianfu ziyou	天赋自由
tianhe	天和
tianli	天理
tianliang	天良
tianliangshu	田粮署
tianqian	天谴
tiaoweipin	调味品
tidu yamen	提督衙门
tongmenghui	同盟会
tongsheng	童生
tongxiangguan	同乡官
tongzheng shisi	通政使司
tuzaishui	屠宰税
weirenmin fuwu	为人民服务
weixin	威信
wenguan baohufa	文官保护法
wenguan chengjie weiyuanhui	文官惩戒委员会
wenjing zhizhi	文景之治

wuquan xianfa	五权宪法
xianfa	宪法
xianfa yuanze	宪法原则
xianjinxian	先进县
xianming lingxiu	贤明领袖
xianzheng	宪政
xianzhi xianjuezhe	先知先觉者
xiaobao	小报
xinfang lingdao xiaozu	信访领导小组
xinfang tiaoli	信访条例
xinfang zhidu	信访制度
xingbu	刑部
xingzheng	行政
xingzheng caipanfa	行政裁判法
xingzheng caipanyuan guanzhi caoan	行政裁判管制草案
xingzheng fayuan	行政法院
xingzheng fayuan zuzhifa	行政法院组织法
xingzheng fuyi	行政复议
xingzheng fuyifa	行政复议法
xingzheng jiuji	行政救济
xingzheng shenpan	行政审判
xingzheng shenpan jigou	行政审判机构
xingzheng shenpansuo	行政审判所
xingzheng shenpanting	行政审判庭
xingzheng susong	行政诉讼
xingzheng susongfa	行政诉讼法
xingzheng zhuguan guanshu	行政主管官署
xingzhengquan	行政权
xinqingnian	新青年
xinzheng	新政
xishi	细事
xun'an jiancha yushi	巡按监察御史
xunzheng	训政
yanlu	言路
yipin	一品
yiqie xiangqiankan	一切向前看
yique	诣阙
yiyi shenli	异议审理
youqing	右倾
yubu langzhong	虞部郎中
yuesu	越诉
yushi gejue	与世隔绝
yushitai	御史台
yuya	鱼牙
zaisuyuan	再诉愿

zhangguan	长官
zhejiang jinyan zongjü	浙江禁烟总局
zhengfeng yundong	整风运动
zhengwuyuan	政务院
zhiguishi	知匦使
zhisu	直诉
zhonghua minguo Ezhou yuefa	中华民国鄂州约法
zhonghua minguo linshi yuefa	中华民国临时约法
zhonghua minguo linshi zhengfu zuzhifa caoan	中华民国临时政府组织草案
zhonghua minguo xunzheng shiqi yuefa	中华民国训政时期约法
zhonghua minguo yuefa	中华民国约法
zhonggong zhongyang bangongting	中共中央办公厅
zhongjü	终局
zhongshusheng	中书省
zhongyan	忠言
zhongyang jilü jiancha weiyuanhui	中央纪律委员会
zhongyang shujichu	中央书记处
zhongyang shujichu zhengzhi mishushi	中央书记处政治秘书室
zhongyang zhengfa xiaozu	中央政法小组
zhongyang yanjiuyuan	中央研究院
zhongwai ribao	中外日报
zhouli	周礼
zhuangshipin	装饰品
zhuanyehu	专业户
zhuanzhi	专制
zhuanzhi sixiang	专制思想
zhubo	主薄
zhudong	主动
zhuji shangsu	逐级上诉
zhuquan	主权
ziyou	自由
zongli qinqixin xiaozu	总理亲启信小组
zuimin	罪民
zuzhibu	组织部
zunzhong renge	尊重人格
zuzhu	族诛

Notes

Introduction

1 The letters and visits system in the PRC was first designed as a channel between the Communist leaders and the masses. People could use it not only to file complaints but also to offer suggestions. But it was soon flooded by people's complaints. For details about the original aims of the letters and visits system see Diao Jiecheng, *Renmin xinfang shilue*, 1996.
2 Yu Jianrong, "Xinfang zhidu gaige yu xianzheng jianshe," in *Ershiyi shiji*, July 2005. Also see Zhao Ling, "Guonei shoufen xinfang baogao huo gaoceng guanzhu," in *The Southern Weekend*, November 4, 2004.
3 Zhao Ling, "Xinfang gaige yinfa zhengyi," in *The Southern Weekend*, November 18, 2004.
4 Ying Xing, "Zuowei Teshu xingzheng jiuji de xinfang jiuji," in *Faxue Yanjiu*, 2004: 62.
5 Lex Heerma van Voss, ed., *Petitions in Social History*, 2002: 1.
6 Jonathan Haidt and Craig Joseph, "Intuitive Ethics: How Innately Prepared Intuitions Generate Culturally Variable Virtues," in *Daedalus*, 2004: 55.
7 "A Humble Farmer Plead his Own Case: The Workings of Ma'at," in Raymond Hylton, *The World's History Volume I: Documents Set*, 2001: 33–8.
8 Andreas Würgler, "Voices from among the 'Silent Masses': Humble Petitions and Social Conflicts in Early Modern Central Europe," 2002: 18, 33.
9 G. W. S. Barrow, *Feudal Britain*, 1956: 144, 150; A. F. Pollard, *The Evolution of Parliament*, 1964: 36, 264; Goldwin Smith, *A Constitutional and Legal History of England*, 1955: 156, 160; Harold J. Berman, *Law and Revolution*, 1983: 444.
10 Berman, 1983: 323.
11 Colin Turpin, *British Government and the Constitution*, 1999: 528–30.
12 Ibid.
13 Donald C. Rowat, *The Ombudsman Plan*, 1973: 2, 76.
14 Linda C. Reif, *The Ombudsman, Good Governance and the International Human Rights System*, 2004: 2, 11.
15 John A. Hannigan, "The Newspaper Ombudsman and Consumer Complaints," 1977: 698.
16 Ellen Philips, *Shocked, Appalled, and Dismayed*, 1997.
17 William Graebner and Leonard Richards, eds., *The American Record*, 2001: 225–9.
18 Kevin O'Brien, *Rightful Resistance in Rural China*, 2006; Kevin O'Brien, "Rightful Resistance," 1996: 31–55; Kevin O'Brien and Lianjiang Li, "The Politics of Lodging Complaints in Rural China," 1995: 756–83; Kevin O'Brien and Lianjiang Li, "Suing the Local State," 2005: 31–53.
19 Yongshun Cai, *Collective Resistance in China*, 2010: 185.
20 Isabelle Thireau and Hua Linshan, "The Moral Universe of Aggrieved Chinese Workers," 2003: 83–103.

21 Neil J. Diamant, "Hollow Glory," 2005: 131–58.
22 Xi Chen, "The Power of 'Troublemaking' Protest Tactics and Their Efficiency in China," 2009: 451–71.
23 Carl Minzner, "Xinfang," 2006: 179.
24 For Yu's works see *Yuecun zhengzhi*, 2000; "The Reform of the Letters and Visits System and Constitutional Construction"; "Denunciation of China's Xinfang System," in www.yannan.cn; "Dui xinfang zhidu gaige zhenglun de fansi," 2005; "Xinfang de zhiduxing queshi jiqi zhengzhi houguo," 2004.
25 Ying Xing, 2004: 60.
26 Laura M. Luehrmann, "Facing Citizen Complaints in China, 1951–1996," 2003; and her *Officials Face the Masses*, 2000.
27 Diao Jiecheng, 1996.
28 Yang Yifan and Liu Ducai, "Zhongguo gudai guihanzhidu kaolue," 1998.
29 Jonathan Ocko, "I'll Take it All the Way to Beijing," 1988: 314–15.
30 Huang Yuansheng, "Minguo diyi ge xingzheng susong shenpan jiguan," 2002.
31 Guangyuan Zhou, "Illusion and Reality in the Law of the Late Qing," 1993: 453.
32 Elizabeth J. Perry, *Challenging the Mandate of Heaven*, 2002: ix–xxxi.
33 Ying Xing, 2004: 66.
34 Yang and Liu, 1998.
35 David M. Engel, *Code and Custom in a Thai Provincial Court*, 1978.
36 Minzner, 2006: 124.
37 Capital appeals refer only to appeals that finally reach the state capital. They can be all the three forms of gradual/regular, skipping, and direct appeals and both informal and formal appeals. According to my research of the archives of the Qing Board of Punishment (*xingbu*), most capital appeals involved grave crimes such as homicides, forced suicides, or kidnappings.
38 Article 16 of the latest *The Regulations Regarding Xinfangs* (2005) requires appealers to complain by regular steps. See the *Regulations Regarding Xinfangs* in *The People's Daily*, May 1, 2005.
39 Minzner, 2006: 155; for the Human Rights Watch report see http://hrw.org/english/docs/2005/12/08/china12144_txt.htm.
40 O'Brien and Li, 2006.
41 Kung-chuan Hsiao, *A History of Chinese Political Thought*, 1979: 243; also Mo Zi, online; Liang Hong, *Shijing shangshu*, 2003: 133, 215.
42 Liang Hong, 2003: 238.
43 Song philosopher Zhu Xi (1130–1200) argued that heavenly principles were the Three Principles and Five Constant Virtues (*sangang wuchang*). But in the republican periods (1912–), heavenly principles are vague. Many complainants believe that the injustices imposed on them and their grievances violate heavenly principles. Zhu Xi, *Zhuzi daquan*, 1977, Vol. 70, p. 5.
44 Colin A. Ronan, *The Shorter Science and Civilization in China*, 1978: 289; Yu Ronggen, *Tianli guofa renqingde chongtu yuzhenghe*, 1998: 12–19.
45 Liang Hong, 2003: 208. Recent studies show that *minben* has also served as both satisfaction of popular demands and justification for rulers' power. See Edmund S. K. Fung, *The Intellectual Foundations of Chinese Modernity*, 2010: 166.
46 As Jonathan Ocko argues, this kind of state paternalism with which the rulers and officials performed as parents of the "family" (nation/people) and not property was the "missing" root metaphor in the pre-1900 China. Ocko, "Applying Western Legal Scholarship to the Study of Contract and Property in Early Modern China", 2004: 178–208; also see Dali L. Yang and Litao Zhao, *China's Reform at 30*, 2009: 186.
47 For a just and humane God in natural law see Thomas Aquinas, *The Summa Theologica of Saint Thomas Aquinas, Vol. 2*, 1952: 222; Harold J. Berman, 1983: 142.
48 For natural law see Aquinas, 1952: 208; Lloyd L. Weinreb, *Natural Law and Justice*,

1987: 58; for heaven see Feng Youlan, *Zhongguo zhexue jianshi*, 2010: 251; Lydia H. Liu, *Clash of Empires*, 2004: 132.
49 Aquinas, 1952: 209; Terry Hall, "Legislation," 1998: 139; Weinreb, 1987: 59; Feng, 2010: 240–2.
50 Ronan, 1978: 295; Frederick W. Mote, *Intellectual Foundations of China*, 1989: 13.
51 Tu Wei-ming, *Way, Learning, and Politics*, 1993: 99.
52 Jorn Rusen, *Western Historical Thinking*, 2002: 163.
53 See Thoreau, Tolstoi, Gandhi, King.
54 Lowell Turner, *Fighting for Partnership*, 1998: 1–16; Sidney Tarrow, "Silence and Voice in the Study of Contentious Politics: Introduction,", 2001: 2.
55 The theory of "National" contentious politics see Charles Tilly, *The Contentious French*, 1986: 391–8; The theory of "Transnational" see Sidney Tarrow, *Power in Movement*, 1998: 176–95.
56 James C. Scott, *Weapons of the Weak*, 1985: 29 and "Everyday Forms of Resistance," 1990: 5; O'Brien, 2006: 1–5; O'Brien, 1996.
57 Natural resistance contains both large social protests and individual resistance so long as they do not follow the legally required steps. For a study on social protest in China see Perry, 2002.
58 Ron Aminzade and Elizabeth Perry, "The Sacred, Religious, and Secular in Contentious Politics: Blurring Boundaries," 2001: 155–78.
59 Henrietta Harrison, *The Making of the Republican Citizen*, 2000; Peter Zarrow, *Creating Chinese Modernity*, 2006.
60 E. P. Thompson, *The Making of the English Working Class*, 1963: 156–85, 202, 444, 831–2.

1 Hot potatoes: from early times to 1898

1 A portion of this chapter was published by the *Journal of Asian Studies*, Volume 68, Issue 04 (November 2009), pp. 1105–35. I am grateful to Cambridge University Press for the permission to publish.
2 Hsiao Kung-chuan, *A History of Chinese Political Thought*, 1979: 206.
3 Liang Hong, *Shijing Shanshu*, 2003: 128–57.
4 Ibid.
5 Ibid.: 208–46.
6 Tu Wei-ming, *Way, Learning, and Politics*, 1993: 8.
7 Zhu Xi, *Sishu zhangju jizhu*, 1998: 67.
8 Frederick Mote, *Intellectual Foundations of China*, 1989: 51.
9 Mo Zi, online; also see Hsiao, 1979: 243.
10 D. C. Lau, trans., *Tao Te Ching*, 1963: 141.
11 Hsiao Kung-chuan, 1979: 206; also see Zuo Qiuming, *Zuozhuan*, 1991: 73.
12 Zuo Qiuming, 1991: 205.
13 Sima Qian, *Shiji*, 1975: 423.
14 Sun Yirang, *Zhouli zhengyi*, 1987: 2499.
15 Sun, 1987: 2754; Resounding Stone see Charles O. Hucker, *A Dictionary of Official Titles in Imperial China*, 1985: 210.
16 Yang Yifan and Liu Ducai argue that the institutions of the wood and drum of the times of Yao and Shun and the Red Stone of the Western Zhou lasted into the Han. See Yang and Liu, eds., *Zhongguo fazhishi kaozheng*, 2003: 24; for similar arguments see Xi Chen, "An Authoritarian State and a Contentious Society," 2005: 47; Li Qiuxue, *Zhongguo xinfang shilun*, 2010.
17 Sima Guang, of course, was a conservative Confucian scholar-official who opposed Wang Anshi's reforms. His history naturally contains his own political judgments but it has long been admired for its judiciousness and its comprehensiveness. See Sima Guang, ed., *Zizhi tongjian*, 1956: 1796.

18 Similarly Karen Turner argues that in the Qin period, certain complaints could be brought to higher authorities; Herrlee Glessner Creel argues that it was common for complainants to complain to royal officials in the Zhou dynasty. The King of state Lu admitted that he personally dealt with both big and small legal complaints. Turner, "War, Punishment, and The Law of Nature in early Chinese Concepts of the State," 1993: 308; Creel, "Legal Institutions and Procedures during the Chou Dynasty," 1980: 33–4, 40.
19 The Latter Han historian Zheng Xuan, in his comments on the *Zhouli*, noted that there was no formal complaint system in early times although people in the Han could complain informally to upper-level governments. See Zeng Xianyi, *Zhongguo fazhishi*, 2002: 116.
20 Sima Guang, 1956: 126–7.
21 Ban Gu, *The Hanshu*, 1975: 3200.
22 Unfortunately, the Han code has been largely lost and reconstructed fragments do not include any evidence of complaint systems. See A. F. P. Hulsewe, "Ch'in and Han Law," 1995: 520.
23 Sima Guang, 1956: 495.
24 Ban Gu, 1975: 1098.
25 Fan Ye, *Houhanshu*, 1965: 1872.
26 Ibid., 1965: 1076.
27 Ibid.: 1640.
28 Roger Des Forges, *Cultural Centrality and Political Change in Chinese History*, 2003: 318; Qiang Fang and Roger Des Forges, "Were Chinese Rulers above the Law?" 2007.
29 Jin Chunfeng, *Handai sixiangshi*, 1997: 87.
30 Ibid.: 99; Yu Zhirong, ed., *Jiayi xinshu*, 2003: 256.
31 Dong Zhongshu, *Chunqiu fanlu*, 1997: 30, 148; also see John S. Major, *Heaven and Earth in Early Han Thought*, 1993: 175; Hsiao Kung-chuan, 1979: 210, 487; Jin Chunfeng, 1997: 163–72.
32 Ban Gu, 1975: 1108–9.
33 Fan Ye, 1965: 80.
34 Ch'ü Tung-tsu, *Local Government in China under the Ch'ing*, 1962: 202–28.
35 Fan Ye, 1965: 1640–1; also see Hsiao Kung-chuan, 1979: 539; Etienne Balazs, *Chinese Civilization and Bureaucracy*, 1964: 203.
36 Jin law was based on the *Rites of Zhou*. See Zhang Jinfan, *Zhongguo falu de chuantong yu xiandai zhuanxing*, 1997: 29. Liang Wudi invoked Zhou and Han models in ordering leniency in the administration of the law. See Sima Guang, 1956: 145, 256.
37 Zeng Xianyi, 2002: 138.
38 Sima Guang, 1956: 2611.
39 Wei Shou, *Weishu*, 1974: 2874. Skipping complaints were also common in Tokugawa Japan where they were called "end-run complaints." See James White, *IKKI*, 1995: 143.
40 It seems that the wood and the red stone existed in the Liang but there is no indication of precisely when they were set up or whether they existed in other contemporary states. Liang Wudi, see Zhu Mingpan, *Nanchao Lianghuiyao*, 1984: 542.
41 According to Zhu Mingpan, a Qing historian, public grievances in the later years of the reign of Liang Wudi became rampant because of political corruption, officials' negligence of investigating lawsuits, and abuses of power by evil clerks (*jianli*). See Zhu Mingpan, 1984: 539.
42 The law code enacted by Sui Wendi, *Statutes of the Kaihuang Era* (*kaihuanglü*) has been lost, so we do not find any Sui law stipulating punishment for skipping complaints. But, as the Tang adopted most of the Sui law and the Tang did punish such complaints, we may well infer that the Sui did too. For Sui Wendi see Wei Zhengshou, *Suishu*, 1973: 714.

43 Geoffrey MacCormack, *The Spirit of Traditional Chinese Law*, 1996: 28; Wallace Johnson, *The T'ang Code*, 1997: 415–16.
44 Li Linfu, ed., *Tangliudian*, 1992: 192, 378. Also see Qian Daqun and Ai Yongming, *Tangdai xingzheng falu yanjiu*, 1996: 330.
45 Zhangsun Wuji, *Tanglu shuyi*, 1999: 482.
46 Zhangsun Wuji, 1999: 482; Johnson, 1997: 414–15.
47 In 840, Tang Wenzong decreed that only certain complaints, such as those regarding real grievances or criticism concerning state and military affairs, could reach the petition box. In 847, Tang Xuanzong (r. 846–859), being annoyed by many trivial complaints to the Censorate, ordered that all civil cases should be decided by local magistrates or prefects and should not be sent to the Censorate. See Song Minqiu, ed., *Tangda zhaoling ji*, 1959: 82, 473; Wang Fu (Song), *Tanghuiyao*, 1991: 1231.
48 Wang Fu, 1991: 483.
49 Li Linfu, 1992: 192.
50 Liu Junwen, *Tanglü shuyi jianjie*, 1996: 1672; Li Linfu, 1992: 192.
51 Shen Kuo, *Mengxi bitan*, 1996: 247–8.
52 Dong Hao, *Quan Tangwen*, 1990: 20.
53 Liu Xu, *Jiutangshu*, 1975: 4500.
54 Sima Guang, 1956: 6438. Japan later adopted the Chinese Petition box in 1759 which lasted until 1873. The lord of Tosa encouraged persons of any background to petition without punishment. See Luke S. Roberts, "The Petition Box in Eighteenth-Century Japan," 1994: 427; also Dan Fenno Henderson, "Chinese Influences on Eighteenth-Century Tokugawa Codes," 1980: 270–301: 275; White, 1995: 143.
55 Li Linfu, 1992: 282.
56 Although latter Jin (936–946) historian Liu Xu argues that Empress Wu established the petition box to gain popular support, famous historians in the later dynasties, such as Sima Guang and Ouyang Xiu in the Song, and Shen Jiaben in the Qing, argued that the primary aim of the petition box was to encourage secret reports against anyone who attempted to challenge Empress Wu's reign. Liu Xu, 1975: 4500; Sima Guang, 1956: 6438; Ouyang Xiu, *Xintangshu*, 1975: 2144; Shen Jiaben, *Lidai xingfa kao*, 1985: 50–1.
57 Dong Hao, 1990: 78.
58 Wang Fu, 1991: 1123–5.
59 Wu Jing, *Zhenguan zhengyao*, 2001: Vol.1, pp. 37, 348; Gao Changshan, annotated, *Xunzi*, 2003: 538.
60 Liu Xu, 1975: 2147.
61 Bai Juyi, *Baijuyi ji*, 1997: 630.
62 Dong Hao, 1990: 951–2.
63 Ibid.: 1123.
64 Bai Juyi, 1997: 698.
65 Li Xibi, ed., *Tangda zhaolingji bubian*, 2003: 894.
66 Dong Hao, 1990: 543.
67 Li Tao, *Xuzizhi tongjian changbian*, 1979: 4090.
68 Tuotuo, *Songshi*, 1977: 4961–2.
69 Gu Yanwu, *Rizhilu jishi*, 1985: 90.
70 Brian E. McKnight, *The Quality of Mercy*, 1981: 75.
71 Ichisada Miyazaki, "The Administration of Justice during the Sung Dynasty," 1980: 56. Similar arguments also in John D. Langlois, "Living Law in Sung and Yuan Jurisprudence," 1981: 169.
72 For a detailed account the Song complaint systems from county to the capital see Miyazaki, 1980: 60–9.
73 Dou Yi, *Songxingtong*, 1984: 377.
74 Li Tao, 1979: 582.
75 Tuotuo, 1977: 4972.

76 Yang and Liu, 2003: 46.
77 Guo Dongxu, *Songdai fazhi yanjiu*, 2000: 547.
78 Li Tao, 1979: 424.
79 *Songda zhaolingji*, 1962: Vol. 198, p. 729.
80 Ibid.: Vol. 202, p. 751.
81 Robert Hymes, *Statesmen and Gentlemen*, 1986: 210–12.
82 Tuotuo, 1977: 4962.
83 Patricia Buckley Ebrey argues that the Southern Song showed more respect to women than the early Song because its southward move "forced officials to come to grips with practices less common in north China." *The Inner Quarters*, 1993: 246.
84 *Minggong shupan qingming ji*, 2002: 436.
85 Song Xiaozong's decree of 1164, *Songhuiyao jigao*, 1978: 6593.
86 Miyazaki, 1980: 67–9.
87 John B. Henderson, *The Development and Decline of Chinese Cosmology*, 1984: 119–20; the fall of the Han phenomenalism and the rise of superstition and Neo-Confucianism in the Song dynasty see Hsu Dau-lin, "Crime and Cosmic Order," 1970.
88 Li Tao, 1979: 736, 2469.
89 Ibid.: 597.
90 Tuotuo, 1977: 4995–6.
91 Ibid.: 4975.
92 Guo Dongxu, 2000: 597.
93 *Minggong shupan qingming ji*, 2002: 42.
94 Paul Heng-chao Ch'en, *Chinese Legal Tradition under the Mongols*, 1979: 98; also John D. Langlois, "Living Law in Sung and Yuan Jurisprudence," 1981: 169, 174.
95 Ch'en, 1979: 89–93.
96 John D. Langlois, "Political Thought in Chin-hua under Mongol Rule," 1981: 164.
97 Song Lian, *Yuanshi*, 1976: 70, 74. Morris Rossabi argues that Khubilai Khan had created a legal system that incorporated both Mongol and Chinese elements which was more flexible and lenient than the Chinese one. See Rossabi, *Khubilai Khan*, 1989: 130.
98 Rossabi, 1989: 80.
99 Song, 1976: 164, 250, 2617. A similar rule can be found in China today as the Chinese Communist Party stipulated in 2003 that any county with more than three collective complaints annually will not be evaluated as an advanced county (*xian-jinxian*). Interviews: Official I, November 28, 2003.
100 Song Lian, 1976: 2671.
101 Ibid.: 3781.
102 See Edward Farmer, *Zhu Yuanzhang and Early Ming Legislation*, 1995: 2; John Dardess, *Confucianism and Autocracy*, 1983: 187.
103 Farmer, 1995: 100.
104 See, for example, Zeng Xianyi, 2002: 201; Melissa Macauley, *Social Power and Legal Culture*, 1998: 35; Edward Farmer attributes Zhu Yuanzhang's harsh punishments to the mutual distrust between Zhu and his ministers and scholars. See Farmer, 1995: 44–6.
105 Liu Chonglai, Xu Shirui, and Zheng Jiafu, eds., *Mingshilu leizuan*, 1994: 205.
106 Shen Jiaben, *Jiyi wencun*, 1976: Vol. 2, p. 3.
107 Zhang Tingyu, *Mingshi*, 1974: 2280.
108 Liu Hainian and Yang Yifan, eds., *Zhongguo zhenxi falü jicheng*, 1994: Book 2, Vol. 2, p. 43.
109 Huai Xiaofeng, annotated, *Daminglü*, 1989: 173; for English edition see Yonglin Jiang, trans., *Great Ming Code*, 2005: 192.
110 Dardess, 1983: 186.
111 Long Wenbin, *Minghuiyao*, 1956: 864. Edward Farmer refers to Taizu's encouragement of skipping complaints as "imperial populism." See Farmer, 1995: 105.

112 Long Wenbin, 1956: 951; Farmer, 1995: 74–5.
113 Liu Chonglai *et al.*, 1994: 69.
114 Liu Hainian and Yang Yifan, 1994: 256, 300.
115 Huai Xiaofeng, 1989: 173.
116 Long Wenbin, 1956: 1293.
117 Long Wenbin, 1956: 1294; Charles O. Hucker, *The Censorial System of Ming China*, 1966: 100.
118 This evidence would seem to call into question the generalization made by some observers that capital complaints occurred only when social tensions ran high or the quality of governance was low. Guangyuan Zhou, "Illusion and Reality in the Law of the Late Qing," 1993: 432; Jonathan Ocko, "I'll Take it All the Way to Beijing," 1988: 309.
119 Long Wenbin, 1956: 1294.
120 Liu Chonglai *et al.*, 1994: 153–5.
121 Ibid.: 176.
122 Zhang Tingyu, 1974: 2311–12.
123 Liu Chonglai *et al.*, 1994: 22.
124 Ibid.: 6504.
125 Henderson, 1984: 177–89; Timothy Brook, *The Troubled Empire*, 2010: Ch. 1–3 and *passim*.
126 Liu Chonglai *et al.*, 1994: 25, 120.
127 Yan Junyan, *Mengshuizhai Cundu*, 2002: 267.
128 Chen Zilong, ed., *Ming jingshi wenbian*, 1997: 1173.
129 Zhang Tingyu, 1974: 2324.
130 Long Wenbin, 1956: 1295.
131 Fu Fengxiang, ed., *Huangming zhaoling*, 1956: 1910–11.
132 Hai Rui, *Hairui ji*, 1981: 237.
133 Evelyn S. Rawski, *The Last Emperors*, 1998: 7; Pamela Kyle Crossley, *A Translucent Mirror*, 2002; Edward J. M. Rhoads, *Manchu and Han*, 2000; Mark C. Elliot, *The Manchu Way*, 2001: 34.
134 Thomas A. Metzger, *The Internal Organization of Ch'ing Bureaucracy, Legal, Normative, and Communication Aspects*, 1973: 33; Elliot, 2001: 28; Zeng Xianyi, 2002: 220.
135 Metzger, 1973: 22–3.
136 He Changling and Wei Yuan, eds., *Qing jingshi wenbian*, 1992: 2319. Philip C. C. Huang also argues that most "minor matters" relating to family, marriage, and land were resolved by the society or the "Third Realm"—the coparticipation of both society and the state. See Huang, "Between Informal Mediation and Formal Adjudication: The Third Realm of Qing Civil Justice," 1993: 251–98; *Civil Justice in China*, 1998: 6, 128. See also Kathryn Bernhardt and Philip C. C. Huang eds., *Civil Law in Qing and Republican China*, 1994: 1.
137 Crossley, 2000: 3.
138 *Daqing huidian zeli*: Vol. 124, p. 42; Liu Hainain and Yang Yifan, 1994: Vol. 1, p. 386.
139 According to Reed, many such complaints had already been settled on the county level and had no need to go to the upper level. See Bradly W. Reed, *Talons and Teeth*, 2000: 86–8.
140 Reed, 2000: 16.
141 *Daqing lüli genyuan*, 1871: Vol. 89, p. 22.
142 According to thirty-one capital complaints that I randomly selected from among hundreds all over China from the Qianlong to the Guangxu periods, skipping complaints were against local powerful people and local magistrates. See China First Historical Archives, Board of Punishment, Jiangsu division (xingbu jiangsusi dangan). For a pioneering study, see Ocko, 1988: 294.

143 Ocko, 1988: 294.
144 Na Silu, *Qingdai zhongyang sifa shenpan zhidu*, 1992: 412.
145 *Daqing lüli genyuan*, 1871: Vol. 2, p. 10.
146 *Qing huidian shili*, 1991: Vol. 1006, p. 101.
147 *Daqing lüli genyuan*, 1871: Vol. 89, p. 48.
148 Ibid.: Vol. 89, pp. 37–9.
149 Philip A. Kuhn, *Origins of the Modern Chinese State*, 2002: 4–5.
150 *Qing huidian shili*, 1991: 46; Ocko: 1988: 295.
151 Brian McKnight argues that subjects in the Qing would find it difficult to bring civil cases to the court. It appears from the evidence that they continued to do so. See McKnight 1981: 123, and Philip C. C. Huang 1998: 6, 218.
152 *Daqing lüli genyuan*, 1871: Vol., 89, pp. 32–4, 55.
153 For Italian petitioners see Cecilia Nubola, "Supplications between Politics and Justice: The Northern and Central Italian States in the Early Modern Age," 2002: 37. For Russian peasants see Daniel Field, *Rebels in the Name of the Czar*, 1989: 15–17.
154 Records from the First Historical Archives in Beijing. Xingbu jiangsu si [Board of Punishment, Jiangsu Division] Cases No. 08718 and 09103.
155 Ocko, 1988: 302; Thomas Buoye, "Filial Felons: Leniency and Legal Reasoning in Qing China," 2009: 109–24.
156 Stephen Vlastos, *Peasant Protests and Uprisings in Tokugawa Japan*, 1986: 52–6.
157 *Daqing huidian zeli* (Xingbu): Vol. 124, p. 31, Vol. 5, p. 718.
158 Jonathan Spence, *Emperor of China*, 1988: 43; Metzger, 1973: 178.
159 *Daqing huidian zeli*: Vol, 5, p. 719; *Qingding taigui*: Vol. 11, pp. 24–5.
160 Liu Hainian and Yang Yifan, 1994: Book 3, Vol. 1, p. 254. For an English version see Tianquan Cheng, Yongling Jiang, and William C. Jones eds., *The Great Qing Code*, 1994: 314.
161 *Daqing lüli genyuan*, 1871: Vol. 89, pp. 1, 37.
162 *Daqing huidian zeli*: Vol. 5, p. 718.
163 Liu Hainain and Yang Yifan, 1994: Book 3, Vol. 30, pp. 254, 386–7.
164 *Qingding taigui*: Vol, 3, p. 7.
165 *Daqing guangxü xinfaling*, 1908: Vol. 30, p. 11.
166 William T. Rowe, *Saving the World*, 2001: 328.
167 Rawski, 1998: 227.
168 *Qing huidian shili*, 1991: 158.
169 Yang Hegao, *Gudai zhengfa wenxuan*, 1979: Vol. 2, pp. 325–8.
170 Elliot, 1998: 198, 231.
171 Philip A. Kuhn, *Soulstealers*, 1990.
172 Haichang Xiaopenglaizhu, "Bo Wulinsheng gaobai," May 24, 1876.
173 Zhao Xiaohua, *Wanqing songyu zhidu de shehui kaocha*, 2001: 39. Many other scholars also draw similar arguments about the seriousness of bureaucratic protection and connection. See Reed, 2000: 82, 84–5; T'ung-tsu Ch'u, *Local Government in China under the Ch'ing*, 1962: 114–15.
174 Zhang Jixin, *Daoxian huanhai jianwenlu* 1981: 96; Qingshi bianzuan weiyuanhui, eds., *Qingshi*, 1960: Vol. 357, p. 4472.
175 The First Historical Archives in Beijing. Xingbu jiangsu si, Case Volume No. 09103.
176 Guan Hanqing, *Snow in the Summer*, 2002.

2 Halfway revolutions: the late Qing period (1899–1911)

1 A small portion of this chapter was published by the *Journal of Asian History* (46/2012), pp. 97–116. I am grateful to Harrassowitz Verlag for the permission to publish.
2 See China First Historical Archives, Xingbu Anhuisi, Case Volume No. 09640.

3 See China First Historical Archives, Xingbu Henansi, Case Volume No. 14823.

4 For a detailed study of the late Qing's abolition of corporal punishment, see M. J. Meijer, *The Introduction of Modern Criminal Law in China*, 1950: 127–36.

5 Zeng Xianyi, *Zhongguo fazhishi*, 2002: 251.

6 For the 1900 edict see China First Historical Archives, Xingbu Henansi, Case Volume No. 13834; for 1904 edict see ibid., Case Volume No. 13827.

7 Governors Zhang Zhidong and Liu Kunyi argued in 1901 that certain [skipping] complaints to the court were made by pettifoggers whose intention was to extort money. They called for the prohibition of such [skipping] complaints to the court that had been accepted by a local government and severe punishments of the complainants. See Meijer, 1950: 129.

8 See China First Historical Archives, Xingbu Henansi, Case Volume No. 13827.

9 See China First Historical Archives, Xingbu Henansi, Case Volume No. 13832.

10 Ibid.: Xingbu Huguangsi Case Volume No. 12868.

11 Three complainants who had blocked the royal cart in 1903 and mid-1904 were pardoned by the Board of Punishment because of Cixi's 1904 edict. See China First Historical Archives, Xingbu Shanxisi, Case Volume No. 19417.

12 See China First Historical Archives, Xingbu Shandongsi, Case Volume No. 17141.

13 Ibid.: Xingbu Guizhousi, Case Volume No. 22197.

14 Ibid.: Xingbu Guangxisi, Case Volume No. 21048.

15 Ruan Yicheng, *Fazhi lunji*, 1933: 114.

16 Otto Mayer, *Deguo xingzhengfa*, 2002: 19, 20, 56, 123, 127.

17 For prisons, see Frank Dikötter, *Crime, Punishment and the Prison in Modern China*, 2002: 50–1; for police see Frederic Wakeman, Jr., *Policing Shanghai, 1927–1937*, 1995: 19 and his "Models of Historical Change: The Chinese State and Society, 1839–1989," 1991: 82; for codes, see Jerome Bourgon, "Rights, Freedoms, and Customs in the Making of Chinese Civil Law, 1900–1936," 2004: 94.

18 Saneto Keishu, *Zhongguoren liuxue ribenshi*, 1983: 327–34. See also Douglas R. Reynolds. *China, 1898–1912*, 1993: 123–6 and Lydia H. Liu, *Translingual Practice*, 1995.

19 Yoroshi Ota, *Qingguo xingzhengfa*, 2003: 5, 42, 43, 44.

20 The term *zhuanzhi* had its origins in early China where it was associated with the centralized bureaucratic system of the Qin dynasty. It was taken over by the Japanese to translate the English word "autocracy," and has been regularly translated into English as "authoritarian government" or even "dictatorship" or "despotism" (Lydia H. Liu, 1995: 306). In this case Xia may have used the term in the sense of authoritarian government. For some of the complexity in the development of East Asian terminology relating to sovereignty in the nineteenth and twentieth centuries, see Lydia H. Liu, *The Clash of Empires*, 2004, especially Ch. 2–4.

21 Xia Tongsu, *Xingzhengfa*, 1905: 1, 2, 3, 34.

22 In 1903 there were 1000 Chinese visiting Japan; by 1906, after the Japanese victory over Russia, the number jumped to more than 10,000. See Joseph R. Levenson, *Liang Ch'i-ch'ao and the Mind of Modern China*, 1970: 81; Philip C. C. Huang, *Liang Ch'i-ch'ao and Modern Chinese Liberalism*, 1972: 41; Saneto Keishu, 1983: 1.

23 Zhao Yongqing, *Dongyou jilue*, 2002: 277–83.

24 Xie Zhenmin, *Zhonghua minguo lifashi*, 2000: 28.

25 *Daqing xuantong xinfaling*, 1910: Vol. 15, p. 7.

26 Zhang Demei, *Conggongtang zouxiang fating qingmo mingchu susong zhidu gaige yanjiu*, 2010: 37–8.

27 Guo Shu, "Zhongguo jindai xingzheng fayuan zhidu zhi bianqian," July 21, 2003.

28 "Xingzheng caipanyuan guanzhi caoan," 1909: 115–16.

29 With a few revisions, *The Organizing Law of the Court System* was provisionally adopted by the early republic. Xie Zhenmin, 2000: 28.

30 Joan Judge, *Print and Politics*, 1996: 17. Also see Barbara Mittler, *A Newspaper for China?* 2004: 24–5, 178; Li Bingyan, *Zhongguo xinwenshi*, 1986: 19.

31 Lin Yutang, *A History of the Press and Public Opinion in China*, 1936.
32 Li Bingyan, 1986: 41–2.
33 Ibid.: 245.
34 Zheng Guanying, *Shengshi weiyan*, 2002: 142–3.
35 Seungjoo Yoon, "Literati-Journalists of the Chinese Progress (Shiwu bao) in Discord, 1896–1898," 2002: 53; Levenson, 1970: 24–5.
36 For Egypt's fate see Rebecca E. Karl, *Staging the World*, 2002: 178–9; for the other thinkers see Xiaobing Tang, *Global Space and the Nationalist Discourse of Modernity*, 1996: 56, 80–115, 123.
37 Zhongguo lishi xuehui, *Wuxu bianfa*, 2000: Vol. 3, pp. 323, 324.
38 Natasha Vittinghoff, "Unity vs. Uniformity," 2002: 100, 101.
39 Yuan Shikai, *Yuanshikai zouyi*, 1987: 272.
40 Ren Hengjun, *Wanqing guanchang guize yanjiu*, 2003: 282.
41 Haichang Xiaopenlaizhu (pen name), "Bo Wulinsheng gaobai," May 24, 1876.
42 William P. Alford, "Of Arsenic and Old Laws," 1984: 1180–256; Wang Celai, *Yangnaiwu yu xiaobaicai an*, 2002: 150, 164.
43 Alford, 1984: 1242.
44 Jonathan Spence, *The Gate of Heavenly Peace*, 1981; Mary Backus Rankin, *Early Chinese Revolutionaries*, 1971: 154–5.
45 "Lunshaoxing yuanyu," July 23, 1907; Also see Li Xizhu, "Qingmo minjian yulun yu guanfu zuowei zhi hudong guanxi," 2004: 8–10. *Vernacular Journal* 1971: 187.
46 Judge, 1996: 1–2.
47 Yue Fei (1103–1142) was a patriotic general in the Northern Song dynasty (960–1127) who fought wars against the invasion of the Jurchens but was executed under charges of "There needs no reason." See ibid.: 28. For a different view see Mary Backus Rankin, *Elite Activism and Political Transformation in China*, 1986.
48 *Shibao* here might have adopted the tactic of making sensational claims to sell more of its newspapers. Judge, 1996: 80.
49 For the Subao case see J. Lust, "The 'Su-pao' Case," 1964.
50 Ma Hongmo, *Minhu minyu minlibao xuanji* 1909.5–1910.2, 1982. For a recent study of aspects of the media in Shanghai, see Alexander Des Forges, *Mediasphere Shanghai*, 2007.
51 Ma Hongmo, 1982: 85–8.
52 For the debate over the "public sphere" see the articles by Frederic Wakeman, Jr., William Rowe, Mary Backus Rankin, and Philip C. C. Huang in *Modern China*, Vol. 19, No. 2, Symposium: "Public Sphere"/"Civil Society" in China? 1993; Timothy Brook and Bernard Frolic, eds., *Civil Society in China*, 1997; for Habermas see Wakeman, 1993: 127: see also Jürgen Habermas, *The Structural Transformation of the Public Sphere*, 1989.
53 For the Han see Ch'en Ch'i-Yun, "Confucian, Legalist, and Taoist Thought in Late Han,", 1986: 796–7; for the Southern Song see Lin Yutang, 1936: 46–57; for the Ming see John W. Dardess, *Blood and History in China*, 2002. Also see Etienne Balazs, *Chinese Civilization and Bureaucracy*, 1964: Ch. 13; William S. Atwell, "From Education to Politics: the Fu She," 1975: 333–68.
54 For France see Lex Heerma van Voss, *Petitions in Social History*, 2002: 4; for Japan see Andrew Gordon, *A Modern History of Japan*, 2003: 30.
55 See Tsing Yuan, "Urban Riots and Disturbances," 1979: 277–320; C. K. Yang, "Some Preliminary Statistical Patterns of Mass Actions in Nineteenth-Century China," 1975: 174–210.
56 Sun Zhongshan, *Sunzhongshan quanji*, 1981: Vol. 1, p. 548. For a recent study of the Sino-Japanese war, see S. C. M. Paine, *The Sino-Japanese War of 1894–1895*, 2003.
57 Wang Shi, *Weixin yundong*, 1986: 119.
58 Zhongguo lishi xuehui, 2000: Vol. 2, p. 30.

59 Mary C. Wright, ed., *China in Revolution*, 1968; Jean Chesneaux, ed., *Popular Movements and Secret Societies in China, 1840–1950*, 1972.
60 Roxann Prazniak, *Of Camel Kings and Other Things*, 1999: 68–9; Kristin Stapleton, *Civilizing Chengdu*, 2000: 164–5.
61 For the background on the railway company, see Roger Des Forges, *Popular Movements and Secret Societies in China, 1840–1950*, 1973: Ch. 6; Stapleton 2000.
62 Ma Hongmo, 1982: 498–563.
63 For 1911 in three provinces, see Edward J. M. Rhoads, *China's Republican Revolution*, 1975; Joseph W. Esherick, *Reform and Revolution in China*, 1976. For collective protests in Shanghai in the republican period, see Jeffrey N. Wasserstrom, *Student Protests in Twentieth Century China*, 1991; Elizabeth J. Perry, *Shanghai on Strike*, 1993.
64 Zhongguo lishi xuehui, 2000: Vol. 1, pp. 28, 38.
65 For Chinese science and technology, see Benjamin A. Elman, *On Their Own Terms*, 2005, ch.10.
66 Zheng Guanying, 2002: 10, 31.
67 Zhongguo lishi xuehui, 2000: Vol 2, pp. 152, 176 and Peter Zarrow, "The Reform Movement, the Monarchy, and Political Modernity," 2002: 32. Other renowned scholars such as Liang Qichao and Yan Fu (1853–1921) have also expressed similar arguments about political reform. For Liang see Zhongguo lishi xuehui, 2000: Vol. 2, p. 34; Levenson, 1970: 15–51; for Yan see Zhongguo lishi xuehui, 2000: Vol. 3, pp. 48, 52, 58; Hao Chang, *Liang Ch'i-ch'ao and Intellectual Transition in China 1890–1907*, 1971: 104–5; for a detailed study of Kang's support of modern Western democracy see Kung-chuan Hsiao, *A Modern China and a New World*, 1975: 198–205.
68 Cixi did not oppose reform per se, but she differed with her nephew over how to carry it out and led powerful officials in putting an end to the 100 days. See Yang Tianshi, "Wengtonghe baguan wenti kaocha," 2005: Vol. 3, pp. 199, 203; for a sympathetic biography of Cixi, see Sterling Seagrave, *Dragon Lady*, 1992.
69 For four recent studies of the Boxers, see Joseph W. Esherick, *Origins of Boxer Uprising*, 1988; Paul A. Cohen, *History in Three Keys*, 1997; James L. Hevia, *English Lessons*, 2003: Ch. 7–8; Robert Bickers and R. G. Tiedemann, eds., *The Boxers, China, and the World*, 2007.
70 Ma Hongmo, 1982: 102; Song Jiaoren, *Songjiaoren ji*, 1981: 436.
71 The classic study of the Censorate is Charles O. Hucker, *The Censorial System of Ming China*, 1966.
72 Shen Jiaben, *Jiyi wencun*, 1976: Vol. 3, p. 41. An excellent study on [those with or aspiring to power] using the power of the past to suit their particular needs in Chinese history see William A. Alford, *To Steal a Book is an Elegant Offense*, 1995: 21.
73 Zhu Mingpan, *Nanchao lianghuiyao*, 1984: 539.
74 Arthur F. Wright, "The Sui Dynasty (581–617)," 1979: 103–5.
75 Sima Guang, *Zizhi tongjian*, 1956: 495.
76 *Songda zhaolingji*, 1962: Vol. 202, p. 751; Guo Dongxu, *Songchao falü shilun*, 2001: 340.
77 Chen Guyuan, *Zhongguo fazhishi gaiyao*, 1977: 27. See also the essays in *Realms of Freedom in Modern China*, edited by William C. Kirby in 2004 for more on this theme.
78 Gu Ban, *The Hanshu*, 1975: Vol. 83, p. 3399.
79 Tsing Yuan, 1979: 286–92.
80 The historian Marinus J. Meijer does suggest that Shen's point was more a tactical maneuver to get support for reform than a serious historical interpretation, 1950: 76. But the matter may not be that simple.
81 Shen Jiaben, 1976: Vol. 1, pp. 11, 15.
82 In 1907, Ze Gong, Commissioner for Reorganizing the Governmental System, arguably

for the first time voiced the Western term of protecting human rights. See Xiaoqun Xu, *Trial of Modernity*, 2008: 29.

83 Shen Jiaben, 1976: Vol. 1, p. 20; Saneto Keishu 1983: 327.

84 "People as the root (*minben*)" is not identical to the Western idea of "people as the masters" (*minzhu*). As Liang Qichao argued before, *minben* contained notions of "for the people and of the people" but not of "by the people," a key content of democracy in President Lincoln's Gettysburg speech in 1863. For the argument of a renowned legal scholar in the republican period that notions such as "protecting human rights came from the West," see Yang Honglie, *Zhongguo falü sixiangshi*, 1998: 300; Liang Qichao, *Xianqin zhengzhi sixiangshi*, 1986: 4–5.

85 Haichang Xiaopenglaizhu, "Bo Wulinsheng gaobai," May 24, 1876.

86 Guo Hanmin, *Zhongguo jindaishi zhengwu*, 1989: 239–40.

87 First Historical Archives, Xingbu henansi, Category "Cases of marriage, rape, kidnap, and family dispute," Case No. 14864.

88 *Guangxüchao donghualu*, 1984: 5352.

89 Ibid.: 5112; also see Prazniak, 1999 and Stapleton, 2000.

90 *Daqing xuantong xinfaling*, 1910: Vol. 12, p. 34.

91 Prazniak, 1999: 68–71.

92 Ma Hongmo, 1982: 594.

93 *Daqing xuantong xinfaling*, 1910: Vol. 5, p. 18.

94 Archival Section of Ming and Qing at the Old Palace Museum, ed., *Qingmo choubei lixian dangan shi liao*, 1979: Vol. 1, p. 94.

95 Zhongguo lishi xuehui, 2000: Vol. 1, p. 272; Vol. 2, p. 182.

96 *Guangxüchao donghualu*, 1984: 5193.

97 *Zhengzhi guanbao*, 1965: Vol. 1, p. 418.

3 A golden age: the early republic (1912–1927)

1 Li Liejun made this claim in 1916, four years after the formation of the republic. See Zhou Yuangao, Meng Pengxing, and Shu Yingyun, eds., *Liliejun ji*, 1996: Vol. 1, p. 197.

2 Sun Yat-sen, "Sunda zongtong jiuzhi xuanyanshu," in Sun Yao, *Zhonghua minguo shiliao*, 1966: Vol. 13, p. 69.

3 Sun Yat-sen in Sun Zhongshan, *Sunzhongshan quanji*, 1981: Vol. 10, p. 460; for a similar speech also see John Fitzgerald, *Awakening China*, 1996: 44–5.

4 Shen Yunlong and Sun Yao, 1966. *Zhonghua minguo shiliao*, 1966: Vol. 13, p. 111; Julia Strauss, "The Evolution of Republican Government" in Frederic Wakeman, Jr. and Richard Louis Edmonds, eds., *Reappraising Republican China*, 2000: 77; Frank Dikötter, *Crime, Punishment and the Prison in Modern China*, 2002: 62.

5 Sun see *Zhonghua minguo linshi zhengfu xinfaling*, 1912: 23–4.

6 Fitzgerald, 1996: 55–7; for an early review of Western monographs about the 1911 revolution, see Joseph Esherick. "1911: A Review", 1976. For social reforms see Ernest P. Young, *The Presidency of Yuan Shih-k'ai*, 1977: 78. For new ideas of citizenship, see Henrietta Harrison, *The Making of the Republican Citizen*, 2000.

7 Hou Yijie, *Yuanshikai yisheng*, 1982: 383.

8 *Zhengfu gongbao*, 1971: 25, May 1914.

9 James E. Sheridan, *Chinese Warlord*, 1966: 3–10.

10 Gavan MacCormack, *Chang Tso-lin in Northeast China, 1911–1928*, 1977: 9.

11 Song Jiaoren, *Songjiaoren ji*, 1981: 350–4.

12 Huang Yuansheng, "Minguo diyi ge xingzheng susong shenpan jiguan: minchu ping zhengyuan caijueshu zhengbian yu chutan," 2002: 194.

13 *Zhongguo jindai fazhishi ziliao xuanji*, 1985: 58–62.

14 Ibid.: 84.
15 *Zhengfu gongbao*, 1971: Vol. 25, p. 250.
16 The role of supervising and punishing unlawful officials belonged solely to the Discipline Department. After it was abolished in 1916, this responsibility was shared by government organs such as the Administrative Court and the Interior Ministry. See *Zhonghua minguo faling daquan*, 1917: Vol. 12, p. 4.
17 The difference between a complaint and a lawsuit lies in that a complaint could only be made at a local or central government unit, while a lawsuit could be filed at the Administrative Court. Without first submitting complaints to government units, complainants were not allowed to take lawsuits to the Administrative Court.
18 China Second Historical Archives, "[An Organizational Draft of the Administrative Court]," Archival Category: The Administrative Court; No. 1002–661.
19 Ibid.
20 Detailed studies on the 1913–1914 financial crisis can be found in Xu Xiaoqun, *Trial of Modernity*, 2008: 149–86; for similar arguments see Albert Feuerwerker, "Economic Trends, 1912–49" and Ernest P. Young, "Politics in the Aftermath of Revolution: The Era of Yuan Shih-k'ai, 1912–16,", 1983: 100, 232; Mary Backus Rankin, "State and Society in Early Republican Politics, 1912–18," 2000: 11; Dikötter, 2002: 116; Peter Zarrow, *China in War and Revolution 1985–1949*, 2005: 77; Ding Xianjun and Yu Zuofeng, eds., *Wutingfang ji*, 1993: 577; Zhou, Meng, and Shu, 1996: 39, 77; Philip C. C. Huang, *Code, Custom, and Legal Practice in China*, 2001: 40.
21 *Zhonghua minguo faling daquan*, 1917: Vol. 2, p. 64.
22 Ibid. Also see Feng Zhen, *Minguo zhengzhishi*, 1989: Book 1, Vol. 24, p. 97.
23 Like many direct complaints (e.g., *yique*, the public petition drum) in the dynasties, the Discipline Department allowed only complaints against serious official misbehavior to be made to the department. Other complaints involving civil or criminal ones were still required by the Complaint Law to take regular steps.
24 China Second Historical Archives, "Regulations on Complains to the Department for Disciplining Government," Archival Category: The Administrative Court; No. 1002.
25 *Zhonghua minguo faling daquan*, 1917: Vol. 12, p. 9.
26 Feng Zhen, 1989: Vol. 1, p. 97; also see Nie Xin, "Congsanfasi daosifayuan," 2009: 40–8.
27 Nie Xin, 2009: 43.
28 *Zhonghua minguo faling daquan*, 1917: Vol. 1, pp. 1, 5, 6, 7.
29 As late as 1936, over 1400 counties did not have enough money to establish courts. See Pan Zhenqiu, ed., *Zhonghua minguo shishi jiyao (chugao)*, 1996: January 1936: 17; also see Xu Xiaoqun, 2008: 65, 102.
30 Unfortunately the results of many cases in the book are not available in the archives. See China Second Historical Archives, The Decision of third Branch of the Administrative Court, Archival Category-1003. No. 408.
31 *Zhengfu gongbao*, 1971: Vol. 51, pp. 33–41.
32 Some complaints, of course, were false, but the investigations of the Discipline Department and later the Administrative Court were sometimes unreliable. They were sometimes done by local officials because the center did not have enough money and personnel to conduct their own investigations. As in the past, local officials naturally tended to protect each other, especially when they knew each other. Ibid.
33 This case and the following one are cited in *Pingzhengyuan caijuelu*. I found its first edition of 1916 at the law library of Chinese Academy of Social Science in Beijing. Like many other old books, it lacks any indication of the publisher. Perhaps it was published by the Administrative Court itself. August 15–18, 1916: 2, pp. 4–8.
34 Ibid.: Vol. 2, pp. 1–8.

35 John K. Fairbank, ed. *The Cambridge History of China*, 1983: 100; Ding Xianjun and Yu Zuafeng, 1993: 577; Zhou, Meng, and Shu, 1996: 39, 77.
36 China Second Historical Archives, "Administrative Lawsuits Decided by Pingzhengyuan," Archival Category: The Administrative Court; No. 1005. 86
37 Ibid., No. 1005. "Accusations of People from Zhili, Jilin, and other Provinces against Judicial Personnel at all Levels," September 1914–August 1915.
38 Ruan Yicheng, *Fazhi lunj*, 1933: 115.
39 Guo Shu, "Zhongguo jindai xingzheng fayuan zhiduzhi bianqian," July 21, 2003.
40 *Zhengfu gongbao*, 1971: Vol. 47, p. 545.
41 Ibid.: Vol. 50, p. 385.
42 Ibid.: Vol. 95, p. 416–17.
43 *Xianxing faling quanshu*, 1922: Vol. 2, p. 268.
44 Under direct control of the state department, this bureau was first established in the Nanjing Interim Government (*Nanjing linshi zhengfu*) from January to March 1912). Its functions were: first, drafting laws and regulations; second, making suggestions regarding legislating, annulling, and revising laws and regulations; third, supervising the laws and regulations drafted by all ministries; fourth, preserving the passed laws and regulations; fifth, drafting and deciding on the ritual system (*lizhi*). See Qian Shifu, *Beiyang zhengfu shiqi de zhengzhi zhidu*, 1984: Vol. 1, p. 158.
45 China Second Historical Archives, "Administrative Lawsuits Decided by Pingzhengyuan," Archival Category: The Administrative Court; No. 1005. 44.
46 Under the rules of both the Guomindang (GMD) and especially the CCP, the judicial organs have been politicized and the Administrative Court, as we shall see, has had far less power and independence than it enjoyed in the early republic. For GMD see Xu Xiaoqun, 2008: 90–2.
47 As both Jeffery N. Wasserstrom and Peter Zarrow argue, most students in the republican period belonged to privileged class and were regarded as "flower of the youth" whose protests and sufferings would usually have more social impact than other groups. See Jeffery N. Wasserstrom, *Student Protests in Twentieth-Century China*, 1991: 109; Zarrow, 2005: 122.
48 Zhang Jianan and Jin Ren, eds., *Minguo mingren susongan*, 2004: 19–51.
49 According to *Zhengfu gongbao*, in 1919 alone the Administrative Court had judged 237 complaints. But Huang's chart shows a mere fifteen cases in that year. My own research in the republican archives also shows that the number of cases accepted by the Administrative Court is very incomplete and there is no way to determine it. This is probably due to the contemporary civil wars and political tumults.
50 Huang Yuansheng, "Minguo diyi ge xingzheng susong shenpan jiguan," 2002: 211–12.
51 Andrew Nathan, "A Constitutional Republic: The Peking Government, 1916–28," 1983: 259–83.
52 Sun Yat-sen talked about the purpose of the revolution in a talk with Wang Jingwei, one of his trusted his followers. Sun Yat-sen in Sun Zhongshan, *Sunzhongshan quanji*, 1981: Vol. 1, pp. 289–90.
53 Ding Xianjun and Yu Zuofeng, 1993: 517.
54 Song Jiaoren, 1981: 456.
55 Han Xiutao, *Sifa duli yu jindai zhongguo*, 2003: 158–9.
56 Ding Xianjun and Yu Zuofeng, 1993: 502–10.
57 *Zhengfu gongbao*, 1971: Vol. 8, p. 358.
58 Zhang Sheng, "Minchu daliyuan shenpan duli de zhidu yu shijian," 2002: Vol. 20, p. 150.
59 Mei Huaquan, "Guomin dui sifa zhi guannian," 1922: Book 1, Vol. 1, p. 27.
60 Zhang Sheng, "Minguo chuqi minfa de jindaihua: yi guoyoufa yu jishoufa de zhenghe wei zhongxin," 2002: 149.
61 Zhang Jinfan, 2002: 202–4.

62 Some Chinese scholars at the turn of the twentieth century did not have a full picture of the foreign countries they admired. For example, people's rights were limited in early twentieth-century America when segregation, lynching, child labor, and discrimination against the poor and immigrants were common. Only a few travelers such as Liang Qichao and Sun Yat-sen reported on the dark side of the West. For Liang see Jonathan D. Spence, *The Gate of Heavenly Peace*, 1981: 75; David Arkush and Leo O. Lee, eds., *Land without Ghosts*, 1993: 81–95; for Sun's views, see Sun Zhongshan, *Sunzhongshan quanj*, 1981: Vol. 1, pp. 288–9.

63 *Zhonghua minguo faling daquan*, 1917: Vol. 2, pp. 8–10.

64 Ibid.: Vol 2, p. 1.

65 *Zhengfu gongbao*, 1971: Vol. 5, p. 738.

66 China Second Historical Archives, Category: Interior Ministry, No. 1005. December 28, 1919.

67 China Second Historical Archives, "People's Complaints Received by the Interior Ministry," Archival Category: Interior Ministry, No. 1001.

68 China Second Historical Archives, "People's Complaints Received by the Interior Ministry," Archival Category: Interior Ministry, No. 1001, April 19, 1921.

69 The press flourished in the immediate post-1911 period as many more newspapers appeared where they had not existed before. But after Yuan Shikai's suppression of the "Second Revolution," he imposed new regulations on the press. After *The New Youth* magazine began shifting to socialism, the Beijing government stepped in to ban it in Beijing. See Young, 1977: 143; Young, 1983: 243; Andrew J. Nathan, *Chinese Democracy*, 1985: 146–7; Zarrow, 2005: 197; Rankin, 2000: 11.

70 Criticism of government policies published in magazines such as the *Beijing Daily* (*jingbao*), the *New Youth* (*xinqingnian*), and the *Oriental Miscellany* (*dongfang zazhi*) were largely tolerated. For example, on March 28, 1926, the *Attached Magazine of the Beijing Daily* (*jingbao fukan*) published a critical article written by Zhou Shuren (Lu Xun) who sharply reprimanded the government for its repression of a student demonstration. See Wang Dehou and Qian Liqun, eds., *Luxun zuopin quanbian-zawenjuan shang*, 2000: 393. For a detailed account of the *Oriental Miscellany* and its influence on what some call "Chinese modernity" see Leo Ou-fan Lee. "The Cultural Construction of Modernity in Urban Shanghai," 2000: 31–61.

71 See *Shenbao*, January 1 to December 31, 1919; incidents counted by author.

72 *Shenbao*, March 6, 1919.

73 Susan L. Glosser, *Chinese Visions of Family and State, 1915–1953*, 2003: 35–9, 50–1.

74 *Shenghuo zhoukan*, 1928: Vol. 4, p. 80.

75 *Shenbao*, January 16, 1919.

76 Strauss, 2000: 78–9; Kristin Stapleton, *Civilizing Chengdu*, 2000: 184; John E. Schrecker, *The Chinese Revolution in Historical Perspective*, 1991: 138.

77 Young, 1977: 143.

78 *Zhengfu gongbao*, 1971: Vol. 21, p. 60.

79 Leng Shi, "Falü," May 13, 1919.

80 China Second Historical Archives. Archival Category: The Administrative Court; No. 1002. 157.

81 Chen Duxiu, "Jiusixiang yu guoti wenji," 1917: Vol. 4, p. 2.

82 Zhang Dongsun, "Shuineng jiu zhongguo?" 1923: Vol. 12, p. 23.

83 Zhao Hengti, ed., *Wupeifu xianshengji*, 1971: 284; Ernest P. Young also argues that Yuan in 1914 attained fiscal self-sufficiency and supported a universalization of education see Young, 1983: 244–5.

84 Young, 1983: 227–42.

85 Ibid.: 227.

86 Wellington Bartley Willoughby, *Xinzongtong xuanjufa yi*, 1915; for Goodnow's support of Yuan's absolutism see Young, 1977: 172–6. New Authoritarians around

Party Secretary Zhao Ziyang in early 1989 advocated a similar position as we shall see.

87 Shen Yunlong and Sun Yao, 1966: 315–22.

88 For general studies of the warlord period see James E. Sheridan, "The Warlord Era," 1983: 284–321; Sheridan, 1966; Gavan McCormack, *Chang Tso-lin in Northeast China, 1911–1928*, 1977; Odoric Y. K. Wou, *Militarism in Modern China*, 1977.

89 Zhang Sheng, *Minguo chuqi minfa de jindaihua*, 2002: 195.

90 Zhang Yufa, "Minguo chunian shandongsheng xingzheng zhidu de biange 1912–1937," 1992: 523, 537–8.

91 *Dongfang zazhi*, Vol. 19. April 25, 1922: Vol. 8, pp. 1–2.

92 Stapleton, 2000: 184.

93 Zhao Hengti, 1971: 284.

94 Thomas B. Stephens, *Order and Discipline in China*, 1992: 56–7, 82. A similar argument can be seen in Dikötter, 2002: 124; Stapleton, 2000: 191.

95 Xu Xiaoqun, "The Rule of Law without Due Process 2007: 230–57; also Xu, 2008: 277–301.

96 Zhang Yipeng, "Zhongguo sifa zhidu gaijin zhi yange," 1922: Vol. 1, p. 18.

97 Mei Huaquan, 1922: 28–9.

98 Zhang Jianan and Jin Ren, eds., *Minguo mingren susongan*, 2004: 42.

99 *Xinqingnian*, Vol. 7, No. 6, pp. 1–2, 41; Zarrow, 2005: 120–1.

100 "Pingzhengyuan gaosu shoufei banfa [The complaining fee of the Administrative Court]" China Second Historical Archives, "Administrative Lawsuits Decided by Pingzhengyuan," Archival Category: The Administrative Court; No. 1005. 86.

4 A mixed picture: the later republic (1928–1949)

1 An earlier Romanization system yielded the name Kuomintang or KMT. Fitzgerald, *Awakening China*, 1996: 170–1; Peter Zarrow, *China in War and Revolution 1895–1949*, 2005: 196–203; Jonathan Fenby, *Chang Kai-shek*, 2004: 61–6.

2 The Three Stages of Government are military, tutelage, and constitutional governments; the Three People's Principles are nationalism, democracy, and people's livelihood; the Five Yuan are Legislative, Administrative, Judicial, Supervisory, and Examination, a combination of the three branches of government in some Western republics and two branches inherited from the censorate and Hanlin academy of earlier Chinese polities.

3 Contrary to the claim of a head of the complaint office in a major city in 2003. See Interviews: Officials: A, September 10, 2003.

4 Zhang Yuanruo, "Xingzheng caipan zhidu zhi yanjiu yu jianyi," 1933: Vol. 6, p. 945.

5 Lifayuan zhonghua minguo xianfa cao'an xuanchuan weiyuanhui, ed. *Zhonghua minguo xianfa cao'an shuomingshu*, 1940: 18.

6 Xingzheng fayuan, ed. *Xingzheng fayuan panjue huibian* 1933–1947, 1948: 1.

7 Sun Zhongshan, *Sunzhongshan xuanji*, 1981: 166; "Guomin zhengfu jianguo dagang," 1931: 3; Ch'ien Tuan-sheng, *The Government and Politics of China 1912–1949*, 1970: 133–49.

8 Zarrow, 2005: 213. Foreknowers refer to people who understand social issues earlier than others.

9 *The Central Daily*, October 4, 1928; Ch'ien Tuan-sheng, 1970: 250.

10 *The Central Daily*, October 15, 1928.

11 Ibid.: December 27, 1931.

12 Lai Chengzuo, *Xiuzhen Zhonghua liufa quanshu*, 1936: 33.

13 Zhongguo fagui kanxingshe bianshen weiyuanhui, ed., *Zuixin liufa quanshu*, 1948: 427.

14 1914 law see *Zhonghua minguo faling daquan*, 1917: Vol. 12, pp. 1–4. For the 1932

and 1937 laws see Lai Chengzuo, 1936: 25–31. For the 1942 law see *Zuixin liufa quanshu*, 1948: 429–31.

15 Complaining and arguing papers cost 0.5 yuan, while the writing and translation fee was charged from 0.1 to 0.2 yuan per word. The mailing fee cost 0.1 yuan plus the stamp. According to a *Central Daily* article entitled "Jianshao guanli xinshui yandu wubi zhongbao," published on October 21, 1928, the average Chinese worker earned about a dozen yuan a month. Fee and regulation see Lai Chengzuo, 1936: 31.

16 Lai Chengzuo, 1936: 25.

17 According to the 1928 *County Administrative Law of the National Government*, magistrates would also act as judges of the first-level court (*chushen faguan*). See *Guomin zhengfu xian xingzhengfa*, 1928: 76.

18 Ibid.: 209–12.

19 Ibid.: 43–5.

20 Hao Tiechuan and Lu Jinbi, eds., *Yangzhaolong faxue wenxuan*, 2000: 217–19.

21 Zhang Yuanruo, 1933: 956.

22 For Yang Haikun and Yang Yuqing see Yang Haikun, *Zhongguo xingzhengfa jiben lilun*, 1992: 540; Guo Shu see "Zhongguo jindai xingzheng fayuan zhidu zhi bianqian," July 21, 2003.

23 According to the *Organizing Law of the Administrative Court* (*xingzheng fayuan zuzhifa*) passed in 1931, all judges should: first, have profound knowledge of GMD principles; second, have served as officials in the National Government for two years; three, have attained at least thirty years of age. These requirements in reality excluded most non-GMD members from becoming judges. See Zhao Chen, Yang Yuanbiao, and Shen Zhiming, eds., *Zhongguo liufa quanshu*, 1939: 53; Xu Xiaoqun, *Trial of Modernity*, 2008: 87–92.

24 For the influence of the Leninist concept of the party-state on the GMD, see Zarrow, 2005: 213–15; Fitzgerald, 1996: 215–17; Strauss, 2000: 89; Rebecca Nedostup and Liang Hong-ming, "Begging the Sages of the Party-State," 2002: 186–7.

25 Xu Xiaoqun, 2008: 90.

26 Compared with records in the early republic, the contents in this book would appear to be very incomplete. It is reasonable to think that more than ninety-two cases would have been accepted and decided in fourteen years. Unfortunately there is no way to prove (or disprove) this hypothesis.

27 *Xingzheng fayuan panjue huibian* 1948.

28 The word "complain" here is *qingyuan* in Chinese, which normally refers to political complaints or demands such as demanding more political freedom. *Qingyuan* is different from *gaosu* or *konggao* that usually involve legal accusations against alleged criminals or corrupt officials who have violated people's rights. Miu Quanji, ed., *Zhongguo zhixianshi ziliao huibian: xianfapian*, 1989: 360, 618.

29 *Zhonghua minguo xianfa "xiuzheng cao'an" "cao'an" yitong bijiao*, 1947: 12–13.

30 Article 7 of the 1912 *Provisional Constitution of the Republic of China* noted that people had the right to complain to the congress, while Article 6 of the 1914 *Constitution of the Republic of China* gave people the right to complain to the Legislative Yuan. *Zhongguo jindai fazhishi ziliao xuanji*, 1985: Vol. 58, p. 84. For Strauss see Strauss, 2000: 89.

31 Article 20 of the 1931 Provisional Constitution of the Republic of China during the Political Tutelage (*zhonghua minguo xunzheng shiqi yuefa*) said that people had the right to complain; Article 23 of the *1936 Draft Constitution of the Republic of China* (*zhonghua minguo xianfa caoan*) and Article 16 of the *1947 Constitution of the Republic of China* (*zhonghua minguo xianfa*) reiterated that people had the right to complain, and file lawsuits at the court. All these laws can be found in *Zhonghua minguo xianxing faling daquan*, 1934.

32 Pan Zhenqui, ed., *Zhonghua minguo shishi jiyao*, 1936–August 1929: 719.

33 China Second Historical Archives: Category 1, National Government, No. 6662.

34 Ibid.: No. 1.6585.
35 Rong Mengyuan, ed., *Zhongguo Guomindang lici daibiao dahui ji zhongyang quanhui ziliao*, 1985: Vol. 2, p. 1105.
36 Records read at Shanghai Archives: Category Q109, Shanghai Congress, No. 1857.106.
37 Records read at Shanghai Archives: Category Q117, Shanghai Labor Union, No. 153.
38 Records read at Hubei Provincial Archives, LS-3-2852: 32–3.
39 China Second Historical Archives: Category 10, The Legislative Yuan, No. 59.
40 Records read at Hubei Provincial Archives, LS3-3-2852: 83–6.
41 China Second Historical Archives: Category 10, The Legislative Yuan, No. 59.
42 Ibid.: 163–7.
43 Records read at Hubei Provincial Archives, LS3-3-3737-3738: 4–38.
44 Xu Xiaoqun, 2008: Chapter 10.
45 Andrew Nathan, *Chinese Democracy*, 1985: 148.
46 Eugenia Lean, *Public Passions*, 2007: Ch. 2 and Ch. 7.
47 Nedostup and Liang, 2002: 198.
48 *Zhonghua minguo shishi jiyao* – December 1934: 996–7.
49 Geng Yunzhi, *Xifang minzhu zai jindai zhongguo*, 2003: 459.
50 Frederic Wakeman argues that the secret police such as the Lixingshe (Vigorous Society) and Lanyishe (Blueshirts) were forms of Confucian fascism. See Frederic Wakeman, Jr., "A Revisionist View of the Nanjing Decade," 2000.
51 Lloyd E. Eastman, "The May Fourth Movement as a Historical Turning Point Ecological Exhaustion, Militarization, and other Causes of China's Modern Crisis," 1991: 123–38: 129; William C. Jones, "Chinese Law and Liberty in Comparative Historical Perspective," 2004: 49.
52 Sun Yet-san (Sun Zhongshan) *Sunzhongshan xuanji*, 1981: Vol. 1, pp. 288–9.
53 Zhongguo di'er lishi danganguan, ed., *Zhongguo guomindang diyi erci quanguo daibiao dahui huiyi shiliao*, 1986: Vol. 1, p. 86.
54 Rong Mengyuan, 1985: Vol. 1, p. 517.
55 Zarrow, 2005: 212–16; Wakeman, 2000: 195; Harold R. Isaacs, *The Tragedy of the Chinese Revolution*, 1968: 64; *Zhongguo guomindang diyi erci quanguo daibiao dahui huiyi shiliao*, 1986: Vol. 1, p. 14.
56 William C. Kirby, "The Chinese Party-State Under Dictatorship and Democracy on the Mainland and on Taiwan," 2004: 118.
57 Sun Yat-sen in Sun Zhangshan, *Sunzhongshan xuanji*, 1981: 171; Fitzgerald, 1996: 79.
58 Sun Zhangshan, *Sunzhongshan quanji*, 1981: 326–7; Qiao Congqi, *Sunzhongshan falü sixiang tixi yanjiu*, 1992: 122.
59 Zhang Qiyun, *Xian zongtong Jianggong quanji*, 1984: 1230.
60 Ibid.: 823; *Xianzongtong jianggong sixiang yanlun zongji*, 1984: Vol. 12, p. 151; also Fenby, 2004: 225.
61 Fenby, 2004: 230.
62 *Zhongguo guomindang diyi erci quanguo daibiao dahui huiyi shiliao*, 1986: Vol. 1, p. 645. The only exceptions were unspecified "specialists," who played only subordinate roles in the administration.
63 Zhang Qiyun, 1984: 822.
64 Fitzgerald, 1996: 187; *Zhongguo guomindang diyi erci quanguo daibiao dahui huiyi shiliao*, 1986: Vol. 1, p. 28.
65 Zhang Qiyun, 1984: 515.
66 Frederic Wakeman Jr., "Models of Historical Change," 1991; Lloyd E. Eastman, *The Abortive Revolution*, 1974: 31–84 and *Seeds of Destruction*, 1984: 120–1.
67 Roger B. Jeans, Jr., *Democracy and Socialism in Republican China*, 1997: 204; Kirby, 2004: 118–20; *Zhonghua minguo shishi jiyao* – May 1936: 886.

68 Rong Mengyuan, 1985: Vol. 1. pp. 657–9.
69 Zarrow, 2005: 340–1; Fenby, 2004: 226–31; Wakeman, *Spymaster Dai Li and the Chinese Secret Service*, 2003: 146; Eastman, 1974: 46–7; Wang Limin, *Shanghai fazhishi*, 1998: 142–3; Jeffery N. Wasserstrom, *Student Protests in Twentieth-Century China*, 1991: 268; Jeans, 1997: 57.
70 "Fengyuxiang tongdian chenshu shiju yijian," in *Zhonghua minguo shishi jiyao* – November 1932: 704–9.
71 Rong Mengyuan, 1985: Vol. 2, p. 329.
72 Eastman, 1974: 14.
73 Rong Mengyuan, 1985: Vol. 2, p. 1178. A republican observer Yi Gong, like Chiang, argued that the biggest sickness in the Republic was official corruption, law breaking, and irresponsibility. See Yi Gong, "Gaizao zhengzhi zhi jiben tiaojian, 1932: 190.
74 Wakeman, 2003: 173–80.
75 Wang Qisheng, *Dangyuan dangquan yu dangzheng*, 2003: 219.
76 Ruan Yicheng, *Fazhi lunji*, 1933: 7.
77 "Gedi qunzhong kongsu GMD zhengfu fubaide," in China Second Historical Archives: Category 1, The National Government, No. 6662.
78 According to an unofficial history, Chiang Kai-shek stated at the tenth GMD Plenary Session (*shizhong quanhui*十中全会) held in Chongqing in 1942 that a revolutionary party should not follow the law. If it abided by the law, the party would not be revolutionary. See Che Jixin and Wang Xi, eds., *Minguo yeshi*, 2000: 389.
79 Ruan Yicheng, 1933: 32.
80 Qiu Hanping, "Zhongguo zhi zhixian yu xingxian," 1941: 351.
81 Shen Meijuan, ed., *Shenzui zishu*, 1997: 32–3, 90, 136, 185–7.
82 Lloyd E. Eastman, *Seeds of Destruction*, 1984: 1, 7, 219.
83 Rong Mengyuan, 1985: Vol. 2, p. 306.
84 *Zhonghua minguo xianfa cao'an shuomingshu*, 1940: 126.
85 Rong Mengyuan, 1985: Vol. 2, p. 868.
86 Sterling Seagrave, *The Song Dynasty*, 1985: 374; Fenby, 2004: 362; Chalmers Johnson, *Peasant Nationalism and Communist Power*, 1962; for a critique of CCP actions and defense of GMD policies during this period, see Jung Chang and Jon Halliday, *Mao*, 2006. Although detailed and seemingly well documented, this work is actually highly problematic. See Gregor Benton and Lin Chun, eds., *Was Mao Really a Monster*? 2010.
87 *Zhonghua minguo shishi jiyao* – 1929: 653.
88 "Fan geming anjian peichen zanxingfa," in *Zhongguo jindai fazhishi ziliao xuanji*,1985: Vol. 3, pp. 75–80.
89 Qiao, 1992: 282.
90 Lin Houqi wrote this article in the early PRC period and thus his opinion may have been adjusted to favor the PRC. See Lin Houqi, "Guomindang tongzhi shiqi de sifa gaishu," 1989: 14–15.
91 Wang Limin, 1998: 143.
92 Klaus Muhlhahn, *Criminal Justice in China*, 2009: 128–34.
93 Xie Zhenmin, *Zhonghua minguo lifashi*, 2000: 18.
94 Philip C. C. Huang, *Code, Custom, and Legal Practice in China*, 2001: 66.
95 Lin Ji, *Juzhengzhuan*, 1993: Vol. 239, p. 275.
96 Lin Houqi, 1989: 2.
97 Zhu Guonan, "Qixing guaizhuang de jiusifa," 1982: 132.
98 To reduce the number of magistrate judges, the Judicial Yuan on October 26, 1929, planned to establish 828 new courts, 30 new prisons, and 151 new detaining custodies in 1930. The number varied in the next five years. See *Zhonghua minguo shishi jiyao* – October 1929: 382.
99 *Zhonghua minguo shishi jiyao*, January 1936: 17; *Guomin zhengfu xian xingzhengfa*, 1928: 76.

100 Yang Peng, "Woguo sifa xiankuang ji zhan wang," 1936: 271–3.
101 See Zhu Guonan, 1982: 128.
102 Ibid.: 129.
103 Lin Houqi, 1989: 25.

5 Revolutionary idealism: the early People's Republic (1949–1982)

1 "Zhongguo gongchandang di'er'ci dabiao dahui xuanyan," *The People's Daily*, October 16, 2007.
2 Philip Short, *Mao*, 1999: 122.
3 Nick Knight, *Rethinking Mao*, 2007: 238; Lowell Dittmer, *China's Continuous Revolution*, 1989: 78; Maurice Meisner, *Mao's China and After*, 1999: 291; Short, 1999: 525.
4 For the Ming precedent, see Sarah Schneewind, "Visions and Revisions," 2001: 317–59, esp. p. 338.
5 Scholars such as Maurice Meisner and Lee Feigon argue that Mao did not have insurmountable power in the Party and regularly sought the concurrence of the Party leadership before acting. See Meisner, 1999: 170, 184; Feigon, *Mao: A Reinterpretaion*, 2002: 108. For Mao's self-criticisms in the mid 1940s, see Frederic C. Teiwes and Warren Sun, "From a Leninist to a Charismatic Party," 1995: 347; For Mao's self-criticism in the late 1950s, including at the Lushan Conference in 1959, see Li Rui, *Lushan huiyi shilu*, 1994; see also Stuart Schram, *Chairman Mao Talks to the People*, 1974. For Mao's critics see Wang Laidi, "Maozedong de zhishi fenzi zhengce," 2003; Dai Huang, "Yongnian shenzhixiong," 2003: 61; Li Rui, *Lirui lunshuo wenzuan*, 1998: 198, 178–9.
6 Diao Jiecheng, *Renmin xinfang shilue*, 1996: 20.
7 Ilpyong J. Kim, *The Politics of Chinese Communism*, 1973: 164; also see Diao Jiecheng, 1996: 21.
8 Xinan zhengfa xueyuan hanshoubu, ed., *Zhongguo xinminzhu zhuyi geming shiqi fazhi jianshe zilian xuanbian*, 1982: Vol. 1, p. 279.
9 Ibid.: Vol. 1, pp. 29–30.
10 Kim, 1973: 118.
11 Interviews: Official A, September 10, 2003.
12 Diao Jiecheng, 1996: 21.
13 In 1957, Xi Zhongxun, head of the secretariat of the State Council, criticized officials who, unlike in the base period, distanced themselves from the mass. In an interview, the former head of the complaint office in a major city also argued that in the base period the CCP had a close relationship with the masses. For Xi see Zhonggong zhongyang bangongting and Guowuyuan bangongting, eds.; *Quanguo xinfang gongzuo huiyi ziliao huibian*, 1989: 22. Former head of a complaint office see Interviews: Official A, September 10, 2003.
14 Short, 1999: 270–1.
15 See Short, 1999: 385–9; Jonathan Spence, *The Gate of Heavenly Peace*,1981: 334; Kenneth Lieberthal, *Governing China*, 1995: 54; Yung-fa Chen, "Suspect History and the Mass Line," 2003: 169–89: 172–3; Wang Laidi, 2003: 43.
16 Many scholars have argued that the CCP has been heavily influenced from its birth by Lenin and Stalin's organizational and political methods such as the party-state. See John Fitzgerald, *Awakening China*, 1996: 328; Vivienne Shue, "Powers of State, Paradoxes of Dominion: China 1949–1979," 1991: 206. For Lenin's view on political authority see *Sifa gongzuo shouce*, 1952: Vol. 13, p. 49.
17 The law was also consistent with the Soviet model. Sherila Fitzpatrick notes that Soviet leaders in the 1930s regarded complaints as a channel of information from the grassroots. Lenin, the founder of the Soviet Union, pointed out that every citizen had the right to complaint against any official and did not have to complain to the

immediate superior of that official. For the law see Xinan zhengfa xueyuan hanshoubu: Vol. 1, pp. 44–54. For Fitzpatrick see Laura M. Luehrmann, *Officials Face the Masses*, 2000: 11; For Lenin see Yang Haikun, *Zhongguo xingzhengfa jiben lilun*, 1992: 541.

18 Yang Haikun argues that the 1954 *Interim Regulations of the Port Administration in the PRC* (Zhonghua renmin gongheguo haigang guanli zanxing tiaoli) is an administrative law that guides decisions on administrative compensation. See Yang Haikun, 1992: 541.

19 Some city government may have created similar offices even before this. For example, various Tianjin government organs began accepting people's complaints in January 1949. See Tianjin difangzhi bianxiu weiyuanhui, ed., *Tianjin tongzhi difangzhi*, 1997: 19.

20 Diao Jiecheng, 1996: 25–8.

21 Ibid.

22 Ibid.: 32.

23 Tianjin difangzhi bianxiu weiyuanhui, 1997: 20–3.

24 Diao Jiecheng, 1996: 32.

25 Zhonggong zhongyang wenxian yanjiushi, ed. *Mao Zedong wenji*, 2001: Vol. 6, pp. 164–5.

26 Diao Jiecheng, 1996: 349–50.

27 According to Diao's own evidence, however, as late as 1963, the State Council was still asking county governments to establish complaint offices. Diao Jiecheng, 1996: 38, 39, 41, 51, 52, 53. For the 1963 law see Diao Jiecheng, 1996: 378–82.

28 *Quanguo xinfang gongzuo huiyi ziliao huibian*, 1989: 128–31.

29 Diao Jiecheng, 1996: 75, 80, 81. Also see Tianjin difangzhi bianxiu weiyuanhui, 1997: 183, 443.

30 *Quanguo xinfang gongzuo huiyi ziliao huibian*, 1989: 6.

31 Ibid.: 8, 28. Similar conferences were also held in cities like Tianjin in 1957 and the content was similar. See Tianjin difangzhi bianxiu weiyuanhui, 1997: 443.

32 Diao Jiecheng, 1996: 38.

33 "1955 *nian jiancha gongzuo jihua yaodian*," document read at the Shanghai Archives: B2-1-3.

34 Diao Jiecheng, 1996: 38, the remaining 30 percent came from officials.

35 Karl Marx and Friedrich Engels, *The Communist Manifesto*, 2000; Lloyd E. Eastman, *Seeds of Destruction*, 1984: 170.

36 See Fitzgerald, 1996: 326–8.

37 Zhang Renzhong, *Zhongguo nongmin qiyi shihua*, 1991.

38 Thomas P. Bernstein, "Chinese Communism in the Era of Mao Zedong, 1949–1976," 1991: 276.

39 Meisner, 1999: 58.

40 *Dongbiwu faxue wenji*, 2001: 343.

41 Meisner, 1999: 110; Lee Feigon, *Mao*, 2002: 90.

42 Diao Jiecheng, 1996: 56, 78; for the paternalism of the letters and visits system see Minzner, 2006: 133.

43 Short, 1999: 462.

44 *Maozedong wenji*, 2001: Vol. 7, pp. 205–6.

45 Xinan zhengfa xueyuan hanshoubu: Vol. 1, pp. 68–71.

46 *Quanguo xinfang gongzuo huiyi ziliao huibian*: 10.

47 Tianjin difangzhi bianxiu weiyuanhui, 1997: 445, 450.

48 *Dongbiwu faxue wenji*, 2001: 259–60.

49 According to one document, in the first quarter of 1955 Shanghai urban courts accepted 1265 first-judgment civil cases and 951 second-judgment civil cases. All urban courts in the same period solved 10,556 first-judgment civil cases and 680 second-judgment ones. Shanghai Archives: B2-1-3.

50 Diao Jiecheng, 1996: 90.
51 *Quanguo xinfang gongzuo huiyi ziliao huibian*: 6.
52 Tianjin difangzhi bianxiu weiyuanhui, 1997: 183.
53 Elizabeth J. Perry, "Masters of the country? Shanghai Workers in the Early People's Republic,", 2007: 66–7.
54 Zhonggong zhongyang wenxian yanjiushi, ed., *Maozedong shuxin xuanji*, 1983: 493–6.
55 Neil J. Diamant, "Hollow Glory," 2005: 131–58.
56 The role of newspapers in publishing people's complaints in the early PRC has been ignored or even denied by some scholars in the West who have focused instead only on the 1980s. See Luehrmann, 2000: 122.
57 Frederic Wakeman, Jr. "'Cleanup'," 2007: 44.
58 Benjamin L. Liebman, "Watchdog or Demagogue? 2005: 102–3.
59 The number of complaints that had been published by major newspapers was minimal compared to the contemporary statewide surge of complaints. Almost all of the officials who were accused of lawbreaking were relatively lower-ranked. Only very few worked at the provincial-level. See *The China Youth Daily*, August 31, 1951.
60 *China Youth Daily*, March 31, 1953.
61 Tianjin difangzhi bianxiu weiyuanhui, 1997: 22–3.
62 *Quanguo xinfang gongzuo huiyi ziliao huibian*: 79.
63 See Short, 1999: 436–7; also Ezra F. Vogel, *Canton under Communism*, 1980: 114; Meisner, 1999: 72; 98; Frank Dikötter, *Crime, Punishment and the Prison in Modern China*, 2002: 366; Lieberthal, 1995: 66; Dittmer, 1989: 47–8.
64 Dittmer, 1989: 51.
65 *Dongbiwu faxue wenji*, 2001: 159–61; 252–3.
66 Mao's theory differed from Trotsky's. Whereas Trotsky believed that even less industrial societies could march straight to socialism and that the current socialist revolution could become global, Mao argued that there would have to be many successive revolutions before China and the rest of the world could attain socialism and further revolutions might even be necessary under communism. See Knight, 2007: 235; Meisner, 1999: 194; Dittmer, 1989: 33, 66; Short, 1999: 479.
67 Meisner, 1999: 197, 255, 315; Short, 1999: 479–80, 516, 525; Bernstein, 1991: 299; Vogel, 1980: 268, 297, 321; Lieberthal, 1995: 103–12.
68 Diao Jiecheng, 1996: 120; However, according to a Tianjin government report, collective complaints and capital complaints (*jingfang*) increased after 1955 and 1957. See Tianjin difangzhi bianxiu weiyuanhui, 1997: 179, 183.
69 Diao Jiecheng, 1996: 120–1.
70 For Li Rui see Li Rui, *Lirui lunshuo wenxuan*, 1998: 59; for Gu Zhun see Chen Minzhi and Gu Nanjiu, eds., *Guzhun riji*, 2002: 245.
71 Diao Jiecheng, 1996: 121. This would almost certainly have meant the woman's death.
72 Martin King Whyte, "State and Society in the Mao Era," 1991: 266.
73 *Quanguo xinfang gongzuo huiyi ziliao huibian*: 36.
74 For state see Diao Jiecheng, 1996: 163–4; for local see Tianjin difangzhi bianxiu weiyuanhui, 1997: 179.
75 Diao Jiecheng, 1996: 347–7.
76 Ibid.: 378–82.
77 Ibid.: 173.
78 Ibid.: 389–97.
79 In most periods, the majority of complainants, especially those complaining to the capital, were farmers who, unlike urban intellectuals and workers, may have had few means to address their grievances. Rural residents were least likely to trust local governments and they often harbored faith in the uprightness of the upper-levels of

government. Since 1961, the number of people's letters and visits to the central government had increased steadily, becoming a headache to the central government. Ibid.: 370–3.

80 Andrew Nathan, *Chinese Democracy*, 1985: 80; Luehrmann, 2000: 43–5.

81 Li Jiutuan and Wang Junshan, eds., *Xinshiji zhongguo xinfang gongzuo shiwu quanshu*, 2000: 408–28; also see Interviews: Officials K, December 2, 2003; Official J, November 28, 2003.

82 For the decline of complaints during the Cultural Revolution see Diao Jiecheng, 1996: 213–15; for a detailed account of Lin Biao's death see Jin Qiu, *The Culture of Power*, 1999.

83 Diao Jiecheng, 1996: 216–19. In 1972, Tianjin also witnessed a noticeable rise of complaints but many of them were, unlike those lodged with the central government, about personal issues such as finding and changing jobs. See Tianjin difangzhi bianxiu weiyuanhui, 1997: 28.

84 Tianjin difangzhi bianxiu weiyuanhui, 1997: 449.

85 Hubeisheng Geming weiyuanhui laodongjü, ed., *Laodong gongzuo jianbao*, April 20, 1974.

86 Elizabeth J. Perry and Li Xun, *Proletarian Power*, 1997: 45–8.

87 *Quanguo xinfang gongzuo huiyi ziliao huibian*: 163.

88 Diao Jiecheng, 1996: 216–17.

89 Meisner, 1999: 354–5; Short, 1999: 543–85; Spence, 1981: 387; Vogel, 1980: 326–9; John E. Schrecker, *The Chinese Revolution in Historical Perspective*, 1991: 168–82; Lieberthal, 1995: 101, 112; John Pomfret, *Chinese Lessons*, 2006: 21, 36–7.

90 According to Dai Huang, during the Cultural Revolution, one worker was labeled as a counterrevolutionary after he said "Chairman Mao is florid, while Lin Biao is skinny," a point that was regarded as a scoff of vice chairman Lin Biao. See Dai Huang, *Hu Yaobang yu pingfan yuanjia cuoan*, 1998: 152.

91 Nathan, 1985: 25.

92 Li Rui, *Lirui lunshuo wenxuan*, 1998: 59.

93 *Quanguo xinfang gongzuo huiyi ziliao huibian*: 175–6.

94 Dai Huang, 1998: 28, 67.

95 Jerome Cohen, *Criminal process in the PRC, 1949–1963*, 1968: 9.

96 *Wenhuibao*, June 30, 1957.

97 Elya J. Zhang, "To Be Somebody,", 2006.

98 *Quanguo xinfang gongzuo huiyi ziliao huibian*: 340.

99 Tianjin difangzhi bianxiu weiyuanhui, 1997: 73, 453.

100 Ezra F. Vogel, *Deng Xiaoping and the Transformation of China*, 2011: 368.

101 Dittmer, 1989: 232; Merle Goldman, "The Reassertion of Political Citizenship in the Post-Mao Era: The Democracy Wall Movement," 2002: 179.

102 For Central and Shandong governments see Diao Jiecheng, 1996: 213; for Tianjin see Tianjin difangzhi bianxiu weiyuanhui, 1997: 30–4, 439, 457.

103 *Quanguo xinfang gongzuo huiyi ziliao huibian*: 174.

104 Nathan, 1985: 7, 27.

105 *Quanguo xinfang gongzuo huiyi ziliao huibian*: 161.

106 Ibid.: 190.

107 Albert H. Y. Chen, "Legal Thought and Legal Development in the PRC 1949–2008," 2010: 54.

108 Randall Peerenboom, *China's Long March toward Rule of Law*, 2002: 57, and Yuanyuan Shen, "Conceptions and Receptions of Legality," 2000.

109 *Quanguo xinfang gongzuo huiyi ziliao huibian*: 415.

110 Diao Jiecheng, 1996: 229.

111 *The People's Daily*, January 27, 1979.

112 Diao Jiecheng, 1996: 230.

113 Ibid.: 236–41.

114 *The People's Daily*, October 22, 1979.
115 The newspapers did not publish all letters of complaint they received, but they would pass many of the unpublished ones directly to the government organs that were supposed to deal with them. When they had positive responses from the responsible officials, the newspapers would publish some of them. See the *China Youth Daily*, September 24, 1981; Nathan, 1985: 82, 183–5. For a general study evaluating and using such sources in the 1980s, see Luo Xu, *Searching for Life's Meaning*, 2002.
116 *The People's Daily*, April 24, 1979.
117 Ibid. June 7, 1979.
118 Ibid.: 416–17.
119 Tianjin difangzhi bianxiu weiyuanhui, 1997: 459.
120 *Quanguo xinfang gongzuo huiyi ziliao huibian*: 170–1.
121 The primary mission of the one thousand cadres was to address grievances at the local level. See Diao Jiecheng, 1996: 242.
122 *Quanguo xinfang gongzuo huiyi ziliao huibian*: 403.
123 Zhang Cheng, "Hewei dangde lingdao," in *The People's Daily*, January 15, 1979.
124 Nathan, 1985: 184.
125 Shao Xuyang, "Duzhe laixin weisheme yinbuqi zhongshi," in *The People's Daily*, November 24, 1979.
126 Mao's personal doctor Li Zhisui proposes that Mao's neurasthenia (chronic fatigue) might have contributed to his continuing fear of other leaders' disloyalty. See Li Zhisui, *The Private Life of Chairman Mao*, 1994: 110.
127 *Maozedong wenji*, 2001: Vol. 6, p. 120.
128 Feigon, 2002: 112–16; Meisner, 1999: 171–87; Lieberthal, 1995: 100–1; Short, 1999: 466–7.
129 Meisner, 1999: 262–74; Short, 1999: 506–18.
130 Li Rui, *Lirui riji*, 1998: 280; Lieberthal, 1995: 110; Meisner, 1999: 291; Feigon, 2002: 140–1.
131 The full story of links between China's Cultural Revolution and the U.S. war in Vietnam has yet to be told. For preliminary studies, see Ho Ping-ti and Tang Tsou, eds., *China in Crisis*, 1968: Ch. 1–2.
132 Like Sun Yat-sen and Chiang Kai-shek, as early as the 1920s Mao advocated one-party rule as the necessary means for carrying out a successful revolution. See Fitzgerald, 1996: 188.
133 Lieberthal, 1995: 151.
134 Li Rui, *Lirui lunshuo wenxuan*, 1998: 178.
135 *Mao Zedong wenji*, 2001: Vol. 6, p. 294.
136 In the summer of 1967, Liu Shaoqi tried several times to protest or complain to Mao about his dangerous situation and possible grievances, but he never got any response. See Huang Zheng, ed., *Liushaoqi de zuihou suiyue 1966–1969*, 2002: 49.
137 *Pengzhen wenxuan*, 1991: 257; also see Pitman B. Potter, *From Leninist Discipline to Socialist Legalism*, 2003: 65–7.
138 *Dongbiwu faxue wenji*, 2001: 236. This idea had roots in an ancient saying that the rites do not extend down to the people and the law does not extend up to the officials.
139 "Qieshi jiejue shangfang wenti," in *The People's Daily*, September 17, 1979.
140 *Quanguo xinfang gongzuo huiyi ziliao huibian*, 1989: 22. Also see Tianjin difangzhi bianxiu weiyuanhui, 1997: 443; Meisner, 1999: 125–7.
141 Diao Jiecheng, 1996: 44.
142 Bernstein, 1991: 289. Meisner argues that the Cultural Revolution ironically failed to reduce the number of officials and actually added to the number of bureaucratic posts. Meisner, 1999: 371.
143 *Quanguo xinfang gongzuo huiyi ziliao huibian*, 1989: 187.

144 *The People's Daily*, January 27, 1979.
145 *Maozedong wenji*, 2001: Vol. 7, p. 206.
146 Wang Hongchang and Liu Mengyi, "Dangnei cunzai yige guanliao zhuyizhe jieji ma," in *The China Youth Daily*, February 7, 1981.
147 Carl Minzner argues that the letters and visits system of the PRC is an extra-legal institution and it also overlaps with the formal judicial system. See Minzner, 2006: 124.
148 *Dongbiwu faxue wenji*, 2001: 15.
149 Ibid.: 92.
150 Wei Ming, "Renmin sifa gongzuo burong youpai wumie," in *Wenhuibao*, September 4, 1957.
151 *Sifa gongzuo shouce*, 1952: Vol. 13, p. 31.
152 *Dongbiwu faxue wenji*, 2001: 121.
153 *Sifa gongzuo shouce*, 1952: Vol. 13, p. 4.
154 *Sifa gongzuo shouce*, 1952: Vol. 13, p. 105.
155 Potter, 2003: 64–7.
156 *Renmin sifa zai yuejin*, 1958: 3.
157 Ibid.
158 "Weiweihu fazhi shou chufen de zhengfa ganbu huifu mingyu," in *The People's Daily*, April 18, 1979.
159 For Peng Zhen see *Pengzhen wenxuan*, 1991: 368 and Potter, 2003: 114; Wan Li, *Wanli wenxuan*, 1995: 147.
160 "Xiongyifu de si shuoming le shenme," in *The People's Daily*, August 25, 1979.
161 *Quanguo xinfang gongzuo huiyi ziliao huibian*: 188.
162 "Xinfang gongzuozhe de husheng," in *The People's Daily*, July 27, 1979.
163 *Quanguo xinfang gongzuo huiyi ziliao huibian*: 188.

6 Bureaucratic pragmatism: the reform period (after 1982)

1 Deng Xiaoping, "Minzhu yu fazhi liangshou doubunengruo," 1983: 2: 189; for a general account of Deng Xiaoping's role in the post-1978 see Ezra F. Vogel, *Canton under Communism*, 2011.
2 Gong Pixiang, ed., *Dangdai zhongguo de falü geming*, 1999: 316.
3 Pitman B. Potter, *From Leninist Discipline to Socialist Legislation*, 2003: 117.
4 Ching Kwan Lee, *Against the Law*, 2007: 18; Qiang Fang, "The Case of the Virgin Prostitute: Chinese Media and Legal Reform," 2002: 26–7.
5 *1982 nian zhongguo xianfa*, 1982: 14.
6 Andrew Nathan, *Chinese Democracy*, 1985: 108–9.
7 Xia Yong, *Yifa zhiguo-guojia yu shehui*, 2004: 99.
8 See Stanley Lubman, *Bird in a Cage*, 1999: 123.
9 Jiang Zemin, "Gaojü dengxiaoping lilunweida qizhi, bayouzhongguo tese shehui zhuyi shiye quanmian tuixiang ershiyi shiji," *The People's Daily*, September 22, 1997.
10 Deng Liqun, "Falü yaowei renmin suozhangwo," in *The China Youth Daily*, June 21, 1985.
11 The poll was made by a Shanghai-based magazine *The Youth Generation* [qingnian yidai] in *The China Youth Daily*, September 2, 1986.
12 For more studies on the correlations between Chinese media and rising legal consciousness see Benjamin L. Liebman, "Watchdog or Demagogue?" 2005: 28–31; Mary E. Gallagher, "Mobilizing the Law in China," 2006.
13 Interviews: Others H (migrant workers from Anhui), December 23, 2003.
14 Kevin O'Brien and Lianjiang Li, "The Politics of Lodging Complaints in Rural China," 2005: 31–53.
15 Carl F. Minzner, "Xinfang: An Alternative to the Formal Chinese System," 2006: 124, 162.

16 Yongshun Cai, *Collective Resistance in China*, 2010: 185.
17 Laura M. Luehrmann, *Officials Face the Masses*, 2000: 84, 124.
18 Liebman, 2005: 102–3.
19 Diao Jiecheng, *Renmin xinfang shilüe*, 1996: 398.
20 Ibid.: 389.
21 Ibid.: 398–9.
22 *The People's Daily*, November 1, 1995.
23 Ibid.
24 For a detailed discussion see Pitman B. Potter, "The Administrative Litigation Law of the PRC," 1994: 270–304.
25 Ibid.: 290; Luehrmann, 2000: 100–1.
26 2002 *Zhonghua renmin gongheguo xingzheng susongfa* and *Zhonghua renmin gongheguo xingzheng fuyifa*: 6.
27 Ibid.: 22.
28 Both republican complaint laws allowed people to complain against improper government activities. For unlawful government activities, people should first complain to the immediately higher government. If dissatisfied, they could then bring suits to the administrative court. For republican laws see Zhongguo fagui kanxingshe bianshen weiyuanhui, ed., *Zuixin liufa quanshu*, 1948: 427–9. For the PRC *Administrative Reconsideration Law* see 2002 *Zhonghua renmin gongheguo xingzheng fuyifa*: 48–9.
29 Ibid.: 52–6.
30 Potter, 1994: 273.
31 Figures from 1989 to 1992 come from "Mingaoguan shinian pandian," in *The China Youth Daily*, April 16, 1999. For the others, see *1987–1997 Zhongguo falü nianjian* published from 1987 to 2004.
32 Ren Jianxin, "Zuigao renmin fayuan gognzuo baogao," in *The People's Daily*, April 10, 1990.
33 Ma Huaide, *Zhongguo xingzhengfa*, 1997: 15.
34 The percentage of successful administrative suits is unevenly distributed. Some areas may have lower percentages while others may have higher ones. According to former Prime Minister Zhu Rongji, in the late 1990s some counties had lost 40 percent of their administrative suits and some townships had even lost as high as 70 percent of their suits. See Zhu Rongji, "Renzhen guanche yifa zhiguo fanglue, qieshi quanmian tuijin yifa xingzheng," 1999: 4.
35 Minzner, 2006: 65.
36 Min Jie, "Yi xingzhengting tingzhang de kunao," in *The China Youth Daily*, July 31, 2002.
37 Kevin O'Brien and Lianjiang Li, "Suing the Local State," 2005: 35.
38 For a good study on the issue that Party secretaries and local governments in China are generally above the law see He Weifang, *Yunsong zhengyide fangshi*, 2002: 7, 191, 199.
39 *The China Youth Daily*, April 16, 1999.
40 Guo Guosong, "Shenshi xinfang," in *The Southern Weekend*, November 13, 2003; for a detailed study of the "abstract administrative activities" see Jiang Bixin, "Xingzheng susongfa yuchouxiang xingzheng xingwei," 2009.
41 O'Brien and Li, 2005: 36–7.
42 Ibid.
43 See Table 6.1. For a similar argument see Wang Xiuquan, "Mingaoguan weihe banshu chesu," in *The China Youth Daily*, April 16, 1999.
44 "Gaoguan lushi wunai piaobo," in *The Southern Weekend*, February 7, 2002.
45 A judge in Shanghai Intermediate Court disagreed with the view that officials did not want to present. On the contrary, he told me that in some administrative suits, officials would appear while common witnesses would not present. The judge did

not say that common witnesses might fear official retaliation if they presented. Instead, he explained that it was because commoners disrespected the court. Interviews: Official C (Shanghai judge), September 26, 2003.

46 O'Brien and Li, 2005: 37.

47 *Legal Encyclopedia* reported in 2002 that no official in a eastern city had ever appeared to any People-Accuse-Official case. See *Fazhi bolan*, 2002: Vol. 12, p. 12. Yangtze News see "Tongzhou mingaoguan rangren fuqi," in *The Yangtze Evening News*, September 15, 2003.

48 See O'Brien and Li: 35; Lubman 1999: 209; Jiang Mingan believes that government power will serious restrict the function of administrative litigations before Chinese judiciary can gain full independence. See Guo Guosong, "Shenshi xinfang," *The Southern Weekend*. November 13, 2003.

49 *Fazhi bolan*. 2002: Vol. 12, p. 12.

50 O'Brien and Li, 2005: 42.

51 In the well-known case of "Virgin Prostitute," Ma Dandan who was charged with prostitution and was tortured by policemen in 2001. But the local court only gave her $9 as state compensation. For the case of Ma Dandan see Qiang Fang, 2002.

52 Wang Peirong, an associate professor in Xuzhou, Jiangsu, won a suit in 2002 against the Xuzhou Price Bureau. But he lost two later suits against more powerful governmental units such as the Xuzhou city government and police bureau. See Interviews: Complainant D (Wang Peirong), October 28, 2003. Lubman argues that the Administrative Litigation Law could to some extent check certain officials' arbitrariness. But those officials who fear administrative suits are mostly lower-ranking officials because the Party committee remains unchallengeable by the courts. See Lubman 1999: 209, 215 and Potter, 1994.

53 Minzner, 2006: 162; Yongshen Cai, 2010: 57.

54 Maurice Meisner, *Mao's China and After*, 1999: 451; Kenneth Lieberthal, *Governing China*, 1995: 301; Michel Oksenberg, "The Deng Era's Uncertain Political Legacy," 1991: 323.

55 Qiu Haiping, "Xianqiankan shi fazhan shengchan de zuli," in *The China Youth Daily*, October 22, 1983.

56 Interviews: Official A (Former head of Shanghai Letters and Visits Bureau), September 10, 2003; for Tianjin see Tianjin difangzhi bianxiu weiyuanhui, *Tianjin tongzhi difangzhi*, 1997: 128–48.

57 Interviews: Official K (Two heads of letters and visits office in a northern township), December 2, 2003.

58 Maurice Meisner, *The Deng Xaioping Era*, 1996: 110.

59 Both Xi Zhongxun and Zhou Jie acknowledged that many new complaints related to the Open policy and economic reform. See Zhonggong zhongyang bangongting, *Quanguo xinfang gongzuo huiyi ziliao huibian*, 1989: 577, 583, 589.

60 Tianjin difangzhi bianxiu weiyuanhui, 1997: 470.

61 Chang Xiaoquan, "Ganbu haile hongyanbing, qiangqu liuqian paotongmiao," in *The China Youth Daily*, July 31, 1984.

62 For higher-level courts' right to meddle in lower-level courts' decisions see *Renmin fayuan zuzhifa*, 2006; Lubman, 1999: 269.

63 "Falü de shengli," in *The China Youth Daily*, November 13, 1985.

64 Ying Xing, *Dahe yimin shangfang de gushi*, 2001: 57–191.

65 Zheng Yongzhen, "Shenwei sifa ganbu, weihe jianta falü," in *The China Youth Daily*, May 10, 1983.

66 Nathan, 1985: 26; Tianjin difangzhi bianxiu weiyuanhui, 1997: 41, 181.

67 Liu Xiaomeng, *Zhongguo zhiqing koushushi*, 2004: 562–4.

68 A current head of a township letters and visits office in north China said that there was only one person in charge of the office in the 1980s and there were only a few complaints. More complaints started in the late 1980s and in 1986, most farmers did

not have any idea what the meaning of Xinfang. Interviews: Official M (A township Party secretary in northern China), December 3, 2003; Tianjin difangzhi bianxiu weiyuanhui, 1997: 182.

69 Liebman, 2005: 28–31; Gallagher, 2006.

70 Wang Hui, *China's New Order*, 2003: 117.

71 Meisner, 1999: 516–17. See also Vogel 1980 for Deng's organization of that tour—very interesting.

72 Jiang Zemin, "Gaojü dengxiaoping lilunweida qizhi, bayouzhongguo tese shehui zhuyi shiye quanmian tuixiang ershiyi shiji," *The People's Daily*, September 22, 1997.

73 Lieberthal, 1995: 316; Randall Peerenboom, *China's Long March toward Rule of Law*, 2002: 429.

74 Liu Zuoxiang, "Zhongguo sifa defang baohu zhuyi zhi pipan," 2003: Vol 1, p. 89.

75 Wang, 2003: 26, 83, 177; Dorothy J. Solinger, *Contesting Citizenship in Urban China*, 1999: 131; Peter J. Seybolt, *Throwing the Emperor from his Horse*, 1996: 127; Lieberthal, 1995: 267.

76 Meisner 1996: 303.

77 Chiang Kwan Lee, 2007: 27; Gallagher, 2006; "Tanfang chengshi shangfangzu de yingmi shijie," in *The Worker's Daily*, March 25, 2002.

78 "Zhouzhanshun tongzhi zaiquanguo xinfangjuzhang huiyishangde jianghua," in *Renmin zinfang*, 1999.

79 Qiu Dengchang, "Wosheng xinfang gongzuo mianlin de xinxingshi," 2000: Vol 2, pp. 39–40; like Henan, Shannxi also experienced large scale illegal collective complaints, see Zhou Hulin, "Zengyang ladong qunzhong jifangde zhidong lianhuan," 2000: Vol 2, p. 25.

80 Interviews: Official M, December 3, 2003.

81 *1987–1997 Zhongguo falü nianjian* 1998: 773 and *2000 Zhongguo falü nianjian* 2000: 1210.

82 Geng Zhisheng, "Renzhen xuexi guanche shiliuda jingshen nuli zuohao xinshiji xinjieduan dexinfang gongzuo," 2003: Vol 1, pp. 6–11.

83 Hu Kui and Jiang Shu, "2003 nian zhongguo zaoyu xinfang hongfeng, xin lingdaoren mianlin feichang kaoyan," 2003.

84 Farmers between 1978 and 1984 may have enjoyed higher living standard and low taxes due to the early agricultural reform, but that changed after 1985. See Wang, 2003: 48–9; Seybolt, 1996: 84; Meisner, 1996: 229; "Zhizhi xiang nongmin luanpaikuan luanshoufei," in *The China Youth Daily*, November 1, 1985.

85 O'Brien and Li, 2006: 41; Solinger, 1999: 170; Lieberthal, 1995: 273; Meisner, 1996: 489. Seybolt, 1996: 122–3.

86 "Lipeng yaoqiu zhongshi nongmin fudan zhuyi gongzuo fangfa," in *The China Youth Daily*. April 19, 1990.

87 "Tanpai Mengyuhu," in *The China Youth Daily*. November 19, 1992.

88 Chen Guidi and Chun Tao, *Zhongguo nongmin diaocha*, 2004: 60–77.

89 Yongshen Cai, 2010: 80–1.

90 Peter S. Goodman. "A New Use for Good Earth," in *The Washington Post*, April 13, 2004.

91 For the question why so many people complained to Beijing, the heads of a county letters and visits office in northern China said complainants still believed that rulers were the "head of the family [state] (*dangjiade*)"—a *minben* concept—and would address their grievances better than local officials. Interviews: Official K.

92 Liu Jianping and Dai Dunfeng, "Bieduozou wode maitian," in *The Southern Weekend*, January 8, 2004.

93 Jim Yardley, "Farmers Being Moved Aside by China's Booming Market in Real Estate" in the *New York Times*, December 8, 2004.

94 Yang Jun, "Wanqian louyu zhuhuazhang," in *Xinmin Evening News*, October 6, 2003.

95 Interviews: Official E (An officer in Xuzhou government), October 29, 2003.
96 Zhao Ling, "Chaiqian shinian beixiju," in *The Southern Weekend*, September 4, 2003.
97 Ling Bo, "Huajie dongqian maodun yicheng dangwu zhiji," 2003: Vol. 8, p. 10.
98 "Shiwei fumishuzhang shenhongguang zai quxian ji bufen weibanju xinfang bumen fuzeren huiyishang de jianghua," 2003: Vol. 9, p. 4.
99 Yongshen Cai, 2010: 90.
100 Interviews: Complainant F (Beijing complainant Pi Shufeng), November 6, 2003.
101 "Xinhua shiping tongchi chaiqian zhongde bawang xieyi," in *Xinmin Evening News*, September 15, 2003.
102 "Zifenzhe siwang, nanjing chaiqian jiaoting," in *Bund Picture News* (*waitan huabao*), September 11, 2003.
103 Xie Chunlei, "Yici youzhengyi de shimin xuanchuan xianfa xingdong," in *The Southern Weekend*, December 4, 2003.
104 O'Brien and Li, 2006: 54–63.
105 Chang Kwan Lee, 2007.
106 Solinger, 1999: 87, 135.
107 Interviews: Complainant H (Hu Yuanjin from Hubei), November 18, 2003.
108 But Wang's latest letters show that he is unsatisfied with the solution of the Xuzhou government because the punishment of Yan is only nominal. Yan was simply sentenced for one and a half years with a penalty of mere 200,000 yuan (Yan earned millions of yuan). Interview with Wang (Complainant D), and materials, newspaper reports, and letters provided and sent by Wang.
109 In his latest complaint against the more powerful Xuzhou vice mayor, Wang lost his teaching job in the university and was beaten by the mayor's supporters. All his skipping complaints to CCP leaders such as President Hu Jintao and Premier Wen Jiabao failed to reach their hands. Materials and letters provided and sent by Wang (Complainant D).
110 Two quotations from Guo Guangyun, *Wogao chengweigao*, 2004: Vol. 193, p. 190; Lu Rong, "Weile zhengyi: ta yu chengweigao jiaoliang le banian," in *The Southern Weekend*, August 14, 2003.
111 Interviews: Complainant G (Complainant from Tangshan, Hebei), November 10, 2003.
112 Ke Kuanzhi and He Yinmin, "Qingrong xinfangde aimin fumuguan," 1998.
113 For Jiao's complaints see http://hi.baidu.com/jjt1962/blog/item/ 2f31c5efd10d76e-9ce1b3e97.html.
114 "Liaoning zhuanhe minzhong zhengfu menqian xiagui," in *Nanfang dushibao*, April 13, 2010.
115 For "rightful resistance" see O'Brien and Li, 2006; for "justice from below" see Ethan Michelson, "Justice from Above or Below?" 2008: 43–64; for "issue linkage" and "disruptive tactics" see Yongshen Cai, 2010: 110–34.
116 Interviews: Complainant B (Businessman from Fujian), September 9, 2003.
117 Yongshen Cai, 2010: 112.
118 See Interviews: Official I (A magistrate in north China), November 28, 2003.
119 Ibid.
120 Fu Xingyu, "Baixing gaozhuang weihe nan," in *The Legal Daily*, January 5, 2002.
121 Jim Yardley, "Chinese Complaint to Beijing to Resolve Local Complaints," in the *New York Times*, March 8, 2004.
122 Zhao Ling, "Guonei shoufen xinfang baogao hou gaoceng guanzhu," in *The Southern Weekend*, November 4, 2004. Also see Liu Xiaobo, "Atop a Volcano" in *The Journal of Human Rights in China*, 2005; for Yu see Yu Jianrong, "Xinfang de zhiduxing queshi jiqi zhengzhi houguo," 2004.
123 Minzner, 2006: 157; O'Brien and Li, 2006: 61; Yongshen Cai, "Managed Participation in China," 2004: 440 and Yongshen Cai, 2010: 52.

124 Michelson, 2008: 52–5.
125 Douglass C. North, *Structure and Change in Economic History*, 1981: 21–2.
126 Minzner, 2006: 155.
127 "Xingfang shourong dangxiuyi," in *The Law Service Times* (*falü fuwu shibao*), August 22, 2003.
128 O'Brien and Li, 2006: 35.
129 Ying Xing, 2001: 190.
130 "Zhigong shangfang yao fakuan," in *Baokan wenzhai*, September 17, 2003.
131 Dong Yueling, "Zhongguo xinfang renqun diaocha: manman xinfanglu hechu shi guicheng," 2005.
132 "Complainant Sentenced for Internet Postings," March 3, 2004.
133 Solinger, 1999: 87.
134 Jiang Zemin, "Gaojü dengxiaoping lilunweida qizhi, bayouzhongguo tese shehui zhuyi shiye quanmian tuixiang ershiyi shiji," *The People's Daily*, September 22, 1997.
135 Deng Xiaoping gave officials more lenient treatment in repudiation of Mao. Jiang Zemin, Deng's protégé, articulated in 1995 that the most important condition of a leader is resoluteness and clearness in politics. This actually means loyalty to Jiang is the precondition to be a leader. See *The China Youth Daily*, July 1, 1995.
136 Similar famous cases include "Xiamen Yuanhua and Shenyang Muma." Xiangfan case see Huang Guangming, "Xiangfan guanchang," in *The Southern Weekend*. October 30, 2003.
137 Jiang Zemin, "Jiada lidu tuijin yifa zhiguo," in *The China Youth Daily*, December 26, 1997; Lubman, 1999: 257.
138 *Zuigao fayuan gongbao*, 2003: Vol 2, p. 3.
139 *Makesi engesi lun guojia yufa*, 1958: 381–2.
140 Yu Xiangyang, "Dang yige haofaguan haonan," 2003: Vol. 4, pp. 16–17; Lubman, 1999: 264.
141 Li Yu, "Zhixingnan tianxia dijinan," in *The Legal Daily*, April 29, 2003.
142 Ru Wu, "Gonganju baisu jubu luxing fayuan cheng anjian buhao zhixing," in *The Worker's Daily*, June 8, 2002.
143 Jian Guo, "Quanda haishi fada," in *The China Youth Daily*, September 17, 1986.
144 Minzner, 2006: 105; also see Yongshen Cai, 2010: 56–7; Chen Yingfang, "Pinkun qunti liyi biaoda qudao diaocha," 2003: Vol. 6, p. 89.
145 The head of a northern township complaint office said that his office had no implementing power unless leaders waged pressure. See Interviews: Official O (Head of a township letters and visits office in north China), December 3, 2003.
146 Liu Xiaoyan, "Yige nongfu de shangfang zaoyu," in *The China Youth Daily*, June 10, 2002.
147 "Tanfang chengshi shangfangzu de yinmi shijie," in *The Worker's Daily*, March 25, 2002.
148 "Fanfu kuangren de mengxiang he beicang," in *The Southern Weekend*, August 29, 2002.

Conclusion

1 Zhonggong zhongyang wenxian yanjiushi, ed., *Maozedong wenji*, 2001: Vol. 6, p. 303.
2 *The People's Daily*, July 11, 2003.
3 Interviews: Official I (Hebei magistrate), November 28, 2003.
4 Qin Henhai, "Bo Xilai yaoguanyuan duibaixing youzhenganqing, nitinghou lianhongle meiyou," in *The Chongqing Daily*, March 31, 2008.
5 Liang Hong, *Shijing Shangshu*, 2003: 208, 238.
6 Zhou Daoji, *Woguo minben sixiangde fenxiyu jiantao*, 1977: 16.

7 Zhu Xi, *Sishu zhangju jizhu*, 1998: Vol. 2, pp. 221, 348, 398.
8 Yu Keping, "Chuantong minben sixiangyu xifang minzhu sixiang youzhe benzhi qubie," in *Beijing Daily*, August 8, 2006.
9 Jonathan Fenby, *Chang Kai-shek*, 2004: 240; also see Lloyd E. Eastman, *Seeds of Destruction*, 1984: 143.
10 Kenneth Lieberthal, *Governing China: From Revolution through Reform* 1995: 171, 179.
11 Liang Yanhui, "Ganbu renshi gaige sanshinian: xuanren yongren buzheng zhifeng weihe lüjin buzhi?" in *Xuexi shibao*, June 26, 2008.
12 This is contrary to the view that China's legal system was often satisfactory and fair. William C. Jones, "Chinese Law and Liberty in Comparative Historical Perspective," 2004: 50.
13 *Minggong shupan qingmingji*, 2002: 29.
14 He Changling and Wei Yuan, *Qing jingshi wenbian*, 1992: 512–13, 610.
15 Shen Meijuan, ed., *Shenzui zishu*, 1997: 272.
16 Interviews: Official I (Hebei magistrate). November 28, 2003.
17 This casts doubt on the idea of the system as a social safety valve. Yongshan Cai, "Managed Participation in China," 2004: 448.
18 Qingshi bianzuan weiyuanhui, ed., *Qingshi*: Vol. 6, p. 4472.
19 Guangyuan Zhou, "Illusion and Reaility in the Law of the Late Qing," 1993; Roxann Prazniak, 1999. *Of Camel Kings and Other Things*, 1999: 68–79; Elizabeth Perry, *Challenging the Mandate of Heaven*, 2002.
20 In Weng'an, a young girl named Li Shufen, mysteriously committed suicide on June 21, 2008. A week later, her family and supporters went to the county government and police bureau to complain. No government official was willing to talk to them. Infuriated, people began attacking government buildings and police, resulting in dozens of injuries and arrests. Wang Weibo, "Fengbao yanzhongde weng'an guanyuan: zhengfu miandui kongqian xinren weiji," 2008; Carl G. Minzner, "Xinfang: An Alternative to the Formal Chinese Legal System," 2006: 157.
21 Guo Luoji, "Gaizao peiyu falü wenhua," July 11, 2000.
22 Xi Chen, "An Authoritarian State and a Contentious Society," 2005: 220.

Epilogue: Chinese complaint systems after 2005

1 "Xin xinfang tiaoli de shige liangdian," 2005.
2 Du Wenjuan, "Xin xinfang tiaoli changtong xinfanglu," in *The People's Daily*, January 26, 2005.
3 *Xinfang tiaoli*, January 18, 2005. Some local governments like the Chengdu Police Bureau of Sichuan province also passed their own more specific Xinfang regulations expanding restrictions over certain kinds of complaints. See "Chengdushi gong'anju guanyu jinzhi weifa xinfang weihu shehui zhiande tonggao," *The Chengdu Daily*, April 30, 2007.
4 Zhao Ling, "Shekeyuan baogao chengzhongguo yixingcheng shangfang wenhua," April 5, 2007.
5 Li Yajie and Wei Wu, "Qunzhong fanying qiangliede wufangmian tuchu wenti chengwei xinfang gongzuo zhongdian," March 28, 2007.
6 Interviews with Gao in August 2005 and March 2006 and letters of complaint that he gave to me. Interviews: Complainant I, August 3, 2005.
7 "China: Rampant Violence and Intimidation against Petitioners," December 8, 2005.
8 Calum Macleod, "Chinese Say People's Court Offers Little Help," August 8, 2008; for similar reports also see Andrew Jacobs, "Too Old and Frail to be Re-educated?" *New York Times*, August 21, 2008.
9 Wu Jun, "Liangnüzi weigui shangfang raoluan gonggong changsuo zhixu fenbie beiju shitian," August 24, 2006.

10 Xi Chen, "The Power of 'Troublemaking' Protest Tactics and Their Efficiency in China," 2009: 468–9.

11 Yu Jianrong, "Xinfang zhidu gaige yu xianzheng jianshe," 2005.

12 Zhou Yuede, "Xinfang fazhi jianshe chutan," 2001: 22–3; Li Guohua, "Xinshiqi yifa xinfang gongzuode tansuo yushijian," 2002: 30–1; Wu Chen, "Xinfangquan xinfang fazhihua deluoji qidian," 2002: 67–8.

13 Wu Chen, 2002: 68.

14 Carl F. Minzner, "Xinfang: An Alternative to the Formal Chinese Legal System," 2006: 178.

Bibliography

Primary sources

Archives

The Administrative Court (Pingzhengyuan).
Archives of Judicial Yuan, Supervisory Yuan, Legislative Yuan.
Board of Punishment (Anhui, Jiangsu, Henan, Huguang divisions).
China First Historical Archives in Beijing.
China Second Historical Archives in Nanjing, Jiangsu Province.
Cultural Revolution Archive of Xu Shanzhi (former GMD officer).
Hubei Provincial Archives.
The Interior Ministry.
The National Government.
Shanghai Municipal Archives.

Interviews

All these people contributed to my thinking, though not all of them are quoted in the text.

1 Officials:

A	Former Head of the Xinfang Bureau in a Major City, September 10, 2003.
B	Two Former Heads of a Shanghai Police Bureau in the Cultural Revolution, September 20, 2003.
C	A Judge in a Shanghai Court, September 26, 2003.
D	Vice Head of Xinfang Office in a Major City, October 8, 2003.
E	An Officer in Xuzhou City Government, Jiangsu Province, October 29, 2003.
F	Wei Dong, Former Village Head of Shandong, November 16, 2003.
G	Head of Xinfang Bureau in a Northern City, November 28, 2003.
H	Head of Xinfang Bureau in a Northern County, November 28, 2003.
I	Magistrate of Northern China County, November 28, 2003.
J	County Party Secretary in Northern China, December 2, 2003.
K	Two Heads of County Xinfang Bureau in Northern China, December 2, 2003.
L	Head of County Office in Northern China, December 2, 2003.

M	Township Party Secretary in Northern China, December 3, 2003.
N	Township Vice Party Secretary in Northern China, December 3, 2003.
O	Head of Township Xinfang Office, December 3, 2003.
P	Former Head of Township Xinfang Office, December 3, 2003.
Q	Xinfang Officer in Wuhan, Hubei Province, August 4, 2005.

2 Complainants:

A	Miss Gu in Shanghai, September 17, 2003.
B	Fujian businessman in Shanghai, September 9, 2003.
C	A Shanghai complainant under Urban Relocation, September 30, 2003.
D	Wang Peirong, associate professor at China Mining University, October 28, 2003; June 19, 2008 (telephone call with his wife).
E	A school official complainant in Xuzhou, October 28, 2003.
F	Pi Shufeng and her official son in Beijing, November 6, 2003.
G	Farmer complainant couple from Tangshan, Hebei Province, November 10, 2003.
H	Hu Yuanjin from Hubei Province, November 18, 2003.
I	Gao Chunyuan from Hebei Province, August 3, 2005; March 18, 2006 (telephone).

3 Others—Scholars, lawyers, workers:

A	Shanghai Lawyer, September 14, 2003.
B	A company manager in Shanghai, September 22, 2003.
C	A Shanghai driver, October 8, 2003.
D	Cab driver in Nanjing, October 13, 2003.
E	Ying Xing, associate professor at China Political and Legal University, November 19, 2003.
F	He Weifang, law professor in Beijing University. November 18, 2003.
G	Liang Zhiping, legal scholar in Beijing, November 21, 2003.
H	Liu Zhenxiang and Zhang Yuxia, migrant workers from Anhui, December 23, 2003.
I	Cai Yi and Liang Xiaochun, two migrant workers in Shanghai, October 1, 2003.

Newspapers

The Bright Daily (Guangming ribao).
The Bund Picture News (Waitan huabao).
The Central Daily (Zhongyang ribao).
The Chendhu Daily (Chengdu ribao)
China Newsweek (Zhongguo xinwen zhoukan)
The China Youth Daily (Zhongguo qingnianbao), 1951–2005.
The Chongqing Daily (Chongqing ribao)
The Daily of Collected Articles (Wenhuibao), 1955–2003.
The Eastern Miscellany (Dongfang zazhi), 1904–1916.
The Law Service Times (falü fuwu shibao).
The Legal Daily (Fazhi ribao).
The Life Weekly (Shenghuo zhoukan).
Metropolitan Morning News (Dushi chengbao)
The New Youth (Xinqingnian), 1915–1919.

The People's Court Daily (Renmin fayuanbao).
The People's Daily (Renmin ribao), 1950–2008.
Phoenix Weekly (Fenghuang zhoukan)
The Selected Newspaper Articles (Baokan wenzhai).
The Shanghai Daily (Shenbao), 1907–1930.
The Shanghai Legal Daily (Shanghai fazhibao).
The Southern Metropolitan Daily (Nanfang dushibao).
The Southern Weekend (Nanfang zhoumo), 1984–2005.
The Worker's Daily (Gongren ribao), 1990–2005.
Xinmin Evening News (Xinmin wanbao). 1990–2005.
The Yangtze Evening News (Changjiang wanbao)

Books

1982 nian zhongguo xianfa 1982 年中国宪法 [The 1982 Chinese Constitution]. Beijing: Renmin chubanshe.

2002. *Zhonghua renmin gongheguo xingzheng susongfa* 中华人民共和国行政诉讼法 [Administrative Procedure Law of the People's Republic of China] and *Zhonghua renmin gongheguo xingzheng fuyifa* 中华人民共和国行政复议法 [Law of the People's Republic of China on Administrative Reconsideration]. Beijing: Falü chubanshe.

1998–2004. *Zhongguo falü nianjian* 中国法律年鉴 [The Encyclopedia of Chinese Law 1987–2004]. Beijing: Zhongguo falü nianjianshe (multiple volumes).

Aquinas, Thomas. 1952. *The Summa Theologica of Saint Thomas Aquinas, Vol. 2. in Great Books of the Western World, Vol. 20*. Chicago: University of Chicago Press.

Archival Section of Ming and Qing at the Old Palace Museum, ed. 1979. *Qingmo choubei lixian dangan shi liao* 清末筹备立宪档案史料. Beijing: Zhonghua shujü.

Arkush, David and Lee, Leo O. eds. 1993. *Land without Ghost: Chinese Impressions of America from the Mid-nineteenth Century to the Present*. Berkeley: University of California Press.

Bai, Juyi 白居易, Tang. 1997. *Baijuyi ji* 白居易集 [Collected Works of Bai Juyi]. Changsha: Yuelu shushe.

*Baihuabao*白话报. 1971. [Vernacular Journal] n.p.

Ban, Gu 班固, Latter Han. 1975. *Hanshu* 汉书 [History of the Han Dynasty]. Beijing: Zhonghua shujü.

Chen, Duxiu 陈独秀. 1917. "Jiusixiang yu guoti wenti 旧思想与国体问题 [Old Thought and the State System]." *Xinqingnian*, Vol. 3, pp. 1–3.

Chen, Duxiu 陈独秀. 1918. "Jinri zhongguo zhi zhengzhi wenti 今日中国之政治问题 [Chinese Political Problems in Today]," *Xinqingnian* [*The New Youth*], Vol. 5.

Chen, Duxiu 陈独秀. 1919. "Shixing minzhi de jichu 实行民治的基础 [The Basis of the Rule of People], " *Xinqingnian*[*The New Youth*], Vol. 7, pp. 13–21.

Chen, Minzhi 陈敏之 and Gu, Nanjiu 顾南九, eds. 2002. *Guzhun riji* 顾准日记 [The Diary of Gu Zhun]. Beijing: Zhongguo qingnian chubanshe.

Chen, Zilong 陈子龙, Qing, ed. 1997. *Ming jingshi wenbian* 明经世文编 [Collected Writings on Statecraft from the Qing Dynasty]. Beijing: Zhonghua shujü.

Chengshi fangwu chaiqian guanli tiaoli 城市房屋拆迁管理条例 [Regulations Regarding Urban Disposal]. 2003. Beijing: Zhongguo fazhi chubanshe.

Cohen, Jerome. 1968. *Criminal process in the PRC, 1949–1963: An Introduction*. Cambridge: Harvard University Press.

Daqing guangxü xinfaling 大清光绪新法令. 1908. [New Legislation of the Guangxü reign of the Qing]. Shanghai: Shangwu yinshuguan.

Daqing huidian zeli 大清会典则例 n.d. [Collected Statutes and Regulations of the Great Qing].

Daqing lüli genyuan 大清律例根源 1871. [The Origin of the Qing Code]. Anhui: Anhui fuwen shujü.

Daqing xuantong xinfaling 大清宣统新法令. 1910. [New Laws during the Reign of Xuantong]. Shanghai: Shangwu yinshuguan.

Deng, Xiaoping 邓小平. 1983. "Minzhu yu fazhi liangshou doubu nengruo 民主与法制两手都不能弱 [Neither Democracy and Legal System can be Weak]" in *Dengxiaoping wenxuan* 邓小平文选. Beijing: Renmin chubanshe.

Ding, Xianjun 丁贤俊 and Yu Zuofeng 喻作凤, eds. 1993. *Wutingfang ji* 伍廷芳集 [Collected Works of Wu Tingfang]. Beijing: Zhonghua shujü.

Dong, Hao 董浩, Qing. 1990. *Quan Tangwen* 全唐文 [The Complete Texts of the Tang]. Shanghai: Shanghai Ancient Books Press.

Dong, Zhongshu 董仲舒, Former Han. 1997. *Chunqiu fanlu tianren sance* 春秋繁露-天人三策 [Rich Dews of Spring and Autumn. Three Strategies of Heaven and Human Interaction]. Hunan: Yuelu shushe.

Dongbiwu faxue wenji 董必武法学文集. 2001.[Selected Legal Works of Dong Biwu]. Beijing: Falü chubanshe.

Dou, Yi 窦仪, Song. 1984. *Songxingtong* 宋刑统 [The Penal Law of the Song]. Beijing: Zhonghua shujü.

Erchengji: Henan chengshi yishu 二程集: 河南程氏遗书 [Collection of Two Chengs: The Inherited Books of Henan Chengs]. 1981. Beijing: Zhonghua shujü.

Fan, Ye 范晔, Northern and Southern dynasties. 1965. *Houhanshu* 后汉书 [History of the Late Han]. Beijing: Zhonghua shujü.

Fang, Bao 方苞, Qing. 1979. "Yuzhong zaji 狱中杂记 [Prison Notes]" in Yang Hegao 杨鹤皋. *Gudai zhengfa wenxuan* 古代政法文选 [Selected Materials on the History of Government and Law]. Beijing: Beijing zhengfa xueyuan.

Fazhi bolan 法制博览 [Legal encyclopedia]. 2002, Vol. 12, p. 12.

Fu, Fengxiang 傅凤翔, Ming, ed. 1956. *Huangming zhaoling* 皇明诏令 [The Royal Edicts of the Ming Rulers]. Taiwan: Chengwen chubanshe.

Fu, You 傅优. 1927. *Zuixin fenlei daliyuan jieshili* 最新分类大理院解释例 [The Latest Classified Exemplary cases of the Supreme Court]. Shanghai: Shanghai datong shujü.

Gao, Changshan 高长山. 2003. *Xunzi* 荀子 [Warring States] annotated. Heilongjiang: Heilongjiang renmin chubanshe.

Geng, Zhisheng 耿志声. 2003. "Renzhen xuexi guanche shiliuda jingshen nuli zuohao xinshiji xinjieduan dexinfang gongzuo 认真学习贯彻十六大精神，努力做好新世纪新 阶段的信访工作 [Seriously study and implement the spirit of the sixteenth congress, strive to do well the task of letters and visits in the new century and new era]" in *Renmin xinfang*, Vol. 1, pp. 6–11.

Guangzhou Philosophical and Social Science Research Center of China Scientific Academy, ed. 1963. *Liaozhongkaiji* 廖仲恺集 [Works of Liao Zhongkai]. Beijing: Zhonghua shujü.

Gu, Yanwu 顾炎武, Qing. 1985. *Rizhilu jishi* 日知录集释 [Collected Explanation of The Record of Daily Knowledge]. Shanghai: Shanghai guji chubanshe.

Guangxüchao donghualu 光绪朝东华录. 1984. [Documents of the Guangxü Reign of the Qing]. Beijing: Zhonghua shujü.

Guo, Guangyun 郭光允. 2004. *Wogao chengweigao: yige gognmin yu yige shengwei shuji de zhanzheng* 我告程维高: 一个公民与一个省委书记的战争 [I Accuse Cheng Weugao: A War between a Citizen and a Provincial Party Secretary]. Beijing: Dongfang chubanshe.

Guomin zhengfu xian xingzhengfa 国民政府县行政法 [County Administrative Law of the National Government]. 1928. Nanjing: Minguo fazheng xuehui.

Hai, Rui 海瑞, Ming. 1981. *Hairui ji* 海瑞集 [Collected Works of Hai Rui]. Beijing: Zhonghua shujü.

Haichang, Xiaopenglaizhu 海昌小蓬莱主. 1876. "Bo Wulinsheng gaobai 驳武林生告白 [Opposing the Confession of Wulinsheng]" in *Shenbao* 申报 [*The Shanghai Daily*], May 24.

Hao, Tiechuan 郝铁川 and Lu, Jinbi陆锦碧, eds. 2000. *Yangzhaolong faxue wenxuan* 杨兆龙法学文选 [Selected Legal Works of Yang Zhaolong]. Beijing: Zhongguo zhengfa daxue chubanshe.

He, Changling 贺长龄 and Wei, Yuan 魏源, Late Qing, eds. 1992. *Qing jingshi wenbian* 清经世文编 [Collected Writings on Statecraft from the Qing Dynasty]. Beijing: Zhonghua shujü.

He, Jianzhang 何建章, 1990. *Zhanguoce* 战国策 [Strategems of the Warring States], annotated. Beijing: Zhonghua shujü.

He, Weifang 贺卫方. 2002. *Yunsong zhengyide fangshi* 运送正义的方式 [The Way of Transporting Justice]. Shanghai: Shanghai sanlian shudian chubanshe.

Huai, Xiaofeng 怀效峰, 1989. *Daminglü* 大明律 [The Law of the Ming] annotated. Shenyang: Liaoshen shushe.

Huang, Xing 黄兴. 1981. *Huangxingji* 黄兴集 [Works of Huang Xing]. Beijing: Zhonghua shujü.

Hubeisheng Geming weiyuanhui laodongjü 湖北省革命委员会劳动局, ed. 1974. *Laodong gongzuo jianbao* 劳动工作简报 [Brief Working Report], No. 9, April 20.

Jiang, Yonglin, trans. 2005. *Great Ming Code*. Seattle: University of Washington Press.

Jiang, Zemin 江泽民. 1997. "Gaojü dengxiaoping lilunweida qizhi, bajianshe youzhongguo tese shehui zhuyi shiye quanmian tuixiang ershiyi shiji 高举邓小平理论伟大旗帜, 把建设有中国特色社会主义事业全面推向二十一世纪 [Carrying High the Flag of the Deng Xiaoping Theory and Push the Chinese Special Solicalism to the Twenty-first Century]" in *The People's Daily*, September 22.

Jiang, Zemin 江泽民. 1997. "Jiada lidu tuijin yifa zhiguo 加大力度推进依法治国 [Speeding up the rule of law]" in *The China Youth Daily*, December 26.

"Jianshao guanyuan xinshui yandu wubi zhongbao 减少官员薪水严杜舞弊中饱 [Reducing Official Salaries and Strictly Preventing Corruption]," in *The Central Daily*, October 21, 1928.

Lai, Chengzuo 来承祚. 1936. *Xiuzhen zhonghua liufa quanshu* 袖珍中华六法全书 [A Tiny Book of Chinese Six Laws]. Beijing: Zhonghua shujü.

Lau, D. C., trans. 1963. *Tao Te Ching*. London: Penguin Books.

Leng, Shi 冷氏. 1919. "Falü 法律 [The Law]" in *Shenbao*, May 13.

Li, Fang 李昉. Song, 1985. *Taiping yulan* 太平御览 [Imperial Encyclopedia of the Taiping]. Beijing: Zhonghua shujü.

Li, Linfu 李林甫, Tang. 1992. *Tangliudian* 唐六典 [Six Cannons of the Tang]. Beijing: Zhonghua shujü.

Li, Rui 李锐. 1994. *Lushan huiyi shilu* 庐山会议实录 [Verified Record of Lushan Conference]. Henan, Henan renmin chubanshe.

Li, Rui 李锐. 1998. *Lirui lunshuo wenxuan*李锐论说文选[Arguments of Li Rui]. Beijing: Zhongguo shehui kexue chubanshe.

Li, Rui 李锐. 1998. *Lirui riji* 李锐日记 [Li Rui's Diary]. Beijing: Zuojia chubanshe.

Li, Tao 李焘, Song. 1979. *Xuzizhi tongjian changbian* 续资治通鉴长编 [Supplement to the Comprehensive Mirror for Aid in Government]. Beijing: Zhonghua shujü.

Li, Xibi 李希泌, ed. 2003. *Tangda zhaolingji bubian* 唐大诏令集补编 [Complemented Edition of the Collection of Tang Decrees]. Shanghai: Shanghai guji chubanshe.

Li, Zhisui. 1994. *The Private Life of Chairman Mao*. New York: Random House.

Li, Zongren 李宗仁. 1986. *Lizongren huiyilu* 李宗仁回忆录 [Memoir of Li Zongren]. Canton: Nanyue chubanshe.

Liang, Qichao 梁启超. 1986. Xianqin zhengzhi sixiangshi 先秦政治思想史 [History of Political Thoughts in the Pre-Qin Periods]. Beijing: Zhonghua shuju.

Liang, Hong 梁鸿. 2003. *Shijing Shangshu* 诗经-尚书 [The Book of Songs and the Ancient Book]. Hunan: Shidai wenyi chubanshe.

Lifayuan zhonghua minguo xianfa caoan xuanchuan weiyuanhui 立法院中华民国宪法草案宣传委员会 [The Constitution-draft Propaganda Committee of the Legislative Ministry in the Republic of China], ed. 1940. *Zhonghua minguo xianfa cao'an shuomingshu* 中华民国宪法草案说明书 [Explanatory Book of the Constitutional Draft in the Republic of China]. Zhengzhong shujü.

Liu, Chonglai 刘重来, Xu, Shirui 徐适瑞, and Zheng, Jiafu 郑家福, eds. 1994. *Mingshilu leizuan: sifa jianchajuan* 明实录类纂: 司法监察卷 [Classified Edition of the Veritable Record of the Ming; Volume of Judiciary and Inspection]. Wuhan: Wuhan chubanshe.

Liu, Hainian 刘海年 and Yang, Yifan 杨一凡, eds. 1994. *Zhongguo zhenxi falü jicheng* 中国珍惜 法律集成 [A Collection of the Rare Chinese Laws]. Beijing: Kexue chubanshe.

Liu, Junwen 刘俊文. 1996. *Tanglü shuyi jianjie* 唐律疏议笺解 [Clarification of Tang Code with Commentaries]. Beijing: Zhonghua shujü.

Liu, Shifang 刘世芳. 1936. "Gailiang sifa zhi guanjian 改良司法之管见 [Some Points in Improving the Judicary]," in *Faxue zazhi*, Vol. 9. No. 1, pp. 1–10.

Liu, Xiaomeng 刘小萌. 2004. *Zhongguo zhiqing koushushi* 中国知青口述史 [An Oral History of Chinese Intellectual Youths]. Beijing: Zhongguo shehui kexue chubanshe.

Liu, Xu 刘煦. Tang. 1975. *Jiutangshu* 旧唐书 [The Old History of the Tang]. Beijing: Zhonghua shujü.

Locke, John. 1967. *Two Treatises of Government*. Cambridge: Cambridge University Press.

Long, Wenbin 龙文彬, Ming. 1956. *Minghuiyao* 明会要 [Institutional History of the Ming Dynasty]. Beijing: Zhonghua shujü.

Lu, Rong 卢嵘. 2003. "Weile zhengyi: ta yu chengweigao jiaoliang le banian为了正义: 他与程维高较量了八年 [For Justice: He has Fought against Cheng Weigao for Eight Years]," in *The Southern Weekend*, August 14.

"Lunshaoxing yuanyu 论绍兴冤狱 [The Grievance of Shaoxing]," in *The Shanghai Daily*, July 23, 1907.

Ma, Hongmo 马鸿谟, ed. 1982. *Minhu minyu minlibao xuanji* 1909.5–1910.2 民呼民吁民立报选辑 [Selected Articles of Minfu, Minyu, and Minli News 1909.5 to 1910.2]. Henan: Henan renmin chubanshe.

Mei, Huaquan 梅华铨. 1922. "Guomin dui sifa zhi guannian 国民对司法之观念 [Chinese Concepts of the Judiciary]," *Faxue jikan* 法学季刊 [Legal Quarterly]. pp. 25–30, 1922.

Minggong shupan qingming ji 明公书判清明集, Song. 2002. [Collection of Lucid Decisions by Celebrated Judges *c.*260–1265. 14 juan]. Beijing: Zhonghua shujü.

Miu, Quanji 缪全吉, ed. 1989. *Zhongguo zhixianshi ziliao huibian: xianfapian* 中国制宪史资料汇编：宪法篇 [Collected Materials of the History of Chinese Constitutional Making: Constitution Part]. Taibei: Guoshiguan.

Mo, Zi. Online, available at: http://hi.baidu.com/zhongguowenxue360/blog/item/f2782cee1b882c3cadafd507.html.

Ouyang, Xiu 欧阳修, Song. 1975. *Xintangshu* 新唐书 [New History of the Tang Dynasty]. Beijing: Zhonghua shujü.

Pan, Zhenqiu 潘振球 ed. 1936. *Zhonghua minguo shishi jiyao (chugao)* 中华民国史事纪要 (初稿) [A Draft of Historical Compendium of the Republican China]. Taiwan: Guoshiguan.

Pengzhen wenxuan 彭真文选 [Selected Works of Peng Zhen]. 1991. Beijing: Renmin chubanshe.

Pingzhengyuan caijuelu 平政院裁决录 [Adjudicating Cases of the Administrative Court]. 1916.

Qing huidian shili 清会典事例 1991. [Precedents for the Collected Statutes of the Qing Dynasty]. Beijing: Zhonghua shujü.

Qingding taigui 钦定台规 [Imperially established regulations of the Censorate].

Qingshi bianzuan weiyuanhui 清史编纂委员会 [Editing Committee of the Qing History] ed. 1960. *Qingshi* 清史 [The History of the Qing Dynasty]. Taiwan: Guofang yanjiuyuan.

Qiu, Hanping 丘汉平. 1941. "Zhongguo zhi zhixian yu xingxian 中国之制宪与行宪 [The Making and Implementing of the Constitution in China]" *Faxue zazhi*, Vol. 11, No. 3, pp. 351–65.

*Renmin fayuan zuzhifa*人民法院组织法. [Organization Law of the People's Courts]. 2006. Online, available at: www.hudong.com/wiki.

Renmin sifa zai yuejin 人民司法在跃进 [The People's Judiciary is Leaping Forward]. 1958. Beijing: Falü chubanshe.

Rong, Mengyuan 荣孟源, ed. 1985. *Zhongguo Guomindang lici daibiao dahui ji zhongyang quanhui ziliao* 中国国民党历次代表大会及中央全会资料 [Documents of the past GMD Congresses and the Central Plenary Sessions]. Beijing: Guangming ribao chubanshe.

Ruan, Yicheng 阮毅成. 1933. *Fazhi lunji* 法治论集 [Comments on the Rule of Law]. Nanjing: Shidai gonglun chubanshe.

Shangshu 尚书 [The Book of Venerated Documents]. 2003. Hunan: Shidai wenyi chuabnshe and Hunan wenyi chubanshe.

Shen, Fuxiang 沈福祥. *Wode wenge suiyue* 我的文革岁月[My Times in the Cultural Revolution]. Formerly online at: www.boxun.com/hero/shenfx/9_2.shtml.

Shen, Jiaben 沈家本, Qing. 1976. *Jiyi wencun.* 寄移文存 [Jiyi's Remained Works]. Taiwan: Shangwu yinshuguan.

Shen, Jiaben 沈家本, Qing. 1985. *Lidai xingfakao* 历代刑法考[A Criticism of Dynastic Criminal Laws]. Beijing: Zhonghua shujü.

Shen, Kuo 沈括, Song. 1996. *Mengxi bitan* 梦溪笔谈 [Dream Stream Essays]. Chengdu: Bashu shushe.

Shen, Meijuan 沈美娟, ed. 1997. *Shenzui zishu* 沈醉自述 [A Self Talk of Shen Zui]. Beijing: Shiyue wenyi chubanshe.

Shen, Tongsheng 沈桐生, ed. 1985. *Guangxü zhengyao* 光绪政要 [Major Political Events in the Reign of Guangxü]. Taiwan: Wenhai chubanshe.

Shen, Yunlong 沈云龙 Editor-in-chief; Sun Yao 孙曜 ed. 1966. *Zhonghua minguo shiliao* 中华民国史料 [Historical Sources of the Republic of China]. Taiwan: Wenhai chubanshe.

Shenghuo zhoukan 生活周刊 [The Life Weekly]. 1928. Shanghai: Shenghuo zhoukan, Reprinted by Renmin chubanshe.

Sifa gongzuo shouce 司法工作手册. 1952. [A Pamphlet of Judiciary] Fujian: Fujiansheng renmin fayuan.
Sima, Guang 司马, Song. 1956. *Zizhi tongjian* 资治通鉴 [The Comprehensive Mirror for Aid in Government]. Beijing: Zhonghua shujü.
Sima, Qian 司马迁, Han. 1975. *Shiji* 史记 [The historical records]. Beijing: Zhonghua shujü.
Song, Jiaoren 宋教仁. 1981. *Songjiaorenji* 宋教仁集 [Collected Works of Song Jiaoren]. Beijing: Zhonghua shujü.
Song, Lian 宋濂, Ming. 1976. *Yuanshi* 元史 [The History of the Yuan Dynasty]. Beijing: Zhonghua shujü.
Song, Minqiu 宋敏求. ed. 1959. *Tangda zhaoling ji* 唐大诏令集 [Collection of Tang Decrees]. Beijing: Shangwu yinshuguan.
Songda zhaolingji 宋大诏令集. 1962. [Collection of Song Decrees]. Beijing: Zhonghua shujü.
Songhuiyao jigao 宋会要辑稿. 1978. [Draft Version of the Important Documents of the Song]. Beijing: Zhonghua shujü.
Sun, Yao 孙曜. ed. 1966. *Zhonghua minguo shiliao* 中华民国史料 [Historical Materials of the Republic of China]. Taiwan: Wenhai chubanshe.
Sun, Yat-sen (Sun, Zhongshan) 孙中山. 1981. *Sunzhongshan quanji* 孙中山全集 [Complete Works of Sun Yat-sen]. Beijing: Zhonghua shujü.
Sun, Yat-sen (Sun, Zhongshan) 孙中山. 1981. *Sunzhongshan xuanji* 孙中山选集 [Selected Works of Sun Zhongshan] Beijing: Renmin chubanshe.
Sun, Yirang 孙贻让, Qing. 1987. *Zhouli zhengyi* 周礼正义 [A Commentary on *Zhouli*]. Beijing: Zhonghua shujü.
Tan, Sitong 谭嗣同 2002. *Renxue* 仁学 [A Study of Humaneness]. Beijing: Huaxia chubanshe.
The 1954 Constitution of the People's Republic of China, *The People's Daily*, June 16, 1954.
Tianjin difangzhi bianxiu weiyuanhui 天津地方志编修委员会 [Editing Committee of Tianjin Local History], ed. 1997. *Tianjin tongzhi difangzhi* 天津通志地方志 [Tianjin General and Local History]. Tianjin: Tianjin shehui kexueyuan chubanshe.
Tuotuo 脱脱, Yuan. 1977. *Songshi* 宋史 [The History of the Song Dynasty]. Beijing: Zhonghua shujü.
Wan, Li 万里. 1995. *Wanli wenxuan* 万里文选 [Selected Works of Wan Li]. Beijing: Renmin chubanshe.
Wang, Dehou 王德后 and Qian, Liqun 钱里群 eds. 2000. *Luxun zuopin quanbian-zawenjuan shang* 鲁迅作品全编-杂文卷上 [The Complete Edition of Lu Xun's Works-Miscellaneous Articles I]. Zhejiang: Zhejiang wenyi chubanshe.
Wang, Fu 王溥, Song. 1991. *Tanghuiyao* 唐会要 [Institutional History of the Tang Dynasty] Shanghai: Shanghai guji chubanshe.
Wang, Kangnian 汪康年. 1896. "Lun zhongguo canyong minquan zhi liyi 论中国参用民权之利益" [The Benefits of China to Adopt People's Rights] in *China Progress*: 9.
Wei, Shou 魏收, Northern Qi. 1974. *Weishu* 魏书 [The History of (the Northern) Wei]. Beijing: Zhonghua shujü.
Wei, Zhao 韦昭. 1978. *Guoyu* 国语 [Discourses of the State], annotated. Shanghai: Shanghai guji chubanshe.
Wei, Zhengshou 魏征寿, Tang. 1973. *Suishu* 隋书 [The History of the Sui Dynasty]. Beijing: Zhonghua shujü.
Willoughby, Wellington Bartley 韦罗贝. 1915. *Xinzongtong xuanjufa yi* 新总统选举法议 [A Discussion on the Election Law of the New President].

Wu, Jing吴兢, Tang. 2001. *Zhenguan zhengyao* 贞观政要 [The Important Politics of the Zhenguan Period]. Beijing: Time, Literature, and Art Press.

Xia, Tongsu 夏同稣. 1905. *Xingzhengfa* 行政法 [The Administrative Law]. Tokyo: Namiki kappanjo.

Xianxing faling quanshu 现行法令全书 [A Complete Book on the Contemporary Law]. 1922. Beijing: Zhonghua shujü.

Xianzongtong jianggong sixiang yanlun zongji 先总统蒋公思想言论总集 [Speeches and Papers of Former President Jiang]. 1984. Taiwan: Guomindang dangshi weiyuanhui.

Xinan zhengfa xueyuan hanshoubu 西南政法学院函授部 [The Mail Department of the Xinan Political and Legal Institute], ed. 1982. *Zhongguo xinminzhu zhuyi geming shiqi fazhi jianshe ziliao xuanbian* 中国新民主主义时期法制建设资料选编 [Selected Documents Construction of the Legal System in the Chinese New-Democratic Period]. Sichuan: Xinan zhengfa xueyuan hanshoubu.

Xinfang tiaoli 信访条例 [Regulations Regarding Letters and Visits] in *The People's Daily*, January 18, 2005.

Xingzheng caipanyuan guanzhi caoan 行政裁判员官制草案. 1909. [A Draft of the Official Ranks of the Administrative Personnel]. China Second Historical Archives.

Xingzheng fayuan 行政法院 [The Administrative Court], ed. 1948. *Xingzheng fayuan panjue huibian* 1933–1947 行政法院判决汇编 1933–1947 [Collective Edition of the Administrative Court Judgments]. Shanghai: Shanghai faxue bianyishe.

Yan, Junyan 颜俊彦, Ming. 2002. *Mengshuizhai Cundu* 盟水宅存牍 [Remained Works of Mengshuizhai]. Beijing: Zhongguo zhengfa daxue chubanshe.

Yang, Bojun 杨伯峻. 1981. *Zuozhuan* 左传 [The Zuo Commentary], annotated. Beijing: Zhonghua shujü.

Yang, Hegao 杨鹤皋. 1979. *Gudai zhengfa wenxuan* 古代政法文选 [Selected Materials on the History of Government and Law]. Beijing: Beijing zhengfa xueyuan.

Yi, Gong 翼公. 1932. "Gaizao zhengzhi zhi jiben tiaojian 改造政治之基本条件 [Basic Conditions for Reforming Politics]" in *Shenghuo zhoukan* [Life Weekly], Vol. 4.

Yu, Zhirong 于智荣, ed. 2003. *Jiayi xinshu* 贾谊新书 [New Book of Jia Yi]. Heilongjiang: Heilongjiang renmin chubanshe.

Yuan, Shikai 袁世凯. 1906. *Lixian gangyao* 立宪纲要 [The Principles of Constitutional Establishment]. Beijing: Beiyang guanbaojü.

Yuan, Shikai 袁世凯. 1987. *Yuanshikai zouyi* 袁世凯奏议 [Memorials of Yuan Shikai]. Tianjin Library and History Research Department of Tianjing Social Academy, ed. Tianjin: Tianjing guji chubanshe.

Zhang, Dongsun 张东荪. 1923. "Shuineng jiu zhongguo谁能救中国[Who Can Save China]?" in *Dongfang zazhi*, Vol. 20, pp. 23–5.

Zhang, Jixin 张集馨, Qing. 1981. *Daoxian huanhai jianwenlu* 道咸宦海见闻录 [Report of Things Heard and Seen in the Daoguang and Xianfen Reigns]. Beijing: Zhonghua shujü.

Zhang, Qiyun 张其昀. 1984. *Xian zongtong jianggong quanji* 先总统蒋公全集 [Complete Works of Former President Chang Kai-shek]. Taiwan: Zhongguo wenhua daxue chuban.

Zhang, Tingyu 张廷玉, Qing. 1974. *Mingshi* 明史 [The History of the Ming Dynasty]. Beijing: Zhonghua shujü.

Zhang, Yipeng 张一鹏. 1922. "Zhongguo sifa zhidu gaijin zhi yange 中国司法制度改进之沿革 [The Reforming Experience of the Chinese Judicial System]" in *Faxue jikan*. Vol. 1, pp. 18–24.

Zhang, Yuanruo 章渊若. 1933. "Xingzheng caipan zhidu zhi yanjiu yu jianyi 行政裁判制度之研究与建议 [Study and Suggestion of the Administrative Judging System]," in *Faxue zazhi*, Vol. 6.

Zhangsun, Wuji 长孙无忌, Tang. 1999. *Tanglü shuyi* 唐律疏议 [Tang Code with Commentaries] Beijing: Falü chubanshe.

Zhao, Chen 赵琛, Yang, Yuanbiao 杨元彪, and Shen, Zhiming 沈志明. eds. 1939. *Zhongguo liufa quanshu* 中国六法全书 [Complete Book of Chinese Six Laws]. Shanghai: Shijie shujü.

Zhao, Hengti 赵恒惕, ed. 1971. *Wupeifu xianshengji* 吴佩孚先生集 [Works of Mr. Wu Peifu]. Taiwan: Wenhai chubanshe.

Zhao, Yongqing 赵永清. 2002. *Dongyou jilue* 东游纪略 [A Summary of an Eastern Visit] in Sun Xuemei 孙雪梅, ed. *Riben zhengfa kaochaji* 日本政法考察记 [An Examination of Japan's Political and Legal System]. Shanghai: Shanghai guji chubanshe.

Zheng, Guanying 郑观应 2002. *Shengshi weiyan* 盛世危言 [Alarming Reminder for the Flourishing Age]. Beijing: Huaxia chubanshe.

"Zhengdun baozhi chuyan 整顿报纸刍言 [Casual Talks on Disciplining Newspapers]" in *Shenbao* [The Shanghai Daily], June 28, 1898.

Zhengfu gongbao 政府公报 [Government Gazette]. 1971. Taiwan: Wenhai chubanshe. Vols. 1–55.

Zhengzhi guanbao 政治官报. [Official Newspapers]. 1965. Taiwan: Wenhai chubanshe.

Zhi, Fu 直夫. 1927. "Falü zhi weixin 法律之威信 [The Prestige of the Law]" in *Falü Pinglun* [The Law Weekly Review] Vols. 183–208.

Zhonggong zhongyang bangongting 中共中央办公厅 [The General Office of the CCP], guowuyuan bangongting 国务院办公厅 [The Office of the State Council], ed. 1989. *Quanguo xinfang gongzuo huiyi ziliao huibian* 全国信访工作会议资料汇 编 [Complete Edition of the State-Wide Complaint Conference Documents] (internal edition).

Zhonggong zhongyang wenxian yanjiushi 中共中央文献研究室 [Studying Unit of the Central Committee of the CCP], ed.1983. *Maozedong shuxin xuanji* 毛泽东书 信选集 [Selected Letters of Mao Zedong]. Beijing: Renmin chubanshe.

Zhonggong zhongyang wenxian yanjiushi 中共中央文献研究室 [Archive Research Unit of the Central CCP], ed. 2001. *Maozedong wenji* 毛泽东文集 [Collected Works of Mao Zedong]. Beijing: Renmin chubanshe.

Zhongguo di'er lishi danganguan 中国第二历史档案馆 [China Second Historical Archives], ed. 1986. *Zhongguo guomindang diyi erci quanguo daibiao dahui huiyi shiliao* 中国国民党第一二次全国代表大会会议史料 [Historical Documents of the First and Second National Congress of the Chinese GMD]. Jiangsu: Jiangsu guji chubanshe.

Zhongguo fagui kanxingshe bianshen weiyuanhui 中国法规刊行社编审委员会 [Editing Committee of Chinese Legal Regulations Press], ed. 1948. *Zuixin liufa quanshu* 最新六法全书 [The Latest Six-Law Book]. Shanghai: Shanghai chunming shudian.

Zhongguo jindai fazhishi ziliao xuanji 中国近代法制史资料选辑 (1840–1949) [Selected Documents of Chinese Modern Legal History]. 1985. Shannxi: Xibei zhengfa xueyuan fazhishi jiaoyanshi bianyin.

Zhongguo lishi xuehui 中国历史学会 Chinese Historical Association], ed. 2000. *Wuxü bianfa* 戊戌变法 [The 1898 Reforms]. Shanghai: Shanghai renmin chubanshe, Shanghai shudian chubanshe. Vols. 1–3.

"Zhongguo xianxing faling yu geren ziyou 中国现行法令与个人自由 [The Present Chinese Law and Rules and the Personal Freedom]." 1922. in *Faxue jikan* Vol. 1, pp. 45–52.

Zhonghua minguo faling daquan 中华民国法令大全 [Comprehensive Laws of the Republic of China]. 1917. Shanghai: Shanghai shangwu yinshuguan.

Zhonghua minguo linshi zhengfu xinfaling 中华民国临时政府新法令 [New Laws and Orders of the Provisional Government of the Republic of China]. 1912. Shanghai: Shanghai ziyou chubanshe.

Zhonghua minguo xianfa "xiuzheng cao'an" "cao'an" yitong bijiao 中华民国宪法"修正草案", "草案"异同比较 [A Comparison between the "Draft Revision" and "Draft" of the Constitution of the Republic of China]. 1947.

Zhonghua minguo xianxing fagui daquan 中华民国现行法规大全 [A Complete Collection of the Current Laws and Regulations in the Republic of China]. 1931. Shanghai: Shangwu yinshuguan.

Zhou, Yuangao 周元高, Meng Pengxing 孟彭兴, and Shu Yingyun 舒颖云, eds. 1996. *Liliejun ji* 李烈钧集 [Collective Works of Li Liejun]. Beijing: Zhonghua shujü.

Zhou, Zhenfu 周振甫. 2006. *Shijing* 诗经 [The Book of Songs], annotated. Jiangsu: Jiangsu jiaoyü chubanshe.

Zhu, Guonan 朱国南. 1982. "Qixing guaizhuang de jiusifa 奇形怪状的旧司法 [The Strange Old Judiciary]" in Zhongguo renmin zhengzhi xieshang huiyi quanguo weiyuan hui wenshi ziliao yanjiu weiyuanhui 中国人民政治协商会 议全国委员会文史资料研究委员会 [The Literary and Historical Studying Committee of the National Committee of the Chinese Political Consultation Conference] *Wenshi ziliao xuanji* 文史资料选辑 [Selected Literary and Historical Documents]. Vol. 78. Beijing: Wenshi ziliao chubanshe.

Zhu, Mingpan 朱铭盘, Qing. 1984. *Nanchao lianghuiyao* 南朝梁会要 [The Administrative System of Liang in the Southern Dynasties]. Shanghai: Shanghai guji chubanshe.

Zhu, Qingqi 祝文祺, Bao Shuyun 鲍书芸, Pan Wenfang 潘文舫, and He Weikai 何文楷, eds. 2004. *Xingan huilan* 刑案汇览 [Conspectus of Criminal Cases]. Beijing: Beijing guji chubanshe.

Zhu, Rongji 朱镕基. 1999. "Renzhen guanche yifa zhiguo fanglue, qieshi quanmian tuijin yifa xingzheng 认真贯彻依法治国方略, 切实全面推进依法行政 [Seriously Implementing the Rule of Law Strategy and Practically and Comprehensively Forwarding Administration by Law]" in *Quanguo yifa xingzheng gongzuo huiyi zhuanji* 全国依法行政工作会议专辑 [A Special Edition of the Nation-wide Work Conference of Administration by Law]. Beijing: Zhongguo fazhi chubanshe.

Zhu, Xi 朱熹, Song. 1977. *Zhuzi quanshu* 朱子全书 [Zhu Xi's Complete Works]. Originally published in 1713, reprinted. Taibei: Guangxue.

Zhu, Xi 朱熹, Song. 1998. *Sishu zhangju jizhu* 四书章句集注 [Annotation of Four Books] Liaonin: Liaonin jiaoyu chubanshe.

Zuigao fayuan gongbao 最高法院公报 [The Supreme Court Report]. 2003.

Zuo, Qiuming左丘明, Warring States Era. 1991. *Zuozhuan* 左传 [The Commentary of Zuo]. Hunan: Yuelu shushe.

Secondary sources

Alford, William. 1984. "Of Arsenic and Old Laws: Looking Anew at Criminal Justice in Late Imperial China" in *California Law Review*, Vol. 72, No. 6, pp. 1180–256.

Alford, William. 1995. *To Steal a Book is an Elegant Offense: Intellectual Property Law in Chinese Civilization.* Stanford: Stanford University Press.

Aminzade, Ron and Perry, Elizabeth. 2001. "The Sacred, Religious, and Secular in Contentious Politics: Blurring Boundaries," in Doug McAdam, Sidney Tarrow, and Charles

Tilly, eds. *Silence and Voice in the Study of Contentious Politics*. Cambridge: Cambridge University Press.
Atwell, William S. 1975. "From Education to Politics: The Fu She," in William Theodore de Bary, ed., *The Unfolding of Neo-Confucianism*. New York: Columbia University Press, pp. 333–68.
Balazs, Etienne. 1964. *Chinese Civilization and Bureaucracy: Variation on a Theme*. New Haven: Yale University Press.
Bao, Ruowang (Jean Pasqualini) and Chelminski, Rudolph. 1973. *Prisoner of Mao*. New York: Penguin Books.
Barrow, G. W. S. 1956. *Feudal Britain: The Completion of the Medieval Kingdoms 1066–1314*. London: Edward Arnold Ltd.
Benton, Gregor and Chun, Lin, eds. 2010. *Was Mao Really a Monster? The Academic Response to Chang and Halliday's Mao: The Unknown Story*. London/New York: Routledge.
Berman, Harold J. 1983. *Law and Revolution: The Formation of the Western Legal Tradition*. Cambridge: Harvard University Press.
Bernhardt, Kathryn and Huang, Philip C. C., eds. 1994. *Civil Law in Qing and Republican China*. Stanford: Stanford University Press.
Bernstein, Thomas P. 1991. "Chinese Communism in the Era of Mao Zedong, 1949–1976," in Kenneth Lieberthal, Joyce Kallgren, Roderick MacFarquhar, and Frederic Wakeman, Jr., eds., *Perspectives on Modern China: Four Anniversaries*. Armonk: M. E. Sharpe.
Bickers, Robert and Tiedemann, R. G., eds. 2007. *The Boxers, China, and the World*. Lanham: Rowman and Littlefield.
Bloom, Irene. 2004. "The Moral Autonomy of the Individual in Confucian Tradition," in William C. Kirby, ed., *Realms of Freedom in Modern China*. Stanford: Stanford University Press, pp. 19–43.
Bodde, Derk. 1973. *Law in Imperial China*. Philadelphia: University of Pennsylvania Press.
Bourgon, Jerome. 2004. "Rights, Freedoms, and Customs in the Making of Chinese Civil Law, 1900–1936," in William C. Kirby, *Realms of Freedom in Modern China*. Stanford: Stanford University Press, pp. 84–112.
Brook, Timothy. 2010. *The Troubled Empire: China in the Yuan and Ming Dynasties*. Cambridge: The Belknap Press of Harvard University Press.
Brook, Timothy and Frolic, Bernard, eds. 1997. *Civil Society in China*. Armonk: M. E. Sharpe.
Brown, Jeremy and Pickowicz, Paul G., eds. 2007. *Dilemmas of Victory: The Early Years of the People's Republic of China*. Cambridge: Harvard University Press.
Buoye, Thomas. 2006. *Manslaughter, Markets, and Modral Economy: Violent Disputes over Property Rights in Eighteenth-Century China*. Cambridge: Cambridge University Press.
Buoye, Thomas. 2009. "Filial Felons: Leniency and Legal Reasoning in Qing China," in Robert E. Hegel and Katherine Carlitz, eds., *Writing and Law in Late Imperial China: Crimes, Conflict, and Judgment*. Seattle: University of Washington Press.
"Burang jishaoshu hujiao mancha zhe deli 不让极少数胡搅蛮缠者得利 [Do not Let Those Vexatious People Benefit]," in *Shanghai Legal Daily*. September 17, 2003.
Cai, Guanhua 蔡冠华. 1990. "Zhengchu duomen dailaide biduan 政出多门带来的弊端 [The Problems Caused by Reundant Governments]" in *The China Youth Daily*, November 13.
Cai, Yongshun. 2004. "Managed Participation in China," in *Political Science Quarterly*. Vol. 119, No. 3, pp. 425–51.

Cai, Yongshun. 2010. *Collective Resistance in China: Why Popular Protests Succeed or Fail*. Stanford: Stanford University Press.

Cao, Jinqing 曹锦清. 2000. *Huanghe biande zhongguo* 黄河边的中国 [China on the Riverside of the Yellow River]. Shanghai: Shanghai wenyi chubanshe.

Ch'en, Ch'i-Yun. 1986. "Confucian, Legalist, and Taoist Thought in Late Han," in Denis Twitchett and John K. Fairbank, eds., *The Cambridge History of China, Vol I, The Ch'in and Han Empires, 221 B.C.–A.D. 220*. Cambridge: Cambridge University Press.

Ch'en, Paul Heng-chao. 1979. *Chinese Legal Tradition under the Mongols: The Code of 1291 as Reconstructed*. Princeton: Princeton University Press.

Ch'ien, Tuan-sheng. 1970. *The Government and Politics of China 1912–1949*. Stanford: Stanford University Press.

Ch'ü, T'ung-tsu. 1962. *Local Government in China under the Ch'ing*. Cambridge: Harvard University Press.

Ch'ü, T'ung-tsu. 1965. *Law and Society in Traditional China*. Paris: Mouton and La Haye.

Ch'ü, T'ung-tsu. 1972. *Han Social Structure*. Seattle: University of Washington Press.

Ch'ü, T'ung-tsu, Fan Zhongxin 范忠信, and Yan Feng 晏锋, trans. 2003. *Qingdai difang zhengfu* 清代地方政府 [Local Government in China under the Ch'ing]. Beijing: Falü chubanshe.

Chang, Jung and Halliday, Jon. 2006. *Mao: The Unknown Story*. New York: Anchor.

Chang, Xiaoquan 常孝全. 1984. "Ganbu haile hongyanbing, qiangqu liuqian paotong-miao 干部害了红眼病，抢去六千泡桐苗 [Officials Suffers Red Eyes and Rob Six Thousand Saplings]," in *The China Youth Daily*. July 31.

Chao, Zhongchen 晁中辰. 1993. *Mingchengzu zhuan* 明成祖传 [Biography of Ming Chengzu]. Beijing: Renmin chubanshe.

Che, Jixin 车吉心 and Wang, Xi 王熹, eds. 2000. *Minguo yeshi* 民国野史 [An Unofficial History of the Republic of China]. Shandong: Taishan chubanshe.

Chen, Albert H. Y. 2010. "Legal Thought and Legal Development in the PRC 1949–2008," in John Gillespie and Albert H. Y. Chen, eds., *Legal Reforms in China and Vietnam: A Comparison of Asian Communist Regimes*. London: Routledge, pp. 51–77.

Chen, Guidi 陈桂棣 and Chun, Tao 春桃. 2004. *Zhongguo nongmin diaocha* 中国农民调查 [The Investigation of Chinese Farmers]. Beijing: Renmin wenxue chubanshe.

Chen, Guyuan 陈顾远. 1977. *Zhongguo fazhishi gaiyao*中国法制史概要 [A Sketch of the Chinese Legal History]. Taibei: Sanmin shujü.

Chen, Yingfang 陈映芳. 2003. "Pinkun qunti liyi biaoda qudao diaocha 贫困群体利益表达渠道调查 [The Investigation of Lower-class People's Interest Expressing Ways]," in *Strategy and Management* (*zhanlue yu guanli*). No. 6, pp. 87–92.

Chen, Yung-fa. 2003. "Suspect History and the Mass Line: Another 'Yan'an Way'," in Jeffrey N. Wasserstrom, ed., *Twentieth-Century China: New Approaches*. London: Routledge.

Chen, Xi. 2005. "An Authoritarian State and a Contentious Society: The Case of China." Columbia University, unpublished dissertation.

Chen, Xi. 2009. "The Power of 'Troublemaking' Protest Tactics and Their Efficiency in China," in *Comparative Politics*, Vol. 41, No. 4, pp. 451–71.

Cheng, Liaoyuan 程燎原. 1999. *Cong fazhi dao fazhi* 从法制到法治 [From the Rule by Law to the Rule of Law]. Beijing: Falü chubanshe.

Cheng, Tianquan, Jiang Yonglin, and Jones, William C., eds. 1994. *The Great Qing Code: A New Translation*. Oxford: Oxford University Press.

"Chengdushi gong'anju guanyu jinzhi weifa xinfang weihu shehui zhiande tonggao 成都

市公安局关于禁止违法信访维护社会治安秩序的通告 [The Note of Chendu Police Bureau that Forbids illegal Petition and Safeguards Social Security Order]," in *Chengdu Daily*, April 30, 2007.

Chesneaux, Jean, ed. 1972. *Popular Movements and Secret Societies in China, 1840–1950*. Stanford: Stanford University Press.

"China: Rampant Violence and Intimidation against Petitioners." 2005. In *Human Right Watch website*. December. Online, available at: http://hrw.org/english/docs/2005/12/08/china12144_txt.htm.

Cohen, Jerome Alan, Edwards, Randle R., and Chen, Fu-mei Chang. 1980. *Essays on China's Legal Tradition*. Princeton: Princeton University Press.

Cohen, Paul A. 1992. "The Contested Past: The Boxers as History or Myth," in *Journal of Asian Studies*, Vol. 51, No. 1, pp. 82–113.

Cohen, Paul A. 1997. *History in Three Keys: The Boxers as Event, Experience, and Myth*. New York: Columbia University Press.

"Complainant Sentenced for Internet Postings," in *Human Rights in China* press release. March 3, 2004 [accessed online in 2004, press release since taken down].

Creel, Herrlee Glessner. 1980. "Legal Institutions and Procedures during the Chou Dynasty," in Jerome Alan Cohen, R. Randle Edwards, and Fu-mei Chang Chen, eds., *Essays on China's Legal Tradition*. Princeton: Princeton University Press.

Crossley, Pamela Kyle. 2002. *A Translucent Mirror: History and Identity in Qing Imperial Ideology*. Berkeley: University of California Press.

Da, Mo 大漠. 2004. "Han Guizhi yu tahe shaqi miezi mingan 韩桂芝与塔河杀妻灭子命案 [Han Guizhi and the Life Case of Killing both Wife and Son in Tanhe]," in *Morning News of E'zhou* (E'zhou *fazhi zaobao*), December 30.

Dai, Huang 戴煌. 2003. "Yongnian shenzhixiong 永念慎之兄 [Always remember elder brother Li Shenzhi]," in *Modern China Studies*. Fall, pp. 55–66.

Dai, Huang 戴煌. 1998. *Hu Yaobang yu pingfan yuanjia cuoan* 胡耀邦与平反冤假错案 [Hu Yaobang and the Rehabilitation of Cases Involving Grievances and False and Wrong Charges]. Beijing: Zhongguo wenlian chuban gongsi and Xinhua chubanshe.

Dardess, John W. 1983. *Confucianism and Autocracy: Professional Elites in the Founding of the Ming Dynasty*. Berkeley/Los Angeles: University of California Press.

Dardess, John W. 2002. *Blood and History in China: The Donglin Faction and Its Repression, 1620–1627*. Honolulu: University of Hawai'i Press.

Deng, Liqun 邓立群. 1985. "Falü yaowei renmin suozhangwo 法律要为人民所掌握 [Law must be Grasped by People]," *The China Youth Daily*, June 21.

Des Forges, Alexander. 2007. *Mediasphere Shanghai: The Aesthetics of Cultural Production*. Honolulu: University of Hawai'i Press.

Des Forges, Roger. 1973. *Hsi-liang and the Chinese National Revolution*. New Haven: Yale University Press.

Des Forges, Roger. 2003. *Cultural Centrality and Political Change in Chinese History: Northeast Henan in the Fall of the Ming*. Stanford: Stanford University Press.

Des Forges, Roger. 2005. "Toward Another Zhou or Tang? Views from the Central Plain during the Shunzhi Reign," in *Time, Temporality, and Imperial Transition: East Asia from Ming to Qing*, edited by Lynn A. Struve. Honolulu: University of Hawai'i Press, pp. 73–112.

Diamant, Neil J. 2005. "Hollow Glory: The Politics of Rights and Identity among PRC Veterans in the 1950s and 1960s," in Neil J. Diamant, Stanley B. Lubman, and Kevin O'Brien, eds. *Engaging the Law in China: State, Society, and Possibilities for Justice*. Stanford: Stanford University Press, pp. 131–60.

Diao, Jiecheng 刁杰成. 1996. *Renmin xinfang shilüe* 人民信访史略 [A Brief History of People's Letters and Visits]. Beijing: Beijing jingji xueyuan chenbanshe.

Dikötter, Frank. 2002. *Crime, Punishment and the Prison in Modern China*. New York: Columbia University Press.

Dittmer, Lowell. 1989. *China's Continuous Revolution: The Post-Liberal Epoch 1949–1981*. Berkeley: University of California Press.

Dong, Yueling 董月玲. 2005. "Zhongguo xinfang renqun diaocha: manman xinfanglu hechu shi guicheng 中国信访人群调查: 慢慢信访路何处是归程 [A Study on China's Complainants: Where is the Returning Way of the Long Complaint Road]," in *The China Youth Daily*, April 13.

Du, Wenjuan 杜文娟. 2005. "Xin xinfang tiaoli changtong xinfanglu 新信访条例畅通信访路 [The New Regulations Clear the Path of Letters and Visits]," in *The People's Daily*, January 26.

"Dui ganbu de chuli yao zhuoyan yu jiaoyu 对干部的处理要着眼于教育 [Stressing the Means of Education to Deal with Cadres]," in *The People's Daily*, May 9, 1979.

Eastman, Lloyd E. 1974. *The Abotive Revolution: China under Nationalist Rule, 1927–1937*. Cambridge: Harvard University Press.

Eastman, Lloyd E. 1984. *Seeds of Destruction: Nationalist China in War and Revolution, 1937–1949*. Stanford: Stanford University Press.

Eastman, Lloyd E. 1991. "The May Fourth Movement as a Historical Turning Point Ecological Exhaustion, Militarization, and other Causes of China's Modern Crisis," in Kenneth Lieberthal, Joyce Kallgren, Roderick MacFarquhar, and Frederic Wakeman, Jr., eds., *Perspectives on Modern China: Four Anniversaries*. Armonk: M. E. Sharpe.

Ebrey, Patricia Buckley. 1993. *The Inner Quarters: Marriage and the Lives of Chinese Women in the Sung Period*. Berkeley: University of California Press.

Elliot, Morris. 2001. *The Manchu Way: The Eight Banners and Ethnic Identity in Late Imperial China*. Stanford: Stanford University Press.

Elman, Benjamin A. 2000. *A Cultural History of Civil Examinations in Late Imperial China*. Berkeley: University of California Press.

Elman, Benjamin A. 2005. *On Their Own Terms: Science in China, 1550–1900*. Cambridge: Harvard University Press.

"Empty Promise: The Role of Lawyers, Human Rights Protections & China's Criminal Procedure Law in Practice," in *China Rights Forum*, September 2001.

Engel, David M. 1978. *Code and Custom in a Thai Provincial Court*. Tucson: The University of Arizona Press.

Esherick, Joseph W. 1976. *Reform and Revolution in China: The 1911 Revolution in Hunan and Hubei*. Berkeley: University of California Press.

Esherick, Joseph W. 1976. "1911: A Review," in *Modern China*, Vol. 2, No. 2. pp. 141–84.

Esherick, Joseph W. 1988. *Origins of Boxers Uprising*. Berkeley: University of California Press.

Esherick, Joseph W., Pickowica, Paul G., and Walder, Andrew G., eds. 2006. *The Chinese Culture Revolution as History*. Stanford: Stanford University Press.

Fairbank, John K., ed. 1983. *The Cambridge History of China*. Cambridge: Cambridge University Press.

"Falü de shengli 法律的胜利 [The success of the law]," in *The China Youth Daily*, November 13, 1985.

"Fanfu kuangren de mengxiang he beicang 反复狂人的梦想和悲伧 [Dream and Tragedy of a Wild Anti-Corruptionist]," in *The Southern Weekend*. August 29, 2002.

Fang, Qiang. 2002. "The Case of the Virgin Prostitute: Chinese Media and Legal Reform," in *Stanford Journal of East Asian Affairs*, Vol. 2, No. 1, pp. 26–40.

Fang, Qiang. 2008. "The Spirit of the Rule of Law in China," in *Education About Asia*, Vol. 13, No. 1, online, available at: www.asian-studies.org/EAA/TOC/13-1.htm.

Fang, Qiang and Des Forges, Roger. 2007. "Were Chinese Rulers Above the Law? Toward a Theory of the Rule of Law in Chinese History," in *Stanford Journal of International Law*, Vol. 44, No. 1, pp. 101–46.

Farmer, Edward. 1995. *Zhu Yuanzhang and Early Ming Legislation: The Reordering of Chinese Society Following the Era of Mongol Rule*. Leiden: E. J. Brill.

Fei, Xiaotong 费孝通. 1946. *Minzhu, xianfa, and renquan* 民主, 宪法, 人权 [Democracy, Constitution, and Human Rights]. Shanghai: Shenghuo shudian.

Feigon, Lee. 2002. *Mao: A Reinterpretation*. Chicago: Ivan R. Dee.

Fenby, Jonathan. 2004. *Chang Kai-shek: China's Generalissimo and the Nation he Lost*. New York: Carroll & Graf Publishers.

Feng, Youlan 冯友兰. 2010. *Zhongguo zhexue jianshi* 中国哲学简史 [A Brief History of Chinese Philosophy]. Beijing: Beijing daxue chubanshe.

Feng, Zhen 冯震, 1989. *Minguo zhengzhishi* 民国政制史 [History of Political System in the Republic of China] in *Minguo congshu* 民国从书 [Republican Binding] Shanghai: Shanghia shudian chubanshe.

Feuerwerker, Albert. 1983. "Economic Trends, 1912–49," in John K. Fairbank, ed., *The Cambridge History of China. Volume 12. Republican China 1912–1949, Part I.* Cambridge: Cambridge University Press.

Field, Daniel. 1989. *Rebels in the Name of the Czar*. Boston: Unwin Hyman.

Fitzgerald, John. 1996. *Awakening China: Politics, Culture, and Class in the Natioanlist China*. Stanford: Stanford University Press.

Foucault, Michel. 1979. *Discipline and Punish: the Birth of the Prison*. New York: Vintage Books.

Fu, Xingyu 傅兴宇. 2002. "Baixing gaozhuang weihe nan 百姓告状为何难 [Why is it so Difficult for People to Complain?]," in *The Legal Daily*, January 5.

Fung, Edmund S. K. 2010. *The Intellectual Foundations of Chinese Modernity: Cultural and Political Thought in the Republican Era*. Cambridge: Cambridge University Press.

Gallagher, Mary E. 2006. "Mobilizing the Law in China: 'Informed Disenchantment' and the Development of Legal Consciousness," in *Law & Society Review*, Vol. 40, No. 4, pp. 783–816.

"Gaoguan lüshi wunai piaobo 告官律师无奈漂泊 [The Lawyer who Accuses Officials Has to Wander Aimlessly]," in *The Southern Weekend*, February 7, 2002.

Geng, Yunzhi 耿云志. 2003. *Xifang minzhu zai jindai zhongguo* 西方民主在近代中国 [Western Democracy in Modern China]. Beijing: Zhongguo qingnian chubanshe.

Glosser, Susan L. 2003. *Chinese Visions of Family and State, 1915–1953*. Berkeley: University of California Press.

Goldman, Merle. 2002. "The Reassertion of Political Citizenship in the Post-Mao Era: The Democracy Wall Movement," in Merle Goldman and Elizabeth J. Perry, eds., *Changing Meanings of Citizenship in Modern China*. Cambridge: Harvard University Press, pp. 159–86.

Gong, Pixiang 公丕祥, ed. 1999. *Dangdai zhongguo de falü geming* 当代中国的法律革命 [The Current Chinese Legal Revolution]. Beijing: Falü chubanshe.

Goodman, Peter S. 2004. "A New Use for Good Earth: Chinese Farmers Pay Price in Drive to Build Golf Centers," in the *Washington Post*, April 13.

Gordon, Andrew. 2003. *A Modern History of Japan: From Tokugawa Times to the Present.* Oxford: Oxford University Press.

Graebner, William and Richards, Leonard, eds. 2001. *The American Record.* Boston: McGraw-Hill.

Guan, Hanqing. 2002. *Snow in the Summer*. Beijing: New World Press.

Guo, Dongxu 郭东旭. 2000. *Songdai fazhi yanjiu* 宋代法制研究 [Research on the Song Legal System]. Shijiazhuang: Hebei daxue chubanshe.

Guo, Dongxu 郭东旭. 2001. *Songchao falü shilun* 宋朝法律史论 [A Comment on the Song Legal History]. Hebei: Hebei daxue chubanshe.

Guo, Guosong 郭国松. 2003. "Shenshi xinfang 审视信访 [Examining Xinfangs]," in *The Southern Weekend*, November 13.

Guo, Hanmin 郭汉民. 1989. *Zhongguo jindaishi zhengwu* 中国近代史正误 [Correcting Mistakes in Modern Chinese History]. Hunan: Hunan renmin chubanshe.

Guo, Luoji 郭罗基. 2000. "Gaizao peiyu falü wenhua 改造培育法律文化 [Reforming and Nurturing the Legal Culture]," in *Minzhu luntan* (*Democratic Forum*). July 11.

Guo, Shu 郭殊. 2003. "Zhongguo jindai xingzheng fayuan zhidu zhi bianqian 中国近代行政法院制度之变迁 [The Transitions of the Administrative Court System in Modern China]," in *Remin fayuanbao* 人民法院报 [People's Court Daily]. July 21.

Habermas, Jürgen. 1989. *The Structural Transformation of the Public Sphere: An Inquiry into a Category of Bourgeois Society*, trans. Thomas Burger. Cambridge: MIT Press.

Haidt, Jonathan and Joseph, Craig. 2004. "Intuitive Ethics: How Innately Prepared Intuitions Generate Culturally Variable Virtues," in *Daedalus*, Vol. 133, No. 4, pp. 55–66.

Hall, Terry. 1998. "Legislation," in David Forte, ed., *Natural Law and Contemporary Public Policy*. Georgetown: Georgetown University Press pp. 135–56.

Han, Xiutao 韩秀桃. 2003. *Sifa duli yu jindai zhongguo* 司法独立与近代中国 [Judicial Independence and Modern China]. Beijing: Qinghua daxue chubanshe.

Hannigan, John A. 1977. "The Newspaper Ombudsman and Consumer Complaints: An Empirical Assessment," in *Law & Society Review*, Vol. 11, No. 4, pp. 679–99.

Harrison, Henrietta. 2000. *The Making of the Republican Citizen: Political Ceremonies and Symbols in China 1911–1929*. Oxford: Oxford University Press.

Hegel, Robert E. and Carlita, Katherine, eds. 2007. *Writing and Law in Late Imperial China: Crime, Conflict, and Judgment*. Seattle: University of Washington Press.

Henderson, Dan Fenno. 1980. "Chinese Influences on Eighteenth-Century Tokugawa Codes," in Jerome Alan Cohen, R. Randle Edwards and Fu-mei Chang Chen, eds., *Essays on China's Legal Tradition*. Princeton: Princeton University Press, pp. 270–301.

Henderson, John B. 1984. *The Development and Decline of Chinese Cosmology*. New York: Columbia University Press.

Hevia, James L. 2003. *English Lessons: The Pedagogy of Imperialism in Nineteenth-Century China*. Durham: Duke University Press.

Ho, Ping-ti and Tang, Tsou, eds. 1968. *China in Crisis, Vol. 2, China's Policies in Asia and America's Alternatives*. Chicago: Chicago University Press.

Hornbeck, Stanley K. 1926. *Contemporary Politics in the Far East*. Cited from Inagagi naofumi 稻垣直文 in "Xiandai zhongguo 现代中国 [The Modern China. Zhong Yun trans.]," *Dongfang zazhi*. Vol. 23, pp. 29–33.

Hou, Chengchen 侯承琛. 1979. "Buchenzhi de gangu yinggai genghuan 不称职的干部应该更换 [Unqualified Officials Should be Replaced]," in *The People's Daily*. March 11.

Hou Yijie 侯宜杰. 1982. *Yuanshikai yisheng* 袁世凯一生 [The Life of Yuan Shikai]. Henan: Henanrenmin chubanshe.

Hsiao, Kung-chuan. 1975. *A Modern China and a New World: K'ang Yu-wei, Reformer and Utopian, 1858–1927*. Seattle: University of Washington Press.

Hsiao, Kung-chuan. 1979. *A History of Chinese Political Thought: Vol. 1—From the Beginnings to the Sixth Century A.D.* Princeton: Princeton University Press.

Hsu, Dau-lin. 1970. "Crime and Cosmic Order," in *Harvard Journal of Asiatic Studies*, Vol. 30, pp. 111–25.

Hu, Kui 胡奎 and Jiang, Shu 姜抒. 2003. "2003 nian zhongguo zaoyu xinfang hongfeng, xin lingdaoren mianlin feichang kaoyan 2003 年中国遭遇信访洪峰, 新领导人面临非常考验 [Having a Flood Surge in 2003, Chinese New Rulers are Facing a Special Test]," in *Liaowang dongfang*. December 8.

Huang, Guangming 黄广明. 2003. "Xiangfan guanchang 襄樊官场 [The Xiangfan Government Circle]," in *The Southern Weekend*, October 30.

Huang, Philip C. C. 1972. *Liang Ch'i-ch'ao and Modern Chinese Liberalism*. Seattle: Washington University Press.

Huang, Philip C. C. 1993. "'Public Sphere'/'Civil Society' in China? The Third Realm between State and Society," in *Modern China*, Vol. 19, No. 2, pp. 216–40.

Huang, Philip C. C. 1993. "Between Informal Mediation and Formal Adjudication: The Third Realm of Qing Civil Justice," in *Modern China*, Vol. 19, No. 3, pp. 251–98.

Huang, Philip C. C. 1998. *Civil Justice in China: Representation and Practice in the Qing*. Stanford: Stanford University Press.

Huang, Philip C. C. 2001. *Code, Custom, and Legal Practice in China: The Qing and the Republic Compared*. Stanford: Stanford University Press.

Huang, Yong 黄勇. 2002. "Yige fushengzhang de zhengjiguan 一个副省长的政绩观 [The Political Achievement in the Eyes of a Vice Governor]," in *The Southern Weekend*, August 22.

Huang, Yuansheng 黄源盛. 2002. "Minguo diyi ge xingzheng susong shenpan jiguan: minchu ping zhengyuan caijueshu zhengbian yu chutan 民国第一个行政诉讼审 判机关: 民初平政院裁决书整编与初探 [The First Administrative Court in the Early Republic: Editing and Preliminary Study on the Pingzhengyuan in the Early Republic]," in Zhang Jinfanb 张晋藩, ed., *Ershi shiji zhongguo fazhi de huigu yu qianzhan* 二十世纪中国法制的回顾与前瞻 [Retrospect and Prospect of the 20th Century Chinese Legal System]. Beijing: Zhongguo zhengfa daxue chubanshe.

Huang, Zheng 黄峥, ed. 2002. *Liushaoqi de zuihou suiyue 1966–1969* 刘少奇的最后岁 月 1966–1969 [Liu Shaoqi's Last Days: 1966–1969]. Beijing: Zhongyang wenxian chubanshe.

Hucker, Charles O. 1966. *The Censorial System of Ming China*. Stanford: Stanford University Press.

Hucker, Charles O. 1985. *A Dictionary of Official Titles in Imperial China*. Stanford: Stanford University Press.

Hulsewe, A. F. P. 1995. "Ch'in and Han Law," in Denis Twitchett and John K. Fairbank, eds., *The Cambridge History of China: The Ch'in and Han Empires*. Cambridge: Cambridge University Press.

Hunt, Michael H. 1983. *The Making of a Special Relationship: The United States and China to 1914*. New York: Columbia University Press.

Huters, Theodore. 2005. *Bringing the World Home: Appropriating the West in Late Qing and Early Republican China*. Honolulu: University of Hawai'i Press.

Hylton, Raymond, ed. 2001. *The World's History Volume I: Documents Set*. Upper Saddle River: Prentice Hall.

Hymes, Robert. 1986. *Statesmen and Gentlemen: The Elite of Fu-Chou, Chiang-His, in Northern and Southern Sung*. Cambridge: Cambridge University Press.

Ichiko, Chuzo. 1980. "Political and Institutional Reform, 1901–1911," in John K. Fairbank and Kwang-Ching Liu, eds., *Cambridge History of China, Late Qing. Part II, 1800–1911*. Cambridge: Cambridge University Press.

Isaacs, Harold R. 1968. *The Tragedy of the Chinese Revolution*. New York: Atheneum.

Jacobs, Andrew. 2008. "Too Old and Frail to be Re-educated? Not in China," in *The New York Times*, August 21.

Jeans, Roger B. Jr., 1997. *Democracy and Socialism in Republican China: The Politics of Zhang Junmai*. Lanham: Rowan & Littlefield Publishers.

Jian, Guo 建国. 1986. "Quanda haishi fada 权大还是法大 [Which is Bigger: Power or Law]," in *The China Youth Daily*, September 17.

Jiang, Bixin 江必新. 2009. "Xingzheng susongfa yuchouxiang xingzheng xingwei 行政诉讼法 与抽象行政行为 [The Administrative Litigation Law and Abstract Administrative Activities]," in *Xingzheng faxue yanjiu*, No. 3. www.procedurallaw.cn/xzss/zdwz/200911/t20091127_287350.html.

Jiang, Shuangfeng 江霜枫. 1957. "Fanyoupai douzheng shi renmin neibu maodun haishi diwo maodun 反右派斗争是人民内部矛盾还是敌我矛盾 [Does the Anti-Rightist Movement belong to People's Internal Contradiction or Enemy-versus-Ourselves Contradiction]," in *Wenhuibao*, July 4.

Jiang, Yonglin. 2000. "Deepening the Dynastic Order at the Local Level: Central-Local Relations as Seen in a Late-Ming Magistrate's Enforcement of the Law," in *Ming Studies*, Vol. 43, pp. 16–39.

Jin, Chunfeng 金春峰. 1997. *Handai sixiangshi* 汉代思想史 [History of Han Thoughts]. Beijing: Zhongguo shehui kexue chubanshe.

Jin, Qiu. 1999. *The Culture of Power: The Lin Biao Incident in the Cultural Revolution*. Stanford: Stanford University Press.

"Jinri qingguan gengdongren 今日清官更动人 [Today's Qingguan (lit, limpid official) is more Attractive]," in *The People's Daily*, April 13, 1990.

Johnson, Chalmers A. 1962. *Peasant Nationalism and Communist Power: The Emergence of Revolutionary China, 1937–1945*. Stanford: Stanford University Press.

Johnson, Wallace, trans. and ed. 1997. *The T'ang Code: Volume II, Specific Articles*. Princeton: Princeton University Press.

Jones, William C. 2004. "Chinese Law and Liberty in Comparative Historical Perspective," in William C. Kirby, ed., *Realms of Freedom in Modern China* Stanford: Stanford University Press, pp. 44–56.

Judge, Joan. 1996. *Print and Politics: 'Shibao' and the Culture of Reform in Late Qing China*. Stanford: Stanford University Press.

Karl, Rebecca E. 2002. *Staging the World: Chinese Nationalism at the Turn of the Twentieth Century*. Durham: Duke University Press.

Karl, Rebecca E. and Peter Zarrow, eds. 2002. *Rethinking the 1898 Reform Period: Political and Cultural Change in Late Qing China*. Harvard: Harvard University Asian Center.

Ke, Kuanzhi 柯宽智 and He, Yinmin 何映民. 1998. "Qingrong xinfangde aimin fumuguan 情融信 访的 '爱民父母官' [The people-loving parental official's sentiment fills the letters and visits]," in *Minqing yu xinfang*, Vol. 1, pp. 22–4.

Keishu, Saneto. 1983. *Zhongguoren liuxue ribenshi* 中国人留学日本史 [History of Chinese Students in Japan]. Beijing: shenghuo dushu xinzhi sanlian shudian.

Kim, Ilpyong J. 1973. *The Politics of Chinese Communism: Kiangsi under the Soviets*. Berkeley: University of California Press.

Kirby, William C. 2004. "The Chinese Party-State Under Dictatorship and Democracy on the Mainland and on Taiwan," in William C. Kirby, ed., *Realms of Freedom in Modern China*. Stanford: Stanford University Press.

Knight, Nick. 2007. *Rethinking Mao: Exploration in Mao Zedong's Thought*. Lanham: Lexington Books.

Kuhn, Philip A. 1990. *Soulstealers: The Chinese Sorcery Scare of 1768*. Cambridge: Harvard University Press.

Kuhn, Philip A. 2002. *Origins of the Modern Chinese State*. Stanford: Stanford University Press.

Langlois, John D. 1981. "Living Law in Sung and Yuan Jurisprudence," *Harvard Journal of Asiatic Studies*, Vol. 41, No. 1, pp. 165–217.

Langlois, John D. 1981. "Political Thought in Chin-hua under Mongol Rule" in John D. Langlois, ed., *China under Mongol Rule*. Princeton: Princeton University Press, pp. 137–85.

Lean, Eugenia. 2007. *Public Passions: The Trial of Shi Jianqiao and the Rise of Popular Sympathy in Republican China*. Berkeley: University of California Press.

Lee, Ching Kwan. 2007. *Against the Law: Labor Protests in China's Rustbelt and Sunbelt*. Berkeley: University of California Press.

Lee, Leo Ou-fan. 2000. "The Cultural Construction of Modernity in Urban Shanghai: Some Preliminary Explorations," in Wen-hsin Yeh, ed., *Becoming Chinese: Passages to Modernity and Beyond*. Berkeley: University of California.

Levenson, Joseph R. 1970. *Liang Ch'i-ch'ao and the Mind of Modern China*. Berkeley: University of California Press.

Li, Bingyan 李炳炎. 1986. *Zhongguo xinwenshi* 中国新闻史 [The History of Chinese Newspapers]. Taiwan: Taoshi chubanshe.

Li, Guohua 李国华. 2002. "Xinshiqi yifa xinfang gongzuode tansuo yushijian 新时期依法信访 工作的探索与实践 [The investigation and practice of the lawful letters and visits in the new era]," in *Renmin xinfang*, Vol. 7, pp. 30–1.

Li, Jiutuan 李九团 and Wang, Junshan 王俊山, eds. 2000. *Xinshiji zhongguo xinfang gongzuo shiwu quanshu* 新世纪中国信访工作实务全书 [A Practical Compendium of the Chinese Xinfang Work in the New Century]. Beijing: Zhongguo shenji chubanshe.

Li, Qiuxue. 2010. *Zhongguo xinfang shilun* 中国信访史论 [Historical Discussion of Chinese Letters and Visits]. Beijing: Zhongguo shehui kexue chubanshe.

Li, Xizhu 李细珠. 2004. "Qingmo minjian yulun yu guanfu zuowei zhi hudong guanxi 清末民间舆论与官府作为之互动关系 [The Mutual Relationship between Media and Government in the Late Qing]," in *Jindaishi yanjiu* 近代史研究 [Study of Modern History], pp. 1–44.

Li, Yajie 李亚杰 and Wei Wu 魏武. 2007. "Qunzhong fanying qiangliede wufangmian tuchu wenti chengwei xinfang gongzuo zhongdian 群众反映强烈的五方面突出问题成为信访工作重点 [Noticeable Problems in Five Fields Reflected Intensely by the Mass will become the Crucial Points of Xinfang]", in *Xinhuanwang* (New China Net). March 28.

Li, Yu 李郁. 2003. "Zhixingnan tianxia dijinan 执行难, 天下第几难 [What is the rank of the Difficulty of Implementation]," in *The Legal Daily*, April 29.

Liang, Yanhui 梁妍慧. 2008. "Ganbu renshi gaige sanshinian: xuanren yongren buzheng zhifeng weihe lüjin buzhi? 干部人事改革30年:选人用人不正之风为何屡禁不 止? [Thirty Years Reform of Cadre Personnel: Why does Incorrect Selecting and Appointing Policy Proceed with little Check?]," in *Xuexi shibao*, June 26.

"Liaoning zhuanhe minzhong zhengfu menqian xiagui 辽宁庄河民众政府门前下跪 [People from Liaoning Zhuanghe Knelt Down In Front of the Government Gate]," in *Nanfang dushibao*, April 13, 2010.

Lieberthal, Kenneth. 1995. *Governing China: From Revolution through Reform*. New York: W. W. Norton & Company.

Lieberthal, Kenneth, Kallgren, Joyce, MacFarquhar, Roderick, and Wakeman, Frederic Jr., eds. 1991. *Perspectives on Modern China: Four Anniversaries*. Armonk: M. E. Sharpe.

Liebman, Benjamin L. 2005. "Watchdog or Demagogue? The Media in the Chinese Legal System," in *Columbia Law Review*, Vol. 105, No. 1, pp. 1–157.

Lin, Houqi 林厚祺. 1989. "Guomindang tongzhi shiqi de sifa gaishu 国民党统治时期的司法概述 [A Brief Explanation of the Judiciary under the Control of the GMD]," in *Facao neiwai* 法曹内外 [Inside and Outside the Judiciary]. Fujian: Zhongguo zhengxie fujiansheng weiyuanhui and wenshi ziliao yanjiu weiyuanhui, pp. 1–28.

Lin, Ji 林济. 1993. *Juzhengzhuan* 居正传 [A Biography of Ju Zheng]. Hubei: Hubei renmin chubanshe.

Lin, Yutang. 1936. *A History of the Press and Public Opinion in China*. Shanghai: Kelly and Walsh, 1936).

Ling, Bo 凌波. 2003. "Huajie dongqian maodun yicheng dangwu zhiji 化解动拆迁矛盾已成当务之急 [The Top Issue is to Dissolve the Contradiction of Urban Disposal]," in *Shanghai Xinfang* 上海信访 [Shanghai Xinfang] pp. 10–12.

"Lipeng yaoqiu zhongshi nongmin fudan zhuyi gongzuo fangfa 李鹏要求重视农民负担注意工作方法[Li Peng Demands the Emphasis on Farmers' Burden and Attention on Working method]," in *The China Youth Daily*, April 19, 1990.

Liu, Jianping 刘建平 and Dai, Dunfeng 戴敦峰. 2004. "Bieduozou wode maitian 别夺走我 的麦田 [Do not Deprive Me My Wheat Land]," in *The Southern Weekend*, January 8.

Liu, Lydia H. 1995. *Translingual Practice: Literature, National Culture, and Translated Modernity, China, 1900–1937*. Stanford: Stanford University Press.

Liu, Lydia H. 2004. *The Clash of Empires: The Invention of China in Modern World Making*. Cambridge: Harvard University Press.

Liu, Xiaobo. 2005. "Atop a Volcano," in *The Journal of Human Rights in China*, Vol. 1, pp. 39–44, online, available at: www.hrichina.org/sites/default/files/oldsite/PDFs/CRF.1.2005/1.2005AtopAVolcano.pdf.

Liu, Xiaoyan 刘晓燕. 2002. "Yige nongfu de shangfang zaoyu 一个农妇的上访遭遇 [The Experience of a Farmer Woman's Complaint]," in *The China Youth Daily*, June 10.

Liu, Yongping. 1998. *Origins of Chinese Law: Penal and Administrative Law in its Early Development*. Oxford: Oxford University Press.

Liu, Zuoxiang 刘作祥. 2003. "Zhongguo sifa defang baohu zhuyi zhi pipan: jianlun sifa quan guojiahua de gaige silu 中国司法地方保护之批判: 兼论司法权国家化的 改革思路 [A Criticism on China's Local Legal Protectionism: Also Argues about the Reform on the Nationalization of Judicial Power]," in *Faxue yanjiu*, pp. 83–98.

Loewe, Michael. 1995. "The Religious and Intellectual Background" in Denis Twitchett and John K. Fairbank, eds., *The Cambridge History of China: The Ch'in and Han Empires*. Cambridge: Cambridge University Press.

Loewe, Michael and Shaughnessy, Edward L. eds. 1999. *The Cambridge History of Ancient China: From the Origins of Civilization to 221 B.C.* Cambridge: Cambridge University Press.

Lu, Songyue 鲁嵩岳. 1998. *Shenxingxian dianping* 《慎刑宪》点评 [Comments on the *Book of Discreet Punishment*]. Beijing: Falü chubanshe.

Lubman, Stanley. 1999. *Bird in a Cage: Legal Reform in China after Mao*. Stanford: Stanford University Press.

Luehrmann, Laura M. 2000. "Officials Face the Masses: Citizen Contacting in Modern China." Dissertation manuscript, Ohio State University.

Luehrmann, Laura M. 2003. "Facing Citizen Complaints in China, 1951–1996," *Asian Survey*, Vol. 43, No. 5, pp. 845–66.

Lust, J. 1964. "The 'Su-pao' Case: An Episode in the Early Chinese Nationalist Movement," in *Bulletin of the School of Oriental and African Studies*, Vol. 27, No. 2, pp. 408–29.

Ma, Huaide 马怀德. 1997. *Zhongguo xingzhengfa* 中国行政法 [Chinese Administrative Law]. Beijing: Zhongguo zhengfa daxue chubanshe.

Macauley, Melissa. 1998. *Social Power and Legal Culture: Litigation Masters in Late Imperial China*. Stanford: Stanford University Press.

MacCormack, Geoffrey. 1996. *The Spirit of Traditional Chinese Law*. Athens: The University of Georgia Press.

Macleod, Calum. 2008. "Chinese Say People's Court Offers Little Help," in *The USA Today*, August 8.

Major, John S. 1993. *Heaven and Earth in Early Han Thought: Chapter Three, Four, and Five of the Huainanzi*. Albany: State University of New York Press.

Makesi engesi lun guojia yufa 马克思恩格斯论国家与法 [Marx and Engels Arguments on State and Law]. 1958. Beijing: Falü chubanshe.

Marx, Karl and Engels, Friedrich. 2002. *The Communist Manifesto.* New York: Penguin Classics.

Mayer, Otto. 2002. *Deguo xingzhengfa* (Liu Fei 刘飞 trans.) 德国行政法 [German Administrative Law]. Beijing: Shengwu yinshuguan.

McCormack, Gavan. 1977. *Chang Tso-lin in Northeast China, 1911–1928: China, Japan, and the Manchurian Idea*. Stanford: Stanford University Press.

McKnight, Brian E. 1981. *The Quality of Mercy: Amnesties and Traditional Chinese Justice*. Honolulu: The University Press of Hawai'i.

Meijer, M. J. 1950. *The Introduction of Modern Criminal Law in China*. Batavia: De Unie.

Meisner, Maurice. 1996. *The Deng Xaioping Era: An Inquiry into the Fate if Chinese Socialism, 1978–1994*. New York: Hill and Wang.

Meisner, Maurice. 1999. *Mao's China and After: A History of the People's Republic of China*. New York: The Free Press.

Metzger, Thomas A. 1973. *The Internal Organization of Ch'ing Bureaucracy, Legal, Normative, and Communication Aspects*. Cambridge University Press.

Michelson, Ethan. 2008. "Justice from Above or Below? Popular Strategies for Resolving Grievances in Rural China," in *China Quarterly*, Vol. 193, March, pp. 43–64.

Min Jie 闵捷. 2002. "Yi xingzhengting tingzhang de kunao: tudi zhengce tuozhu mingaoguan detui 一行政庭庭长的苦恼: 土地政策拖住民告官的腿 [The Worry of the Head of an Administrative Division]," in *The China Youth Daily*, July 31.

"Mingaoguan shinian pandian 民告官十年盘点 [A Study of People-Accuse-Officials for Ten Years],"in *The China Youth Daily*, April 16, 1999.

Minzner, Carl F. 2006. "Xinfang: An Alternative to the Formal Chinese Legal System" in *Stanford Journal of International Law*, Vol. 42, No. 1, pp. 103–79.

Mittler, Barbara. 2004. *A Newspaper for China? Power, Identity, and Change in Shanghai's News Media*. Cambridge: Harvard University Press.

Miyazaki, Ichisada. 1980. "The Administration of Justice during the Sung Dynasty," in Jerome Alan Cohen, R. Randle Edwards and Fu-mei Chang Chen, eds., *Essays on China's Legal Tradition*. Princeton: Princeton University Press.

Mote, Frederick W. 1989. *Intellectual Foundations of China*. New York: Alfred A. Knopf.

Muhlhahn, Klaus. 2009. *Criminal Justice in China: A History*. Cambridge: Harvard University Press.

Na, Silu 那思陆. 1992. *Qingdai zhongyang sifa shenpan zhidu* 清代中央司法审判制度 [The Central Legal Judging System of the Qing]. Taibei: Wenshizhe chubanshe.

Nathan, Andrew. 1983. "A Constitutional Republic: The Peking Government, 1916–28," in John K. Fairbanks, ed., *The Cambridge History of China, Vol. 12, Republican China 1912–1949, Part I*. Cambridge: Cambridge University Press, pp. 259–83.

Nathan, Andrew. 1985. *Chinese Democracy*. Berkeley: University of California Press.

Nedostup, Rebecca and Liang, Hong-ming. 2002. "'Begging the Sages of the Party-State': Citizenship and Government in Transition in Nationalist China 1927–1937" in Lex Heerma van Voss, ed., *Petitions in Social History*. Cambridge: Cambridge University Press, pp. 185–207.

Nie, Xin 聂鑫. 2009. "Congsanfasi daosifayuan: zhongguo zhongyang sifa chuantongde duanlie yuyanxu 从三法司到司法院: 中国中央司法传统的断裂与延续 [From Three Judiciaries to Judicial Ministry: The Break and Connection of the Central Judicial Tradition of China]," in *Zhengfa luntan*, Vol. 27, No. 1.

North, Douglass C. 1981. *Structure and Change in Economic History*. New York: W. W. Norton & Company.

Nubola, Cecilia. 2002. "Supplications between Politics and Justice: The Northern and Central Italian States in the Early Modern Age," in Lex Heerma van Voss, pp. 35–56.

O'Brien, Kevin 1996. "Rightful Resistance," in *World Politics*. Vol. 49, No. 1, pp. 31–55.

O'Brien, Kevin and Li, Lianjiang. 1995. "The Politics of Lodging Complaints in Rural China," in *The China Quarterly*, Vol. 143, September, pp. 756–83.

O'Brien, Kevin and Li, Lianjiang. 2005. "Suing the Local State: Administrative Litigation in Rural China," in Neil J. Diamant, Stanley B. Lubman, and Kevin O'Brien, eds., *Engaging the Law in China: State, Society, and Possibilities for Justice*. Stanford: Stanford University Press, pp. 31–53.

O'Brien, Kevin and Li, Lianjiang. 2006. *Rightful Resistance in Rural China*. Cambridge: Cambridge University Press.

Ocko, Jonathan. 1988. "I'll Take it All the Way to Beijing: Capital Appeals in the Qing," in *Journal of Asian Studies*, Vol. 47, No. 2, pp. 291–315.

Ocko, Jonathan. 2004. "Applying Western Legal Scholarship to the Study of Contract and Property in Early Modern China," in Medeline Zelin and Robert Gardella, eds., *Contract and Property in Early Modern China*. Stanford: Stanford University Press.

Oksenberg, Michel. 1991. "The Deng Era's Uncertain Political Legacy," in Kenneth Lieberthal, Joyce Kallgren, Roderick MacFarquhar, and Frederic Wakeman, Jr., eds., *Perspectives on Modern China: Four Anniversaries*. Armonk: M. E. Sharpe, pp. 309–40.

Ota, Yoroshi. 2003. *Qingguo xingzhengfa* 清国行政法 (Li Xiuqing, Wang Pei, annotation) [The Administrative Law in the Qing State]. Beijing: Zhongguo zhengfa daxue chubanshe.

Paine, S. C. M. 2003. *The Sino-Japanese War of 1894–1895: Perceptions, Power, and Primacy*. Cambridge: Cambridge University Press.

Peerenboom, Randall. 2002. *China's Long March toward Rule of Law*. Cambridge: Cambridge University Press.

Perry, Elizabeth. 1993. *Shanghai on Strike: the Politics of Chinese Labor*. Stanford: Stanford University Press.

Perry, Elizabeth. 2002. *Challenging the Mandate of Heaven: Social Protest and State Power in China*. New York: M. E Sharpe.

Perry, Elizabeth. 2007. "Masters of the Country? Shanghai Workers in the Early People's

Republic," in Jeremy Brown and Paul G. Pickowicz, eds., *Dilemmas of Victory: The Early Years of the People's Republic of China*. Cambridge: Harvard University Press.

Perry, Elizabeth and Li Xun, 1997. *Proletarian Power: Shanghai in the Cultural Revolution*. Boulder: Westview Press 1997.

"Petitioner Round-up Brings Threat of Psychiatric Incarceration," in *Human Rights in China*, September 19, 2005.

Philips, Ellen. 1997. *Shocked, Appalled, and Dismayed: How to Write Letters of Complaint that Get Results*. New York: Vintage Books.

Ping, Shizheng. 2002. "Local Governance and Crisis Management: A Comprehensive Perspective from Post-1949 China," in Robert J. Antony and Jane Kate Leonard, eds., *Dragons, Tigers, and Dogs: Qing Crisis Management and the Boundaries of State Power in Late Imperial China*. Ithaca: Cornell University East Asian Program, pp. 303–21.

Pollard, A. F. 1964. *The Evolution of Parliament*. New York: Russell & Russell Inc.

Pomfret, John. 2006. *Chinese Lessons: Five Classmates and the Story of the New China*. New York: Henry Holt and Company.

Potter, Pitman B. 1994. "The Administrative Litigation Law of the PRC: Judicial Review and Bureaucratic Reform," in Pitman B. Potter, ed., *Domestic Law Reforms in Post-Mao China*. New York: M. E. Sharpe, pp. 270–304.

Potter, Pitman B. 2003. *From Leninist Discipline to Socialist Legalism: Peng Zhen on Law and Political Authority in the PRC*. Stanford: Stanford University Press.

Prazniak, Roxann. 1999. *Of Camel Kings and Other Things: Rural Rebels against Modernity in Late Imperial China*. Lanham: Rowman & Littlefield Publishers.

Pu, Jian 蒲坚. 1990. *Zhongguo gudai xingzhengfa* 中国古代行政法 [The Chinese Ancient Administrative Law]. Beijing: Beijing daxue chubanshe.

Qian, Daqun 钱大群 and Ai Yongming 艾永明. 1996. *Tangdai xingzheng falü yanjiu* 唐代行政法律研究 [A Study of the Tang Administrative Law]. Nanjing: Jiangsu renmin chubanshe.

Qian, Shifu 钱实甫. 1984. *Beiyang zhengfu shiqi de zhengzhi zhidu* 北洋政府时期的政治制度 [The Political System during the Early Republic]. Beijing: Zhonghua shujü.

Qiao, Congqi 乔从启. 1992. *Sunzhongshan falü sixiang tixi yanjiu* 孙中山法律思想体系研究 [A Study of the System of Sun Yat-sen's Legal Thought]. Beijing: Falü chubanshe.

"Qieshi jiejue shangfang wenti 切实解决上访问题 [Readily Solve the Complaint Problem]," in *The People's Daily*, September 17, 1979.

Qin, Henhai 秦恨海. 2008. "Bo Xilai yaoguanyuan duibaixing youzhenganqing, nitinghou lianhongle meiyou 薄熙来要官员对百姓有真感情，你听后脸红了 没有? [Bo Xilai Wants Officials to have Authentic Emotion to the People, Do you Flush after Hearing it?]," in *The Chongqing Daily*, March 31.

"Qineng zhiyao guansheng buyao minsheng 岂能只要官声不要民生 [How can [they] Want Official Voice and not People's Living]," in *The Workers' Daily*, September 2, 2002.

Qiu, Dengchang 仇登昌. 2000. "Wosheng xinfang gongzuo mianlin de xinxingshi 我省信访工作面临的新形势 [The New Complaint Situation in Our Province]," in *Xuexi luntan* 学习论坛 [Study Forum], pp. 39–40.

Qiu, Haiping 邱海平. 1983. "Xianqiankan shi fazhan shengchan de zuli 向前看是发展生产的阻力 [Looking to Money is the Obstacle of Developing Production]," in *The China Youth Daily*, October 22.

Rankin, Mary Backus. 1971. *Early Chinese Revolutionaries: Radical Intellectuals in Shanghai and Chekiang, 1902–1911*. Cambridge: Harvard University Press.

Rankin, Mary Backus. 1986. *Elite Activism and Political Transformation in China: Zhejiang Province, 1865–1911*. Stanford: Stanford University Press.

Rankin, Mary Backus. 1993. "Some Observations on a Chinese Public Sphere." *Modern China*, Vol. 19, No. 2, pp. 158–82.

Rankin, Mary Backus. 2000. "State and Society in Early Republican Politics, 1912–18" in Kenneth Lieberthal, Joyce Kallgren, Roderick MacFarquhar, and Frederic Wakeman, Jr., eds., *Perspectives on Modern China: Four Anniversaries*. New York: M. E. Sharpe.

Rawski, Evelyn S. 1998. *The Last Emperors: A Social History of Qing Imperial Institutions*. Berkeley: University of California Press.

Reed, Bradly W. 2000. *Talons and Teeth: County Clerks and Runners in the Qing Dynasty*. Stanford: Stanford University Press.

Reif, Linda C. 2004. *The Ombudsman, Good Governance and the International Human Rights System*. Leiden/Boston: Martinus Nijhoff Publishers.

Ren, Hengjun 任恒俊. 2003. *Wanqing guanchang guize yanjiu* 晚清官场规则研究 [Research on Late Qing Government Rules]. Hainan: Hainan chubanshe.

Ren, Jianxin 任建新. 1990. "Zuigao renmin fayuan gongzuo baogao 最高人民法院工作报告 [The Supreme Court Work Report]," in *The People's Daily*. April 10, 1990.

Reynolds, Douglas R. 1993. *China, 1898–1912: The Xinzheng Revolution and Japan*. Cambridge: Harvard University Press.

Rhoads, Edward J. M 1975. *China's Republican Revolution: the Case of Kwangtung, 1895–1913*. Cambridge: Harvard University Press.

Rhoads, Edward J. M. 2000. *Manchu and Han: Ethnic Relations and Political Power in Late Qing and Early Republican China, 1861–1928*. Seattle: University of Washington Press.

Roberts, Luke S. 1994. "The Petition Box in Eighteenth-Century Japan" in *The Journal of Asian Studies*, Vol. 20, No. 2, pp. 423–58.

Ronan, Colin A. 1978. *The Shorter Science and Civilization in China: An Abridgment of Joseph Neeham's Original Text*. Cambridge: Cambridge University Press.

Rossabi, Morris. 1989. *Khubilai Khan: His Life and Times*. Berkeley: University of California Press.

Rowat, Donald C. 1973. *The Ombudsman Plan: Essays on the Worldwide Spread of an Idea*. Toronto: McClelland and Stewart Limited.

Rowe, William T. 1993. "The Problem of 'Civil Society' in Late Imperial China," in *Modern China*. Vol. 19, No. 2, pp. 139–57.

Rowe, William T. 2001. *Saving the World: Chen Hongmou and Elite Consciousness in Eighteenth-Century China*. Stanford: Stanford University Press.

Ru, Wu 茹武. 2002. "Gonganju baisu jubu luxing fayuan cheng anjian buhao zhixing 公 安局败诉拒不履行, 法院称案件不好执行 [Police Bureau Refuses to Follow, the Court States that the Case is not Easy to Implement]," in *The Worker's Daily*. June 8.

Rusen, Jorn. 2002. *Western Historical Thinking: An Intercultural Debate*. New York: Berghahn Books.

Schneewind, Sarah. 2001. "Visions and Revisions: Village Policies of the Ming Founder in Seven Phases," in *T'oung Pao*, Vol. 87, pp. 317–59.

Schram, Stuart. 1974. *Chairman Mao Talks to the People: Talks and Letters, 1956–1971*. New York: Pantheon.

Schrecker, John E. 1991. *The Chinese Revolution in Historical Perspective*. New York: Praeger.

Scott, James C. 1985. *Weapons of the Weak: Everyday Forms of Peasant Resistance* New Haven: Yale University Press.

Scott, James C. 1989. "Everyday Forms of Resistance," in Forrest D. Colburn, ed., *Everyday Forms of Peasant Resistance*. Armonk: M. E. Sharpe.

Scott, James C. 1990. *Domination and the Arts of Resistance: Hidden Transcripts*. New Haven: Yale University Press.

Seagrave, Sterling. 1992. *Dragon Lady: The Life and Legend of the Last Empress of China*. New York: Vintage Books.

Seagrave, Sterling. 1996. *The Soong Dynasty*. New York: Harper Perennial.

Seungjoo, Yoon. 2002. "Literati-Journalists of the Chinese Progress (Shiwu bao) in Discord, 1896–1898," in Rebecca E. Karl and Peter Zarrow, eds., *Rethinking the 1898 Reform Period: Political and Cultural Change in Late Qing China*. Cambridge: Harvard University Asian Center, pp. 48–76.

Seybolt, Peter J. 1996. *Throwing the Emperor from his Horse: Portrait of a Village Leader in China, 1923–1995*. Boulder: Westview Press.

Shao, Xuyang 邵旭阳. 1979. "Duzhe laixin weisheme yinbuqi zhongshi 读者来信为什么引不起重视 [Why can Readers' Letters Attract Enough Emphasis]," in *The People's Daily*, November 24.

Shen, Feng 沈峰. 2004. "Nongmin jianfu genben zaijianguan 农民减负根本在减官 [The Root in Reducing Farmers' Burden is to Cut the Number of Officials]," in *The Daily of Collected Articles*, March 24.

Shen, Yuanyuan. 2000. "Conceptions and Receptions of Legality: Understanding the Complexity of Law Reform in Modern China," in Karen G. Turner, James V. Feinerman, and R. Kent Guy, eds., *The Limits of the Rule of Law in China*. Seattle: University of Washington Press, pp. 20–44.

Sheridan, James E. 1966. *Chinese Warlord: The Career of Feng Yu-hsiang*. Stanford: Stanford University Press.

Sheridan, James E. 1983. "The Warlord Era: Politics and Militarism under the Peking Government, 1916–28" in John K. Fairbank, ed., *The Cambridge History of China. Volume 12. Republican China 1912–1949*. Cambridge: Cambridge University Press.

"Shiwei fumishuzhang Shen Hongguang zai quxian ji bufen weibanju xinfang bumen fuzeren huiyishang de jianghua 市委副秘书长沈红光在区县及部分委办局信 访部门负责人会议上的讲话 [The talk of vice municipal party secretary Shen Hongguang in a meeting attended by leaders of districts, counties, and some local xinfang offices]" in *Shanghai xinfang*, 2003, Vol. 9.

Short, Philip. 1999. *Mao: A Life*. New York: John Macrae/Owl.

Shue, Vivienne. 1991. "Powers of State, Paradoxes of Dominion: China 1949–1979," in Kenneth Lieberthal, Joyce Kallgren, Roderick MacFarquhar, and Frederic Wakeman, Jr., eds., *Perspectives on Modern China: Four Anniversaries*. Armonk: M. E. Sharpe.

"Sici qiangxia liuren hebeisheng gaoyuan riqian gongkai tingshen qi'an 四次抢下留人: 河北省高院日前公开庭审奇案 [Saving a Person Four Times from Death: Hebei High Court Recently Adjudicates a Strange Case in Public]," in *The Chinese Commercial Daily* (*huashangbao*) August 1.

Smith, Goldwin. 1955. *A Constitutional and Legal History of England*. New York: Charles Scribner's Sons.

Solinger, Dorothy J. 1999. *Contesting Citizenship in Urban China: Peasant Migrants, the State, and the Logic of the Market*. Berkeley: University of California Press.

Spence, Jonathan. 1981. *The Gate of Heavenly Peace: The Chinese and Their Revolution, 1895–1980*. New York: Penguin Books.

Spence, Jonathan. 1988. *Emperor of China: Self-Portrait of K'ang-hsi*. New York: Vintage Books.

Spence, Jonathan. 1990. *The Search for Modern China*. New York: W. W. Norton & Company.

Stapleton, Kristin. 2000. *Civilizing Chengdu: Chinese Urban Reform 1895–1937*. Cambridge: Harvard University Press.

Stapleton, Kristin. 1997. "County Administration in Late-Qing Sichuan: Conflicting Models of Rural Policing," in *Late Imperial China*, Vol. 18, No. 1, pp. 100–32.

Stephens, Thomas B. 1992. *Order and Discipline in China: The Shanghai Mixed Court 1911–27*. Seattle: University of Washington Press.

Strauss, Julia. 2002. "The Evolution of Republican Government" in Frederic Wakeman, Jr. and Richard Louis Edmonds, eds., *Reappraising Republican China*. Oxford: Oxford University Press, pp. 57–97.

Struve, Lynn A., ed. 2004. *The Qing Formation in World-Historical Time*. Cambridge: Harvard University Asia Center.

Struve, Lynn A., ed. 2005. *Time, Temporality, and Imperial Transition: East Asia from Ming to Qing*. Honolulu: University of Hawai'i Press.

"Tamen weishenme gan wushi falü 他们为什么敢无视法律 [Why Dare They Ignore the Law]," in *The China Youth Daily*, September 2, 1986.

"Tanfang chengshi shangfangzu de yingmi shijie 探访城市上访族的隐秘世界 [Exploring the Secret World of the Complaining Group]," in *The Worker's Daily*, March 25, 2002.

Tang, Xiaobing 唐小兵. 1996. *Global Space and the Nationalist Discourse of Modernity: The Historical Thinking of Liang Qichao*. Stanford: Stanford University Press.

"Tanpai Mengyuhu 摊派猛于虎 [The Collection of Fees is More Fierce than a Tiger]," in *The China Youth Daily*, November 19, 1992.

Tarrow, Sidney. 1998. *Power in Movement: Social Movement and Contentious Politics*. Cambridge: Cambridge University Press.

Tarrow, Sidney. 2001. "Silence and Voice in the Study of Contentious Politics: Introduction," in Doug McAdam, Sidney Tarrow, and Charles Tilly, eds., *Silence and Voice in the Study of Contentious Politics*. Cambridge: Cambridge University Press, pp. 1–13.

Teiwes, Frederic C. and Sun, Warren. 1995. "From a Leninist to a Charismatic Party: The CCP's Changing Leadership, 1937–1945," in Tony Saich and Hans van de Ven, eds., *New Perspectives on the Chinese Communist Revolution*. Armonk: M. E. Sharpe. pp. 339–87.

Thireau, Isabelle and Hua, Linshan. 2003. "The Moral Universe of Aggrieved Chinese Workers: Workers' Appeals to Arbitration Committees and Letters and Visits Offices," in *The China Journal*, No. 50, pp. 83–103.

Thompson, E. P. 1963. *The Making of the English Working Class*. New York: Vintage Books.

Thompson, Roger R. 1995. *China's Local Councils: In the Age of Constitutional Reform, 1898–1911*. Cambridge: Harvard University Press.

Tilly, Charles. 1986. *The Contentious French*. Cambridge: Harvard University Press.

"Tongzhou mingaoguan rangren fuqi 通州民告官让人服气 [People-Accuse-Official Cases in Tongzhou Satisfy People]," in *The Yangtze Evening News*, September 15, 2003.

Tu, Wei-ming. 1993. *Way, Learning, and Politics: Essays on the Confucian Intellectual*. Albany: State University of New York Press.

Turner, Karen. 1993. "War, Punishment, and The Law of Nature in early Chinese Concepts of the State," in *Harvard Journal of Asiatic Studies*, Vol. 53, No. 2, pp. 285–324.

Turner, Karen G., Feinerman, James V., and Guy, R. Kent, eds. 2000. *The Limits of the Rule of Law in China*. Seattle: University of Washington Press.

Turner, Lowell. 1998. *Fighting for Partnership: Labor and Politics in Unified Germany*. Ithaca: Cornell University Press.

Turpin, Colin. 1999. *British Government and the Constitution: Text, Cases, and Materials*. London: Butterworths.

Vittinghoff, Natasha. June, 2002. "Unity vs. Uniformity: Liang Qichao and the Invention of a 'New Journalism' for China," in *Late Imperial China*. Vol. 23, No. 1, pp. 91–143.

Vlastos, Stephen. 1986. *Peasant Protests and Uprisings in Tokugawa Japan*. Berkeley: University of California Press.

Vogel, Ezra F. 1980. *Canton under Communism: Programs and Politics in a Provincial Capital, 1949–1968*. Cambridge: Harvard University Press.

Vogel, Ezra F. 2011. *Deng Xiaoping and the Transformation of China*. Cambridge: Harvard University Press.

Voss, Lex Heerma van, ed. 2002. *Petitions in Social History*. Cambridge: Cambridge University Press.

Wakeman, Frederic Jr. 1991. "Models of Historical Change: The Chinese State and Society, 1839–1989," in Kenneth Liberthal, Joyce Kallgren, Roderick MacFarquhar and Frederic Wakeman, Jr. eds., *Perspectives on Modern China*. Armonk: M. E. Sharpe.

Wakeman, Frederic Jr. 1993. "The Civil Society and Public Sphere Debate: Western Reflections on Chinese Political Culture," in *Modern China*, Vol. 19, No. 2, pp. 108–38.

Wakeman, Frederic Jr. 1995. *Policing Shanghai, 1927–1937*. Stanford: Stanford University Press.

Wakeman, Frederic Jr. 2000. "A Revisionist View of the Nanjing Decade: Confucian Fascism," in Frederick Wakeman, Jr. and Richard L. Edmonds, eds., *Reappraising Republican China*. Oxford: Oxford University Press, pp. 140–78.

Wakeman, Frederic Jr. 2003. *Spymaster Dai Li and the Chinese Secret Service*. Berkeley: University of California Press.

Wakeman, Frederic Jr. 2007. " 'Cleanup': The New Order in Shanghai," in Jeremy Brown and Paul G. Pickowicz, eds., *Dilemmas of Victory: The Early Years of the People's Republic of China*. Cambridge: Harvard University Press. pp. 21–58.

Wakeman, Frederic Jr. and Edmonds, Richard Louis, eds. 2000. *Reappraising Republican China*. Oxford: Oxford University Press.

Wang, Celai 王策来. 2002. *Yangnaiwu yu xiaobaicai an* 杨乃武与小白菜案 [The Case of Yang Naiwu and Xiao Baicai]. Beijing: Zhongguo jiancha chubanshe.

Wang, Hongchang 王洪昌 and Liu, Mengyi 刘梦义. 1981. "Dangnei cunzai yige guanliao zhuyizhe jieji ma 党内存在一个官僚主义者阶级吗 [Does the Party have a Bureaucrat Class]," in *The China Youth Daily*, February 7.

Wang, Hui. 2003. *China's New Order: Society, Politics, and Economy in Transition*, ed. Theodore Huters. Cambridge: Harvard University Press.

Wang, Laidi 王来棣. 2003. "Maozedong de zhishi fenzi zhengce 毛泽东的知识分子政策 [The Intellectual Policy of Mao Zedong]," in *Modern China Studies*, Fall, pp. 38–54.

Wang, Limin 王立民. 1998. *Shanghai fazhishi* 上海法制史 [History of Shanghai Legal System]. Shanghai: Shanghai renmin chubanshe.

Wang, Liming 王礼明. 1979. "Renzhi he fazhi 人治和法治 [The Rule of Man and the Rule of Law]," in the *People's Daily*, January 26.

Wang, Qisheng 王奇生. 2003. *Dangyuan dangquan yu dangzheng: 1924–1949 nian zhongguo Guomindang de zuzhi xingtai* 党员党权与党争: 1924–1949 年中国国民党

的组织形态 [Party Member, Party Power, and Party Struggle: The Organizing Pattern of the Chinese Nationalist Party between 1924 and 1949]. Shanghai: Shanghai shudian chubanshe.

Wang, Shi 王式. 1986. *Weixin yundong* 维新运动 [The Reform Movement]. Shanghai: Shanghai renmin chubanshe.

Wang, Weibo 王维博. 2008. "Fengbao yanzhongde weng'an guanyuan: zhengfu miandui kongqian xinren weiji 风暴眼中的瓮安官员: 政府面对空前信任危机 [Weng'an Officials in the Thunder Eye: Government is Facing Unprecedented Crisis of Trust]," in *China Newsweek* [Zhongguo xinwen zhoukan], July 9.

Wang, Xiuquan 王秀全. 1999. "Mingaoguan weihe banshu chesu 民告官为何半数撤诉 [Why Half People-Accuse-Officials Case are Dropped]," in *The China Youth Daily*, April 16.

"Wangzaoshi jixu sanbu fandang yanlun 王造时继续散布反党言论 [Wang Zaoshi Continued to Spread Anti-Party Words]," in *Wenhuibao*, June 15, 1957.

Wasserstrom, Jeffrey N. 1991. *Student Protests in Twentieth Century China: The View from Shanghai*. Stanford: Stanford University.

Wasserstrom, Jeffrey N., ed. 2003. *Twentieth-Century China: New Approaches*. London: Routledge.

Weber, Max. 1951. *The Religion of China: Confucianism and Taoism*. Glencoe: The Free Press.

Weber, Max. 2003. *Rujiao yu daojiao* 儒教与道教 [Confucianism and Daoism], trans. Wang Rongfen 王容芬. Beijing: Shangwu yinshuguan.

Wei, Ming 魏明. 1957. "Renmin sifa gongzuo burong youpai wumie 人民司法工作不容右派污蔑 [The People's Judiciary Cannot be Smeared by the Rightists]," in *The Daily of Collective Articles*, September 4.

Weinreb, Lloyd L. 1987. *Natural Law and Justice*. Cambridge: Harvard University Press.

"Weiweihu fazhi shou chufen de zhengfa ganbu huifu mingyu 为维护法制受处分的政法干部恢复名誉 [Restoring the reputation of legal cadres who defended the legal system and were disciplined]," in *The People's Daily*, April 18, 1979.

White, James. 1995. *IKKI: Social Conflict and Political Protest in Early Modern Japan*. Ithaca: Cornell University Press.

Whyte, Martin King. 1991. "State and Society in the Mao Era," in Kenneth Lieberthal, Joyce Kallgren, Roderick MacFarquhar, and Frederic Wakeman, Jr., eds., *Perspectives on Modern China: Four Anniversaries*. Armonk: M. E. Sharpe, pp. 255–74.

Wou, Odoric Y. K. 1977. *Militarism in Modern China: The Career of Wu P'ei-fu, 1916–1939*. London: Dawson Publishing.

Wright, Arthur F. 1979. "The Sui Dynasty (581–617)," in Denis Twitchett, ed., *The Cambridge History of China, Vol. 6. Alien Regimes and Border States, 907–1368*. Cambridge: Cambridge University Press, pp. 48–149.

Wright, Mary C., ed. 1968. *China in Revolution, The First Phase, 1900–1913*. New Haven: Yale University Press.

Wu, Chen 吴琛. 2002. "Xinfangquan xinfang fazhihua deluoji qidian 信访权一信访法治化的 逻辑起点 [The right of letters and visits: the logic start of the letters and visits under the rule of law]," in *Renmin xinfang*, Vol. 11–12, pp. 67–8.

Wu, Jun 武军. 2006. "Liangnüzi weigui shangfang raoluan gonggong changsuo zhixu fenbie beiju shitian 两女子违规上访扰乱公共秩序分别被拘十天 [Two Women are Detained for Ten Days due to Unlawful Complaints that have Disturbed Public Order]," in *Dushi chengbao* (Metropolitan Morning News). August 24.

Wu, Yufang 吴雨方. 1983. "Chepi tuiwei, ququ xiaoshi jiaoren paoduantui 扯皮推诿, 区

区小事叫人跑断腿 [Pushing Problems away and Let Me Break My Legs for such a Small Problem]," in *The China Youth Daily*, November 29.

Würgler, Andreas. 2002. "Voices from among the 'Silent Masses': Humble Petitions and Social Conflicts in Early Modern Central Europe," in Lex Heerma van Voss, ed., *Petitions in Social History*. Cambridge: Cambridge University Press, pp. 11–34.

Xia, Yong 夏勇. 2004. *Yifa zhiguo-guojia yu shehui* 依法治国-国家与社会 [Ruling the Country by Law]. Beijing: Shehui kexue wenxian chubanshe.

Xiao, Shu 笑蜀, ed. 1999. *Lishi de xiansheng: Bange shiji qian de Zhuangyan chengnuo* 历史的先声: 半个世纪前的庄严承诺 [The Harbinger of History: Solemn Promises Made a Half Century Ago]. Guangdong: Shantou daxue chubanshe.

Xie Chunlei 谢春雷. 2003. "Yici youzhengyi de shimin xuanchuan xianfa xingdong 一次有争议的市民宣传宪法行动 [One Debatable Citizens' Publicizing Constitution Action]," in *The Southern Weekend*, December 4.

Xie, Zhenmin 谢振民. 2000. *Zhonghua minguo lifashi* 中华民国立法史 [The Legislative History of The Republic of China]. Beijing: Zhongguo zhengfa daxue chubanshe. [First published in 1937 by Zhengzhong shujü.]

"Xin xinfang tiaoli de shige liangdian 新信访条例的十个亮点 [Ten Bright Points of the New Regulations Regarding Letter and Visits]," in *Banyuetan* [The Semi-Monthly Chats], No. 9, 2005.

"Xinfang gongzuozhe de husheng 信访工作者的呼声 [The Voice of Complaint Workers]," in *The People's Daily*, July 27, 1979.

"Xingfang shourong dangxiuyi 信访收容当休矣 [Detainment of Letters and Visits should End]," in *The Law Service Times* (*falü fuwu shibao*), August 22, 2003.

"Xinfang zhongde si'ge baifenzhi bashi shuomingle shenme 信访中的四个80%说明了什么 [What do the Four 80% Mean in Letters and Visits?]," in *Beijing Youth Daily* (Beijing qingnianbao), November 21, 2003.

"Xinhua shiping tongchi chaiqian zhongde bawang xieyi 新华时评痛斥拆迁中的霸王协议 [The Xinhua News Comment Severely Denounces the Hegemonic Agreement in Urban Disposal]," in *Xinmin Evening News*, September 15, 2003.

"Xiongyifu de si shuoming le shenme 熊一福的死说明了什么 [What does the Death of Xiong Yifu Tell Us]," in *The People's Daily*. August 25, 1979.

Xu, Luo. 2002. *Searching for Life's Meaning: Changes and Tensions in the Worldviews of Chinese Youth in the 1980s*. Ann Arbor: University of Michigan Press.

Xu, Xiaoqun. 2007. "The Rule of Law without Due Process: Punishing Robbers and Bandits in early Twentieth-Century China," in *Modern China*, Vol. 33, No. 2, pp. 230–57.

Xu, Xiaoqun. 2008. *Trial of Modernity: Judicial Reform in Early Twentieth-Century China, 1901–1937*. Stanford: Stanford University Press.

Yang, C. K. 1975. "Some Preliminary Statistical Patterns of Mass Actions in Nineteenth-Century China," in *Conflict and Control in Late Imperial China*, Frederick Wakeman, Jr. and Carolyn Grant, eds., Berkeley: University of California Press, pp. 174–210.

Yang, Dali L. and Zhao, Litao. 2009. *China's Reform at 30: Challenges and Prospects*, Singapore: World Scientific Publishing.

Yang, Haikun 杨海坤. 1992. *Zhongguo xingzhengfa jiben lilun* 中国行政法基本理论 [Basic Theories of the Chinese Administrative Law]. Nanjing: Nanjing daxue chubanshe.

Yang, Honglie 杨鸿烈. 1998. *Zhongguo falü sixiangshi* 中国法律思想史 [History of Chinese Legal Thoughts]. Beijing: Shangwu yinchuguan.

Yang, Jun 杨俊. 2003. "Wanqian louyu zhuhuazhang 万千楼宇著华章 [Thousands of Buildings Write Beautiful Chapters]," in *Xinmin Evening News*, October 6.

Yang, Liangqing 杨亮庆. 2002. "Bianhu lushi weihe kunhuo 辩护律师为何困惑 [Why are Lawyers Confused]," in *The China Youth Daily*, July 5.

Yang, Peng 杨鹏. 1936. "Woguo sifa xiankuang ji zhanwang 我国司法现况及展望 [The Present Situation and Prospect of China's Judiciary]," in *Faxua zazhi*, Vol. 9, No. 3, pp. 271–3.

Yang, Tianshi 杨天石. 2005. "Wengtonghe baguan wenti kaocha 翁同禾罢官问题考察 [Study of Weng Tonghe's Dismissal]," in *Jindaishi yanjiu*, pp. 198–216.

Yang, Yifan 杨一凡 and Liu, Ducai 刘笃才. 1998. "Zhongguo gudai guihanzhidu kaolüe 中国古代匦函制度拷略 [Factual Study on the China's Ancient Petition Box System]," in *Faxue yanjiu*, Vol. 1, pp. 79–91.

Yang, Yifan 杨一凡 and Liu, Ducai刘笃才, eds. 2003. *Zhongguo fazhishi kaozheng* 中国社会科学出版社 [A Criticism of the Chinese Legal History]. Beijing: Zhongguo shehui kexue chubanshe.

Yang, Zhaolong 杨兆龙. 1957. "Falüjie de dangyu feidang zhijian 法律界的党与非党之间 [The Legal System between Party and Non-Party]," in *The Daily of Collective Articles*, May 8.

Yardley, Jim. 2004. "Chinese Complaint to Beijing to Resolve Local Complaints," in the *New York Times*, March 8.

Yardley, Jim. 2004. "Farmers Being Moved Aside by China's Booming Market in Real Estate," in the *New York Times*, December 8.

Yasuhiko, Karasawa. 2007. "Between Oral and Written Cultures: Buddhist Monks in Qing Legal Plaints," in Robert E. Hegel and Katherine Carlita, eds., *Writing and Law in Late Imperial China: Crime, Conflict, and Judgment*. Seattle: University of Washington Press, pp. 64–80.

Yeh, Wen-hsin, ed. 2000. *Becoming Chinese: Passages to Modernity and Beyond*. Berkeley: University of California, pp. 31–61.

Yeung, Alison Sau-chu. 2003. "Fornication in the Late Qing Legal Reforms: Moral Teaching and Legal Principles," in *Modern China*, Vol. 29 No. 3, pp. 297–328.

"Yiding yaoba jiguan fengqi gaohao 一定要把机关风气搞好 [Be Sure to Improve the Atmosphere in Organs]," in *The People's Daily*, June 21, 1979.

Ying, Xing 应星. 2001. *Dahe yimin shangfang de gushi*大河移民上访的故事[The Complaint Story of the Dahe Immigrants]. Beijing: Sanlian shudian.

Ying, Xing 应星. 2004. "Zuowei teshu xingzheng jiuji de xinfang jiuji 作为特殊行政救济的信访救济 [The Xinfang Remedy as a Special Form of Administrative Relief]," in *Faxue Yanjiu* 法学研究 [Jurisprudence Research] Vol. 3, pp. 58–71.

Young, Ernest P. 1977. *The Presidency of Yuan Shih-k'ai: Liberalism and Dictatorship in Early Republican China*. Ann Arbor: The University of Michigan Press.

Young, Ernest P. 1983. "Politics in the Aftermath of Revolution: The Era of Yuan Shih-k'ai, 1912–16," in John K. Fairbank, ed., *The Cambridge History of China. Volume 12. Republican China 1912–1949, Part I*. Cambridge: Cambridge University Press.

Yu, Jianrong 于建嵘. "The Reform of the Letter-and-Visit System and Constitutional Construction" and "Denunciation of China's Xinfang System," in www.yannan.cn.

Yu, Jianrong 于建嵘. 2000. *Yuecun zhengzhi* 岳村政治 [Politics in a Village Named Yue]. Beijing: Shangwu yinshuguan.

Yu, Jianrong 于建嵘. 2003. "Nongcun heie shili he jiceng zhengquan tuihua 农村黑恶势力和 基层权力退化 [Mafia in Rural Areas and the Degradation of Local Power]" in *Zhanlue yu guanli*, pp. 1–14

Yu, Jianrong 于建嵘. 2004. "Xinfang de zhiduxing queshi jiqi zhengzhi houguo 信访的制度性 缺失及其政治后果 [The Systematic Failure of the Xinfang and its political

Aftermath]," in *Phoenix Weekly*. No. 32, online, available at: www.chinareform.net/2010/0116/10272.html.

Yu, Jianrong 于建嵘. 2005. "Xinfang zhidu gaige yu xianzheng jianshe 信访制度改革与宪政建设 [The Reform of the Letter-and-Visit System and the Establishment of Constitutional Government" in *Ershiyi shiji* 二十一世纪 [21st Century], online, available at: www.cuhk.edu.hk/ics/21c/supplem/essay/ 0504050g.htm.

Yu, Jianrong 于建嵘. 2005. "Dui xinfang zhidu gaige zhenglun de fansi 对信访制度改革争论的反思 [Rethinking the Debate over Reforming the Xinfang System]" in *Zhongguo dangzheng ganbu luntan* 中国党政干部论坛 [A Forum for China's Party and Political Officials], No. 5.

Yu, Keping 俞可平. 2006. "Chuantong minben sixiangyu xifang minzhu sixiang youzhe benzhi qubie 传统民本思想与西方民主有着本质区别 [Fundamental differences between the concepts of traditional *minben* and Western democracy]," in *Beijing Daily*, August 8.

Yu, Ronggen 俞荣根. 1998. "Tianli guofa renqingde chongtu yuzhenghe 天理国法人情的冲突 与整合 [The Conflicts and Interaction among Heavenly Principles, State Laws and Human Sentiment]," in *Zhonghua wenhua luntan*, April, pp. 12–19.

Yu, Xiangyang 余向阳. 2003. "Dang yige haofaguan haonan 当一个好法官好难 [It is Difficult to be a Good Judge]," in *Fazhi yu shehui* [The Rule of Law and Society], No. 4, pp. 16–17.

Yuan, Tsing. 1979. "Urban Riots and Disturbances," in Jonathan D. Spence and John E. Wills, Jr., eds., *From Ming to Ch'ing: Conquest, Region, and Continuity in Seventeenth-Century China*. New Haven: Yale University Press. pp. 277–320.

Zarrow, Peter. 2002. "The Reform Movement, the Monarchy, and Political Modernity," in Rebecca Karl and Peter Zarrow, eds., *Rethinking the 1898 Reform Period: Political Change in Late Qing China*. Cambridge: Harvard University Press, pp. 17–47.

Zarrow, Peter. 2005. *China in War and Revolution 1895–1949*. London: Routledge.

Zarrow, Peter. 2006. *Creating Chinese Modernity: Knowledge and Everyday Life, 1900–1940*. New York: Peter Long.

Zeng, Xianyi 曾宪义. 2002. *Zhongguo fazhishi* 中国法制史 [History of Chinese Legal System]. Beijing: Beijing University Press.

"Zenneng bi shiliusui shaonü zaohun 怎能逼十六岁少女早婚 [How can [they] Force a Sixteen-Year-Old Girl to Marry]," in *The China Youth Daily*, January 11, 1985.

Zhang, Cheng 张成. 1979. "Hewei dangde lingdao 何谓党的领导 [What is the Party Leadership]," in *The People's Daily*, January 15.

Zhang, Demei 张德美. 2010. *Conggongtang zouxiang fating qingmo mingchu susong zhidu gaige yanjiu* 从公堂走向法庭: 清末民初诉讼制度研究 [From magistrate's office to court: a study on the reform of the litigation system in the late Qing and early Republic]. Beijing: Zhongguo zhengfa daxue chubanshe.

Zhang, Dingtao 张定涛. 1983. "Zhifa fanfa qineng xiaoyao fawai 执法犯法岂能逍遥法外 [How can those Judicial Officials who Violate the Law Face no Punishment]," in *The China Youth Daily*, May 31.

Zhang, Elya J. 2006. "To Be Somebody: Li Qinglin, Run-of-the-Mill Cultural Revolution Showstopper," in Joseph W. Esherick, Paul G. Pickowica, and Andrew G. Walder, eds., *The Chinese Culture Revolution as History*. Stanford: Stanford University Press. pp. 211–39.

Zhang, Guo 张国. 2003. "Xingzheng susong li'an bi shenli gengjiannan 行政诉讼立案比审理更艰难 [Accepting an Administrative Suit is more Difficult than Adjudicating it]," in *The Worker's Daily*, January 4.

Zhang, Jianan 张建安 and Jin, Ren 金人 eds. 2004. *Minguo mingren susongan* 民国名人诉讼案 [Court Cases Involving Famous People in the Republic of China]. Beijing: Qunzhong chubanshe.

Zhang, Jinfan 张晋藩. 1997. *Zhongguo falü de chuantong yu xiandai zhuanxing* 中国法律的传统与现代转型 [The Tradition of Chinese Law and its Modern Transformation]. Beijing: Falü chubanshe.

Zhang, Jinfan 张晋藩, ed. 2002. *Ershi shiji zhongguo fazhi de huigu yu qianzhan* 二十世纪中国法制的回顾与前瞻 [Retrospect and Prospect of the 20th Century Chinese Legal System]. Beijing: Zhongguo zhengfa daxue chubanshe.

Zhang, Jingping 章敬平. 2002. "Faguan zaoyu xinrenweiji 法官遭遇信任危机 [Judges Suffer a Crisis of Trust]," in *Fazhi yu shehui* [The Rule of Law and Society] No. 3.

Zhang, Renzhong 张仁忠. 1991. *Zhongguo nongmin qiyi shihua* 中国农民起义史话 [A Short History of Chinese Peasant Uprisings]. Beijing: Zhonggong zhongyang dangxiao chubanshe.

Zhang, Sheng 张生. 2002. "Minchu daliyuan shenpan duli de zhidu yu shijian 民初大理院审判独立的制度与实践 [The Independent System and Practice of Supreme Court Jurisdiction in the Early Republic]," in *Zhongguo zhengfa daxue xuebao*, pp. 146–52.

Zhang, Sheng 张生. 2002. *Minguo chuqi minfa de jindaihua: yi guoyoufa yu jishoufa de zhenghe wei zhongxin* 民国初期民法的近代化: 以固有法与继受法的整合为中 心 [The Modernization of the Civil Law in the Early Republic: Centered on the Integration of the Native Law and the Foreign Law]. Beijing: Zhongguo zhengfa daxue chubanshe.

Zhang, Yufa 张玉法. 1992. "Minguo chunian shandongsheng xingzheng zhidu de biange 1912–1937 民国初年山东省行政制度的变革 1912–1937 [The Reform of the Administrative System in Shandong Province in the Early Republican Period 1912–1937]," in *Zhongyang yanjiuyuan jindaishisuo jikan*, Vol. 21, pp. 523–52.

Zhao, Ling 赵凌. 2003. "Chaiqian shinian beixiju 拆迁十年悲喜剧 [Ten Years Tragedies and Comedies of Urban Disposal]," in *The Southern Weekend*, September 4.

Zhao, Ling 赵凌. 2004. "Guonei shoufen xinfang baogao huo gaoceng guanzhu 国内首份 信访报告获高层关注 [The First Report onXinfangs in China Has Obtained Attention from the Top]," in *The Southern Weekend*, November 4.

Zhao, Ling 赵凌. 2004. "Xinfang gaige yinfa zhengyi 信访改革引发争议 [The Reform of Xinfang Sparks Debates]," in *The Southern Weekend*, November 18.

Zhao, Ling 赵凌. 2007. "Shekeyuan baogao chengzhongguo yixingcheng shangfang wenhua 社科院报告称中国已形成上访文化 [The Report of the Chinese Academy of Social Science Claims that China has Developed Complaint Culture]," in *The Southern Weekend*, April 5.

Zhao, Mingzhong 赵铭忠 and Li, Zuoming 李祚明. 1994. *Zhongguo dier lishi danganguan zhinan* 中国第二历史档案馆指南 [A Guide to the Chinese Second Historical Archives]. Beijing: Zhongguo dangan chubanshe.

Zhao, Xiaohua 赵晓华. 2001. *Wanqing songyu zhidu de shehui kaocha* 晚清讼狱制度的社会考察 9 [A social survey of the appeal and prison systems in the late Qing]. Beijing: Zhongguo renmin daxue chubanshe.

Zheng, Yongzhen 郑永贞. 1983. "Shenwei sifa ganbu, weihe jianta falü 身为司法干 部, 为何践踏法律 [As a Judicial Official, Why does [he] Violate the Law]," in *The China Youth Daily*, May 10.

"Zhigong shangfang yao fakuan 职工上访要罚款 [Workers Who Complain Will be Fined]" in *Baokan wenzhai*, September 17, 2003.

"Zhizhi xiang nongmin luanpaikuan luanshoufei 制止向农民乱派款乱收费 [Do not

Illegally Collect Money and Fees from Farmers]," in *The China Youth Daily*. November 1, 1985.

Zhou, Daoji 周道济. 1977. *Woguo minben sixiangde fenxiyu jiantao* 我国民本思想的分析与检讨 [A Review and analysis of Chinese *minben* thought]. Taibei: Academia Sinica.

Zhou, Guangyuan. 1993. "Illusion and Reality in the Law of the Late Qing: A Sichuan Case Study," in *Modern China*, Vol. 19, No. 4, pp. 427–56.

Zhou, Hulin 周虎林. 2002. "Zengyang ladong qunzhong jifangde zhidong lianhuan 怎样拉动 群众集访的制动链环 [How to pull the braking hoop of the mass collective complaints]," in *Minqing yuxinfang*, Vol. 2, p. 25.

Zhou, Yuede 周悦德. 2001. "Xinfang fazhi jianshe chutan 信访法治初探 [Preliminary study of rule of law in letters and visits]," in *Renmin xinfang*, Vol. 8, pp. 22–3.

"Zhou Zhanshun tongzhi zaiquanguo xinfangjuzhang huiyishangde jianghua 周占顺同志在全国信访局长会议上的讲话 [The talk of comrade Zhou Zhanshun at the national meeting of heads of letters and visits bureaus]," in *Renmin xinfang*, Vol. 1, 1999, pp. 11–15.

"Zifenzhe siwang, nanjing chaiqian jiaoting 自焚者死亡南京拆迁叫停 [After the Death of a Self-burning Person, Nanjing Stops all Disposal Projects]." in *Bund Picture News* (*waitan huabao*), September 11, 2003.

Index

Page numbers in *italics* denote tables.